# BOOK OF
# BLESSINGS

# THE ROMAN RITUAL

REVISED BY DECREE OF THE
SECOND VATICAN ECUMENICAL
COUNCIL AND PUBLISHED BY
AUTHORITY OF POPE JOHN PAUL II

THE LITURGICAL PRESS
Collegeville, Minnesota
1989

# BOOK OF BLESSINGS

APPROVED FOR USE IN THE DIOCESES OF THE
UNITED STATES OF AMERICA BY THE
NATIONAL CONFERENCE OF CATHOLIC BISHOPS
AND CONFIRMED BY THE APOSTOLIC SEE

*Prepared by*
*International Commission on English in the Liturgy*
*A Joint Commission of Catholic Bishops' Conferences*

*Concordat cum originali:* Ronald F. Krisman

Published by authority of the Bishops' Committee on the Liturgy, National Conference of Catholic Bishops

## ACKNOWLEDGMENTS

The English translation of *Book of Blessings* © 1987, International Committee on English in the Liturgy, Inc. (ICEL), 1275 K Street, NW, Suite 1202, Washington, DC 20005-4097 USA. All rights reserved.

Additional blessings for use in the United States of America © 1988, United States Catholic Conference (USCC), 3211 Fourth Street, NE, Washington, DC 20017-1194 USA. All rights reserved.

Excerpts from the English translation of *The Roman Missal* © 1973, International Committee on English in the Liturgy, Inc. (ICEL), 1275 K Street, NW, Suite 1202, Washington, DC 20005-4097 USA; excerpts from the English translation of the *Liturgy of the Hours* © 1970, 1973, 1975, ICEL; excerpts from the English translation of *Rite of Christian Initiation of Adults* © 1985, ICEL; excerpts from the English translation of *Pastoral Care of the Sick: Rites of Anointing and Viaticum* © 1982, ICEL; excerpts from the English translation of *Order of Christian Funerals* © 1985, ICEL; excerpts from the English translation of *Rite of Commissioning Special Ministers of Holy Communion* © 1978, ICEL; excerpts from the English translation of *Dedication of a Church and an Altar* © 1978, ICEL; excerpts from the English translation of *Holy Communion and Worship of the Eucharist outside Mass* © 1974, ICEL; excerpts from the English translation of *Rite of Penance* © 1975, ICEL; excerpts from *A Book of Prayers* © 1982, ICEL. All rights reserved.

Scripture selections are taken from *The New American Bible with Revised New Testament* © 1986 and 1970 by the Confraternity of Christian Doctrine, Washington, DC, and are used by license of the copyright owner. All rights reserved.

Printed in the United States of America.

ISBN 0-8146-1875-8

NATIONAL CONFERENCE OF CATHOLIC BISHOPS
UNITED STATES OF AMERICA

## DECREE

In accord with the norms established by decree of the Sacred Congregation of Rites in *Cum, nostra aetate* (27 January 1966), this edition of the *Book of Blessings* containing the additional proper blessings approved for use in the United States of America is declared to be the vernacular typical edition of *De Benedictionibus* in the dioceses of the United States of America, and is published by authority of the National Conference of Catholic Bishops.

The *Book of Blessings* and the additional proper blessings for use in the United States of America were canonically approved for use *ad interim* by the Administrative Committee of the National Conference of Catholic Bishops on 22 March 1988 and were subsequently confirmed by the Apostolic See by decree of the Congregation for Divine Worship on 27 January 1989 (Prot. N. 699/88).

On 1 October 1989 the *Book of Blessings* may be published and used in the liturgy. From 3 December 1989, the First Sunday of Advent, the use of the *Book of Blessings* is mandatory in the dioceses of the United States of America. From that day forward no other English version may be used.

Given at the General Secretariat of the National Conference of Catholic Bishops, Washington, DC, on 19 March 1989, the solemnity of Saint Joseph, Husband of Mary.

✠ John L. May
Archbishop of Saint Louis
President
National Conference of Catholic Bishops

Robert N. Lynch
General Secretary

# CONGREGATION FOR DIVINE WORSHIP

Prot. N. 699/88

## DECREE

At the request of His Excellency John L. May, Archbishop of St. Louis and President of the National Conference of Catholic Bishops, on 19 January 1989, and in virtue of the faculty granted to this Congregation by the Supreme Pontiff, Pope John Paul II, we gladly approve, that is, confirm *ad interim* the English text of *De Benedictionibus* (Green Book), as it appears in the appended copy.

In addition we gladly approve, that is, confirm the proper Supplement to this book, as it appears in the appended copy.

This decree, by which the requested confirmation is granted by the Apostolic See, is to be included in its entirety in the published text. Two copies of the printed text should be sent to this Congregation.

Anything to the contrary notwithstanding.

From the Congregation for Divine Worship, 27 January 1989.

✠ Eduardo Cardinal Martinez
Prefect

✠ Virgilio Noè
Titular Archbishop of Voncaria
Secretary

# CONTENTS

PART I
## BLESSINGS DIRECTLY PERTAINING TO PERSONS

PART II
BLESSINGS RELATED TO BUILDINGS
AND TO VARIOUS FORMS OF HUMAN ACTIVITY

PART III
BLESSINGS OF OBJECTS THAT ARE DESIGNED OR ERECTED
FOR USE IN CHURCHES, EITHER IN THE LITURGY
OR IN POPULAR DEVOTIONS

PART IV
BLESSINGS OF ARTICLES MEANT TO FOSTER
THE DEVOTION OF THE CHRISTIAN PEOPLE

PART VI

BLESSINGS FOR VARIOUS NEEDS AND OCCASIONS

## APPENDICES

# FOREWORD

This edition of the *Book of Blessings* contains the approved English translation of *De Benedictionibus* prepared by the International Commission on English in the Liturgy (ICEL), as well as the forty-two orders and prayers of blessing prepared by the Committee on the Liturgy of the National Conference of Catholic Bishops and approved for use in the dioceses of the United States of America. The *Book of Blessings* and the new blessings for the United States have been given provisional or interim approval. Eventually the English translation of the Roman blessings will be revised by the International Commission on English in the Liturgy, and the American blessings will be revised by the Bishops' Committee on the Liturgy. In both cases, the revision will be based on the comments received concerning this edition of the *Book of Blessings*.

The additional blessings contained in this volume have been inserted at the appropriate places throughout the book. As a result, the numbering of this edition differs from that of the Latin edition. The new blessings prepared and approved specifically for use in the dioceses of the United States of America are designated "USA" in the margin.

A new *Part V: Blessings for Feasts and Seasons* has been added to the *Book of Blessings* and, as the title indicates, it consists of blessings related to the feasts and seasons of the liturgical year. All the orders of blessing contained in this section, except the last, are newly composed for use in the United States.

Part V of the Latin edition has been renumbered as *Part VI: Blessings for Various Needs and Occasions*. Only the last two orders of blessing (Chapters 70 and 71) are found in the Latin edition of the *Book of Blessings*. The blessings contained in this section are primarily related to the parish, its pastoral and liturgical ministries, and its organizations.

The final portion of the book contains two appendices: Appendix 1: Order for the Installation of a Pastor; Appendix 2: Solemn Blessings and Prayers over the People. Although not properly a blessing, the Order for the Installation of a Pastor complements the blessings of Part VI and has been included for pastoral convenience. It is a new rite which has been patterned on the various rites in use throughout the country during the past two decades. The second appendix consists of the solemn blessings and prayers over the people found in the *Sacramentary*. Since these blessings may be used to conclude the hours of the Liturgy of the Hours and other liturgical rites and services, they have been included here so that all the major blessings of the Church may be found in one convenient collection.

The *Book of Blessings* was approved by the Administrative Committee of the National Conference of Catholic Bishops on 22 March 1988 and confirmed by the Apostolic See on 27 January 1989 (Prot. N. 699/88).

Blessed be God: Father, Son, and Holy Spirit, now and for ever. Amen.

✝ Joseph P. Delaney
Bishop of Fort Worth
Chairman, Committee on the Liturgy
National Conference of Catholic Bishops

20 March 1989

# CONGREGATION FOR DIVINE WORSHIP

Prot. N. 1200/84

## DECREE

The celebration of blessings holds a privileged place among all the sacramentals created by the Church for the pastoral benefit of the people of God. As a liturgical action, the celebration leads the faithful to praise God and prepares them for the principal effect of the sacraments. By celebrating a blessing the faithful can also sanctify various situations and events in their lives.

In ordering the reform of sacramentals, Vatican Council II decreed that in their celebration special attention should be given to the full, conscious, and active participation of the faithful and that any elements should be eliminated that in the course of time had obscured the true nature and purpose of sacramentals.

The Council further decreed that the number of reserved blessings should be limited, with reservation made in favor only of bishops or Ordinaries, and that provision should be made for qualified laypersons to impart some blessings, at least in certain circumstances and at the discretion of the Ordinary.

Complying with the conciliar decrees, this Congregation for Divine Worship has prepared a new title for the Roman Ritual, which, by apostolic authority, John Paul II has approved and ordered to be published.

Therefore by order of the Pope the Congregation now publishes the *Book of Blessings*. The Latin edition becomes effective as soon as it is published. Once the conference of bishops has prepared a vernacular edition and the translation has been reviewed by the Apostolic See, this edition becomes effective on the date to be decreed by the conference of bishops.

All things to the contrary notwithstanding.

Congregation for Divine Worship, 31 May 1984.

✛ Augustin Mayer, O.S.B.
Titular Archbishop of Satriano
Pro-Prefect

✛ Virgilio Noè
Titular Archbishop of Voncaria
Secretary

# GENERAL INTRODUCTION

## I. BLESSINGS IN THE HISTORY OF SALVATION

1     The source from whom every good gift comes[1] is God, who is above all, blessed for ever.[2] He who is all good has made all things good, so that he might fill his creatures with blessings[3] and even after the Fall he has continued his blessings as a sign of his merciful love.

2     But when the fullness of time arrived, the Father sent his own Son and through him, who took our flesh, gave us a new gift in every spiritual blessing.[4] The ancient curse upon us was thus changed into a blessing: when ''the glorious Sun of Justice, Christ our God, appeared, he freed us from the age-old curse and filled us with holiness.''[5]

3     Christ, the Father's supreme blessing upon us, is portrayed in the gospel as blessing those he encountered, especially the children,[6] and as offering to his Father prayers of blessing.[7] Glorified by the Father, after his ascension Christ sent the gift of his Spirit upon the brothers and sisters he had gained at the cost of his blood. The power of the Spirit would enable them to offer the Father always and everywhere praise, adoration, and thanksgiving and, through the works of charity, to be numbered among the blessed in the Father's kingdom.[8]

4     In Christ the blessing of God upon Abraham[9] reached its complete fulfillment. Through the Spirit sent by Christ, those who are called to a new life, ''showered with every blessing,''[10] become children by adoption and so as members of Christ's Body spread the fruits of the same Spirit in order to bring God's healing blessings to the world.

5     In anticipation of Christ's coming as Savior, the Father had reaffirmed his original covenant of love toward us by the outpouring of many gifts. Thus he prepared a chosen people to welcome the Redeemer and he intervened to make them ever more worthy of the covenant. By walking in the

---

[1] See Roman Missal (Sacramentary), Solemn Blessing no. 3, Beginning of the New Year.

[2] See Romans 9:5.

[3] See Roman Missal, Eucharistic Prayer IV, Preface.

[4] See Galatians 4:4; Ephesians 1:3.

[5] See *The Liturgy of the Hours*, Birthday of Mary, 8 September, antiphon for the Canticle of Zechariah.

[6] See Acts 3:26; Mark 10:16, 6:41; Luke 24:50, etc.

[7] See Matthew 9:31, 14:19, 26:26; Mark 6:41, 8:7 and 9, 14:22; Luke 9:16, 4:30; John 6:11.

[8] See Roman Missal, Common of Holy Men and Women, 9: For those who work for the underprivileged, Opening Prayer.

[9] See Genesis 12:3.

[10] Basil the Great, *De Spiritu Sancto*, cap. 15, 36: PG 32, 131. See Ambrose, *De Spiritu Sancto*, I, 7, 89: PL 16, 755; CSEL 79, 53.

path of righteousness, they had the power to honor God with their lips and with their hearts and thus to become before the world a sign and sacrament of divine blessings.

6      The God from whom all blessings flow favored many persons—particularly the patriarchs, kings, priests, Levites, and parents[11]—by allowing them to offer blessings in praise of his name and to invoke his name, so that other persons or the works of creation would be showered with divine blessings.

Whether God blessed the people himself or through the ministry of those who acted in his name, his blessing was always a promise of divine help, a proclamation of his favor, a reassurance of his faithfulness to the covenant he had made with his people. When, in turn, others uttered blessings, they were offering praise to the one whose goodness and mercy they were proclaiming.

In a word, God bestows his blessing by communicating or declaring his own goodness; his ministers bless God by praising him and thanking him and by offering him their reverent worship and service. Whoever blesses others in God's name invokes the divine help upon individuals or upon an assembled people.

7      Scripture attests that all the beings God has created and keeps in existence[12] by his gracious goodness declare themselves to be blessings from him and should move us to bless him in return. This is above all true after the Word made flesh came to make all things holy by the mystery of his incarnation.

Blessings therefore refer first and foremost to God, whose majesty and goodness they extol, and, since they indicate the communication of God's favor, they also involve human beings, whom he governs and in his providence protects. Further, blessings apply to other created things through which, in their abundance and variety, God blesses human beings.[13]

## II. BLESSINGS IN THE LIFE OF THE CHURCH

8      Taught by the Savior's own command, the Church shares the cup of blessing,[14] as it gives thanks for the inexpressible gift received first in Christ's paschal mystery and then brought to us in the eucharist. From the grace and power received in the eucharist the Church itself becomes a blessing existing in the world. The Church as the universal sacrament of salva-

---

[11] See Genesis 14:19-20; Hebrews 7:1; Genesis 27:27-29, 38, 40; Hebrews 11:20; Genesis 49:1-28; Hebrews 11:21; Deuteronomy 21:5; Deuteronomy 33; Joshua 14:13, 22:6; 2 Chronicles 30:27; Leviticus 9:22-23; Nehemiah 8:6; Sirach 3:9-11.

[12] See, for example, Daniel 3:57-88; Psalm 66:8; Psalm 103; Psalm 135; 1 Timothy 4:4-5.

[13] See Genesis 27:27; Exodus 23:25; Deuteronomy 7:13, 28:12; Job 1:10; Psalm 65:11; Jeremiah 31:23.

[14] See 1 Corinthians 10:16.

tion[15] continues the work of sanctifying and in the Holy Spirit joins Christ its Head in giving glory to the Father.

9    As the Church, through the working of the Holy Spirit, fulfills its many-sided ministry of sanctifying, it has accordingly established many forms of blessing. Through them it calls us to praise God, encourages us to implore his protection, exhorts us to seek his mercy by our holiness of life, and provides us with ways of praying that God will grant the favors we ask.

The blessings instituted by the Church are included among those signs perceptible to the senses by which human sanctification in Christ and the glorification of God are "signified and brought about in ways proper to each of these signs."[16] Human sanctification and God's glorification are the ends toward which all the Church's other activities are directed.[17]

10   Blessings are signs that have God's word as their basis and that are celebrated from motives of faith. They are therefore meant to declare and to manifest the newness of life in Christ that has its origin and growth in the sacraments of the New Covenant established by the Lord. In addition, since they have been established as a kind of imitation of the sacraments, blessings are signs above all of spiritual effects that are achieved through the Church's intercession.[18]

11   Because of these considerations, the Church has a profound concern that the celebration of blessings should truly contribute to God's praise and glory and should serve to better God's people. In order that this intent of the Church might stand out more clearly, blessing formularies have, from age-old tradition, centered above all on glorifying God for his gifts, on imploring favors from him, and on restraining the power of evil in this world.

12   The Church gives glory to God in all things and is particularly intent on showing forth his glory to those who have been or will be reborn through his grace. For them and with them therefore the Church in celebrating its blessings praises the Lord and implores divine grace at important moments in the life of its members. At times the Church also invokes blessings on objects and places connected with human occupations or activities and those related to the liturgy or to piety and popular devotions. But such blessings are invoked always with a view to the people who use the objects to be blessed and frequent the places to be blessed. God has given into our use and care the good things he has created, and we are also the recipients of his own wisdom. Thus the celebration of blessings becomes

---

[15] See Vatican Council II, Dogmatic Constitution on the Church *Lumen gentium*, no. 48.

[16] Vatican Council II, Constitution on the Liturgy *Sacrosanctum Concilium* (hereafter SC), art. 7.

[17] SC, art. 7 and 10.

[18] See SC, art. 60.

the means for us to profess that as we make use of what God has created we wish to find him and to love and serve him with all fidelity.

13     Through the guidance of faith, the assurance of hope, and the inspiration of charity the faithful receive the wisdom to discern the reflections of God's goodness not only in the elements of creation but also in the events of human life. They see all of these as signs of that fatherly providence by which God guides and governs all things. At all times and in every situation, then, the faithful have an occasion for praising God through Christ in the Holy Spirit, for calling on divine help, and for giving thanks in all things, provided there is nothing that conflicts with the letter and spirit of the Gospel. Therefore every celebration of a blessing must be weighed beforehand with pastoral prudence, particularly if there is any danger of shocking the faithful or other persons.

14     This pastoral evaluation of the blessings of creation is in keeping with another text of Vatican Council II: ''Thus, for well-disposed members of the faithful, the effect of the liturgy of the sacraments and the sacramentals is that almost every event in their lives is made holy by divine grace that flows from the paschal mystery of Christ's passion, death, and resurrection, the fount from which all the sacraments and sacramentals draw their power. The liturgy means also that there is hardly any proper use of material things that cannot thus be directed toward human sanctification and the praise of God.''[19]

The celebration of a blessing, then, prepares us to receive the chief effect of the sacraments and makes holy the various situations of human life.

15  ''But in order that the liturgy may possess its full effectiveness, it is necessary that the faithful come to it with proper dispositions.''[20] When through the Church we ask for God's blessing, we should intensify our personal dispositions through faith, for which all things are possible;[21] we should place our assurance in the hope that does not disappoint;[22] above all we should be inspired by the love that impels us to keep God's commandments.[23] Then, seeking what is pleasing to God,[24] we will fully appreciate his blessing and will surely receive it.

### III. OFFICES AND MINISTRIES

16     Blessings are a part of the liturgy of the Church. Therefore their com-

---

[19] SC, art. 61.

[20] SC, art. 11.

[21] See Mark 9:23.

[22] See Romans 5:5.

[23] See John 14:21.

[24] See Romans 12:2; Ephesians 5:17; Matthew 12:50; Mark 3:35.

---

munal celebration is in some cases obligatory but in all cases more in accord with the character of liturgical prayer; as the Church's prayer places truth before the minds of the faithful, those who are present are led to join themselves with heart and voice to the voice of the Church.

For the more important blessings that concern the local Church, it is fitting that the diocesan or parish community assemble, with the bishop or pastor (parish priest) presiding, to celebrate the blessing.

Even in the case of other blessings, the presence of an assembly of the faithful is preferable, since what is done on behalf of any group within the community redounds in some way to the good of the entire community.

17    Whenever there is no assembly of the faithful for the celebration, the person who wishes to bless God's name or to ask God's favor and the minister who presides should still keep in mind that they represent the Church in celebration. In this way from their shared prayer and petition a blessing results that "although a human being pronounces it, does not have a merely human source,"[25] a blessing that is "the longed-for bestowal of sanctification and divine favor."[26]

The celebration of the blessing of things or places according to custom should not take place without the participation of at least some of the faithful.

18    The ministry of blessing involves a particular exercise of the priesthood of Christ and, in keeping with the place and office within the people of God belonging to each person, the exercise of this ministry is determined in the following manner:

a. It belongs to the ministry of the *bishop* to preside at celebrations that involve the entire diocesan community and that are carried out with special solemnity and with a large attendance of the faithful. The bishop, accordingly, may reserve certain celebrations to himself, particularly those celebrated with special solemnity.[27]

b. It belongs to the ministry of a *presbyter or priest,* in keeping with the nature of his service to the people of God, to preside at those blessings especially that involve the community he is appointed to serve. Priests therefore may preside at the celebration of all the blessings in this book, unless a bishop is present as presider.

c. It belongs to the ministry of a *deacon* to preside at those blessings that are so indicated in place in this book, because, as the minister of the altar, of the word, and of charity, the deacon is the assistant of the bishop and the college of presbyters.

But whenever a priest is present, it is more fitting that the office

---

[25] Caesarius of Arles, *Serm.* 77, 5: CCL 103, 321.

[26] Ambrose, *De benedictionibus patriarcharum* 2, 7: PL 14, 709; CSEL, *De Patriarchis,* 32, 2, 18.

[27] See SC, art. 79.

of presiding be assigned to him and that the deacon assist by carrying out those functions proper to the diaconate.

d. An *acolyte* or a *reader* who by formal institution has this special office in the Church is rightly preferred over another layperson as the minister designated at the discretion of the local Ordinary to impart certain blessings.

Other *laymen* and *laywomen*, in virtue of the universal priesthood, a dignity they possess because of their baptism and confirmation, may celebrate certain blessings, as indicated in the respective orders of blessings, by use of the rites and formularies designated for a lay minister. Such laypersons exercise this ministry in virtue of their office (for example, parents on behalf of their children) or by reason of some special liturgical ministry or in fulfillment of a particular charge in the Church, as is the case in many places with religious or catechists appointed by decision of the local Ordinary,[28] after ascertaining their proper pastoral formation and prudence in the apostolate.

But whenever a priest or a deacon is present, the office of presiding should be left to him.

19    The participation of the faithful will be the more active in proportion to the effectiveness of their instruction on the importance of blessings. During the celebration of a blessing and in preaching and catechesis beforehand, priests and ministers should therefore explain to the faithful the meaning and power of blessings. There is a further advantage in teaching the people of God the proper meaning of the rites and prayers employed by the Church in imparting blessings: this will forestall the intrusion into the celebration of anything that might replace genuine faith with superstition and/or a shallow credulity.

## IV. CELEBRATION OF A BLESSING

### TYPICAL STRUCTURE

20    The typical celebration of a blessing consists of two parts: first, the proclamation of the word of God, and second, the praise of God's goodness and the petition for his help.

In addition there are usually rites for the beginning and conclusion that are proper to each celebration.

21    The purpose of the first part of the celebration is to ensure that the blessing is a genuine sacred sign, deriving its meaning and effectiveness from God's word that is proclaimed.[29]

---

[28] See SC, art. 79.

[29] See Lectionary for Mass, (2nd ed., 1981), General Introduction, nos. 3–9.

---

Thus the proclamation of God's word is the central point of the first part and the word proclaimed should provide a basis for the introductory comments and the brief instruction on the readings, as well as for any exhortation or homily that may be given, as occasion suggests.

Particularly when there are several readings, an intervening psalm or song or an interval of prayerful silence may be included, in order to intensify the faith of those taking part in the celebration.

22    The purpose of the second part of the celebration is that through its rites and prayers the community will praise God and, through Christ in the Holy Spirit, implore divine help. The central point of this part, then, is the blessing formulary itself, that is, the prayer of the Church, along with the accompanying proper outward sign.

But intercessions may also be added as a way of fostering the prayerful petition of those present; the intercessions usually precede, but also may follow the prayer of blessing.

23    In the adaptation of celebrations a careful distinction must be made between matters of less importance and those principal elements of the celebrations that are here provided, namely, the proclamation of the word of God and the Church's prayer of blessing. These may never be omitted even when the shorter form of a rite is used.

24    For the planning of a celebration these are the foremost considerations:

a. in most cases a communal celebration is to be preferred,[30] and in such a way that a deacon, reader, cantor or psalmist, and choir all fulfill their proper functions;

b. a primary criterion is that the faithful are able to participate actively, consciously, and easily;[31]

c. provision should be made for the particular circumstances and persons involved,[32] but with due regard for the principles of the liturgical reform and the norms laid down by the responsible authority.

## SIGNS TO BE USED

25    The purpose of the outward signs frequently accompanying prayer is above all to bring to mind God's saving acts, to express a relationship between the present celebration and the Church's sacraments, and in this way to nurture the faith of those present and move them to take part in the rite attentively.[33]

---

[30] See SC, art. 27.

[31] See SC, art. 79.

[32] See SC, art. 38.

[33] See SC, art. 59–60.

26 The outward signs or gestures that are especially employed are: the outstretching, raising, or joining of the hands, the laying on of hands, the sign of the cross, sprinkling with holy water, and incensation.

> a. Because the blessing formulary is before all else an *oratio*, the minister stretches out his hands, joins them, or raises them during it, according to the rubrics in each order of blessing.

> b. The laying on of hands holds a special place among gestures of blessing. Christ often used this sign of blessing, spoke of it to his disciples, saying: "They will lay hands on the sick and these will recover" (Mark 16:18), and continues to use it in and through the Church.

> c. In keeping with an ancient tradition, the tracing of the sign of the cross also often accompanies a blessing.

> d. Some of the orders of blessing provide for sprinkling with holy water, and in these cases ministers should urge the faithful to recall the paschal mystery and renew their baptismal faith.

> e. Some orders of blessing provide for incensation, which is a sign of veneration and honor and, in some uses, a symbol of the Church's prayer.

27 The outward signs of blessing, and particularly the sign of the cross, are in themselves forms of preaching the Gospel and of expressing faith. But to ensure active participation in the celebration and to guard against any danger of superstition, it is ordinarily not permissible to impart the blessing of any article or place merely through a sign of blessing and without either the word of God or any sort of prayer being spoken.

MANNER OF JOINING THE CELEBRATION OF A BLESSING
WITH OTHER CELEBRATIONS OR WITH OTHER BLESSINGS

28 Because some blessings have a special relationship to the sacraments, they may sometimes be joined with the celebration of Mass.

This book specifies what such blessings are and the part or rite with which they are to be joined; it also provides ritual norms that may not be disregarded. No blessings except those so specified may be joined with the eucharistic celebration.

29 As indicated in the individual orders of blessing, some blessings may be joined with other liturgical celebrations.

30 At times it may suit the occasion to have several blessings in a single celebration. The principle of arrangement for such a celebration is that the rite belonging to the more important blessing is to be used, and in the introductory comments and in the intercessions suitable words and signs are added that indicate the intention also of bestowing the other blessings.

31    The minister should keep in mind that blessings are intended, first of all, for the faithful. But they may also be celebrated for catechumens and, in view of the provision of can. 1170, for non-Catholics, unless there is a contrary prohibition of the Church.

    Whenever the celebration of a blessing is shared with Christians with whom we do not have full communion, the provisions laid down by the local Ordinary are to be respected.

32    With a view to the particular circumstances and taking into account the wishes of the faithful, the celebrant or minister is to make full use of the options authorized in the various rites, but also is to maintain the structure of the celebration and is not to mix up the order of the principal parts.

33    In planning a communal celebration care must be taken to ensure that all, both ministers and faithful, exercise their proper functions and carry them out devoutly and with proper decorum and order.

34    Due attention must also be paid to the character proper to the liturgical season, in order that the minister's introductory comments and the people's prayers and intercessions will be linked with the annual cycle of the mysteries of Christ.

## VESTMENTS

35    A bishop when presiding at major celebrations wears the vestments prescribed in the *Ceremonial of Bishops.*

36    A priest or deacon when presiding at blessings celebrated communally, especially those that are celebrated in a church or with special solemnity, is to wear an alb with stole. A surplice may replace the alb when a cassock is worn; a cope may be worn for more solemn celebrations.

37    Vestments are to be either white or of a color corresponding to the liturgical season or feast.

38    A formally instituted minister when presiding at blessings celebrated communally is to wear the vesture prescribed for liturgical celebrations by the conference of bishops or by the local Ordinary.

# V. ADAPTATIONS BELONGING TO THE
# CONFERENCES OF BISHOPS

39    In virtue of the Constitution on the Liturgy,[34] each conference of

---

[34] See SC, art. 63, b.

bishops has the right to prepare a particular ritual, corresponding to the present title of the Roman Ritual, adapted to the needs of the respective region. Once the decisions of the conference have been reviewed by the Apostolic See,[35] the ritual prepared by the conference is to be used in the region concerned.

In this matter the conference of bishops has the following responsibilities:

a. to decide on adaptations, in keeping with the principles established in the present book, and preserving the proper structure of the rites;

b. to weigh carefully and prudently what elements from the traditions and culture of individual peoples may be appropriately admitted into divine worship, then to propose further adaptations that the conference considers to be necessary or helpful;[36]

c. to retain or to adapt blessings belonging to particular rituals or those of the former Roman Ritual that are still in use, as long as such blessings are compatible with the tenor of the Constitution on the Liturgy, with the principles set out in this General Introduction, and with contemporary needs;

d. to add different texts of the same kind to the various orders of blessing whenever the present book gives a choice between several alternative texts;

e. not only to translate in their entirety but also, where necessary, to expand the Introductions in this book, so that the ministers will fully understand the meaning of the rites and carry them out effectively and the faithful will take part more consciously and actively;

f. to supply elements missing from this book, for example, to provide other readings that may be useful and to indicate what songs are suited to the celebrations;

g. to prepare translations of the texts that are adapted to the idiom of the different languages and to the genius of the diverse cultures;

h. to arrange the contents of editions of a book of blessings in a format that will be as convenient as possible for pastoral use; to publish sections of the book separately, but with the major introductions always included.

---

[35] See *Codex Iuris Canonici* (hereafter CIC), can. 838, 2 and 3; see also CIC, can. 1167, 1.

[36] See SC, art. 37–40 and 65.

# Part I
# BLESSINGS DIRECTLY PERTAINING TO PERSONS

CHAPTER 1

# ORDERS FOR THE BLESSING OF FAMILIES AND MEMBERS OF FAMILIES

## INTRODUCTION

40    Marriage, a communion of life and wedded love established by the Creator, was transformed by Christ to be one of the sacraments of the New Covenant, patterned on the mystery of his own fruitful union with the Church, and one of the states and orders of the Christian life. The Church has therefore always made marriage a primary concern of its pastoral ministry. For marriage is the source of the family and in the life of the family husband and wife possess their distinctive charism and vocation within the people of God, in order that for each other, their children, and their friends they may be cooperators in the working of God's grace and witnesses to faith and to Christ's love. As the Church of the household, the Christian family has the duty of upholding clearly before all people the values of the kingdom of God in this world and hope in the life to come by fulfilling its divinely appointed mission and carrying out its proper apostolate.[1]

41    There is need for husbands and wives, as well as other family members, to become continually better fitted for their responsibilities and to carry them out guided by the Gospel and motivated by Christian love. The Church has therefore established certain sacramentals that in particular situations enrich the life of the family by the proclamation of the word of God and a special blessing. Chief among these sacramentals are the orders of blessing set out in the present chapter.

---

[1] See Vatican Council II, Dogmatic Constitution on the Church *Lumen gentium*, nos. 11 and 35; Decree on the Apostolate of the Laity *Apostolicam actuositatem*, nos. 7 and 11; Pastoral Constitution on the Church in the Modern World *Gaudium et spes*, nos. 47–52.

# I. ORDER FOR THE BLESSING OF A FAMILY

## INTRODUCTION

42    The celebration of the blessing provided here is a suitable means of fostering the Christian life in the members of a family, whenever a blessing is requested by the family or suggested by pastoral considerations. To ensure that the celebration serves its purpose, it is to be adapted to each individual situation.

43    The blessing of a family may also be carried out within Mass, by use of the order provided in nos. 62–67.

44    The present order may be used by a priest or deacon. It may also be used by a layperson, who follows the rites and prayers designated for a lay minister.

45    While maintaining the structure and chief elements of the rite, the minister should adapt the celebration to the circumstances of the place and the people involved.

## A. ORDER OF BLESSING

### INTRODUCTORY RITES

46    When the family has gathered, the minister says:

**In the name of the Father, and of the Son, and of the Holy Spirit.**

All make the sign of the cross and reply:

**Amen.**

47    A minister who is a priest or deacon greets those present in the following or other suitable words, taken mainly from sacred Scripture.

**The grace and peace of God our Father and the Lord Jesus Christ be with you all.**

All make the following or some other suitable reply.

**And also with you.**

Or:

**Blessed be God for ever.**

**48**     A lay minister greets those present in the following words.

**The grace of our Lord Jesus Christ be with us all, now and for ever.**

**R̸. Amen.**

**49**     In the following or similar words, the minister prepares those present for the blessing.

**My dear friends, from the sacrament of marriage the family has received newness of life and the grace of Christ. The family is specially important to the Church and to civil society, for it is the primary life-giving community.**

**In our celebration today we call down the Lord's blessing upon you, so that you may continually be instruments of God's grace to one another and witnesses to faith in all the circumstances of life.**

**With God as your help you will fulfill your mission by conforming your entire life to the Gospel and so witness to Christ before the world.**

## READING OF THE WORD OF GOD

**50**     One of those present or the minister reads one of the following texts of sacred Scripture.

**Brothers and sisters, listen to the words of the first letter of Paul to the Corinthians:**     12:12-14

*We are all one body.*

**As a body is one though it has many parts, and all the parts of the body, though many, are one body, so also Christ. For in one Spirit we were all baptized into one body, whether Jews or Greeks, slaves or free persons, and we were all given to drink of one Spirit.**

**Now the body is not a single part, but many.**

51    Or:

**Brothers and sisters, listen to the words of the apostle Paul to the Ephesians:**

*4:1-6*

*Bear with one another lovingly.*

**I, then, a prisoner for the Lord, urge you to live in a manner worthy of the call you have received, with all humility and gentleness, with patience, bearing with one another through love, striving to preserve the unity of the spirit through the bond of peace: one body and one Spirit, as you were also called to the one hope of your call; one Lord, one faith, one baptism; one God and Father of all, who is over all and through all and in all.**

52    Or:

Romans 12:4-16—*Love each other with mutual affection.*

1 Corinthians 12:31b—13:7—*Love is always ready to excuse, to trust, to hope, and to endure whatever comes.*

53    As circumstances suggest, the following responsorial psalm may be sung or said, or some other suitable song.

R̊. **Happy are those who fear the Lord.**

Psalm 128

**Happy are you who fear the LORD,
who walk in his ways!
For you shall eat the fruit of your handiwork;
happy shall you be, and favored.** R̊.

**Behold, thus is the man blessed
who fears the LORD.
The LORD bless you from Zion:
may you see the prosperity of Jerusalem
all the days of your life;
May you see your children's children.** R̊.

54    As circumstances suggest, the minister may give those present a brief explanation of the biblical text, so that they may understand through faith the meaning of the celebration.

# INTERCESSIONS

55    The intercessions are then said. The minister introduces them and an assisting minister or one of those present announces the intentions. From the following intentions those best suited to the occasion may be used or adapted, or other intentions that apply to the particular circumstances may be composed.

The minister says:

**Christ the Lord, the Word coeternal with the Father, lived among us and chose to be part of a family and to enrich it with his blessings. Let us humbly ask for his favor and protection on this family.**

Ry. **Lord, keep our family in your peace.**

Or:

Ry. **Lord, hear our prayer.**

Assisting minister:

**Through your own obedience to Mary and Joseph you consecrated family life; make this family holy by your presence. (For this we pray:)** Ry.

Assisting minister:

**Your heart was set on the concerns of your Father; make every home a place where he is worshiped with reverence. (For this we pray:)** Ry.

Assisting minister:

**You made your own family the model of prayer, of love, and of obedience to your Father's will; by your grace make this family holy and make it rich with your gifts. (For this we pray:)** Ry.

Assisting minister:

**You loved those who were close to you and they returned your love; bind all families together in the bonds of peace and of love for each other. (For this we pray:)** Ry.

Assisting minister:

**At Cana in Galilee, when a new family was beginning, you gladdened it with your first miracle, changing water into wine; alleviate the sorrows and worries of this family and change them into joy. (For this we pray:)** ℟.

Assisting minister:

**In your concern for the integrity of the family you said: "Let no one separate those whom God has bound together"; bind this husband and wife ever more closely together in the bond of your own love. (For this we pray:)** ℟.

56    After the intercessions, the minister, in the following or similar words, invites all present to sing or say the Lord's Prayer:

**Let us pray with confidence to the Father in the words our Savior taught us:**

All:

**Our Father . . .**

## PRAYER OF BLESSING

57    A minister who is a priest or deacon says the prayer of blessing with hands outstretched over the family members; a lay minister says the prayer with hands joined.

**O God,**
**you have created us in love and saved us in mercy,**
**and through the bond of marriage**
**you have established the family**
**and willed that it should become a sign of Christ's love**
  **for his Church.**

**Shower your blessings on this family gathered here**
  **in your name.**
**Enable those who are joined by one love**
**to support one another**
**by their fervor of spirit and devotion to prayer.**
**Make them responsive to the needs of others**
**and witnesses to the faith in all they say and do.**

**We ask this through Christ our Lord.**

**℟. Amen.**

58     Or:

**We bless your name, O Lord,**
**for sending your own incarnate Son**
**to become part of a family,**
**so that, as he lived its life,**
**he would experience its worries and its joys.**

**We ask you, Lord,**
**to protect and watch over this family,**
**so that in the strength of your grace**
**its members may enjoy prosperity,**
**possess the priceless gift of your peace,**
**and, as the Church alive in the home,**
**bear witness in this world to your glory.**

**We ask this through Christ our Lord.**

**R℣. Amen.**

59     As circumstances suggest, the minister in silence may sprinkle the family with holy water.

## Concluding Rite

60     The minister concludes the rite by saying:

**May the Lord Jesus,**
**who lived with his holy family in Nazareth,**
**dwell also with your family,**
**keep it from all evil,**
**and make all of you one in heart and mind.**

**R℣. Amen.**

61     It is preferable to end the celebration with a suitable song.

# B. ORDER OF BLESSING WITHIN MASS

**62**     With due respect for the requirements of law, the priest who plans the Mass should readily make use of options in selecting various parts of the Mass, especially so that these serve the spiritual well-being of the family members.

     When the blessing of the family is carried out within a Mass celebrated at the family's home, the rite must be arranged in accord with the principles and provisions of the Instruction on Masses with small groups, *Actio pastoralis*,[2] or, where applicable, of the *Directory for Masses with Children*.[3] The celebration should also include appropriate comments on the rites.

**63**     After the gospel reading, the celebrant in the homily gives those present an explanation of the biblical text and of the graces belonging to family life and of the mission of the family in the life of the Church.


## GENERAL INTERCESSIONS

**64**     The general intercessions follow, either in the form usual at Mass or in the form given here. The celebrant concludes the general intercessions with the prayer of blessing, unless it is thought better to have the prayer of blessing at the end of Mass as a prayer over the people. The celebrant introduces the intercessions and an assisting minister or one of those present announces the intentions. From the following intentions those best suited to the occasion may be used or adapted, or other intentions that apply to the family and the particular circumstances may be composed.

The celebrant says:

**Christ the Lord, the Word coeternal with the Father, lived among us and chose to be part of a family and to enrich it with his blessings. Let us humbly ask for his favor and protection on this family.**

R̸. **Lord, keep our family in your peace.**

Or:

R̸. **Lord, hear our prayer.**

---

[2] Congregation for Divine Worship, 15 May 1969: AAS 61 (1969), pp. 806–811; English tr., International Commission on English in the Liturgy, *Documents on the Liturgy, 1963–1979: Conciliar, Papal, and Curial Texts* (hereafter DOL), The Liturgical Press (Collegeville, Minn., 1982), nos. 2120–2133.

[3] Congregation for Divine Worship, 1 November 1973: AAS 66 (1974), pp. 30–46; English tr., DOL, nos. 2134–2188.

*Assisting minister:*

**Through your own obedience to Mary and Joseph you consecrated family life; make this family holy by your presence. (For this we pray:) R⁊.**

*Assisting minister:*

**Your heart was set on the concerns of your Father; make every home a place where he is worshiped with reverence. (For this we pray:) R⁊.**

*Assisting minister:*

**You made your own family the model of prayer, of love, and of obedience to your Father's will; by your grace make this family holy and make it rich with your gifts. (For this we pray:) R⁊.**

*Assisting minister:*

**You loved those who were close to you and they returned your love; bind all families together in the bonds of peace and of love for each other. (For this we pray:) R⁊.**

*Assisting minister:*

**At Cana in Galilee, when a new family was beginning, you gladdened it with your first miracle, changing water into wine; alleviate the sorrows and worries of this family and change them into joy. (For this we pray:) R⁊.**

*Assisting minister:*

**In your concern for the integrity of the family you said: ''Let no one separate those whom God has bound together''; bind this husband and wife ever more closely together in the bond of your own love. (For this we pray:) R⁊.**

## PRAYER OF BLESSING

65    With hands outstretched over the family members, the celebrant continues with the prayer of blessing.

**O God,
you have created us in love and saved us in mercy,**

and through the bond of marriage
you have established the family
and willed that it should become a sign of Christ's love for
   his Church.

Shower your blessings on this family gathered here
   in your name.
Enable those who are joined by one love
to support one another
by their fervor of spirit and devotion to prayer.
Make them responsive to the needs of others
and witnesses to the faith in all they say and do.

We ask this through Christ our Lord.

R̸. Amen.

66    Or:

We bless your name, O Lord,
for sending your own incarnate Son
to become part of a family,
so that, as he lived its life,
he would experience its worries and its joys.

We ask you, Lord,
to protect and watch over this family,
so that in the strength of your grace
its members may enjoy prosperity,
possess the priceless gift of your peace,
and, as the Church alive in the home,
bear witness in this world to your glory.

We ask this through Christ our Lord.

R̸. Amen.

67    But as an alternative, if this seems more opportune, the
prayer of blessing may be used at the end of Mass after the following or some other invitation:

Bow your heads and pray for God's blessing.

After the prayer of blessing, the celebrant always adds:

And may almighty God bless you,
the Father, and the Son, ✝ and the Holy Spirit.

R̸. Amen.

# II. ORDER FOR THE ANNUAL BLESSING OF FAMILIES IN THEIR OWN HOMES

## INTRODUCTION

68    Pastors must regard as one of their primary pastoral duties the faithful visitation of families to bring the message of Christ's peace. They will thus obey the command of Christ to his disciples: "On entering any house, first say: 'Peace to this house'" (Luke 10:5).

69    Pastors and their assistants must therefore consider as a sacred trust the custom of an annual visit, particularly during the Easter season, to the families living in their parish. The occasion is a rich opportunity to fulfill pastoral responsibilities that grow in effectiveness the more the priests come to know the families.

70    The order for the annual blessing of families in their homes directly pertains to the family and therefore requires the presence of the family members.

71    No house is to be blessed unless the residents are present.

72    The present order may be used by a priest or deacon.

73    Normally the blessing is celebrated in each individual home. But for pastoral reasons and in the interest of increased unity between families living in the same building or locale, the blessing may be celebrated for several families gathered together in one convenient place. The text of the prayer of blessing is then adapted accordingly.

74    While maintaining the structure and chief elements of the rite, the celebrant should adapt the celebration to the circumstances of the place and the families involved. The celebrant's manner of presiding at the celebration should manifest the attentive concern of charity toward all present, particularly the young, the elderly, and the sick.

# ORDER OF BLESSING

## INTRODUCTORY RITES

75    When the community has gathered, the celebrant greets those present in the following or other suitable words, taken mainly from sacred Scripture.

**Peace be with this house and with all who live here.**

Or:

**The grace and peace of God our Father and the Lord Jesus Christ be with you.**

All make the following or some other suitable reply.

**And also with you.**

76    In the following or similar words, which should always be adapted to suit the particular situation, the celebrant prepares those present for the blessing.

**The purpose of the parish visit is that through the ministry of the priest (deacon) Christ may enter your home to bring you peace and joy. This happens above all through the reading of the word of God and the prayer of the Church.**

**Let us, then, prepare ourselves inwardly, so that, through the Holy Spirit, Christ himself will speak to us in this celebration and bring us the comfort of his presence.**

## READING OF THE WORD OF GOD

77    One of those present or the celebrant reads a text of sacred Scripture, taken preferably from those indicated here.

**Brothers and sisters, listen to the words of the holy gospel according to Matthew:**     7:24-28

*A house built on rock.*

**Jesus said to his disciples: ''Everyone who listens to these words of mine and acts on them will be like a wise man who built his house on rock. The rain fell, the floods came, and the winds blew and buffeted the house. But it did not collapse; it had been set solidly on rock. And everyone who listens to**

these words of mine but does not act on them will be like a fool who built his house on sand. The rain fell, the floods came, and the winds blew and buffeted the house. And it collapsed and was completely ruined.''

When Jesus finished these words, the crowds were astonished at his teaching.

78     Or:

Ephesians 4:1-6—*Bear with one another lovingly.*

Colossians 3:12-25—*Over all these virtues put on love.*

Acts 2:44-47—*In their homes they broke bread. With exultant and sincere hearts they took their meals in common.*

Luke 19:1-10—*Today salvation has come to this house.*

John 1:35-39—*They stayed with him that day.*

79     As circumstances suggest, one of the following responsorial psalms may be sung or said, or some other suitable song.

R℣. **We are his people: the sheep of his flock.**

Psalm 100

**Sing joyfully to the LORD, all you lands;
serve the LORD with gladness;
come before him with joyful song.** R℣.

**Know that the LORD is God;
he made us, his we are;
his people, the flock he tends.** R℣.

**Enter his gates with thanksgiving,
his courts with praise;
Give thanks to him; bless his name.** R℣.

**For he is good:
the LORD, whose kindness endures forever,
and his faithfulness, to all generations.** R℣.

Psalm 128:1-2, 3, 4-6a

R℣. **(4) See how the Lord blesses those who fear him.**

Psalm 148:1-2, 3-4, 12-13

R℣. **(13a) Let all praise the name of the Lord.**

80    As circumstances suggest, the celebrant may give those present a brief explanation of the biblical text, so that they may understand through faith the meaning of the celebration.

## INTERCESSIONS

81    The intercessions are then said. The celebrant introduces them and an assisting minister or one of those present announces the intentions. From the following intentions those best suited to the occasion may be used or adapted, or other intentions that apply to the particular circumstances may be composed.

During the Easter season

The celebrant says:

**My brothers and sisters, these are the days of our Easter gladness. Prompted by the Holy Spirit, let us pray to the risen Christ, whom the Father has made the beginning and foundation of our communion with each other. Calling on his name, let us say to him:**

℟. **Lord, stay with us.**

Or:

℟. **Lord, hear our prayer.**

Assisting minister:

**Lord Jesus Christ, after the resurrection you appeared to your disciples and gladdened them with the gift of your peace; make this family aware of your presence and help them to strive to remain close to you in the serenity of your peace. (For this we pray:)** ℟.

Assisting minister:

**You reached the glory of the resurrection through the humiliation of your passion; teach all the members of this family how to use even their daily trials to build up a household of love. (For this we pray:)** ℟.

Assisting minister:

**While you were at table with the disciples you showed yourself to them through the breaking of the bread; as the mem-**

bers of this family share in the eucharist with the Christian community, make them strong in faith and eager witnesses before the world to their faith in you. (For this we pray:) R̸.

Assisting minister:

With the power of the Holy Spirit you filled the house where the disciples were gathered; send the same Holy Spirit upon this family with the gifts of peace and joy. (For this we pray:) R̸.

82    Or:

Outside the Easter season

The celebrant says:

My brothers and sisters, as we ask the blessing of the Lord on this family, we must remember that a way of life that is a true communion can only endure and grow if the Lord is its source. Let us therefore call upon him, saying:

R̸. **Lord, make us holy.**

Or:

R̸. **Lord, hear our prayer.**

Assisting minister:

Lord Jesus Christ, through whom every family is like a building constructed by the Holy Spirit to become a temple of your glory, grant that this family of yours may be bonded together in your name. May you be the unshakeable foundation of their life together. (For this we pray:) R̸.

Assisting minister:

With Mary and Joseph you sanctified domestic life; teach all who live here that self-giving is the way to guide and uphold their life as a family. (For this we pray:) R̸.

Assisting minister:

Through Christian initiation you have joined the natural family to a larger spiritual family, the Church; help the members of this family to carry out faithfully their responsibility in your Church. (For this we pray:) R̸.

*Assisting minister:*

**You gathered the first members of the Church together in the upper room around Mary your mother; grant that the members of this household Church may learn from her to keep your words in their hearts, to be constant in prayer, and to be generous in giving of themselves and of all they possess to others. (For this we pray:)** ℟.

83    After the intercessions the celebrant, in the following or similar words, invites all present to sing or say the Lord's Prayer:

**Let us pray with confidence to the Father in the words our Savior taught us:**

*All:*

**Our Father . . .**

## PRAYER OF BLESSING

84    With hands outstretched over the family members, the celebrant continues with the prayer of blessing.

*During the Easter season*

**Blessed are you, O Lord.**
**In the Passover of the Old Testament**
**you kept unharmed the houses of your people**
**that were sprinkled with the blood of a lamb.**
**The fulfillment of your signs is the true paschal lamb,**
**the Son you gave to us.**
**He was crucified for us and raised from the dead,**
**so that we might all be filled with the grace of**
   **the Holy Spirit.**
**Bless ✙ this family and this home,**
**so that the joy of your love**
**may gladden the hearts of all who live here.**

**We ask this through Christ our Lord.**

℟. **Amen.**

85    Or:

*Outside the Easter season*

**Almighty and eternal God,**

**18**  ANNUAL BLESSING OF FAMILIES IN THEIR OWN HOMES

your fatherly tenderness never ceases to provide for our needs.
We ask you to bestow on this family and this home
the riches of your ✝ blessing.
With the gift of your grace sanctify those who live here,
so that, faithful to your commandments,
they will care for each other,
ennoble this world by their lives,
and reach the home you have prepared for them in heaven.

We ask this through Christ our Lord.

℞. Amen.

86    Or:

Blessed are you, God our Father,
for your gift of this house as the dwelling place of this family.
Grant that those who live here
may obtain the gifts of the Holy Spirit.
Through their works of charity let them show
what grace your ✝ blessing brings,
so that all who visit this home
will find the spirit of love and peace
which only you can give.

We ask this through Christ our Lord.

℞. Amen.

87    After the prayer of blessing, the celebrant sprinkles those present and the home with holy water and, as circumstances suggest, may say:

Let this water call to mind our baptism into Christ,
who has redeemed us by his death and resurrection.

## Concluding Rite

88    The celebrant concludes the rite by saying:

May the God of hope fill you with every joy in believing.
May the peace of Christ abound in your hearts.
May the Holy Spirit enrich you with his gifts,
now and for ever.

℞. Amen.

89    It is preferable to end the celebration with a suitable song.

# III. ORDERS FOR THE BLESSING OF A MARRIED COUPLE

## INTRODUCTION

90    A major wedding anniversary, for example, the 25th, 50th, or 60th, is a fitting occasion for a special remembrance of the sacrament of marriage by means of the celebration of the proper Mass and prayers provided in the Roman Missal.[4]

91    The blessing of a married couple may be celebrated within Mass, by use of the orders of blessing provided in nos. 94–106 and 107–114, or by a blessing outside Mass, celebrated according to the orders given in nos. 115–131 and 132–134.

92    A married couple may also request a blessing at a time other than an anniversary for the special needs of their lives or for such occasions as retreats or pilgrimages. If several couples are to be blessed at the same time, the prayer of blessing and the final blessing are adapted accordingly.

93    While maintaining the structure and chief elements of the rite, the minister should adapt the celebration to the circumstances of the place and the married couple and the families involved.

## A. ORDER OF BLESSING WITHIN MASS ON THE ANNIVERSARY OF MARRIAGE

94    Depending on the provisions of the rubrics, in the liturgy of the word the readings may be taken either from the lectionary of the *Rite of Marriage*[5] or from the Lectionary for Mass, Masses for Various Needs and Occasions, ''In Thanksgiving.''[6]

95    The homily follows the gospel reading. In it the celebrant, basing himself on the sacred text, gives an explanation of the grace and mystery of Christian married life pertinent to the life of the couple.

---

[4] See Roman Missal, Ritual Masses: Wedding Mass, 2. The Anniversaries of Marriage.

[5] See Roman Ritual, *Rite of Marriage*, nos. 67–105; Lectionary for Mass (2nd ed., 1981), nos. 801–805 (Ritual Masses: VI. Marriage).

[6] See Lectionary for Mass (2nd ed., 1981), nos. 943–947 (Masses for Various Needs and Occasions, III. For Various Public Needs, 26. In Thanksgiving).

96    Then the celebrant invites the couple to pray in silence and to renew before God their sacred matrimonial commitment to each other.

97    The celebrant may say the following prayer and then incense the couple's wedding rings.

**Lord,**
**increase and consecrate the love which N. and N.**
  **have for one another.**
**The wedding rings they once exchanged**
**are the sign of their fidelity.**
**May they continue to prosper**
**in the grace of the sacrament.**

**We ask this through Christ our Lord.**

**R⁊. Amen.**


98    Or if the couple renews the exchange of rings, the celebrant says the following prayer of blessing.

**Lord,**
**bless and consecrate the love which N. and N.**
  **have for one another.**
**May these rings be a symbol**
**of their true faith in each other**
**and of the grace of the sacrament.**

**We ask this through Christ our Lord.**

**R⁊. Amen.**


99    One of the following formularies may also be used:[7]

**Lord,**
**bless these rings which we bless ✢ in your name.**
**Grant that those who wear them**
**may always have a deep faith in each other.**
**May they continue to enjoy your peace and goodwill**
**and live together in love.**

**We ask this through Christ our Lord.**

**R⁊. Amen.**

---

[7] See *Rite of Marriage*, nos. 110–111.

Or:

**Lord,**
**bless ✝ and consecrate the love which N. and N.**
**have for one another.**
**May these rings be a symbol**
**of their true faith in each other**
**and always remind them of their love.**

**We ask this through Christ our Lord.**

℟. **Amen.**

## GENERAL INTERCESSIONS

**100** The general intercessions follow, either in the form usual at Mass or in the form given here.

The celebrant says:

**In the tender plan of his providence, God our almighty Father has given married love, its faithfulness, (and its fruitfulness,) a special significance in the history of salvation. Let us therefore call upon him, saying:**

℟. **Lord, renew in your servants their fidelity to each other.**

Or:

℟. **Lord, hear our prayer.**

Assisting minister:

**Father all-holy, the faithful one, you ask for and respond to fidelity to your covenant; fill with your blessings your servants who are celebrating their (25th, 50th, 60th, *other*) wedding anniversary. (For this we pray:)** ℟.

Assisting minister:

**You live in eternity with the Son and the Holy Spirit in oneness of life and communion of love; grant that these your servants will be mindful of the covenant of love they pledged to each other through the sacrament of marriage and never fail in fidelity. (For this we pray:)** ℟.

Assisting minister:

**In your providence you have ordained that all genuinely human experiences should become ways of leading the faithful to share in the mystery of Christ; grant to your servants serenity in good times and bad and the will to stay close to Christ and to live for him alone. (For this we pray:) R⁊.**

Assisting minister:

**It is your will that married life should be a lesson in Christian living; grant that all husbands and wives may be witnesses to the wonders of your Son's love. (For this we pray:) R⁊.**

101   The celebrant immediately adds the following or some other suitable prayer.

**O God,**
**the life of the family is founded on the plan of your**
**  own providence.**
**In your mercy receive the prayers of your servants.**
**Grant that by imitating the Holy Family**
**they may reach the joys of your home**
**and together praise you for ever.**

**We ask this through Christ our Lord.**

**R⁊. Amen.**

102   In the liturgy of the eucharist the Order of Mass is observed, with the few modifications indicated.

As circumstances suggest, the husband and wife may bring the bread and wine to the altar for the presentation of the gifts.

## Prayer of Blessing

103   After the Lord's Prayer, and omitting the embolism "Deliver us," the celebrant faces the couple and, with hands outstretched, says:

**Lord God and Creator,**
**we bless and praise your name.**
**In the beginning you made man and woman,**
**so that they might enter a communion of life and love.**
**You likewise blessed the union of N. with N.,**
**so that they might reflect the union of Christ**
**  with his Church:**

look with kindness on them today.
Amid the joys and struggles of their life
you have preserved the union between them;
renew their marriage covenant,
increase your love in them,
and strengthen their bond of peace,
so that (surrounded by their children)
they may always rejoice in the gift of your blessing.

We ask this through Christ our Lord.

R̸. Amen.

104    As circumstances suggest and in keeping with local custom,
after the celebrant says: "The peace of the Lord be with you,"
the husband and wife and all present may offer to each other some
sign of peace and love.

105    The couple may receive communion under both kinds.

106    At the end of Mass the celebrant blesses the couple, either
in the usual manner or by using a more solemn formulary, for
example:

In the following or similar words, the assisting deacon invites
those present to prepare for the blessing.

Bow your heads and pray for God's blessing.

Then with hands outstretched over the couple, the celebrant says:

May God, the almighty Father, give you joy.

R̸. Amen.

May the only Son of God have mercy on you
and help you in good times and in bad.

R̸. Amen.

May the Holy Spirit
always fill your hearts with love.

R̸. Amen.

Then he blesses all present.

And may almighty God bless you all,
the Father, and the Son, ✝ and the Holy Spirit.

R̸. Amen.

# B. ORDER OF BLESSING WITHIN MASS ON OTHER OCCASIONS

**107** Depending on the provisions of the rubrics, in the liturgy of the word the readings may be taken from the Lectionary for Mass, from either Ritual Masses, "Wedding Mass" or the Masses for Various Needs and Occasions, "In Thanksgiving."[8]

**108** The homily follows the gospel reading. In it the celebrant, basing himself on the sacred text, gives an explanation of the grace and mystery of Christian married life pertinent to the life of the couple.

**109** Then the celebrant invites the couple to pray in silence and to renew before God their sacred matrimonial commitment to each other.

## GENERAL INTERCESSIONS

**110** The general intercessions follow, either in the form usual at Mass or in the form given here.

The celebrant says:

**In the tender plan of his providence, God our almighty Father has given married love, its faithfulness, (and its fruitfulness,) a special significance in the history of salvation. Let us therefore call upon him, saying:**

℟. **Lord, renew in your servants their fidelity to each other.**

Or:

℟. **Lord, hear our prayer.**

Assisting minister:

**Father all-holy, you have made marriage the great symbol of Christ's love for his Church; bestow on these your servants the fullness of your own love. (For this we pray:)** ℟.

---

[8] See Lectionary for Mass (2nd ed., 1981), nos. 801–805 (Ritual Masses: VI. Marriage) and nos. 943–947 (Masses for Various Needs and Occasions, III. For Various Public Needs, 26. In Thanksgiving).

Assisting minister:

You live in eternity with the Son and the Holy Spirit in one-ness of life and communion of love; grant that these your servants will be mindful of the covenant of love they pledged to each other through the sacrament of marriage and never fail in fidelity. (For this we pray:) ℟.

Assisting minister:

In your providence you have ordained that all genuinely human experiences should become ways of leading the faith-ful to share in the mystery of Christ; grant to your servants serenity in good times and bad and the will to stay close to Christ and to live for him alone. (For this we pray:) ℟.

Assisting minister:

It is your will that married life should be a lesson in Christian living; grant that all husbands and wives may be witnesses to the wonders of your Son's love. (For this we pray:) ℟.

## PRAYER OF BLESSING

111    With hands outstretched, the celebrant concludes the inter-cessions by saying:

Almighty and eternal God,
you have so exalted the unbreakable bond of marriage
that it has become the sacramental sign
of your Son's union with the Church as his spouse.

Look with favor on N. and N., whom you have united
    in marriage,
as they ask for your help
and the protection of the Virgin Mary.
They pray that in good times and in bad
they will grow in love for each other;
that they will resolve to be of one heart
in the bond of peace.

Lord, in their struggles let them rejoice
that you are near to help them;
in their needs let them know
that you are there to rescue them;

in their joys let them see
that you are the source and completion of every happiness.

We ask this through Christ our Lord.

R℣. Amen.

> 112 In the liturgy of the eucharist the Order of Mass is observed, with the few modifications indicated.
>
> As circumstances suggest, the husband and wife may bring the bread and wine to the altar for the presentation of the gifts.
>
> 113 As circumstances suggest and in keeping with local custom, after the celebrant says: "The peace of the Lord be with you," the husband and wife and all present may offer to each other some sign of peace and love.
>
> 114 At the end of Mass the celebrant blesses the couple, either in the usual manner, or by using a more solemn formulary, for example:
>
> In the following or similar words, the assisting deacon invites those present to prepare for the blessing.

Bow your heads and pray for God's blessing.

> Then with hands outstretched over the couple, the celebrant says:

May God, the almighty Father, give you joy.

R℣. Amen.

May the only Son of God have mercy on you
and help you in good times and in bad.

R℣. Amen.

May the Holy Spirit
always fill your hearts with love.

R℣. Amen.

> Then he blesses all present.

And may almighty God bless you all,
the Father, and the Son, ✝ and the Holy Spirit.

R℣. Amen.

# C. ORDER OF BLESSING OUTSIDE MASS

**115**    The present order may be used by a priest or deacon. It may also be used by a layperson, who follows the rites and prayers designated for a lay minister.

**116**    While maintaining the structure and chief elements of the rite, the minister should adapt the celebration to the circumstances of the place and the couple involved.

Whenever a couple is to receive a blessing without the participation of a community of the faithful, the minister may use the shorter rite provided in nos. 132–134.

## Introductory Rites

**117**    When the community has gathered, Psalm 34 or some other suitable song may be sung. After the singing, the minister says:

**In the name of the Father, and of the Son, and of the Holy Spirit.**

All make the sign of the cross and reply:

**Amen.**

**118**    A minister who is a priest or deacon greets those present in the following or other suitable words, taken mainly from sacred Scripture.

**The grace and peace of God our Father, who exalted the marriage bond and made it the sign of Christ and his Church, be with you all.**

All make the following or some other suitable reply.

**And also with you.**

---

**119**    A lay minister greets those present in the following words.

**Blessed be the God of all consolation, who has shown us his great mercy. Blessed be God now and for ever.**

℟. **Amen.**

---

120    In the following or similar words, which should always be adapted to suit the particular occasion, the minister prepares the couple and all present for the blessing.

**We have come together to celebrate the anniversary of the marriage of our brother and sister. As we join them in their joy, we join them also in their gratitude. God has set them among us as a sign of his love and through the years they have remained faithful (and have fulfilled their responsibilities as parents). Let us give thanks for all the favors N. and N. have received during their married life. May God keep them in their love for each other, so that they may be more and more of one mind and one heart.**

## READING OF THE WORD OF GOD

121    A reader or another person present reads a text of sacred Scripture, taken preferably from the texts provided in the *Rite of Marriage* and the Lectionary for Mass.[9] The readings chosen should be those that best apply to the life of the couple.

**Brothers and sisters, listen to the words of the first letter of Paul to the Corinthians:**    1:4-9

*I never stop thanking God because of the grace of God which was given you.*

**I give thanks to my God always on your account for the grace of God bestowed on you in Christ Jesus, that in him you were enriched in every way, with all discourse and all knowledge, as the testimony to Christ was confirmed among you, so that you are not lacking in any spiritual gift as you wait for the revelation of our Lord Jesus Christ. He will keep you firm to the end, irreproachable on the day of our Lord Jesus Christ.**

**God is faithful, and by him you were called to fellowship with his Son, Jesus Christ our Lord.**

122    As circumstances suggest, the following responsorial psalm may be sung or said, or some other suitable song.

---

[9] See Roman Ritual, *Rite of Marriage*, nos. 67–105; Lectionary for Mass (2nd ed., 1981), nos. 801–805 (Ritual Masses, VI. Marriage) or nos. 943–947 (Masses for Various Needs and Occasions, III. For Various Public Needs, 26. In Thanksgiving).

℟. **Happy are those who fear the Lord.**

Psalm 128

**Happy are you who fear the LORD,
who walk in his ways!
For you shall eat the fruit of your handiwork;
happy shall you be, and favored. ℟.**

**Your wife shall be like a fruitful vine
in the recesses of your home;
Your children like olive plants
around your table. ℟.**

**Behold, thus is the man blessed
who fears the LORD.
The LORD bless you from Zion:
may you see the prosperity of Jerusalem
all the days of your life. ℟.**

123    As circumstances suggest, the minister may give those present a brief explanation of the biblical text and of the grace and mystery of Christian married life, so that they may understand through faith the meaning of the celebration.

Then the minister invites the couple to pray in silence and to renew before God their sacred matrimonial commitment to each other.

124    On a wedding anniversary the minister may say the following prayer and then incense the couple's wedding rings.

**Lord,
increase and consecrate the love which N. and N.
 have for one another.
The wedding rings they once exchanged
are the sign of their fidelity.
May they continue to prosper
in the grace of the sacrament.**

**We ask this through Christ our Lord.**

℟. **Amen.**

125    Or, if the couple renews the exchange of rings, the minister says the following prayer of blessing.

**Lord,**
**bless and consecrate the love which N. and N.**
    **have for one another.**
**May these rings be a symbol**
**of their true faith in each other**
**and of the grace of the sacrament.**

**We ask this through Christ our Lord.**

℞. **Amen.**

> **126** A minister who is a priest or a deacon may also use one of the following formularies.[10]

**Lord,**
**bless these rings which we bless ✝ in your name.**
**Grant that those who wear them**
**may always have a deep faith in each other.**
**May they continue to enjoy your peace and goodwill**
**and live together in love.**

**We ask this through Christ our Lord.**

℞. **Amen.**

> Or:

**Lord,**
**bless ✝ and consecrate the love which N. and N.**
    **have for one another.**
**May these rings be a symbol**
**of their true faith in each other**
**and always remind them of their love.**

**We ask this through Christ our Lord.**

℞. **Amen.**

## INTERCESSIONS

> **127** The intercessions are then said. The minister introduces them and an assisting minister or one of those present announces the intentions. From the following intentions those best suited to the occasion may be used or adapted, or other intentions that apply to the particular circumstances may be composed.

---

[10] See *Rite of Marriage*, nos. 110–111.

In the tender plan of his providence, God our almighty Father has given married love, its faithfulness, (and its fruitfulness,) a special significance in the history of salvation. Let us therefore call upon him, saying:

℞. **Lord, renew in your servants their fidelity to each other.**

Or:

℞. **Lord, hear our prayer.**

Assisting minister:

**Father all-holy, you have made marriage the great symbol of Christ's love for his Church; bestow on these your servants the fullness of your own love. (For this we pray:)** ℞.

---

On the 25th, 50th, 60th, or other wedding anniversary

Assisting minister:

**Father all-holy, the faithful one, you ask for and respond to fidelity to your covenant; fill with your blessings your servants who are celebrating their (25th, 50th, 60th, *other*) wedding anniversary. (For this we pray:)** ℞.

---

Assisting minister:

**You live in eternity with the Son and the Holy Spirit in oneness of life and communion of love; grant that these your servants will be mindful of the covenant of love they pledged to each other through the sacrament of marriage and never fail in fidelity. (For this we pray:)** ℞.

Assisting minister:

**In your providence you have ordained that all genuinely human experiences should become ways of leading the faithful to share in the mystery of Christ; grant to your servants serenity in good times and bad and the will to stay close to Christ and to live for him alone. (For this we pray:)** ℞.

Assisting minister:

**It is your will that married life should be a lesson in Christian living; grant that all husbands and wives may be witnesses to the wonders of your Son's love. (For this we pray:)** ℟.

## PRAYER OF BLESSING

128   A minister who is a priest or deacon says the appropriate prayer of blessing with hands outstretched; a lay minister says the prayer with hands joined.

A   On the 25th, 50th, 60th, or other anniversary

**Lord God and Creator,**
**we bless and praise your name.**
**In the beginning you made man and woman,**
**so that they might enter a communion of life and love.**
**You likewise blessed the union of N. with N.,**
**so that they might reflect the union of Christ**
**   with his Church:**
**look with kindness on them today.**
**Amid the joys and struggles of their life**
**you have preserved the union between them;**
**renew their marriage covenant,**
**increase your love in them,**
**and strengthen their bond of peace,**
**so that (surrounded by their children)**
**they may always rejoice in the gift of your blessing.**

**We ask this through Christ our Lord.**

℟. **Amen.**

B   On other occasions

**Almighty and eternal God,**
**you have so exalted the unbreakable bond of marriage**
**that it has become the sacramental sign**
**of your Son's union with the Church as his spouse.**

**Look with favor on N. and N., whom you have united**
**   in marriage,**
**as they ask for your help**
**and the protection of the Virgin Mary.**

They pray that in good times and in bad
they will grow in love for each other;
that they will resolve to be of one heart
in the bond of peace.

Lord, in their struggles let them rejoice
that you are near to help them;
in their needs let them know
that you are there to rescue them;
in their joys let them see
that you are the source and completion of every happiness.

We ask this through Christ our Lord.

R̶. Amen.

## CONCLUDING RITE

129    A minister who is a priest or deacon concludes the rite by first blessing the couple and saying, with hands outstretched toward them:

May God, the almighty Father, give you joy.

R̶. Amen.

May the only Son of God have mercy on you
and help you in good times and in bad.

R̶. Amen.

May the Holy Spirit
always fill your hearts with love.

R̶. Amen.

Then he blesses all present.

And may almighty God bless you all,
the Father, and the Son, ✠ and the Holy Spirit.

R̶. Amen.

130     A lay minister concludes the rite by signing himself or herself with the sign of the cross and saying:

**May the God of hope fill you with every joy in believing.**
**May the peace of Christ abound in your hearts.**
**May the Holy Spirit enrich you with his gifts,**
**now and for ever.**

**R℣. Amen.**

131     It is preferable to end the celebration with a suitable song.

# D. SHORTER RITE

132     The minister says:

**Our help is in the name of the Lord.**

All reply:

**Who made heaven and earth.**

133     One of those present or the minister reads a text of sacred Scripture, for example:

Mark 10:8-9

**Jesus answered the Pharisees, saying: "They are no longer two but one flesh. Therefore what God has joined together, no human being must separate."**

John 15:9, 10, 11

**Jesus said: "Remain in my love. If you keep my commandments, you will remain in my love, just as I have kept my Father's commandments and remain in his love.**

**"I have told you this so that my joy might be in you and your joy might be complete."**

**134** A minister who is a priest or deacon says the appropriate prayer of blessing with hands outstretched; a lay minister says the prayer with hands joined.

A     On the 25th, 50th, 60th, or other anniversary

**Lord God and Creator,**
**we bless and praise your name.**
**In the beginning you made man and woman,**
**so that they might enter a communion of life and love.**
**You likewise blessed the union of N. with N.,**
**so that they might reflect the union of Christ**
**    with his Church:**
**look with kindness on them today.**
**Amid the joys and struggles of their life**
**you have preserved the union between them;**
**renew their marriage covenant,**
**increase your love in them,**
**and strengthen their bond of peace,**
**so that (surrounded by their children)**
**they may always rejoice in the gift of your blessing.**

**We ask this through Christ our Lord.**

**R̶. Amen.**

B     On other occasions

**Almighty and eternal God,**
**you have so exalted the unbreakable bond of marriage**
**that it has become the sacramental sign**
**of your Son's union with the Church as his spouse.**

**Look with favor on N. and N., whom you have united**
**    in marriage,**
**as they ask for your help**
**and the protection of the Virgin Mary.**
**They pray that in good times and in bad**
**they will grow in love for each other;**
**that they will resolve to be of one heart**
**in the bond of peace.**

**Lord, in their struggles let them rejoice**
**that you are near to help them;**
**in their needs let them know**
**that you are there to rescue them;**

in their joys let them see
that you are the source and completion of every happiness.

We ask this through Christ our Lord.

℟. **Amen.**

# IV. ORDERS FOR THE BLESSING OF CHILDREN

## INTRODUCTION

135     There are many pastoral occasions for giving praise to God and praying for children who have already been baptized: for example, when the parents request a blessing, when special feasts are held for children, when the school year begins. The celebration of a blessing is to be adapted to the circumstances.

136     The present orders may be used by a priest or a deacon. They may also be used by a layperson, particularly a catechist and also a person in charge of the children's education, who follows the rites and prayers designated for a lay minister.

137     While maintaining the structure and chief elements of the rite, the minister should adapt the celebration to the circumstances of the families and children involved.

138     When the blessing is for just one child, the minister adapts the texts accordingly or, if this seems more opportune, uses the shorter rite provided in nos. 170–172.

## A. ORDER FOR THE BLESSING OF BAPTIZED CHILDREN

### INTRODUCTORY RITES

139     When the community has gathered, Psalm 113 or some other suitable song may be sung. After the singing, the minister says:

**In the name of the Father, and of the Son, and of the Holy Spirit.**

All make the sign of the cross and reply:

**Amen.**

140     A minister who is a priest or deacon greets the children (child) and all present in the following or other suitable words, taken mainly from sacred Scripture.

**The grace and peace of God our Father and his Son Jesus Christ, who showed his love for children, be with you all.**

All make the following or some other suitable reply.

**And also with you.**

---

141    A lay minister greets those present in the following words.

**Brothers and sisters, let us praise and thank the Lord, who took little children into his arms and blessed them. Praised be the Lord now and for ever.**

R̸. **Praised be the Lord now and for ever.**

Or:

R̸. **Amen.**

---

142    In the following or similar words, the minister prepares the children (child) and all present for the blessing.

**When he came into the world, our Lord, the Son of God, became a child and grew in wisdom, age, and grace in the eyes of God and of all who knew him. Jesus welcomed children, believed in their dignity, and held them up as a model for all who are seeking the kingdom of God.**

**But children do need the help of grown-ups if they are to develop their individual gifts, and their moral, mental, and physical powers, and so reach human and Christian maturity.**

**Let us therefore ask for God's blessing, so that we will devote ourselves to the Christian upbringing of these children (this child) and so that they (he/she) will accept willingly the guidance they (he/she) need (needs).**

## READING OF THE WORD OF GOD

143    A reader, another person present, or the minister reads a text of sacred Scripture.

**Brothers and sisters, listen to the words of the holy gospel according to Mark:** 10:13-16

*Jesus blessed the children.*

**People were bringing children to Jesus that he might touch them, but the disciples rebuked them. When Jesus saw this he became indignant and said to the disciples, "Let the children come to me; do not prevent them, for the kingdom of God belongs to such as these. Amen, I say to you, whoever does not accept the kingdom of God like a child will not enter it." Then he embraced the children and blessed them, placing his hands on them.**

144 Or:

**Brothers and sisters, listen to the words of the holy gospel according to Matthew:** 18:1-5, 10

*Whoever welcomes one such child for my sake welcomes me.*

**At that time the disciples approached Jesus and said, "Who is the greatest in the kingdom of heaven?" He called a child over, placed it in their midst, and said, "Amen, I say to you, unless you turn and become like children, you will not enter the kingdom of heaven. Whoever humbles himself like this child is the greatest in the kingdom of heaven. And whoever receives one child such as this in my name receives me.**

**"See that you do not despise one of these little ones, for I say to you that their angels in heaven always look upon the face of my heavenly Father."**

145 Or:

Matthew 19:13-15—*Let the children come to me.*

Matthew 21:14-16—*From the speech of infants and children you have framed a hymn of praise.*

Luke 2:46-52—*Jesus progressed in wisdom, age, and grace.*

146 As circumstances suggest, the minister may give those present a brief explanation of the biblical text, so that they may understand through faith the meaning of the celebration.

The explanation should be short and suited to the children's (child's) understanding, but it should also be helpful to the adults.

**147**    After the reading or after the instruction, a psalm, a hymn, or some other song familiar to the children (child) may be sung.

R℣. **We are his people: the sheep of his flock.**

Psalm 100

**Sing joyfully to the LORD, all you lands;**
**serve the LORD with gladness;**
**come before him with joyful song.** R℣.

**Know that the LORD is God;**
**he made us, his we are;**
**his people, the flock he tends.** R℣.

**Enter his gates with thanksgiving,**
**his courts with praise;**
**Give thanks to him; bless his name.** R℣.

**For he is good:**
**the LORD, whose kindness endures forever,**
**and his faithfulness, to all generations.** R℣.

Psalm 150:1-2, 3-4, 5

R℣. **(5c) Let everything that breathes praise the Lord!**

## INTERCESSIONS

**148**    The intercessions are then said. The minister introduces them and an assisting minister or one of those present announces the intentions. From the following intentions those best suited to the occasion may be used or adapted, or other intentions that apply to the particular circumstances may be composed.

Two formularies are provided here, the second of which is a model that invites a response by the children (child) or allows for their adding their own intentions.

A        The minister says:

**The Lord Jesus held up to all his followers the simplicity and trust of children as a condition for entering the kingdom of heaven. Let us therefore call on Jesus in prayer, saying:**

R℣. **Lord, in children let us welcome you.**

Or:

R℣. **Lord, hear our prayer.**

**Lord Jesus, born of the Virgin Mary, you sanctified childhood; grant that these children (this child) may grow as you did in wisdom, age, and grace. (For this we pray:) R̂.**

Assisting minister:

**Through their (his/her) parents and the Church you show these children (this child) the tenderness of your own love; grant that those entrusted with their (his/her) care will be tireless in watching over them (him/her). (For this we pray:) R̂.**

Assisting minister:

**In baptism you have given all of us rebirth to a new childhood and opened to us the doors to your Father's house; grant that as faithful servants we may follow wherever you lead. (For this we pray:) R̂.**

Assisting minister:

**Even as a child you had to undergo persecution and exile; grant that all children who are victims of the evil of these times may find help and protection. (For this we pray:) R̂.**

B      149    The minister says:

**Lord Jesus, you welcomed and blessed little children; listen kindly to our prayer.**

**R̂. Lord, hear us.**

Or:

**R̂. Lord, hear our prayer.**

Assisting minister:

**Protect us from all dangers. R̂.**

Assisting minister:

**Watch over our life and our upbringing. R̂.**

Assisting minister:

**May we grow in wisdom, age, and grace in the eyes of God and of our neighbors. R̂.**

Assisting minister:

**Help all of today's children. R⁊.**

Assisting minister:

**Let us thank you for your gifts to us. R⁊.**

Assisting minister:

**Bless our parents, friends, and all who are kind to us. R⁊.**

## PRAYER OF BLESSING

150   A minister who is a priest or deacon may, as circumstances suggest, hold his hands outstretched over the children (child), as he says the prayer of blessing.

**Lord, our God,**
**out of the speech of little children**
**you have fashioned a hymn of praise.**
**Look with kindness on these children (this child)**
**whom the faith of the Church commends to your tender care.**
**Your Son, born of the Virgin Mary, gladly welcomed**
  **little children.**
**He took them in his arms, blessed them,**
**and held them up as an example for all.**

**We pray that you, Father,**
**will also send your blessing on them (him/her),**
**so that they (he/she) may grow in Christian maturity**
**and, by the power of the Holy Spirit,**
**become Christ's witnesses (witness) in the world,**
**spreading and defending the faith.**

**We ask this through Christ our Lord.**

**R⁊. Amen.**

151   A lay minister says the following prayer of blessing with hands joined.

**Lord Jesus Christ,**
**you loved children so much that you said:**
**"Whoever welcomes a child welcomes me."**

Hear our prayers and, with your unfailing protection,
watch over these children (this child)
whom you have blessed with the grace of baptism.
When they (he/she) have (has) grown to maturity,
grant that they (he/she) will confess your name
  in willing faith,
be fervent in charity,
and persevere courageously in the hope of reaching
  your kingdom,
where you live and reign for ever and ever.

R̶⁊. **Amen.**

---

152    After the prayer of blessing, the minister may sprinkle the children (child) with holy water and, as circumstances suggest, may say:

**Let this water call to mind our baptism into Christ,
who has redeemed us by his death and resurrection.**

## CONCLUDING RITE

153    A minister who is a priest or deacon concludes the rite by saying:

**May the Lord Jesus, who loved children,
bless you and keep you in his love,
now and for ever.**

R̶⁊. **Amen.**

---

154    A lay minister concludes the rite by signing himself or herself with the sign of the cross and saying:

**May the Lord Jesus, who loved children,
bless us and keep us in his love,
now and for ever.**

R̶⁊. **Amen.**

---

155    It is preferable to end the celebration with a suitable song.

# B. ORDER FOR THE BLESSING OF A CHILD NOT YET BAPTIZED

**156**     A gathering in preparation for a baptism soon to be celebrated is an opportune occasion for the blessing of a child not yet baptized through a celebration similar to the blessings imparted during the catechumenate. Pastoral practice should include an explanation of why the parents or the minister trace the sign of the cross upon the child, namely, as an indication that the child is marked by the sign of salvation, is already dedicated to God, and is being prepared for the reception of baptism.

**157**     The present order may be used by a priest or deacon. It may also be used by a layperson, particularly a catechist, who follows the rites and prayers designated for a lay minister.

## INTRODUCTORY RITES

**158**     When the family has gathered, the minister says:

**In the name of the Father, and of the Son, and of the Holy Spirit.**

All make the sign of the cross and reply:

**Amen.**

**159**     A minister who is a priest or deacon greets the child and all present in the following or other suitable words, taken mainly from sacred Scripture.

**The grace and peace of God our Father and his Son Jesus Christ, who showed his love for children, be with you all.**

All make the following or some other suitable reply.

**And also with you.**

Or:

**Blessed be God for ever.**

160   A lay minister greets the child and all present in the following words.

**Brothers and sisters, let us praise and thank the Lord, who took little children into his arms and blessed them. Praised be the Lord now and for ever.**

R̰. **Praised be the Lord now and for ever.**

Or:

R̰. **Amen.**

161   In the following or similar words, the minister prepares those present for the blessing.

**When he came into the world, our Lord, the Son of God, became a child and grew in wisdom, age, and grace in the eyes of God and of all who knew him. Jesus welcomed children, believed in their dignity, and held them up as a model for all who are seeking the kingdom of God.**

**But children do need the help of grown-ups if they are to develop their individual gifts, and their moral, mental, and physical powers, and so reach human and Christian maturity.**

**Let us therefore ask for God's blessing, so that we will devote ourselves to the Christian upbringing of N. and so that he/she will accept willingly the guidance he/she needs.**

## READING OF THE WORD OF GOD

162   One of those present or the minister reads a text of sacred Scripture, taken preferably from the texts given in the *Rite of Baptism for Children* and the Lectionary for Mass.[11] A reading should be chosen that best serves the preparation of the parents for their child's baptism.

---

[11] See *Rite of Baptism for Children*, nos. 186–215; Lectionary for Mass (2nd ed., 1981), nos. 751–763 (Ritual Masses, I. Christian Initiation, 1. Order of Catechumens and Christian Initiation of Adults, Christian Initiation Apart from the Easter Vigil and 2. Christian Initiation of Children).

**Brothers and sisters, listen to the words of the holy gospel according to Mark:** 10:13-16

*Jesus blessed the children.*

**People were bringing children to Jesus that he might touch them, but the disciples rebuked them. When Jesus saw this he became indignant and said to the disciples, ''Let the children come to me; do not prevent them, for the kingdom of God belongs to such as these. Amen, I say to you, whoever does not accept the kingdom of God like a child will not enter it.'' Then he embraced the children and blessed them, placing his hands on them.**

163 As circumstances suggest, the minister may give those present a brief explanation of the biblical text, so that they may understand through faith the meaning of the celebration.

164 After the reading or after the instruction, a psalm, a hymn, or some other song familiar to the child may be sung.

R⁊. **Let everything that breathes praise the Lord!**

Psalm 150

**Alleluia.**
**Praise the Lord in his sanctuary,**
**praise him in the firmament of his strength.**
**Praise him for his mighty deeds,**
**praise him for his sovereign majesty.** R⁊.

**Praise him with the blast of the trumpet,**
**praise him with lyre and harp.**
**Praise him with timbrel and dance,**
**praise him with strings and pipe.** R⁊.

**Praise him with sounding cymbals,**
**praise him with clanging cymbals.**
**Let everything that has breath**
**praise the LORD! Alleluia.** R⁊.

## INTERCESSIONS

165 The intercessions are then said. The minister introduces them and an assisting minister or one of those present announces the intentions. From the following intentions those best suited

to the occasion may be used or adapted, or other intentions that apply to the particular circumstances may be composed.

The minister says:

**The Lord Jesus held up to all his followers the simplicity and trust of children as a condition for entering the kingdom of heaven. Let us therefore call on Jesus in prayer, saying:**

R̶. **Lord, in children let us welcome you.**

Or:

R̶. **Lord, hear our prayer.**

Assisting minister:

**Lord Jesus, you will new children to be begotten for the Church not by human birth but by God; grant that the time of awaiting baptism may be one of a more complete preparation for its celebration. (For this we pray:)** R̶.

Assisting minister:

**Through his/her parents and the Church you show this child the tenderness of your own love; grant that those entrusted with his/her care will be tireless in watching over him/her. (For this we pray:)** R̶.

Assisting minister:

**In baptism you have given all of us rebirth to a new childhood and opened to us the doors to your Father's house; grant that as faithful servants we may follow wherever you lead. (For this we pray:)** R̶.

Assisting minister:

**Even as a child you had to undergo persecution and exile; grant that all children who are victims of the evil of these times may find help and protection. (For this we pray:)** R̶.

## PRAYER OF BLESSING

166    A minister who is a priest or deacon says the prayer of blessing while laying hands on the child; a lay minister says the prayer with hands joined.

**All-powerful God and Father,**
**you are the source of all blessings, the protector**
**of infants,**
**whose gift of children enriches and brightens a marriage.**
**Look with favor on this child**
**and, when he/she is reborn of water and the Holy Spirit,**
**bring him/her into your own spiritual family, the Church,**
**there to become a sharer in your kingdom**
**and with us to bless your name for ever.**

**We ask this through Christ our Lord.**

**R⁷. Amen.**

168     In silence the minister and the parents trace the sign of the
cross on the child's forehead.

## Concluding Rite

168     A minister who is a priest or deacon concludes the rite by
saying:

**May the Lord Jesus, who loved children,**
**bless you and keep you in his love,**
**now and for ever.**

**R⁷. Amen.**

169     A lay minister concludes the rite by signing himself or herself with the sign of the cross and saying:

**May the Lord Jesus, who loved children,**
**bless us and keep us in his love,**
**now and for ever.**

**R⁷. Amen.**

# C. SHORTER RITE

**170** The minister says:

**Our help is in the name of the Lord.**

All reply:

**Who made heaven and earth.**

**171** One of those present or the minister reads a text of sacred Scripture, for example:

Mark 10:14

**When Jesus saw the disciples rebuking the people he became indignant and said to them, "Let the children come to me; do not prevent them, for the kingdom of God belongs to such as these."**

Matthew 18:3

**Jesus said to his disciples: "Amen, I say to you, unless you turn and become like children, you will not enter the kingdom of heaven."**

Matthew 18:5

**Jesus said to his disciples: "Whoever receives one child such as this in my name receives me."**

1 Corinthians 14:20

**Brothers, stop being childish in your thinking. In respect to evil be like infants, but in your thinking be mature.**

**172** A minister who is a priest or deacon says the appropriate prayer of blessing while laying hands on the child; a lay minister says the prayer with hands joined.

A    A child already baptized

**Lord Jesus Christ,**
**you loved children so much that you said:**
**"Whoever welcomes a child welcomes me."**
**Hear our prayers and, with your unfailing protection,**
**watch over this child**

whom you have blessed with the grace of baptism.
When he/she has grown to maturity,
grant that he/she will confess your name in willing faith,
be fervent in charity,
and persevere courageously in the hope of reaching your
   kingdom,
where you live and reign for ever and ever.

R7. **Amen.**

B          A child not yet baptized

All-powerful God and Father,
you are the source of all blessings, the protector
   of infants,
whose gift of children enriches and brightens a marriage.
Look with favor on this child
and, when he/she is reborn of water and the Holy Spirit,
bring him/her into your own spiritual family, the Church,
there to become a sharer in your kingdom
and with us to bless your name for ever.

We ask this through Christ our Lord.

R7. **Amen.**

## SHORT FORMULARY

173    As circumstances suggest, a priest or deacon may use the
following short blessing formulary.

May the Lord Jesus, who loved children,
bless ✝ you, N., and keep you in his love,
now and for ever.

R7. **Amen.**

# V. ORDER FOR THE BLESSING OF SONS AND DAUGHTERS

## INTRODUCTION

174    The gospels record that children were presented to Jesus, so that he might bless them and lay hands on them. Christian parents wish to bestow this blessing of the Lord on their own children and the practice of a blessing by parents is a tradition treasured by many peoples. The blessing may be celebrated on special occasions in the life of the children or whenever the family gathers for prayer or for reflection on sacred Scripture.

175    When a priest or deacon is present, the ministry of blessing more fittingly belongs to him. This is particularly the case on the occasion of the regular parish visitations that are scheduled for the blessing of families.

176    The present order may be used by the parents or by a priest or deacon. While maintaining the structure and chief elements of the rite, the minister should adapt the celebration to the circumstances of the place and the people involved.

177    When a child is to be blessed as part of the celebration of another blessing, the short formulary provided in no. 194 may be used.

178    When a child who is sick is to be blessed, the ritual provided in chapter 2, nos. 309–402 may be used.


## ORDER OF BLESSING

### INTRODUCTORY RITES

179    When the family has gathered, the minister says:

**In the name of the Father, and of the Son, and of the Holy Spirit.**

All make the sign of the cross and reply:

**Amen.**

180    A minister who is a priest or deacon greets those present in the following or other suitable words, taken mainly from sacred Scripture.

---

**The grace of God our Father, who has made us his children by adoption, be with you all.**

All make the following or some other suitable reply.

**And also with you.**

---

181    A lay minister greets those present in the following words.

**My brothers and sisters, let us praise God our Father, who has made us his children by adoption. To God be glory now and for ever.**

℟. **To God be glory now and for ever.**

Or:

℟. **Amen.**

---

182    In the following or similar words, the minister prepares the children and all present for the blessing.

**In Psalm 128 we read: "Your children will be like olive shoots around the table." For children are the sign and pledge of God's blessing. They are living proof of God's presence, because when God blesses the family with the gift of children, he fills its life with joy and happiness. Children should therefore be cherished and respected. But they should also be taught reverence for God, so that with a sense of responsibility they will grow in wisdom and grace, hold in their thoughts and actions to whatever is true, upright, and virtuous, and live in the world as Christ's witnesses and heralds.**

## READING OF THE WORD OF GOD

183    One of those present or the minister reads a text of sacred Scripture.

**Brothers and sisters, listen to the words of the holy gospel according to Matthew:** 19:13-15

*Let the children come to me.*

Children were brought to Jesus that he might lay his hands on them and pray. The disciples rebuked the parents, but Jesus said, ''Let the children come to me, and do not prevent them; for the kingdom of heaven belongs to such as these.'' After he placed his hands on the children, he went away.


184    Or:

**Brothers and sisters, listen to the words of the book of Tobit:** 4:5-7, 19

*My son, keep in mind my commandments.*

Tobit said: ''Through all your days, my son, keep the Lord in mind, and suppress every desire to sin or to break his commandments. Perform good works all the days of your life, and do not tread the paths of wrongdoing. For if you are steadfast in your service, your good works will bring success, not only to you but also to all those who live uprightly. Give alms from your possessions. Do not turn your face away from any of the poor, and God's face will not be turned away from you.

''At all times bless the Lord God, and ask him to make all your paths straight and to grant success to all your endeavors and plans. For no pagan nation possesses good counsel, but the Lord himself gives all good things. If the Lord chooses, he raises a man up; but if he should decide otherwise, he casts him down to the deepest recesses of the nether world. So now, my son, keep in mind my commandments, and never let them be erased from your heart.''


185    Or:

**Brothers and sisters, listen to the words of the book of Proverbs:** 4:1-7

*Hear, children, a father's instruction.*

Hear, O children, a father's instruction,
be attentive, that you may gain understanding!
Yes, excellent advice I give you;
my teaching do not forsake.

When I was my father's child,
frail, yet the darling of my mother,
He taught me, and said to me:
"Let your heart hold fast my words:
keep my commands, that you may live!
Get wisdom, get understanding!
Do not forget or turn aside from the words I utter.
Forsake her not, and she will preserve you;
love her, and she will safeguard you;
The beginning of wisdom is: get wisdom;
at the cost of all you have, get understanding.

186   Or:

Matthew 18:1-5, 10—*Anyone who welcomes a little child such as this in my name welcomes me.*

187   As circumstances suggest, the following responsorial psalm may be sung or said, or some other suitable song may be sung.

R℣. **See how the Lord blesses those who fear him.**

Or:

R℣. **Happy are those who fear the Lord.**

Psalm 128

**Happy are you who fear the LORD,
who walk in his ways!
For you shall eat the fruit of your handiwork;
happy shall you be, and favored.** R℣.

**Your wife shall be like a fruitful vine
in the recesses of your home;
Your children like olive plants
around your table.** R℣.

**Behold thus is the man blessed
who fears the LORD.
The LORD bless you from Zion;
may you see the prosperity of Jerusalem
all the days of your life;
May you see your children's children.** R℣.

188   As circumstances suggest, the minister may give those present a brief explanation of the biblical text, so that they may understand through faith the meaning of the celebration.

# INTERCESSIONS

189    The intercessions are then said. The minister introduces them and an assisting minister or one of those present announces the intentions. From the following intentions those best suited to the occasion may be used or adapted, or other intentions that apply to the particular circumstances may be composed.

The minister says:

**The Lord Jesus taught us to call the almighty God our Father. Let us then pray to him saying:**

℟. **Father all-holy, watch over your children.**

Or:

℟. **Lord, hear our prayer.**

Assisting minister:

**Loving Father, you so loved the world that you gave your only Son; keep us, your children reborn in baptism, in your love. (For this we pray:)** ℟.

Assisting minister:

**Your favor rested fully on the Son you loved; grant that each one of us may successfully carry out the responsibilities entrusted to us in the world and in the Church. (For this we pray:)** ℟.

Assisting minister:

**As your Son was growing up, you placed him in the tender care of Mary and Joseph; grant that your children may grow to the full maturity of Christ. (For this we pray:)** ℟.

Assisting minister:

**You show a special love for those who are alone and abandoned; through the help of the Christian community let all children who are deprived of a family's love know that you are their Father. (For this we pray:)** ℟.

# Prayer of Blessing

190  As circumstances suggest, the parents may trace the sign of the cross on their children's forehead; they then say the prayer of blessing.

**Father,
inexhaustible source of life and author of all good,
we bless you and we thank you
for brightening our communion of love by your gift
  of children.
Grant that our children (child) will find in the life
  of this family such inspiration
that they (he/she) will strive always for what is right
  and good
and one day, by your grace,
reach their (his/her) home in heaven.**

**We ask this through Christ our Lord.**

℞. **Amen.**

---

191  A minister who is not a parent of the children says the following prayer of blessing.

**Lord Jesus Christ,
you loved children so much that you said:
"Whoever welcomes a child welcomes me."
Hear our prayers and, with your unfailing protection,
watch over these children (this child)
whom you have blessed with the grace of baptism.
When they (he/she) have (has) grown to maturity,
grant that they (he/she) will confess your name
  in willing faith,
be fervent in charity,
and persevere courageously in the hope of reaching
  your kingdom,
where you live and reign for ever and ever.**

℞. **Amen.**

## Concluding Rite

**192**　The parents (or other lay minister) conclude the rite by signing themselves with the sign of the cross and saying:

**May the Lord Jesus, who loved children,**
**bless us and keep us in his love,**
**now and for ever.**

℟. **Amen.**

---

**193**　A minister who is a priest or deacon concludes the rite by saying:

**May the Lord Jesus, who loved children,**
**bless you and keep you in his love,**
**now and for ever.**

℟. **Amen.**

---

## Short Formulary

**194**　As circumstances suggest, the following short blessing formulary may be used.

**May the Lord keep you**
**and make you grow in his love,**
**so that you may live worthy of the calling he has given you,**
**now and for ever.**

℟. **Amen.**

# VI. ORDER FOR THE BLESSING OF AN ENGAGED COUPLE

## INTRODUCTION

195    Besides seeing to the upbringing of their children, Christian parents have the further serious responsibility, an exercise of their own apostolate, of helping the children to prepare themselves properly for marriage.

The betrothal of a young Christian couple therefore is a special occasion for their families, who should celebrate it together with prayer and a special rite. In this way they ask God's blessing that the happiness promised by the children's engagement will be brought to fulfillment.

In order that the celebration will better achieve its purpose, it should be adapted to suit the particular circumstances.

196    When the engagement is celebrated within the circle of the two families, one of the parents should preside. But when a priest or a deacon is present, the office of presiding more fittingly belongs to him (provided it is clear to all that the blessing is not the celebration of the sacrament of marriage itself).

197    The present order may be used by the parents, a priest, a deacon, or a lay minister. While maintaining the structure and chief elements of the rite, the minister should adapt the celebration to the circumstances of the place and the people involved.

198    The present order may also be celebrated during the engagement period on an occasion when couples are brought together for premarital instruction. Neither a formal betrothal nor the special blessing of an engaged couple is ever to be combined with the celebration of Mass.

## ORDER OF BLESSING

### INTRODUCTORY RITES

199    When the families have gathered, the minister says:

**In the name of the Father, and of the Son, and of the Holy Spirit.**

All make the sign of the cross and reply:

**Amen.**

200     A minister who is a priest or deacon greets those present in the following or other suitable words, taken mainly from sacred Scripture.

**The grace and peace of our Lord Jesus Christ, who loved us and gave himself for us, be with you all.**

All make the following or some other suitable reply.

**And also with you.**

---

201     A lay minister greets those present in the following words.

**Brothers and sisters, let us praise our Lord Jesus Christ, who loved us and gave himself for us. Let us bless him now and for ever.**

**R̷. Amen.**

---

202     In the following or similar words, the minister prepares the couple and all present for the blessing.

**We know that all of us need God's blessing at all times; but at the time of their engagement to be married, Christians are in particular need of grace as they prepare themselves to form a new family.**

**Let us pray, then, for God's blessing to come upon this couple, our brother and sister: that as they await the day of their wedding, they will grow in mutual respect and in their love for one another; that through their companionship and prayer together they will prepare themselves rightly and chastely for marriage.**

## READING OF THE WORD OF GOD

203 .     One of those present or the minister reads a text of sacred Scripture.

**Brothers and sisters, listen to the words of the holy gospel according to John:**        John 15:9-12

*This is my commandment: love one another as I have loved you.*

**Jesus said to his disciples: ''As the Father loves me, so I also love you. Remain in my love. If you keep my commandments,**

you will remain in my love, just as I have kept my Father's commandments and remain in his love.

"I have told you this so that my joy might be in you and your joy might be complete. This is my commandment: love one another as I love you."

204 Or:

**Brothers and sisters, listen to the words of the first letter of Paul to the Corinthians:** 13:4-13

*There is no limit to love's forbearance, to its trust, its hope, its power to endure.*

**Love is patient, love is kind. It is not jealous, love is not pompous, it is not inflated, it is not rude, it does not seek its own interests, it is not quick-tempered, it does not brood over injury, it does not rejoice over wrongdoing but rejoices with the truth. It bears all things, believes all things, hopes all things, endures all things.**

**Love never fails. If there are prophecies, they will be brought to nothing; if tongues, they will cease; if knowledge, it will be brought to nothing. For we know partially and we prophesy partially, but when the perfect comes, the partial will pass away. When I was a child, I used to talk as a child, think as a child, reason as a child; when I became a man, I put aside childish things. At present we see indistinctly, as in a mirror, but then face to face. At present I know partially; then I shall know fully as I am fully known. So faith, hope, love remain, these three; but the greatest of these is love.**

205 Or:

Hosea 2:21-26—*I will espouse you in fidelity.*

Philippians 2:1-5—*United in spirit and ideals.*

206 As circumstances suggest, the following responsorial psalm may be sung or said, or some other suitable song.

R̶⁊. **The Lord is good to all.**

Psalm 145

**The Lord is gracious and merciful,
slow to anger and of great kindness.**

**The LORD is good to all**
**and compassionate toward all his works.** R℣.

**Let all your works give you thanks, O LORD,**
**and let your faithful ones bless you.**
**The eyes of all look hopefully to you,**
**and you give them their food in due season.** R℣.

**The LORD is just in all his ways**
**and holy in all his works.**
**The LORD is near to all who call upon him,**
**to all who call upon him in truth.** R℣.

207   As circumstances suggest, the minister may give those present a brief explanation of the biblical text, so that they may understand through faith the meaning of the celebration and its difference from the celebration of marriage.

## INTERCESSIONS

208   The intercessions are then said. The minister introduces them and an assisting minister or one of those present announces the intentions. From the following intentions those best suited to the occasion may be used or adapted, or other intentions that apply to the particular circumstances may be composed.

The minister says:

**God our Father has so loved us that in Christ he makes us his children and the witnesses to his love before the entire world. Let us, therefore, call upon him in all confidence, saying:**

R℣. **Lord, help us to remain always in your love.**

Assisting minister:

**God our Father, you willed that your true children, brothers and sisters in Christ, should be known by their love for one another.** R℣.

Assisting minister:

**You place upon us the sweet demands of love so that we may find happiness by responding to them.** R℣.

Assisting minister:

**You join a man and a woman together by their love for each other, so that in the family they establish they may rejoice in children, the crown of their love.** R℣.

Assisting minister:

**Through the paschal offering, Christ espoused the Church as his Bride and in his blood offered it to you, holy and immaculate. In this you have given us the ideal of the love that should exist between husband and wife in the sacrament of marriage. R℣.**

Assisting minister:

**You call N. and N. to the communion of life and love that binds the Christian family together, mind and heart. R℣.**

209    In accord with local custom, before the prayer of blessing, the engaged couple may express some sign of their pledge to each other, for example, by signing a document or by exchanging rings or gifts.

210    The engagement rings or gifts may be blessed by use of the following formulary.

**In due course may you honor the sacred pledge symbolized by these gifts which you now exchange.**

**R℣. Amen.**

## PRAYER OF BLESSING

211    A lay minister says the following prayer of blessing with hands joined. A priest or deacon says the following prayer with hands outstretched.

**We praise you, Lord,**
**for your gentle plan draws together your children,**
**    N. and N.,** *Zoe & Drew*
**in love for one another.**
**Strengthen their hearts,**
**so that they will keep faith with each other,**
**please you in all things,**
**and so come to the happiness of celebrating the sacrament**
**    of their marriage.**

**We ask this through Christ our Lord.**

**R℣. Amen.**

212    Or a minister who is a priest or deacon may say the following prayer of blessing.

*START HERE*

Lord God,
**the source of all love,**
**the wise plan of your providence has brought these**
**young people together.**
**As they prepare themselves for the sacrament of marriage**
**and pray for your grace,**
**grant that, strengthened by your blessing,** ✝
**they may grow in their respect for one another**
**and cherish each other with a sincere love.**

**We ask this through Christ our Lord.**

℟. **Amen.**

*READ THIS* ✓

## CONCLUDING RITE

213   The minister concludes the rite by saying:

*ZOE + DREW*

**May the God of love and peace**
**abide in you, guide your steps,**
**and confirm your hearts in his love,**
**now and for ever.**

℟. **Amen.** *HUG BOTH OF THEM*

214   It is preferable to end the celebration with a suitable song.

# VII. ORDER FOR THE BLESSING OF PARENTS BEFORE CHILDBIRTH

## INTRODUCTION

215   A husband and wife participate in God's love through the sacrament of marriage and cooperate in the gift of life through the conception of a child. It is appropriate that they receive God's blessing together as they wait in faith and hope for the birth of their child.

When only the mother is present, the *Order for the Blessing of a Mother before Childbirth*, nos. 240–252, is used.

216   The blessing may be celebrated at any time during the pregnancy.

217   These orders may be used by a priest or a deacon, and also by a lay-person, who follows the rites and prayers designated for a lay minister, or a family member.

## A. ORDER OF BLESSING

### INTRODUCTORY RITES

218   When the community has gathered, a suitable song may be sung. After the singing, the minister says:

**In the name of the Father, and of the Son, and of the Holy Spirit.**

All make the sign of the cross and reply:

**Amen.**

219   A minister who is a priest or deacon greets those present in the following or other suitable words, taken mainly from sacred Scripture.

**May Christ, who became like us in the womb of the Virgin Mary, be with you all.**

And all reply:

**And also with you.**

**Brothers and sisters, let us bless the Lord Jesus, who in the womb of the Virgin Mary became like us. Blessed be God for ever.**

℞. **Blessed be God for ever.**

**God, the Lord of life, brings every human creature into being and rules and sustains the life of each one of us. He has particular care for those born of a Christian marriage, since through the sacrament of baptism they will receive the gift of divine life itself. These parents-to-be are partners in God's love and seek his blessing because they already cherish the child they have conceived and because they await the hour of their child's birth in faith and hope.**

## READING OF THE WORD OF GOD

**Brothers and sisters, listen to the words of the first book of Samuel:**                                                     1:19-20, 24—2:1

*The birth of Samuel.*

**Early the next morning Elkanah and Hannah worshiped before the LORD, and then returned to their home in Ramah. When Elkanah had relations with his wife Hannah, the LORD remembered her. She conceived, and at the end of her term bore a son whom she called Samuel, since she had asked the LORD for him.**

**Once he was weaned, she brought him up with her, along with a three-year-old bull, an ephah of flour, and a skin of wine, and presented him at the temple of the LORD in Shiloh. After the boy's father had sacrificed the young bull, Hannah, his**

**mother, approached Eli and said: "Pardon, my lord! As you live, my lord, I am the woman who stood near you here, praying to the LORD. I prayed for this child, and the LORD granted my request. Now I, in turn, give him to the LORD; as long as he lives, he shall be dedicated to the LORD."**

**She left him there; and as she worshiped the LORD, she said:**

**"My heart exults in the LORD,**
**my horn is exalted in my God.**
**I have swallowed up my enemies;**
**I rejoice in my victory."**

223 Or:

Luke 1:39-45—*The baby leapt in my womb for joy.*

Luke 1:26-38—*You shall conceive and bear a son.*

Luke 2:1-14—*She gave birth to her firstborn son.*

224 As circumstances suggest, the following responsorial psalm may be sung, or some other suitable song.

℟. **The earth is full of the goodness of the Lord.**

Psalm 33

**Happy the nation whose God is the LORD,**
**the people he has chosen for his own inheritance.** ℟.

**Our soul waits for the LORD,**
**who is our help and our shield,**
**For in him our hearts rejoice;**
**in his holy name we trust.** ℟.

**May your kindness, O LORD, be upon us**
**who have put our hope in you.** ℟.

225 As circumstances suggest, the minister may give those present a brief explanation of the biblical text, so that they may understand through faith the meaning of the celebration.

## LITANY

226 The litany is then said. The minister introduces it and an assisting minister or one of those present announces the invocations. From the following those best suited to the occasion may be used or adapted, or other invocations that apply to the particular circumstances may be composed.

The minister says:

**Christ the Lord, the blessed fruit of Mary's womb, by the mystery of his incarnation filled the world with his grace and goodness. Let us therefore raise our voices to praise him, saying:**

**R℣. Blessed are you, O Lord, for your loving kindness.**

Assisting minister:

**Christ our Lord, you bless the love of husband and wife through the sacrament of marriage. We pray: R℣.**

Assisting minister:

**Christ our Lord, you assumed our nature in order that we may be reborn as children of God. We pray: R℣.**

Assisting minister:

**Christ our Lord, you give the example of Mary and Joseph to N. and N., that they may be loving parents. We pray: R℣.**

Assisting minister:

**Christ our Lord, through the ministry of parents you fill the Church with joy by enriching it with new children. We pray: R℣.**

227   After the litany the minister, in the following or similar words, invites all present to sing or say the Lord's Prayer.

**Remember us, Lord, when you come to your kingdom, and teach us how to pray:**

All:

**Our Father . . .**

## PRAYER OF BLESSING

228   A minister who is a priest or deacon says the prayer of blessing with hands outstretched over the parents; a lay minister says the prayer with hands joined.

**Gracious Father,**
**your Word, spoken in love, created the human family**
**and, in the fullness of time,**
**your Son, conceived in love, restored it to your friendship.**

Hear the prayers of N. and N.,
who await the birth of their child.
Calm their fears when they are anxious.
Watch over and support these parents
and bring their child into this world
safely and in good health,
so that as members of your family
they may praise you and glorify you
through your Son, our Lord Jesus Christ,
now and for ever.

R̸. Amen.

## CONCLUDING RITE

**229** A minister who is a priest or deacon concludes the rite by saying:

May God, the source of all life,
protect you by his goodness.

R̸. Amen.

May the Son nourish your faith,
build up your hope,
and deepen in you the gift of his love.

R̸. Amen.

May the Spirit of love be attentive to your prayers
and strengthen you as the hour of childbirth draws near.

R̸. Amen.

Then he blesses all present.

And may almighty God bless you all,
the Father, and the Son, ✛ and the Holy Spirit.

R̸. Amen.

230    A lay minister concludes the rite by signing himself or herself with the sign of the cross and saying:

**May God, who chose to give us the joys of eternal salvation through the motherhood of Mary and the protection of Joseph, bless and keep us in his care, now and for ever.**

℞. **Amen.**

231    It is preferable to end the celebration with a suitable song.

# B. SHORTER RITE

232    All make the sign of the cross as the minister says:

**Blessed be the name of the Lord.**

All reply:

**Now and for ever.**

233    One of those present or the minister reads a text of sacred Scripture, for example:

**Brothers and sisters, listen to the words of the first book of Samuel:**    1:19-20, 24—2:1

*The birth of Samuel.*

**Early the next morning Elkanah and Hannah worshiped before the LORD, and then returned to their home in Ramah. When Elkanah had relations with his wife Hannah, the LORD remembered her. She conceived, and at the end of her term bore a son whom she called Samuel, since she had asked the LORD for him.**

**Once he was weaned, she brought him up with her, along with a three-year-old bull, an ephah of flour, and a skin of wine, and presented him at the temple of the LORD in Shiloh. After the boy's father had sacrificed the young bull, Hannah, his mother, approached Eli and said: "Pardon, my lord! As you live, my lord, I am the woman who stood near you here, praying to the LORD. I prayed for this child, and the LORD granted**

my request. Now I, in turn, give him to the LORD; as long as he lives, he shall be dedicated to the LORD.''

She left him there; and as she worshiped the LORD, she said:
"My heart exults in the LORD,
my horn is exalted in my God.
I have swallowed up my enemies;
I rejoice in my victory.''

234    Or:

Luke 1:39-45—*The baby leapt in my womb for joy.*

Luke 1:26-38—*You shall conceive and bear a son.*

Luke 2:1-14—*She gave birth to her firstborn son.*

235    A minister who is a priest or deacon says the prayer of blessing with hands outstretched over the parents; a lay minister says the prayer with hands joined.

Gracious Father,
your Word, spoken in love, created the human family
and, in the fullness of time,
your Son, conceived in love, restored it to your friendship.

Hear the prayers of N. and N.,
who await the birth of their child.
Calm their fears when they are anxious.
Watch over and support these parents
and bring their child into this world
safely and in good health,
so that as members of your family
they may praise you and glorify you
through your Son, our Lord Jesus Christ,
now and for ever.

R/. Amen.

# VIII. ORDERS FOR THE BLESSING OF A MOTHER BEFORE CHILDBIRTH AND AFTER CHILDBIRTH

## INTRODUCTION

236    The blessing before childbirth provided here may be celebrated for an individual mother, particularly in the company of her own family. It may also be celebrated for several mothers together, for example, in a hospital, and then the formularies are said in the plural wherever necessary.

237    But the blessing after childbirth provided here is intended only for a mother who was unable to take part in the celebration of her child's baptism; therefore it is celebrated only for an individual mother.

238    The present order may be used by a priest, a deacon, or a lay minister. While maintaining the structure and chief elements of the rite, the minister should adapt the celebration to the circumstances of the place and the mother involved.

239    In special situations, a priest or a deacon may use the short formulary given at the end of each of the shorter rites, nos. 256 and 278.

## A. ORDER FOR THE BLESSING OF A MOTHER BEFORE CHILDBIRTH

### INTRODUCTORY RITES

240    When the family or a community of the faithful has gathered, the minister says:

**In the name of the Father, and of the Son, and of the Holy Spirit.**

All make the sign of the cross and reply:

**Amen.**

241    A minister who is a priest or deacon greets those present in the following or other suitable words, taken mainly from sacred Scripture.

**May Christ, who became one of us in the womb of the Virgin Mary, be with you all.**

All make the following or some other suitable reply.

**And also with you.**

---

242    A lay minister greets those present in the following words.

**Brothers and sisters, let us bless the Lord Jesus, who in the womb of the Virgin Mary became one of us. Blessed be God now and for ever.**

R̝. **Blessed be God now and for ever.**

Or:

R̝. **Amen.**

---

243    In the following or similar words, the minister prepares the mother and all present for the blessing.

**God, the Lord of life, by his will brings every human being into existence and he rules and sustains the life of every one of us. Our faith tells us of God's particular care over those born of a Christian marriage, since through the sacrament of baptism they will receive the gift of sharing in the divine life itself. The reason for the blessing of a mother-to-be is that she may await her hour of delivery in faith and hope and, as the partner of God's own love, may already cherish with her maternal love the child in her womb.**

## READING OF THE WORD OF GOD

244    A reader, another person present, or the minister reads a text of sacred Scripture.

**Brothers and sisters, listen to the words of the holy gospel according to Luke:**       1:39-45

*The baby leapt in my womb for joy.*

**During those days Mary set out and traveled to the hill country in haste to a town of Judah, where she entered the house of Zechariah and greeted Elizabeth. When Elizabeth heard Mary's greeting, the infant leaped in her womb, and Elizabeth,**

filled with the holy Spirit, cried out in a loud voice and said, "Most blessed are you among women, and blessed is the fruit of your womb. And how does this happen to me, that the mother of my Lord should come to me? For at the moment the sound of your greeting reached my ears, the infant in my womb leaped for joy. Blessed are you who believed that what was spoken to you by the Lord would be fulfilled."

245  Or:

Luke 1:26-38—*You shall conceive and bear a son.*

Luke 2:1-14—*She gave birth to her firstborn son.*

246  As circumstances suggest, the following responsorial psalm may be sung or said, or some other suitable song.

R͞. **The earth is full of the goodness of the Lord.**

Psalm 33

**Happy the nation whose God is the LORD,**
**the people he has chosen for his own inheritance.**
**But see, the eyes of the LORD are upon those who fear him,**
**upon those who hope for his kindness.** R͞.

**Our soul waits for the LORD,**
**who is our help and our shield,**
**For in him our hearts rejoice;**
**in his holy name we trust.** R͞.

**May your kindness, O LORD, be upon us**
**who have put our hope in you.** R͞.

247  As circumstances suggest, the minister may give those present a brief explanation of the biblical text, so that they may understand through faith the meaning of the celebration.


# INTERCESSIONS

248  The intercessions are then said. The minister introduces them and an assisting minister or one of those present announces the intentions. From the following intentions those best suited to the occasion may be used or adapted, or other intentions that apply to the mother and the particular circumstances may be composed.

The minister says:

**Christ the Lord, the blessed fruit of Mary's womb, by the mystery of his incarnation filled the world with his grace and goodness. Let us therefore raise our voices to praise him.**

R℣. **Blessed are you, O Lord, for your loving kindness.**

Or:

R℣. **Blessed be God for ever.**

Assisting minister:

**You were born of a woman, so that we might become God's adopted children. (Let us bless the Lord:) R℣.**

Assisting minister:

**You took life from Mary and willed that the womb that bore you and the breasts that nursed you would be called blessed. (Let us bless the Lord:) R℣.**

Assisting minister:

**Through the Virgin Mary, blessed among women, you have honored the female sex. (Let us bless the Lord:) R℣.**

Assisting minister:

**As you hung on the cross you made Mary, your own Mother, the Mother of the Church. (Let us bless the Lord:) R℣.**

Assisting minister:

**Through the ministry of mothers you increase the joy and exultation of the Church by enriching it with new children. (Let us bless the Lord:) R℣.**

## PRAYER OF BLESSING

**249** A minister who is a priest or deacon may, as circumstances suggest, extend his hands over the mother or trace the sign of the cross on her forehead, as he says the prayer of blessing; a lay minister says the prayer with hands joined.

**Lord God,**
**Creator of the human race,**
**your Son, through the working of the Holy Spirit,**
**was born of a woman,**
**so that he might pay the age-old debt of sin**
**and save us by his redemption.**

**Receive with kindness the prayer of your servant**
**as she asks for the birth of a healthy child.**
**Grant that she may safely deliver a son or a daughter**
**to be numbered among your family,**
**to serve you in all things,**
**and to gain eternal life.**

**We ask this through Christ our Lord.**

**R̸. Amen.**

250    After the prayer of blessing, the minister invites all present to pray for the protection of the Blessed Virgin. They may do so by singing or reciting the following antiphon, or other Marian prayers, for example, *Loving Mother of the Redeemer (Alma Redemptoris Mater), Hail, Mary,* or *Hail, Holy Queen.*

**We fly to you for protection,**
**holy Mother of God.**
**Listen to our prayers**
**and help us in our needs.**
**Save us from every danger,**
**glorious and Blessed Virgin.**

## CONCLUDING RITE

251    After the invitation, ''Bow your heads and pray for God's blessing,'' or something similar is said, a minister who is a priest or deacon concludes the rite by facing the mother and saying:

**May God, the source of all life,**
**protect you by his goodness.**

**R̸. Amen.**

**May he deepen your faith,**
**build up your hope,**
**and constantly increase the gift of his love in you.**

**R̸. Amen.**

At the hour of your delivery
may he be attentive to your prayers
and strengthen you with his grace.

R̸. Amen.

Then he blesses all present.

And may almighty God bless you all,
the Father, and the Son, ✝ and the Holy Spirit.

R̸. Amen.

252    A lay minister invokes God's blessing on the mother and
all present by signing himself or herself with the sign of the cross
and saying:

May God, who chose to make known and to send
   the blessings of eternal salvation
   through the motherhood of the Blessed Virgin,
bless us and keep us in his care,
now and for ever.

R̸. Amen.

# B. SHORTER RITE

253    The minister says:

Our help is in the name of the Lord.

All reply:

Who made heaven and earth.

254    One of those present or the minister reads a text of sacred
Scripture, for example:

Isaiah 44:3

I will pour out water upon the thirsty ground,
and streams upon the dry land;
I will pour out my spirit upon your offspring,
and my blessing upon your descendants.

Luke 1:41-42a

**When Elizabeth heard Mary's greeting, the infant leaped in her womb, and Elizabeth, filled with the holy Spirit, cried out in a loud voice and said, "Most blessed are you among women, and blessed is the fruit of your womb."**

255　A minister who is a priest or deacon says the following prayer of blessing with hands outstretched over the mother; a lay minister says the prayer with hands joined.

**Lord God,**
**Creator of the human race,**
**your Son, through the working of the Holy Spirit,**
**was born of a woman,**
**so that he might pay the age-old debt of sin**
**and save us by his redemption.**

**Receive with kindness the prayer of your servant**
**as she asks for the birth of a healthy child.**
**Grant that she may safely deliver a son or a daughter**
**to be numbered among your family,**
**to serve you in all things,**
**and to gain eternal life.**

**We ask this through Christ our Lord.**

R̶⁊. **Amen.**

## SHORT FORMULARY

256　As circumstances suggest, a priest or deacon may use the following short blessing formulary.

**God has brought gladness and light to the world**
**through the Virgin Mary's delivery of her child.**
**May Christ fill your heart with his holy joy**
**and keep you and your baby safe from harm.**
**In the name of the Father, ✝ and of the Son, and of the**
　**Holy Spirit.**

R̶⁊. **Amen.**

# C. ORDER FOR THE BLESSING OF A MOTHER
## AFTER CHILDBIRTH

**257**   The blessing of a mother after childbirth is contained in the *Rite of Baptism for Children*.[12]

**258**   When a new mother has been unable to take part in the celebration of her child's baptism, it is fitting to have a special celebration in order to provide the opportunity for her to benefit from the blessing that in the rite of baptism prompts the mother and all present to thank God for the gift of the newborn child.

## INTRODUCTORY RITES

**259**   When the family or community of the faithful has gathered, the minister says:

**In the name of the Father, and of the Son, and of the Holy Spirit.**

All make the sign of the cross and reply:

**Amen.**

**260**   A minister who is a priest or deacon greets those present in the following or other suitable words, taken mainly from sacred Scripture.

**May Christ, who became one of us in the womb of the Virgin Mary, be with you all.**

All make the following or some other suitable reply.

**And also with you.**

---

**261**   A lay minister greets those present in the following words.

**Brothers and sisters, let us bless the Lord Jesus, who in the womb of the Virgin Mary became one of us. Blessed be God now and for ever.**

℟. **Blessed be God now and for ever.**

Or:

℟. **Amen.**

---

[12] See Roman Ritual, *Rite of Baptism for Children*, no. 105.

262 In the following or similar words, the minister prepares the mother and all present for the blessing.

**The Christian community has already welcomed with joy the child you have borne and in the celebration of (his/her) baptism has prayed that you will fully recognize the gift you have received and the responsibility entrusted to you in the Church and that, like Mary, you will proclaim the greatness of the Lord. Today we all wish to join with you in glad thanksgiving as we call on God to bless you.**

## READING OF THE WORD OF GOD

263 A reader, another person present, or the minister reads a text of sacred Scripture.

**Brothers and sisters, listen to the words of the first book of Samuel:**
1:20-28

*The Lord granted my request.*

**Hannah conceived, and at the end of her term bore a son whom she called Samuel, since she had asked the LORD for him. The next time her husband Elkanah was going up with the rest of his household to offer the customary sacrifice to the LORD and to fulfill his vows, Hannah did not go, explaining to her husband, ''Once the child is weaned, I will take him to appear before the LORD and to remain there forever; I will offer him as a perpetual nazirite.'' Her husband Elkanah answered her: ''Do what you think best; wait until you have weaned him. Only, may the LORD bring your resolve to fulfillment!'' And so she remained at home and nursed her son until she had weaned him. Once he was weaned, she brought him up with her, along with a three-year-old bull, an ephah of flour, and a skin of wine, and presented him at the temple of the LORD in Shiloh. After the boy's father had sacrificed the young bull, Hannah, his mother, approached Eli and said, ''Pardon, my lord! As you live, my lord, I am the woman who stood near you here, praying to the LORD. I prayed for this child, and the LORD granted my request. Now I, in turn, give him to the LORD; as long as he lives, he shall be dedicated to the LORD.''**

**264** Or:

1 Samuel 2:1-10—*Prayer of Hannah.*

Luke 1:67-79—*Blessed be the Lord.*

**265**　　As circumstances suggest, the following responsorial psalm may be sung or said, or some other suitable song.

R̸. **Your children are like shoots of the olive.**

Psalm 128

**Happy are you who fear the LORD,
who walk in his ways!
For you shall eat the fruit of your handiwork;
happy shall you be, and favored.** R̸.

**Your wife shall be like a fruitful vine
in the recesses of your home;
Your children like olive plants
around your table.** R̸.

**Behold, thus is the man blessed
who fears the LORD.
The LORD bless you from Zion:
may you see the prosperity of Jerusalem
all the days of your life;
May you see your children's children.** R̸.

**266**　　Then the minister gives a brief explanation of the biblical text, so that the mother and all present may give thanks for God's gift of the newborn child and may accept the role entrusted to them for the Christian upbringing of the child.

## PRAYER OF THANKSGIVING

**267**　　A prayer of thanksgiving is then said. The invocations may be said by an assisting minister or another person present. Those given here may be used or adapted or others that apply to the mother and the particular circumstances may be composed.

Assisting minister:

**For the new life that has begun in this family, let us thank the Lord, saying:**

R̸. **We thank you, Lord.**

*Assisting minister:*

**For the child that this mother has so happily received from your hands.** ℟.

*Assisting minister:*

**For your gift of health to mother and child.** ℟.

*Assisting minister:*

**For the sacrament of baptism that has made the heart of her child the temple of your glory.** ℟.

*Assisting minister:*

**For the gladness that has delighted all our hearts at this birth.** ℟.

*Assisting minister:*

**For all the favors that your fatherly love continually bestows on us.** ℟.

**268** All then sing or recite the Canticle of Mary, or a hymn of thanksgiving may be sung.

## Prayer of Blessing

**269** A minister who is a priest or deacon says the prayer of blessing with hands outstretched; a lay minister says the prayer with hands joined.

**O God,**
**author and sustainer of human life,**
**from your goodness your servant N. has received the joy**
  **of becoming a mother.**
**Graciously accept our thanks**
**and give ear to our prayers:**
**defend this mother and child from every evil,**
**be their companion along their pathway through life,**
**and welcome them one day**
**into the joys of your eternal home.**

**We ask this through Christ our Lord.**

**℟. Amen.**

270    Or:

**O God,
our every blessing comes from you
and you welcome the simple prayers
of those who bless your name.
Grant that this mother may live
in reliance on your goodness and in thankfulness to you.
Give to her and to her child the joyful reassurance
that you are always near to protect them.**

**We ask this through Christ our Lord.**

℞. **Amen.**

## CONCLUDING RITE

271    A minister who is a priest or deacon concludes the rite by facing the mother and saying:

**Almighty God has brought you the joy of motherhood:
may he now bless ✝ you.
You thank him today for the gift of your child:
may he bring you and your child one day
to a share in the unending joys of heaven.**

**We ask this through Christ our Lord.**

℞. **Amen.**

272    Or, after the invitation, "Bow your heads and pray for God's blessing," or something similar is said, he says, with hands outstretched:

**May God, the source of all life,
protect you by his goodness.**

℞. **Amen.**

**May he deepen your faith,
build up your hope,
and constantly increase the gift of his love in you.**

℞. **Amen.**

**May he keep your child
strong in body and in spirit.**

℞. **Amen.**

Then he blesses all present.

**And may almighty God bless you all,
the Father, and the Son, ✚ and the Holy Spirit.**

℟. **Amen.**

---

273    A lay minister invokes God's blessing on the mother and
all present by signing himself or herself with the sign of the cross
and saying:

**May the tender love of the Father,
the peace of his Son, Jesus Christ,
the grace and strength of the Holy Spirit
preserve you to live by the light of faith
and to reach the promise of eternal happiness.**

**And may almighty God bless us all,
the Father, and the Son, and the Holy Spirit.**

℟. **Amen.**

---

274    It is preferable to end the celebration with a suitable song.

# D. SHORTER RITE

275    The minister says:

**Blessed be the name of the Lord.**

All reply:

**Now and for ever.**

276    One of those present or the minister reads a text of sacred
Scripture, for example:

1 Samuel 1:27

**I prayed for this child, and the LORD granted my request.**

Luke 1:68-69

**Zechariah prayed:**
**Blessed be the Lord, the God of Israel,**
**for he has visited and brought redemption to his people.**
**He has raised up a horn for our salvation**
**within the house of David his servant.**

1 Thessalonians 5:18

**In all circumstances give thanks, for this is the will of God**
**for you in Christ Jesus.**

277    A minister who is a priest or deacon says the prayer of
blessing with hands outstretched; a lay minister says the prayer
with hands joined.

**O God,**
**our every blessing comes from you**
**and you welcome the simple prayers**
**of those who bless your name.**
**Grant that this mother may live**
**in reliance on your goodness and in thankfulness to you.**
**Give to her and to her child the joyful reassurance**
**that you are always near to protect them.**

**We ask this through Christ our Lord.**

**R̸. Amen.**

## SHORT FORMULARY

278    As circumstances suggest, a priest or deacon may use the
following short blessing formulary.

**May the Lord God almighty,**
**who through the earthly birth of his own Son**
**has filled the whole world with joy,**
**so bless + you**
**that the child he has given you**
**will always bring joy to your heart.**

**R̸. Amen.**

# IX. ORDER FOR THE BLESSING OF PARENTS AFTER A MISCARRIAGE

## INTRODUCTION

279    In times of death and grief the Christian turns to the Lord for consolation and strength. This is especially true when a child dies before birth. This blessing is provided to assist the parents in their grief and console them with the blessing of God.

280    The minister should be attentive to the needs of the parents and other family members and to this end the introduction to the *Order of Christian Funerals*, Part II: Funeral Rites For Children will be helpful.

281    These orders may be used by a priest or a deacon, and also by a layperson, who follows the rites and prayers designated for a lay minister.

## A. ORDER OF BLESSING

### INTRODUCTORY RITES

282    When the community has gathered, a suitable song may be sung. The minister says:

**In the name of the Father, and of the Son, and of the Holy Spirit.**

All make the sign of the cross and reply:

**Amen.**

283    A minister who is a priest or deacon greets those present in the following or other suitable words, taken mainly from sacred Scripture.

**May the Father of mercies, the God of all consolation, be with you all.**

And all reply:

**And also with you.**

**284**   A lay minister greets those present in the following words:

**Let us praise the Father of mercies, the God of all consolation. Blessed be God for ever.**

℟. **Blessed be God for ever.**

**285**   In the following or similar words, the minister prepares those present for the blessing.

**For those who trust in God,
in the pain of sorrow there is consolation,
in the face of despair there is hope,
in the midst of death there is life.
N. and N., as we mourn the death of your child we place ourselves in the hands of God and ask for strength, for healing, and for love.**

## READING OF THE WORD OF GOD

**286**   A reader, another person present, or the minister reads a text of sacred Scripture.

**Brothers and sisters, listen to the words of the book of Lamentations:**
                        3:17-26

*Hope in the Lord.*

**My soul is deprived of peace,
I have forgotten what happiness is;
I tell myself my future is lost,
all that I hoped for from the Lord.
The thought of my homeless poverty
is wormwood and gall;
Remembering it over and over
leaves my soul downcast within me.
But I will call this to mind,
as my reason to have hope:
The favors of the LORD are not exhausted,
his mercies are not spent;
They are renewed each morning,
so great is his faithfulness.**

My portion is the LORD, says my soul;
therefore will I hope in him.
Good is the LORD to one who waits for him,
to the soul that seeks him;
It is good to hope in silence
for the saving help of the LORD.

287    Or:

Isaiah 49:8-13—*In a time of favor I answer you, on the day of salvation I help you.*

Romans 8:18-27—*In hope we were saved.*

Romans 8:26-31—*If God is for us, who can be against us?*

Colossians 1:9-12—*We have been praying for you unceasingly.*

Hebrews 5:7-10—*Christ intercedes for us.*

Luke 22:39-46—*Agony in the garden.*

288    As circumstances suggest, one of the following responsorial psalms may be sung, or some other suitable song.

R̃. **To you, O Lord, I lift up my soul.**

Psalm 25

**Your ways, O LORD, make known to me;
teach me your paths,
Guide me in your truth and teach me,
for you are God my savior,
and for you I wait all the day.** R̃.

**Remember that your compassion, O LORD,
and your kindness are from of old.
The sins of my youth and my frailties remember not;
in your kindness remember me
because of your goodness, O LORD.** R̃.

**Look toward me, and have pity on me,
for I am alone and afflicted.
Relieve the troubles of my heart,
and bring me out of my distress.** R̃.

**Preserve my life, and rescue me;
let me not be put to shame, for I take refuge in you.
Let integrity and uprightness preserve me,
because I wait for you, O LORD.** R̃.

Psalm 143:1, 5-6, 8, 10

R℣. (v. 1) **O Lord, hear my prayer.**

289    As circumstances suggest, the minister may give those present a brief explanation of the biblical text, so that they may understand through faith the meaning of the celebration.

## INTERCESSIONS

290    The intercessions are then said. The minister introduces them and an assisting minister or one of those present announces the intentions. From the following those best suited to the occasion may be used or adapted, or other intentions that apply to the particular circumstances may be composed.

The minister says:

**Let us pray to God who throughout the ages has heard the cries of parents.**

R℣. **Lord, hear our prayer.**

Assisting minister:

**For N. and N., who know the pain of grief, that they may be comforted, we pray.** R℣.

Assisting minister:

**For this family, that it may find new hope in the midst of suffering, we pray.** R℣.

Assisting minister:

**For these parents, that they may learn from the example of Mary, who grieved by the cross of her Son, we pray.** R℣.

Assisting minister:

**For all who have suffered the loss of a child, that Christ may be their support, we pray.** R℣.

291    After the intercessions the minister, in the following or similar words, invites all present to sing or say the Lord's Prayer.

**Let us pray to the God of consolation and hope, as Christ has taught us:**

All:

**Our Father . . .**

## PRAYER OF BLESSING

**292** A minister who is a priest or deacon says the prayer of blessing with hands outstretched over the parents; a lay minister says the prayer with hands joined.

**Compassionate God,**
**soothe the hearts of N. and N.,**
**and grant that through the prayers of Mary,**
**who grieved by the cross of her Son,**
**you may enlighten their faith,**
**give hope to their hearts,**
**and peace to their lives.**

**Lord,**
**grant mercy to all the members of this family**
**and comfort them with the hope**
**that one day we will all live with you,**
**with your Son Jesus Christ, and the Holy Spirit,**
**for ever and ever.**

**R℣. Amen.**

**293** Or:

**Lord,**
**God of all creation**
**we bless and thank you for your tender care.**
**Receive this life you created in love**
**and comfort your faithful people in their time of loss**
**with the assurance of your unfailing mercy.**

**We ask this through Christ our Lord.**

**R℣. Amen.**

As circumstances suggest, the minister in silence may sprinkle the parents with holy water.

## CONCLUDING RITE

**294** A minister who is a priest or deacon concludes the rite by saying:

**May God be with you in your sorrow,
and give you light and peace.**

℟. **Amen.**

**May God raise you up from your grief.**

℟. **Amen.**

**May God grant you encouragement and strength to accept
his will.**

℟. **Amen.**

Then he blesses all present.

**And may almighty God bless you all,
the Father, and the Son, ✝ and the Holy Spirit.**

℟. **Amen.**

---

295    A lay minister concludes the rite by signing himself or herself with the sign of the cross and saying:

**May God give us peace in our sorrow,
consolation in our grief,
and strength to accept his will in all things.**

℟. **Amen.**

---

296    It is preferable to end the celebration with a suitable song.

# B. SHORTER RITE

297    All make the sign of the cross as the minister says:

**Our help is in the name of the Lord.**

All reply:

**Who made heaven and earth.**

298 One of those present or the minister reads a text of sacred Scripture, for example:

**Brothers and sisters, listen to the words of the book of Lamentations:**                                              3:17-26

*Hope in the Lord.*

**My soul is deprived of peace,
I have forgotten what happiness is;
I tell myself my future is lost,
all that I hoped for from the LORD.
The thought of my homeless poverty
is wormwood and gall;
Remembering it over and over
leaves my soul downcast within me.
But I will call this to mind,
as my reason to have hope:
The favors of the LORD are not exhausted,
his mercies are not spent;
They are renewed each morning,
so great is his faithfulness.
My portion is the LORD, says my soul;
therefore will I hope in him.
Good is the LORD to one who waits for him,
to the soul that seeks him;
It is good to hope in silence
for the saving help of the LORD.**

299 Or:

Romans 8:26-31—*If God is for us, who can be against us?*

Colossians 1:9-12—*We have been praying for you unceasingly.*

300 A minister who is a priest or deacon says the prayer of blessing with hands outstretched over the parents; a lay minister says the prayer with hands joined.

**Compassionate God,
soothe the hearts of N. and N.,
and grant that through the prayers of Mary,
who grieved by the cross of her Son,
you may enlighten their faith,
give hope to their hearts,
and peace to their lives.**

**Lord,**
**grant mercy to all the members of this family**
**and comfort them with the hope**
**that one day we will all live with you,**
**with your Son Jesus Christ, and the Holy Spirit,**
**for ever and ever.**

R̸. **Amen.**

301   Or:

**Lord,**
**God of all creation,**
**we bless and thank you for your tender care.**
**Receive this life you created in love**
**and comfort your faithful people in their time of loss**
**with the assurance of your unfailing mercy.**

**We ask this through Christ our Lord.**

R̸. **Amen.**

# X. ORDER FOR THE BLESSING OF PARENTS AND AN ADOPTED CHILD

USA

## INTRODUCTION

302    The adoption of a child is an important event in the lives of a married couple or a single parent. This blessing serves as a public thanksgiving for the precious gift of a child and as a welcome of the child into its new family.

303    If the child is old enough to respond, provision is made for the child to accept the new parents as his or her own. In this case, the introduction of the rite should be adapted to the circumstances, and a more appropriate reading may be chosen.

304    If there is only one parent, the rite should be adapted to the circumstances by the minister.

305    This order may be used by a priest or a deacon, and also by a layperson, who follows the rites and prayers designated for a lay minister.

## ORDER OF BLESSING

### INTRODUCTORY RITES

306    When the community has gathered, a suitable song may be sung. After the singing, the minister says:

**In the name of the Father, and of the Son, and of the Holy Spirit.**

All make the sign of the cross and reply:

**Amen.**

307    A minister who is a priest or deacon greets those present in the following or other suitable words, taken mainly from sacred Scripture.

**May the love of God be with you always.**

And all reply:

**And also with you.**

308      A lay minister greets those present in the following words:

**Let us praise our loving God.
Blessed be God for ever.**

℟. **Blessed be God for ever.**

309      In the following or similar words, the minister prepares those present for the blessing.

**It has pleased God our heavenly Father to answer the earnest prayers of N. and N. for the gift of a child. Today we join them in offering heartfelt thanks for the joyful and solemn responsibility which becomes theirs by the arrival of N. into their family.**

## READING OF THE WORD OF GOD

310      A reader, another person present, or the minister reads a text of sacred Scripture.

**Brothers and sisters, listen to the words of the holy gospel according to Mark:**          10:13-16

*Jesus blesses the little children.*

**People were bringing children to Jesus that he might touch them, but the disciples rebuked the people. When Jesus saw this he became indignant and said to the disciples, ''Let the children come to me; do not prevent them, for the kingdom of God belongs to such as these. Amen, I say to you, whoever does not accept the kingdom of God like a child will not enter it.'' Then he embraced the children and blessed them, placing his hands on them.**

311     Or:

Deuteronomy 6:4-7—*Diligently teach your children.*

Deuteronomy 31:12-13—*Do this that your children may hear.*

1 Samuel 1:9-11, 20-28; 2:26—*The birth and presentation of Samuel.*

Matthew 18:1-4—*Those who humble themselves like children will be the greatest.*

Luke 2:22-32, 52—*Presentation of Jesus in the temple.*

312   As circumstances suggest, one of the following responsorial psalms may be sung, or some other suitable song.

℟. **O Lord, our God, how wonderful your name in all the earth!**

Psalm 8

**O Lᴏʀᴅ, our Lord,**
**how glorious is your name over all the earth!**
**You have exalted your majesty above the heavens.**
**Out of the mouths of babes and sucklings**
**you have fashioned praise because of your foes,**
**to silence the hostile and the vengeful.** ℟.

**When I behold your heavens, the work of your fingers,**
**the moon and the stars which you set in place—**
**What is man that you should be mindful of him,**
**or the son of man that you should care for him?** ℟.

**You have made him little less than the angels,**
**and crowned him with glory and honor.**
**You have given him rule over the works of your hands,**
**putting all things under his feet:** ℟.

**All sheep and oxen,**
**yes, and the beasts of the field,**
**The birds of the air, the fishes of the sea,**
**and whatever swims the paths of the seas.** ℟.

**O Lᴏʀᴅ, our Lord,**
**how glorious is your name over all the earth!** ℟.

Psalm 78:1-7

℟. **(v. 4) Tell the coming generations the glorious deeds of the Lord.**

313   As circumstances suggest, the minister may give those present a brief explanation of the biblical text, so that they may understand through faith the meaning of the celebration.

## Aᴄᴋɴᴏᴡʟᴇᴅɢᴍᴇɴᴛ ʙʏ ᴛʜᴇ Cʜɪʟᴅ ᴀɴᴅ Pᴀʀᴇɴᴛs

314   The minister asks the parents:

**You have received N. into your family;
will you (continue to) love and care for him/her?**

Parents:

**We will.**

315    If the child is old enough to answer, the minister asks:

**You have accepted N. and N. as your parents;
will you love and respect them?**

The child replies:

**I will.**

316    The minister says:

**As God has made us all his children by grace and adoption,
may this family always abide in his love.**

The Canticle of Mary or another hymn of praise may then be sung.

## INTERCESSIONS

317    The intercessions are then said. The minister introduces
them and an assisting minister or one of those present announces
the intentions. From the following those best suited to the occasion may be used or adapted, or other intentions that apply to
the particular circumstances may be composed.

The minister says:

**God is the author of all life and calls us into his loving fam-
ily; with thankful hearts we pray:**

R⁊. **Loving Father, hear us.**

Assisting minister:

**For the Church throughout the world, that it may nurture,
guide, protect and love all who are joined to it in baptism, let
us pray to the Lord.** R⁊.

Assisting minister:

**For N. and N. and their new son/daughter, N., that God may bind them together in love as a family in Christ, let us pray to the Lord. R℔.**

Assisting minister:

**[For the brother(s) and sister(s) of N., that they may grow in friendship and love, let us pray to the Lord. R℔.]**

Assisting minister:

**For married couples who desire the gift of a child, that God may hear their prayers, let us pray to the Lord. R℔.**

Assisting minister:

**For all Christian families, that the love of Christ may dwell in their homes, let us pray to the Lord. R℔.**

318    After the intercessions the minister, in the following or similar words, invites all present to sing or say the Lord's Prayer.

**As God's children by adoption, we pray:**

All:

**Our Father . . .**

## PRAYER OF BLESSING

319    A minister who is a priest or deacon says the prayer of blessing with hands outstretched over the parents and child; a lay minister says the prayer with hands joined.

**Loving God,
your Son has taught us
that whoever welcomes a child in his name,
  welcomes him.
We give you thanks for N.,
whom N. and N. have welcomed into their family.
Bless this family.**

**Confirm a lively sense of your presence with them
and grant to these parents patience and wisdom,
that their lives may show forth the love of Christ
as they bring N. up to love all that is good.**

**We ask this through Christ our Lord.**

**R̝. Amen.**

> As circumstances suggest, the minister in silence may sprinkle
> the family with holy water.

## CONCLUDING RITE

320    A minister who is a priest or deacon concludes the rite by
saying:

**May almighty God, who has called us into the family of Christ,
fill you with grace and peace,
now and for ever.**

**R̝. Amen.**

> Then he blesses all present.

**And may almighty God bless you all,
the Father, and the Son, ✠ and the Holy Spirit.**

**R̝. Amen.**

---

321    A lay minister concludes the rite by signing himself or herself with the sign of the cross and saying:

**May almighty God, who has called us into the family of Christ,
fill us with grace and peace, now and for ever.**

**R̝. Amen.**

---

322    It is preferable to end the celebration with a suitable song.

# XI. ORDER OF BLESSING ON THE OCCASION OF A BIRTHDAY

USA

## INTRODUCTION

323    It is always appropriate to give thanks to God, but especially so on the occasion of a birthday. The birthday celebration provides an opportunity for acknowledging and giving thanks to God as the author and giver of life.

324    A birthday is also an appropriate occasion for children to express love and thanks to their parents who have shared the gift of life and love with them.

325    These orders may be used by a priest or a deacon, and also by a layperson, who follows the rites and prayers designated for a lay minister, or by a family member.

## A. ORDER OF BLESSING

### INTRODUCTORY RITES

326    When all have gathered a suitable song may be sung. After the singing, the minister says:

**In the name of the Father, and of the Son, and of the Holy Spirit.**

All make the sign of the cross and reply:

**Amen.**

327    A minister who is a priest or deacon greets those present in the following or other suitable words, taken mainly from sacred Scripture.

**May God who loves you and fills your life with joy, be with you always.**

And all reply:

**And also with you.**

**Praise be to God, who loves us and fills our lives with joy, now and for ever.**

**R̸. Amen.**

329    In the following or similar words, the minister prepares those present for the blessing.

**Each year as we celebrate another birthday we recall the gift of life which we have received from God. Today we give thanks for our parents and all those who have loved, nourished, and taught us of God's love.**

## READING OF THE WORD OF GOD

330    A reader, another person present, or the minister reads a text of sacred Scripture.

**Brothers and sisters, listen to the words of the apostle Paul to the Philippians:**                                              1:3-11

*Thanks be to God.*

**I give thanks to my God at every remembrance of you, praying always with joy in my every prayer for all of you, because of your partnership for the gospel from the first day until now. I am confident of this, that the one who began a good work in you will continue to complete it until the day of Christ Jesus. It is right that I should think this way about all of you, because I hold you in my heart, you who are all partners with me in grace, both in my imprisonment and in the defense and confirmation of the gospel. For God is my witness, how I long for all of you with the affection of Christ Jesus. And this is my prayer: that your love may increase ever more and more in knowledge and every kind of perception, to discern what is of value, so that you may be pure and blameless for the day of Christ, filled with the fruit of righteousness that comes through Jesus Christ for the glory and praise of God.**

331 Or:

Hosea 11:1-4—*Israel was a child.*

1 Thessalonians 3:9-11—*May you grow in holiness.*

1 Peter 1:3-5—*New birth in Christ.*

Matthew 5:1-12—*The beatitudes.*

Luke 2:21-32—*Presentation of Jesus in the temple.*

332    As circumstances suggest, one of the following responsorial psalms may be sung, or some other suitable song.

℟. **Teach us to number our days aright.**

Psalm 90

**Before the mountains were begotten**
**and the earth and the world were brought forth,**
**from everlasting to everlasting you are God.** ℟.

**You turn man back to dust,**
**saying, "Return, O children of men."**
**For a thousand years in your sight**
**are as yesterday, now that it is past,**
**or as a watch of the night.** ℟.

**You make an end of them in their sleep;**
**the next morning they are like the changing grass,**
**Which at dawn springs up anew,**
**but by evening wilts and fades.** ℟.

**Teach us to number our days aright,**
**that we may gain wisdom of heart.**
**Return, O LORD! How long?**
**Have pity on your servants!** ℟.

**Fill us at daybreak with your kindness,**
**that we may shout for joy and gladness all our days.**
**Make us glad, for the days when you afflicted us,**
**for the years when we saw evil.**
**Let your work be seen by your servants**
**and your glory by their children.** ℟.

Psalm 128:1-2, 3-4, 5-6

℟. (v. 5) **The Lord bless you all the days of your life.**

Psalm 103:1-2, 13-14, 15-16, 17-18

℟. (v. 1) **Bless the Lord, O my soul.**

333    As circumstances suggest, the minister may give those present a brief explanation of the biblical text, so that they may understand through faith the meaning of the celebration.

## LITANY

334    The litany is then said. The minister introduces it and an assisting minister or one of those present announces the invocations. From the following those best suited to the occasion may be used or adapted, or other invocations that apply to the particular circumstances may be composed.

The minister says:

**Let us praise the Lord God of all creation.**

℟. **Blessed be God for ever.**

Assisting minister:

**Blessed be God, who has shaped us from dust and breathed life into us.** ℟.

Assisting minister:

**Blessed be God, who in his great love has sent his only Son to save us.** ℟.

Assisting minister:

**Blessed be God, who guides our feet along right paths.** ℟.

Assisting minister:

**Blessed be God, the Father, the Son, and the Holy Spirit.** ℟.

335    After the litany the minister, in the following or similar words, invites all present to sing or say the Lord's Prayer.

**Let us pray to God, the author and giver of life, in the words his Son taught us:**

All:

**Our Father . . .**

# Prayer of Blessing

336    A minister who is a priest or deacon says the prayer of blessing with hands outstretched over the one who is to be blessed; a lay minister says the prayer with hands joined.

A          For adults

**God of all creation,
we offer you grateful praise for the gift of life.
Hear the prayers of N., your servant,
who recalls today the day of his/her birth
and rejoices in your gifts of life and love,
    family and friends.**

**Bless him/her with your presence
and surround him/her with your love
that he/she may enjoy many happy years,
all of them pleasing to you.**

**We ask this through Christ our Lord.**

**R⁊. Amen.**

B          For children

**Loving God,
you created all the people of the world
and you know each of us by name.
We thank you for N., who today celebrates his/her birthday.
Bless him/her with your love and friendship
that he/she may grow in wisdom, knowledge, and grace.
May he/she love his/her family always
and be faithful to his/her friends.**

**Grant this through Christ our Lord.**

**R⁊. Amen.**

As circumstances suggest, the minister in silence may sprinkle the person with holy water.

337    A minister who is a priest or deacon concludes the rite by saying:

**May the Lord bless you and keep you.**

℟. **Amen.**

**May his face shine upon you
and be gracious to you.**

℟. **Amen.**

**May he look upon you with kindness and give you his
    peace.**

℟. **Amen.**

Then he blesses all present.

**And may almighty God bless you all,
the Father, and the Son, ✛ and the Holy Spirit.**

℟. **Amen.**

338    A lay minister concludes the rite by signing himself or herself with the sign of the cross and saying:

**May the Lord bless us and keep us.**

℟. **Amen.**

**May his face shine upon us
and be gracious to us.**

℟. **Amen.**

**May he look upon us with kindness and give us his peace.**

℟. **Amen.**

339    It is preferable to end the celebration with a suitable song.

# B. SHORTER RITE

340     All make the sign of the cross as the minister says:

**Blessed be the name of the Lord.**

All reply:

**Now and for ever.**

341     One of those present or the minister reads a text of sacred Scripture, for example:

**Brothers and sisters, listen to the words of the apostle Paul to the Philippians:**      1:3-11

*Thanks be to God.*

**I give thanks to my God at every remembrance of you, praying always with joy in my every prayer for all of you, because of your partnership for the gospel from the first day until now. I am confident of this, that the one who began a good work in you will continue to complete it until the day of Christ Jesus. It is right that I should think this way about all of you, because I hold you in my heart, you who are all partners with me in grace, both in my imprisonment and in the defense and confirmation of the gospel. For God is my witness, how I long for all of you with the affection of Christ Jesus. And this is my prayer: that your love may increase ever more and more in knowledge and every kind of perception, to discern what is of value, so that you may be pure and blameless for the day of Christ, filled with the fruit of righteousness that comes through Jesus Christ for the glory and praise of God.**

342     Or:

1 Thessalonians 3:9-11—*May you grow in holiness.*

Matthew 5:1-12—*The beatitudes.*

343     A minister who is a priest or deacon says the prayer of blessing with hands outstretched; a lay minister says the prayer with hands joined.

A        For adults

**God of all creation,
we offer you grateful praise for the gift of life.**

Hear the prayers of N., your servant,
who recalls today the day of his/her birth
and rejoices in your gifts of life and love,
  family and friends.

Bless him/her with your presence
and surround him/her with your love
that he/she may enjoy many happy years,
all of them pleasing to you.

We ask this through Christ our Lord.

℞. Amen.

B          For children

Loving God,
you created all the people of the world
and you know each of us by name.
We thank you for N., who today celebrates his/her birthday.
Bless him/her with your love and friendship
that he/she may grow in wisdom, knowledge, and grace.
May he/she love his/her family always
and be faithful to his/her friends.

Grant this through Christ our Lord.

℞. Amen.

# XII. ORDERS FOR THE BLESSING OF ELDERLY PEOPLE CONFINED TO THEIR HOMES

## INTRODUCTION

344    The faithful who are elderly and infirm, confined at home or in a nursing home, need their brothers and sisters in Christ to help them feel that they are still part of the family and the ecclesial community. The purpose of the present blessing is that the elderly may receive from the community a mark of respect and affection and together with the community thank God for his favors and for the good he has enabled them to do in their lives.

345    The present orders may be used by a priest, a deacon, or a lay minister. While maintaining the structure and chief elements of the rite, the minister should adapt the celebration to the circumstances of the place and the people involved.

346    In nos. 363–368 the selection of certain elements from the present order (nos. 348–362) provides for a blessing of the elderly within Mass (after the homily or at the end of Mass) or on an occasion when communion is brought to them at home. In the second case, the blessing may also be celebrated by an acolyte or by a duly appointed special minister of the eucharist, who follows the rites and texts designated for use by lay ministers.

347    When just one elderly person is to be blessed, a priest or a deacon may use the short formulary given in no. 375.

# A. ORDER OF BLESSING

## INTRODUCTORY RITES

348    When the family or community has gathered, the minister says:

**In the name of the Father, and of the Son, and of the Holy Spirit.**

All make the sign of the cross and reply:

**Amen.**

349 A minister who is a priest or deacon greets the elderly people and all present in the following or other suitable words, taken mainly from sacred Scripture.

**The grace of our Lord Jesus Christ and the love of God and the fellowship of the Holy Spirit be with you all.**

All make the following or some other suitable reply.

**And also with you.**

350 A lay minister greets the elderly people and all present in the following words.

**Brothers and sisters, let us bless the Lord Jesus, whom the aged Simeon held in his arms. The child he held was his Lord and Master. Blessed be God now and for ever.**

℟. **Blessed be God now and for ever.**

Or:

℟. **Amen.**

351 In the following or similar words, the minister may prepare the elderly people and all present for the blessing.

**The period of old age is a gift that should be received from God with gratitude. Elderly people have the opportunity to share with us the riches of their experience and of their Christian lives. Let us therefore now join them in thanking God and in asking that he will keep high their hopes and strengthen their trust in him.**

## READING OF THE WORD OF GOD

352 A reader, another person present, or the minister reads a text of sacred Scripture. As circumstances suggest, the following reading may be shortened.

**Brothers and sisters, listen to the words of the holy gospel according to Luke:** 2:25-32, 36-38

*Awaiting the consolation of Israel.*

Now there was a man in Jerusalem whose name was Simeon. This man was righteous and devout, awaiting the consolation of Israel, and the holy Spirit was upon him. It had been revealed to him by the holy Spirit that he should not see death before he had seen the Messiah of the Lord. He came in the Spirit into the temple; and when the parents brought in the child Jesus to perform the custom of the law in regard to him, he took him into his arms and blessed God, saying:

"Now, Master, you may let your servant go
    in peace, according to your word,
for my eyes have seen your salvation,
    which you prepared in sight of all the peoples,
a light for revelation to the Gentiles,
    and glory for your people Israel."

There was also a prophetess, Anna, the daughter of Phanuel, of the tribe of Asher. She was advanced in years, having lived seven years with her husband after her marriage, and then as a widow until she was eighty-four. She never left the temple, but worshiped night and day with fasting and prayer. And coming forward at that very time, she gave thanks to God and spoke about the child to all who were awaiting the redemption of Jerusalem.

353    Or:

Sirach 3:2-18—*Take care of your father when he is old.*

Sirach 25:6-8, 13-16 (Greek, 25:4-6, 10-12)—*The glory of the old is their fear of the Lord.*

Wisdom 4:8-9—*An unsullied life, the attainment of old age.*

Philippians 3:20—4:1—*We eagerly await the coming of our Savior.*

354    As circumstances suggest, one of the following responsorial psalms may be sung or said, or some other suitable song.

R̰. **My God, come quickly to help me.**

Psalm 71

**In you, O LORD, I take refuge;**
**let me never be put to shame.**
**In your justice rescue me, and deliver me;**
**incline your ear to me, and save me.** R̰.

**Be my rock of refuge,
a stronghold to give me safety,
for you are my rock and my fortress.
O my God, rescue me from the hand of the wicked,
from the grasp of the criminal and the violent.** R̶/.

**For you are my hope, O LORD;
my trust, O God, from my youth.
On you I depend from birth;
from my mother's womb you are my strength;
constant has been my hope in you.** R̶/.

**But I will always hope
and praise you ever more and more.
My mouth shall declare your justice,
day by day your salvation,
though I know not their extent.** R̶/.

Psalm 126:1-2b, 2d-3, 4-5, 6

R̶/. **(v. 3) The Lord has done great things for us; we are filled
with joy.**

355    As circumstances suggest, the minister may give those
present a brief explanation of the biblical text, so that they may
understand through faith the meaning of the celebration.

## INTERCESSIONS

356    The intercessions are then said. The minister introduces
them and an assisting minister or one of those present announces
the intentions. From the following intentions those best suited
to the occasion may be used or adapted, or other intentions that
apply to the particular circumstances may be composed.

The minister says:

**God, our almighty Father, gives us new strength and power
by his life-giving grace all through our lives. Let us then pray
to him saying:**

R̶/. **Lord, do not forsake us.**

Or:

R̶/. **Lord, hear our prayer.**

Assisting minister:

**O God, you rewarded the expectations of Simeon and Anna by revealing your Son to them; grant that these servants of yours may in faith see your salvation and rejoice in the consolation of the Holy Spirit. (For this we pray:) R⁊.**

Assisting minister:

**You sent your Son into the world to tell all who are weary that in him they would find rest; help these your servants to take up their cross with patience each day. (For this we pray:) R⁊.**

Assisting minister:

**Your generous kindness can never be surpassed by anyone; grant that these your servants may receive from their families and friends the tender care owed to them. (For this we pray:) R⁊.**

Assisting minister:

**In your love you never turn away from anyone, least of all those who are weak and afflicted; grant that society will acknowledge and unfailingly respect the dignity of the elderly. (For this we pray:) R⁊.**

## Prayer of Blessing

357    A minister who is a priest or deacon may, as circumstances suggest, extend his hands over the elderly people, individually or as a group, or trace the sign of the cross on the forehead of each, as he says the prayer of blessing; a lay minister says the prayer with hands joined.

**Lord, our God,**
**you have given these your faithful**
**the grace to maintain their hope in you**
**through all life's changes**
**and to taste and see your goodness.**
**We bless you for the gifts you have showered on them**
  **for so many years.**

We ask that they may find joy in a renewed strength
of spirit,
that they may have good health,
and that they may inspire us by the example of their
serene way of life.

We ask this through Christ our Lord.

R̶7. **Amen.**

358    Or:

All-powerful and ever-living God,
in whom we live and move and have our being,
we thank you and praise you
for giving N. and N. (the members of this community)
long years,
lived in faith and in doing good.

Grant that they may have the loving support
of their friends and relatives,
that in good health they may be cheerful,
and in poor health not lose hope.
Sustained by the help of your blessing,
let them spend their old age giving praise to your name.

We ask this through Christ our Lord.

R̶7. **Amen.**

359    Or:

Lord God almighty,
bless these your servants,
to whom you have given a long life.
Let them be aware of your nearness,
so that, when they worry about past failings,
they will rejoice in your mercy
and, when they think of the future,
they will faithfully rely on you as their hope.

We ask this through Christ our Lord.

R̶7. **Amen.**

# CONCLUDING RITE

360    After the invitation, "Bow your heads and pray for God's blessing," or something similar is said, a minister who is a priest or deacon concludes the rite by facing the elderly people and, with hands outstretched, saying:

**May the Lord Jesus Christ be with you**
**to protect you.**

R⁊. **Amen.**

**May he go before you**
**to lead you**
**and follow after you**
**to give you strength.**

R⁊. **Amen.**

**May he watch over you,**
**keep you in his care,**
**and bless you with his peace.**

R⁊. **Amen.**

Then he blesses all present.

**And may almighty God bless you all,**
**the Father, and the Son, ✝ and the Holy Spirit.**

R⁊. **Amen.**

---

361    A lay minister invokes God's blessing on the elderly people and all present by signing himself or herself with the sign of the cross and saying:

**May the Lord bless us,**
**protect us from all evil,**
**and bring us to everlasting life.**

R⁊. **Amen.**

---

362    It is preferable to end the celebration with a suitable song.

# B. ORDER OF BLESSING WITHIN MASS

## GENERAL INTERCESSIONS

**363** After the homily the general intercessions follow either in the form usual at Mass or in the form given here. From the following intentions those best suited to the occasion may be used or adapted, or other intentions that apply to the elderly people and the particular circumstances may be composed. But the celebrant is always to use the prayer of blessing provided here.

The minister says:

**God, our almighty Father, gives us new strength and power by his life-giving grace all through our lives. Let us then pray to him saying:**

R̲. **Lord, do not forsake us.**

Or:

R̲. **Lord, hear our prayer.**

Assisting minister:

**O God, you rewarded the expectations of Simeon and Anna by revealing your Son to them; grant that these servants of yours may in faith see your salvation and rejoice in the consolation of the Holy Spirit. (For this we pray:)** R̲.

Assisting minister:

**You sent your Son into the world to tell all who are weary that in him they would find rest; help these your servants to take up their cross with patience each day. (For this we pray:)** R̲.

Assisting minister:

**Your generous kindness can never be surpassed by anyone; grant that these your servants may receive from their families and friends the tender care owed to them. (For this we pray:)** R̲.

Assisting minister:

**In your love you never turn away from anyone, least of all those who are weak and afflicted; grant that society will acknowledge and unfailingly respect the dignity of the elderly. (For this we pray:)** R̲.

## PRAYER OF BLESSING

**364** With hands outstretched over the elderly people as a group, the celebrant immediately says:

**Lord, our God,**
**you have given these your faithful**
**the grace to maintain their hope in you**
**through all life's changes**
**and to taste and see your goodness.**
**We bless you for the gifts you have showered on them for**
**so many years.**
**We ask that they may find joy in a renewed strength**
**of spirit,**
**that they may have good health,**
**and that they may inspire us by the example of their**
**serene way of life.**

**We ask this through Christ our Lord.**

**R̿. Amen.**

**365** But as an alternative, if circumstances suggest, at the end of Mass after the invitation, "Bow your heads and pray for God's blessing," or something similar is said, the celebrant invites the elderly people to receive a special blessing. Then the celebrant, with hands outstretched, says the following blessing, no. 366, or else the prayer of blessing, nos. 367 and 368, and all make the responses.

## BLESSING

**366** Facing the elderly people, the celebrant says:

**May the Lord Jesus Christ be with you**
**to protect you.**

**R̿. Amen.**

**May he go before you**
**to lead you**
**and follow after you**
**to give you strength.**

**R̿. Amen.**

May he watch over you,
keep you in his care,
and bless you with his peace.

℟. Amen.

Then he blesses all present.

And may almighty God bless you all,
the Father, and the Son, ✝ and the Holy Spirit.

℟. Amen.

## PRAYER OF BLESSING

367   With hands outstretched over the elderly people, the celebrant says:

All-powerful and ever-living God,
in whom we live and move and have our being,
we thank you and praise you
for giving N. and N. (the members of this community)
   long years,
lived in faith and in doing good.

Grant that they may have the loving support
   of their friends and relatives,
that in good health they may be cheerful,
and in poor health not lose hope.
Sustained by the help of your blessing,
let them spend their old age giving praise to your name.

We ask this through Christ our Lord.

℟. Amen.

368   After the prayer, the celebrant adds:

And may the blessing of almighty God,
the Father, and the Son, ✝ and the Holy Spirit,
come upon you and remain with you for ever.

℟. Amen.

# C. ORDER OF BLESSING WITH COMMUNION OUTSIDE MASS

369     When the rite is combined with an extended celebration of the word of God, the texts of sacred Scripture may be taken from those indicated already in nos. 352–354.

370     The intercessions may take the form given in no. 356, but a minister who is a priest or deacon always concludes the intercessions with the following prayer of blessing, said with hands outstretched over the elderly people.

**Lord, our God,**
**you have given these your faithful**
**the grace to maintain their hope in you**
**through all life's changes**
**and to taste and see your goodness.**
**We bless you for the gifts you have showered on them for**
**    so many years.**
**We ask that they may find joy in a renewed strength**
**    of spirit,**
**that they may have good health,**
**and that they may inspire us by the example of their serene**
**way of life.**

**We ask this through Christ our Lord.**

R̚. **Amen.**

---

371     A lay minister says the following prayer of blessing with hands joined.

**Lord God almighty,**
**bless these your servants,**
**to whom you have given a long life.**
**Let them be aware of your nearness,**
**so that, when they worry about past failings,**
**they will rejoice in your mercy**
**and, when they think of the future,**
**they will faithfully rely on you as their hope.**

**We ask this through Christ our Lord.**

R̚. **Amen.**

---

# D. SHORTER RITE

372 The minister says:

**Our help is in the name of the Lord.**

All reply:

**Who made heaven and earth.**

373 One of those present or the minister reads a text of sacred Scripture, for example:

Wisdom 4:8

**For the age that is honorable comes not
with the passing of time,
nor can it be measured in terms of years.**

James 5:7-8

**Be patient, therefore, brothers and sisters, until the coming
of the Lord. See how the farmer waits for the precious fruit
of the earth, being patient with it until it receives the early
and the late rains. You too must be patient.**

Luke 9:23

**Then Jesus said to all, "If anyone wishes to come after me,
he must deny himself and take up his cross daily and follow
me."**

374 A minister who is a priest or deacon may, as circumstances suggest, extend his hands over the elderly person or trace the sign of the cross on the elderly person's forehead, as he says the prayer of blessing; a lay minister says the prayer with hands joined.

**Lord God almighty,
bless your servant, N.,
to whom you have given a long life.
Let him/her be aware of your nearness,
so that, when he/she worries about past failings,
he/she will rejoice in your mercy
and, when he/she thinks of the future,
he/she will faithfully rely on you as his/her hope.**

**We ask this through Christ our Lord.**

℟. **Amen.**

## Short Formulary

375 As circumstances suggest, a priest or deacon may use the following short blessing formulary.

**May almighty God bless ✠ you,**
**for he forsakes no one,**
**but with fatherly care**
**sustains you, his child,**
**even in old age and failing strength.**

℟. **Amen.**

## CHAPTER 2

# ORDERS FOR THE BLESSING OF THE SICK

## INTRODUCTION

376    The blessing of the sick by the ministers of the Church is a very ancient custom, having its origins in the practice of Christ himself and his apostles. When ministers visit those who are sick, they are to respect the provisions of *Pastoral Care of the Sick: Rites of Anointing and Viaticum*, nos. 42–56, but the primary concern of every minister should be to show the sick how much Christ and his Church are concerned for them.

377    The text of *Pastoral Care of the Sick* indicates many occasions for blessing the sick and provides the blessing formularies.[13]

378    The present order may be used by a priest or deacon. It may also be used by a layperson, who follows the rites and prayers designated for a lay minister. While maintaining the structure and chief elements of the rite, the minister should adapt the celebration to the circumstances of the place and the people involved.

379    When just one sick person is to be blessed, a priest or a deacon may use the short formulary given in no. 406.

---

[13] See Roman Ritual, *Pastoral Care of the Sick: Rites of Anointing and Viaticum*, no. 54.

# I. ORDER OF BLESSING

## A. ORDER FOR THE BLESSING OF ADULTS

### INTRODUCTORY RITES

380    When the community has gathered, the minister says:

**In the name of the Father, and of the Son, and of the Holy Spirit.**

All make the sign of the cross and reply:

**Amen.**

381    A minister who is a priest or a deacon greets those present in the following or other suitable words, taken mainly from sacred Scripture.

**Peace be with you (this house) and all who live here.**

Or:

**The peace of the Lord be with you always.**

All the make the following or some other suitable reply.

**And also with you.**

---

382    A lay minister greets those present in the following words.

**Brothers and sisters, let us bless the Lord, who went about doing good and healing the sick. Blessed be God now and for ever.**

R̸. **Blessed be God now and for ever.**

Or:

R̸. **Amen.**

---

383    In the following or similar words, the minister prepares the sick and all present for the blessing.

**The Lord Jesus, who went about doing good works and healing sickness and infirmity of every kind, commanded his disciples to care for the sick, to pray for them, and to lay hands on them. In this celebration we shall entrust our sick brothers and sisters to the care of the Lord, asking that he will enable them to bear their pain and suffering in the knowledge that, if they accept their share in the pain of his own passion, they will also share in its power to give comfort and strength.**

## READING OF THE WORD OF GOD

384   A reader, another person present, or the minister reads a text of sacred Scripture, taken preferably from the texts given in *Pastoral Care of the Sick* and the Lectionary for Mass.[14] The readings chosen should be those that best apply to the physical and spiritual condition of those who are sick.

**Brothers and sisters, listen to the words of the second letter of Paul to the Corinthians:**                      1:3-7

*The God of all consolation.*

**Blessed be the God and Father of our Lord Jesus Christ, the Father of compassion and God of all encouragement, who encourages us in our every affliction, so that we may be able to encourage those who are in any affliction with the encouragement with which we ourselves are encouraged by God. For as Christ's sufferings overflow to us, so through Christ does our encouragement also overflow. If we are afflicted, it is for your encouragement and salvation; if we are encouraged, it is for your encouragement, which enables you to endure the same sufferings that we suffer. Our hope for you is firm, for we know that as you share in the sufferings, you also share in the encouragement.**

385   Or:

**Brothers and sisters, listen to the words of the holy gospel according to Matthew:**                      11:28-30

*Come to me and I will refresh you.*

---

[14] See ibid., no. 297; Lectionary for Mass (2nd ed., 1981), nos. 790–795, 796–800 (Ritual Masses: V. Pastoral Care of the Sick and the Dying, 1. Anointing of the Sick and 2. Viaticum), and nos. 933–937 (Masses for Various Needs and Occasions, III. For Various Public Needs, 24. For the Sick).

Jesus said to the crowds: "Come to me, all you who labor and are burdened, and I will give you rest. Take my yoke upon you and learn from me, for I am meek and humble of heart; and you will find rest for yourselves. For my yoke is easy, and my burden light."

386    Or:

Brothers and sisters, listen to the words of the holy gospel according to Mark:                                              6:53-56

*They laid the sick in the marketplace.*

After making the crossing, Jesus and his disciples came to land at Gennesaret and tied up there. As they were leaving the boat, people immediately recognized him. They scurried about the surrounding country and began to bring in the sick on mats to wherever they heard he was. Whatever villages or towns or countryside he entered, they laid the sick in the marketplaces and begged him that they might touch only the tassel on his cloak; and as many as touched it were healed.

387    As circumstances suggest, one of the following responsorial psalms may be sung or said, or some other suitable song.

R̃. **Lord, you have preserved my life from destruction.**

Isaiah 38

Once I said,
"In the noontime of life I must depart!
To the gates of the nether world I shall
be consigned
for the rest of my years." R̃.

I said, "I shall see the LORD no more
in the land of the living.
No longer shall I behold my fellow men
among those who dwell in the world." R̃.

My dwelling, like a shepherd's tent,
is struck down and borne away from me;
You have folded up my life, like a weaver
who severs the last thread. R̃.

Those live whom the LORD protects;
yours . . . the life of my spirit.
You have given me health and life. R̃.

Psalm 102:2-3, 24-25

℟. (v. 2) **O Lord, hear my prayer, and let my cry come to you.**

**388**    As circumstances suggest, the minister may give those present a brief explanation of the biblical text, so that they may understand through faith the meaning of the celebration.

## INTERCESSIONS

**389**    The intercessions are then said. The minister introduces them and an assisting minister or one of those present announces the intentions. From the following intentions those best suited to the occasion may be used or adapted, or other intentions that apply to those who are sick and to the particular circumstances may be composed.

The minister says:

**The Lord Jesus loves our brothers and sisters who are ill. With trust let us pray to him that he will comfort them with his grace, saying:**

℟. **Lord, give those who are sick the comfort of your presence.**

Assisting minister:

**Lord Jesus, you came as healer of body and of spirit, in order to cure all our ills.** ℟.

Assisting minister:

**You were a man of suffering, but it was our infirmities that you bore, our sufferings that you endured.** ℟.

Assisting minister:

**You chose to be like us in all things, in order to assure us of your compassion.** ℟.

Assisting minister:

**You experienced the weakness of the flesh in order to deliver us from evil.** ℟.

Assisting minister:

**At the foot of the cross your Mother stood as companion in your sufferings, and in your tender care you gave her to us as our Mother.** ℟.

**It is your wish that in our own flesh we should fill up what is wanting in your sufferings for the sake of your Body, the Church. ℟.**

390    Instead of the intercessions or in addition to them, one of the following litanies taken from *Pastoral Care of the Sick,* nos. 245 and 138 may be used.

Minister:

**You bore our weakness and carried our sorrows: Lord, have mercy.**

**℟. Lord, have mercy.**

Minister:

**You felt compassion for the crowd, and went about doing good and healing the sick: Christ, have mercy.**

**℟. Christ, have mercy.**

Minister:

**You commanded your apostles to lay their hands on the sick in your name: Lord, have mercy.**

**℟. Lord, have mercy.**

391    Or:

The minister says:

**Let us pray to God for our brothers and sisters and for all those who devote themselves to caring for them.**

Assisting minister:

**Bless N. and N. and fill them with new hope and strength: Lord, have mercy.**

**℟. Lord, have mercy.**

Assisting minister:

**Relieve their pain: Lord, have mercy. ℟.**

Assisting minister:

**Free them from sin and do not let them give way to temptation: Lord, have mercy. ℟.**

*Assisting minister:*

**Sustain all the sick with your power: Lord, have mercy. ℟.**

*Assisting minister:*

**Assist all who care for the sick: Lord, have mercy. ℟.**

*Assisting minister:*

**Give life and health to our brothers and sisters on whom we lay our hands in your name: Lord, have mercy. ℟.**

## PRAYER OF BLESSING

392 A minister who is a priest or deacon may, as circumstances suggest, lay his hands on the head of each sick person, and then say the prayer of blessing.

**Lord, our God,**
**you sent your Son into the world**
**to bear our infirmities**
**and to endure our sufferings.**
**For N. and N., your servants who are sick,**
**we ask that your blessing will give them strength**
**to overcome their weakness**
**through the power of patience and the comfort of hope**
**and that with your aid they will soon be restored to health.**

**We ask this through Christ our Lord.**

**℟. Amen.**

393 Or, without the laying on of hands:

**Lord Jesus,**
**who went about doing good and healing all,**
**we ask you to bless your friends who are sick.**
**Give them strength in body, courage in spirit,**
  **and patience with pain.**
**Let them recover their health,**
**so that, restored to the Christian community,**
**they may joyfully praise your name,**
**for you live and reign for ever and ever.**

**℟. Amen.**

394 A lay minister traces the sign of the cross on the forehead of each sick person and says the following prayer of blessing.

**Lord, our God,**
**who watch over your creatures with unfailing care,**
**keep us in the safe embrace of your love.**
**With your strong right hand raise up your servants**
 **(N. and N.)**
**and give them the strength of your own power.**
**Minister to them and heal their illnesses,**
**so that they may have from you the help they long for.**

**We ask this through Christ our Lord.**

**R̸. Amen.**

395 Or, for one sick person:

**Lord and Father, almighty and eternal God,**
**by your blessing you give us strength and support**
 **in our frailty:**
**turn with kindness toward this your servant N.**
**Free him/her from all illness and restore him/her to health,**
**so that in the sure knowledge of your goodness**
**he/she will gratefully bless your holy name.**

**We ask this through Christ our Lord.**

**R̸. Amen.**

396 After the prayer of blessing, the minister invites all present to pray for the protection of the Blessed Virgin. They may do so by singing or reciting a Marian antiphon, for example, *We turn to you for protection (Sub tuum praesidium)* or *Hail, Holy Queen.*

## Concluding Rite

397 A minister who is a priest or a deacon concludes the rite by facing the sick and saying:

**May God the Father bless you.**

**R̸. Amen.**

**May God the Son comfort you.**

℞. **Amen.**

**May God the Holy Spirit enlighten you.**

℞. **Amen.**

> Then he blesses all present.

**And may almighty God bless you all,
the Father, and the Son, ✝ and the Holy Spirit.**

℞. **Amen.**

---

**398**  A lay minister invokes the Lord's blessing on the sick and all present by signing himself or herself with the sign of the cross and saying:

**May the Lord Jesus Christ,
who went about doing good and healing the sick,
grant that we may have good health
and be enriched by his blessings.**

℞. **Amen.**

---

# B. ORDER FOR THE BLESSING OF CHILDREN

**399**  For the blessing of sick children, the texts already given are to be adapted to the children's level, but special intercessions are provided here and a special prayer of blessing.

## INTERCESSIONS

**400**  To the following intentions others may be added that apply to the condition of the sick children and to the particular circumstances.

---

The minister says:

**The Lord Jesus loved and cherished the little ones with a special love. Let us, then, pray to him for these sick children, saying:**

**R̷. Lord, keep them in all their ways.**

Or:

**R̷. Lord, hear our prayer.**

Assisting minister:

**Lord Jesus, you called the little children to come to you and said that the kingdom of heaven belongs to such as these; listen with mercy to our prayers for these children. (For this we pray:) R̷.**

Assisting minister:

**You revealed the mysteries of the kingdom of heaven, not to the wise of this world, but to little children; give these children the proof of your love. (For this we pray:) R̷.**

Assisting minister:

**You praised the children who cried out their Hosannas on the eve of your passion; strengthen these children and their parents with your holy comfort. (For this we pray:) R̷.**

Assisting minister:

**You charged your disciples to take care of the sick; stand at the side of all those who so gladly devote themselves to restoring the health of these children. (For this we pray:) R̷.**

## Prayer of Blessing

401    A minister who is a priest or deacon may, as circumstances suggest, lay his hands on the head of each sick child, and then say the prayer of blessing.

**Lord, our God,**
**your Son Jesus Christ welcomed little children and**
  **blessed them.**

Stretch out your right hand over these little children,
    N. and N., who are sick.
Grant that, made well again,
they may return to their parents
and to the community of your holy Church
and give you thanks and praise.

We ask this through Christ our Lord.

R̸. Amen.

---

402   A lay minister, and particularly a mother or father when blessing a sick child, traces the sign of the cross on each child's forehead and then says the following prayer of blessing.

Father of mercy and God of all consolation,
you show tender care for all your creatures
and give health of soul and body.
Raise up these children
    (*or* this child *or* the son/daughter you have given us)
    from their (his/her) sickness.
Then, growing in wisdom and grace in your sight and ours,
they (he/she) will serve you all the days of their (his/her) life
in uprightness and holiness
and offer the thanksgiving due to your mercy.

We ask this through Christ our Lord.

R̸. Amen.

---

# C. SHORTER RITE

403   The minister says:

Our help is in the name of the Lord.

All reply:

Who made heaven and earth.

404   One of those present or the minister reads a text of sacred Scripture, for example:

## 2 Corinthians 1:3-4

**Blessed be the God and Father of our Lord Jesus Christ, the Father of compassion and God of all encouragement, who encourages us in our every affliction, so that we may be able to encourage those who are in any affliction with the encouragement with which we ourselves are encouraged by God.**

## Matthew 11:28-29

**Jesus said: "Come to me, all you who labor and are burdened, and I will give you rest. Take my yoke upon you and learn from me, for I am meek and humble of heart; and you will find rest for yourselves."**

405    As circumstances suggest, a minister who is a priest or deacon may lay hands on the sick person while saying the prayer of blessing; a lay minister may trace the sign of the cross on the sick person's forehead while saying the prayer.

**Lord and Father, almighty and eternal God,
by your blessing you give us strength and support
  in our frailty:
turn with kindness toward your servant, N.
Free him/her from all illness and restore him/her to health,
so that in the sure knowledge of your goodness
he/she will gratefully bless your holy name.**

**We ask this through Christ our Lord.**

**R℣. Amen.**

## SHORT FORMULARY

406    As circumstances suggest, a priest or deacon may use the following short blessing formulary.

**May he who alone is Lord and Redeemer
bless + you, N.
May he give health to your body
and holiness to your soul.
May he bring you safely to eternal life.**

**R℣. Amen.**

# II. ORDER FOR THE BLESSING OF A PERSON SUFFERING FROM ADDICTION OR FROM SUBSTANCE ABUSE

## INTRODUCTION

407     Addiction to alcohol, drugs, and other controlled substances causes great disruption in the life of an individual and his or her family. This blessing is intended to strengthen the addicted person in the struggle to overcome addiction and also to assist his or her family and friends.

408     This blessing may also be used for individuals who, although not addicted, abuse alcohol or drugs and wish the assistance of God's blessing in their struggle.

409     Ministers should be aware of the spiritual needs of a person suffering from addiction or substance abuse, and to this end the pastoral guidance on the care of the sick and rites of *Pastoral Care of the Sick* will be helpful.

410     If the recovery process is slow or is marked by relapses, the blessing may be repeated when pastorally appropriate.

411     These orders may be used by a priest or a deacon, and also by a layperson, who follows the rites and prayers designated for a lay minister.

## A. ORDER OF BLESSING

### INTRODUCTORY RITES

412     When the community has gathered, a suitable song may be sung. After the singing, the minister says:

**In the name of the Father, and of the Son, and of the Holy Spirit.**

All make the sign of the cross and reply:

**Amen.**

**413**    A minister who is a priest or deacon greets those present in the following or other suitable words, taken mainly from sacred Scripture.

**The Lord be with you.**

And all reply:

**And also with you.**

---

**414**    A lay minister greets those present in the following words:

**Let us praise God our creator, who gives us courage and strength, now and for ever.**

R̶. **Amen.**

---

**415**    In the following or similar words, the minister prepares those present for the blessing.

**God created the world and all things in it and entrusted them into our hands that we might use them for our good and for the building up of the Church and human society. Today we pray for N., that God may strengthen him/her in his/her weakness and restore him/her to the freedom of God's children. We pray also for ourselves that we may encourage and support him/her in the days ahead.**

## READING OF THE WORD OF GOD

**416**    A reader, another person present, or the minister reads a text of sacred Scripture.

**Brothers and sisters, listen to the words of the second letter of Paul to the Corinthians:**                    4:6-9

*We are afflicted, but not crushed.*

**For God who said, "Let light shine out of darkness," has shone in our hearts to bring to light the knowledge of the glory of God on the face of Jesus Christ.**

**But we hold this treasure in earthen vessels, that the surpassing power may be of God and not from us. We are afflicted**

---

in every way, but not constrained; perplexed, but not driven to despair; persecuted, but not abandoned; struck down, but not destroyed.

417    Or:

Isaiah 63:7-9—*He has favored us according to his mercy.*

Romans 8:18-25—*I consider the sufferings of the present to be as nothing compared with the glory to be revealed in us.*

Matthew 15:21-28—*Woman, you have great faith.*

418    As circumstances suggest, one of the following responsorial psalms may be sung or said, or some other suitable song.

R̸. **Our help is from the Lord who made heaven and earth.**

Psalm 121

**I lift up my eyes toward the mountains;**
**whence shall help come to me?**
**My help is from the LORD**
**who made heaven and earth.** R̸.

**May he not suffer your foot to slip;**
**may he slumber not who guards you:**
**Indeed he neither slumbers nor sleeps,**
**the guardian of Israel.** R̸.

**The LORD is your guardian; the LORD is your shade;**
**he is beside you at your right hand.**
**The sun shall not harm you by day,**
**nor the moon by night.** R̸.

**The LORD will guard you from all evil;**
**he will guard your life.**
**The LORD will guard your coming and your going,**
**both now and forever.** R̸.

Psalm 130:1-2, 3-4, 5-6, 7-8

R̸. **(v. 5) My soul trusts in the Lord.**

419    As circumstances suggest, the minister may give those present a brief explanation of the biblical text, so that they may understand through faith the meaning of the celebration.

## INTERCESSIONS

420    The intercessions are then said. The minister introduces
them and an assisting minister or one of those present announces
the intentions. From the following those best suited to the occasion may be used or adapted, or other intentions that apply to
the particular circumstances may be composed.

The minister says:

**Our God gives us life and constantly calls us to new life; let
us pray to God with confidence.**

℞. **Lord, hear our prayer.**

Assisting minister:

**For those addicted to alcohol/drugs, that God may be their
strength and support, we pray.** ℞.

Assisting minister:

**For N., bound by the chains of addiction/substance abuse, that
we encourage and assist him/her in his/her struggle, we pray.**
℞.

Assisting minister:

**For N., that he/she may trust in the mercy of God through
whom all things are possible, we pray.** ℞.

Assisting minister:

**For the family and friends of N., that with faith and patience
they show him/her their love, we pray.** ℞.

Assisting minister:

**For the Church, that it may always be attentive to those in need,
we pray.** ℞.

421    After the intercessions the minister, in the following or
similar words, invites all present to sing or say the Lord's Prayer.

**Let us pray to our merciful God as Jesus taught us:**

All:

**Our Father . . .**

# PRAYER OF BLESSING

422 **422** A minister who is a priest or deacon says the prayer of blessing with hands outstretched over the person; a lay minister says the prayer with hands joined.

A        For addiction

**God of mercy,
we bless you in the name of your Son, Jesus Christ,
who ministered to all who came to him.
Give your strength to N., your servant,
bound by the chains of addiction.
Enfold him/her in your love
and restore him/her to the freedom of God's children.**

**Lord,
look with compassion on all those
who have lost their health and freedom.
Restore to them the assurance of your unfailing mercy,
and strengthen them in the work of recovery.**

**To those who care for them,
grant patient understanding and a love that perseveres.**

**We ask this through Christ our Lord.**

℟. **Amen.**

B        For substance abuse

**God of mercy,
we bless you in the name of your Son, Jesus Christ,
who ministered to all who came to him.
Give your strength to N., your servant,
enfold him/her in your love
and restore him/her to the freedom of God's children.**

**Lord,
look with compassion on all those
who have lost their health and freedom.
Restore to them the assurance of your unfailing mercy,
strengthen them in the work of recovery,
and help them to resist all temptation.**

**To those who care for them,
grant patient understanding and a love that perseveres.**

**We ask this through Christ our Lord.**

**R̸. Amen.**

> As circumstances suggest, the minister in silence may sprinkle the person with holy water.

## CONCLUDING RITE

423    A minister who is a priest or deacon concludes the rite by saying:

**May God give you light and peace.**

**R̸. Amen.**

**May God raise you up and save you.**

**R̸. Amen.**

**May God give you courage and strength.**

**R̸. Amen.**

> Then he blesses all present.

**And may almighty God bless you all,
the Father, and the Son, ✠ and the Holy Spirit.**

**R̸. Amen.**

424    A lay minister concludes the rite by signing himself or herself with the sign of the cross and saying:

**May our all-merciful God, Father, Son, and Holy Spirit, bless us and embrace us in love for ever.**

**R̸. Amen.**

425    It is preferable to end the celebration with a suitable song.

# B. SHORTER RITE

**426**   All make the sign of the cross as the minister says:

**Our help is in the name of the Lord.**

All reply:

**Who made heaven and earth.**

**427**   One of those present or the minister reads a text of sacred Scripture, for example:

**Brothers and sisters, listen to the words of the second letter of Paul to the Corinthians:**                                4:6-9

*We are afflicted, but not crushed.*

**For God who said, "Let light shine out of darkness," has shone in our hearts to bring to light the knowledge of the glory of God on the face of Jesus Christ.**

**But we hold this treasure in earthen vessels, that the surpassing power may be of God and not from us. We are afflicted in every way, but not constrained; perplexed, but not driven to despair; persecuted, but not abandoned; struck down, but not destroyed.**

**428**   Or:

Isaiah 63:7-9—*He has favored us according to his mercy.*

Matthew 15:21-28—*Woman, you have great faith.*

**429**   A minister who is a priest or deacon says the prayer of blessing with hands outstretched over the person; a lay minister says the prayer with hands joined.

A                For addiction

**God of mercy,**
**we bless you in the name of your Son, Jesus Christ,**
**who ministered to all who came to him.**
**Give your strength to N., your servant,**
**bound by the chains of addiction.**
**Enfold him/her in your love**
**and restore him/her to the freedom of God's children.**

**Lord,**
**look with compassion on all those**
**who have lost their health and freedom.**

Restore to them the assurance of your unfailing mercy,
and strengthen them in the work of recovery.

To those who care for them,
grant patient understanding and a love that perseveres.

We ask this through Christ our Lord.

R⁊. Amen.

B          For substance abuse

God of mercy,
we bless you in the name of your Son, Jesus Christ,
who ministered to all who came to him.
Give your strength to N., your servant,
enfold him/her in your love
and restore him/her to the freedom of God's children.

Lord,
look with compassion on all those
who have lost their health and freedom.
Restore to them the assurance of your unfailing mercy,
strengthen them in the work of recovery,
and help them to resist all temptation.

To those who care for them,
grant patient understanding and a love that perseveres.

We ask this through Christ our Lord.

R⁊. Amen.

# III. ORDER FOR THE BLESSING OF A VICTIM OF CRIME OR OPPRESSION USA

## INTRODUCTION

430     The personal experience of a crime, political oppression, or social oppression can be traumatic and not easily forgotten. A victim often needs the assistance of others, and no less that of God, in dealing with this experience.

431     This blessing is intended to assist the victim and help him or her come to a state of tranquility and peace.

432     These orders may be used by a priest or a deacon, and also by a layperson, who follows the rites and prayers designated for a lay minister.

## A. ORDER OF BLESSING

### INTRODUCTORY RITES

433     When the community has gathered, a suitable song may be sung. After the singing, the minister says:

**In the name of the Father, and of the Son, and of the Holy Spirit.**

All make the sign of the cross and reply:

**Amen.**

434     A minister who is a priest or deacon greets those present in the following or other suitable words, taken mainly from sacred Scripture.

**May the grace and peace of Christ be with you.**

And all reply:

**And also with you.**

435 A lay minister greets those present in the following words:

**May the Lord grant us peace, now and for ever.**

℟. **Amen.**

436 In the following or similar words, the minister prepares those present for the blessing.

**Throughout history God has manifested his love and care for those who have suffered from violence, hatred, and oppression. We commend N. to the healing mercy of God who binds up all our wounds and enfolds us in his gentle care.**

## Reading of the Word of God

437 A reader, another person present, or the minister reads a text of sacred Scripture.

**Brothers and sisters, listen to the words of the holy gospel according to Matthew:** 10:28-33

*Do not fear.*

**Jesus said to his disciples: "Do not be afraid of those who kill the body but cannot kill the soul; rather, be afraid of the one who can destroy both soul and body in Gehenna. Are not two sparrows sold for a small coin? Yet not one of them falls to the ground without your Father's knowledge. Even all the hairs of your head are counted. So do not be afraid; you are worth more than many sparrows. Everyone who acknowledges me before others I will acknowledge before my heavenly Father. But whoever denies me before others, I will deny before my heavenly Father."**

438 Or:

Isaiah 59:6b-8, 15-18—*The Lord is appalled by evil and injustice.*

Job 3:1-26—*Lamentation of Job.*

Lamentations 3:1-24—*I am one who knows affliction.*

Lamentations 3:49-59—*When I called, you came to my aid.*

Micah 4:1-4—*Every person shall sit undisturbed.*

Matthew 5:1-10—*The beatitudes.*

Matthew 5:43-48—*Love your enemies, pray for those who persecute you.*

Luke 10:25-37—*The good Samaritan.*

**439**    As circumstances suggest, one of the following responsorial psalms may be sung, or some other suitable song.

R̵. **The Lord is my strength and my salvation.**

Psalm 140

**Deliver me, O LORD, from evil men;**
**preserve me from violent men,**
**From those who devise evil in their hearts,**
**and stir up wars every day.** R̵.

**Save me, O LORD, from the hands of the wicked;**
**preserve me from violent men**
**Who plan to trip up my feet—**
**the proud who have hidden a trap for me;**
**They have spread cords for a net;**
**by the wayside they have laid snares for me.** R̵.

**Grant not, O LORD, the desires of the wicked;**
**further not their plans.**
**Those who surround me lift up their heads;**
**may the mischief which they threaten overwhelm them.** R̵.

**I know that the LORD renders**
**justice to the afflicted, judgment to the poor.**
**Surely the just shall give thanks to your name;**
**the upright shall dwell in your presence.** R̵.

Psalm 142:2-3, 4b-5, 6-7

R̵. (v. 6) **You, O Lord, are my refuge.**

Psalm 31:2-3a, 4-5, 15-16, 24-25

R̵. (v. 6) **Into your hands I commend my spirit.**

**440**    As circumstances suggest, the minister may give those present a brief explanation of the biblical text, so that they may understand through faith the meaning of the celebration.

# INTERCESSIONS

**441**    The intercessions are then said. The minister introduces them and an assisting minister or one of those present announces the intentions. From the following those best suited to the occasion may be used or adapted, or other intentions that apply to the particular circumstances may be composed.

The minister says:

**Let us pray to the Lord God, the defender of the weak and powerless, who delivered our ancestors from harm.**

**R7. Deliver us from evil, O Lord.**

Assisting minister:

**For N., that he/she may be freed from pain and fear, we pray to the Lord. R7.**

Assisting minister:

**For all who are victims of crime/oppression, we pray to the Lord. R7.**

Assisting minister:

**For an end to all acts of violence and hatred, we pray to the Lord. R7.**

Assisting minister:

**For those who harm others, that they may change their lives and turn to God, we pray to the Lord. R7.**

**442**    After the intercessions the minister, in the following or similar words, invites all present to sing or say the Lord's Prayer.

**The Lord heals our wounds and strengthens us in our weakness; let us pray as Christ has taught us:**

All:

**Our Father . . .**

# PRAYER OF BLESSING

**443**    A minister who is a priest or deacon says the prayer of blessing with hands outstretched over the person to be blessed; a lay minister says the prayer with hands joined.

**Lord God,**
**your own Son was delivered into the hands of the**
**    wicked,**
**yet he prayed for his persecutors**
**and overcame hatred with the blood of the cross.**
**Relieve the suffering of N.;**
**grant him/her peace of mind**
**and a renewed faith in your protection and care.**

**Protect us all from the violence of others,**
**keep us safe from the weapons of hate,**
**and restore to us tranquility and peace.**

**We ask this through Christ our Lord.**

**R̸. Amen.**

> As circumstances suggest, the minister in silence may sprinkle the person with holy water.

## CONCLUDING RITE

> **444**    A minister who is a priest or deacon concludes the rite by saying:

**May God bless you with his mercy,**
**strengthen you with his love,**
**and enable you to walk in charity and peace.**

**R̸. Amen.**

> Then he blesses all present.

**And may almighty God bless you all,**
**the Father, and the Son, ✝ and the Holy Spirit.**

**R̸. Amen.**

> **445**    A lay minister concludes the rite by signing himself or herself with the sign of the cross and saying:

**May God bless us with his mercy,**
**strengthen us with his love,**
**and enable us to walk in charity and peace.**

**R̸. Amen.**

> **446**    It is preferable to end the celebration with a suitable song.

# B. SHORTER RITE

**447**    All make the sign of the cross as the minister says:

**Our help is in the name of the Lord.**

All reply:

**Who made heaven and earth.**

**448**    One of those present or the minister reads a text of sacred Scripture, for example:

**Brothers and sisters, listen to the words of the holy gospel according to Matthew:**                                                      10:28-33

*Do not fear.*

**Jesus said to his disciples: "Do not be afraid of those who kill the body but cannot kill the soul; rather, be afraid of the one who can destroy both soul and body in Gehenna. Are not two sparrows sold for a small coin? Yet not one of them falls to the ground without your Father's knowledge. Even all the hairs of your head are counted. So do not be afraid; you are worth more than many sparrows. Everyone who acknowledges me before others I will acknowledge before my heavenly Father. But whoever denies me before others, I will deny before my heavenly Father."**

**449**    Or:

Isaiah 59:6b-8, 15-18—*The Lord is appalled by evil and injustice.*

Job 3:1-26—*Lamentation of Job.*

Lamentations 3:1-24—*I am a man who knows affliction.*

Lamentations 3:49-59—*When I called, you came to my aid.*

Matthew 5:1-10—*The beatitudes.*

Luke 10:25-37—*The good Samaritan.*

**450**    A minister who is a priest or deacon says the prayer of blessing with hands outstretched over the person; a lay minister says the prayer with hands joined.

**Lord God,**
**your own Son was delivered into the hands of the wicked**
**yet he prayed for his persecutors**
**and overcame hatred with the blood of the cross.**

Relieve the suffering of N.;
grant him/her peace of mind
and a renewed faith in your protection and care.

Protect us all from the violence of others,
keep us safe from the weapons of hate,
and restore to us tranquility and peace.

We ask this through Christ our Lord.

R͡/. Amen.

CHAPTER 3

# ORDER FOR THE BLESSING OF MISSIONARIES SENT TO PROCLAIM THE GOSPEL

## INTRODUCTION

451    The celebration of a blessing should mark the occasion when Christ's disciples, whether clerics, religious, or laypersons, are sent by the lawful pastors of the Church to preach the mystery of salvation to the peoples of the world. The purpose of the rite is to ask God's blessing on the new heralds of the Gospel, to instruct the faithful concerning the nature and significance of missionary activity, and to inspire them to follow with their prayers those who, endowed with a special charism, are about to depart to proclaim the Gospel.

452    As the present chapter provides, the best way to carry out such a rite is either within a celebration of the liturgy of the word or within a celebration of the eucharist.

453    A priest is the celebrant for the orders of blessing in this chapter. While maintaining the structure and chief elements of the rite, he should adapt the celebration to the circumstances of the place and the missionaries involved.

    When, as is desirable, the bishop is the celebrant, everything in the celebration is to be adapted accordingly.

# I. ORDER OF BLESSING WITHIN
# A CELEBRATION OF THE WORD OF GOD

## INTRODUCTORY RITES

**454** When the community has gathered, the celebrant, the assisting deacon, and the other ministers, all wearing their proper vestments, proceed from the sacristy through the body of the church to the sanctuary. They are led by a crossbearer and the assisting deacon, who carries the Book of the Gospels; the choir, joined by the people, sings a suitable song.

**455** The departing missionaries take part in the procession.

**456** After the singing, the celebrant says:

**In the name of the Father, and of the Son, and of the Holy Spirit.**

All make the sign of the cross and reply:

**Amen.**

**457** The celebrant greets those present in the following or other suitable words, taken mainly from sacred Scripture.

**May the Lord, who has called us out of darkness into his marvelous light, be with you all.**

All make the following or some other suitable reply.

**And also with you.**

**458** In the following or similar words, the celebrant prepares those present for the blessing and explains the rite.

**My dear friends, as we take part in today's celebration we are in a sense reliving a practice of the early Church, the eager sending of its members to other peoples, to assist either those who were already of the household of the faith or those who did not yet believe in Christ.**

**The sending of our brothers and sisters to serve the needs of the Church will strengthen our bond of communion with the local Churches to which they are going, and the prayers we offer in this celebration are an expression of that communion.**

---

**459** All pray briefly in silence; then the celebrant continues:

**Our God and Father,**
**your will is that all should be saved**
**and come to the knowledge of your truth.**
**Send workers into your great harvest,**
**so that the Gospel may be preached to every creature**
**and your people, gathered together by the word of life**
**and strengthened by the power of the sacraments,**
**may advance in the way of salvation and love.**

**We ask this through Christ our Lord.**

R̶⁊. **Amen.**

## READING OF THE WORD OF GOD

**460** Readers or the assisting deacon read one or more texts of sacred Scripture, taken from the texts given in the Lectionary for Mass in Masses for Various Needs and Occasions, ''For the Spread of the Gospel.''[15] Between the readings there is a responsorial psalm, related to the reading that preceded it, or an interval of silence. The gospel reading always holds the place of honor.

**461** It is most fitting that, before the proclamation of the gospel reading, the missionaries should be introduced to the community.

The assisting deacon announces to the people the names of those departing for the missions and, as circumstances suggest, he may indicate the rank or office the missionaries hold within the people of God, as well as the Churches to which they are being sent. Thus, for example:

Deacon:

**These are the names of those who, in keeping with the Lord's command, are being sent by our Church of N. to preach the Gospel, accompanied by our prayers:**

**N.N., priest, to the Church in N.**
**N.N., deacon, to the Church in N.**
**N.N., religious of (N.), to the Church in N.**
**N.N., layman/laywoman, to the Church in N.**

---

[15] See Lectionary for Mass (2nd ed., 1981), nos. 872–876 (Masses for Various Needs and Occasions, I. For the Church, 11. For the Spread of the Gospel).

462    But when the group of departing missionaries includes men religious or women religious, the superior of the order or congregation to which they belong, rather than the assisting deacon, announces their names, charges, and destinations. Thus, for example:

Superior:

**From our institute, inspired by charity and strengthened by obedience, these members are going forth to proclaim the Gospel:**

**Brother N.,** (*for example,* **teacher,**) **to N.**
**Sister N.,** (*for example,* **catechist,**) **to N.**

463    When their name is called, the missionaries respond either by word, for example, by saying, "Present," or by gesture, for example, by standing.

464    After the gospel reading by the deacon, the celebrant in the homily explains both the biblical readings and the meaning of the rite.

465    After the homily, the missionaries go and stand near the celebrant, but in such a way as not to obstruct the people's view of the rite.

## INTERCESSIONS

466    In the intercessions that follow all pray together for the missionaries and for the Churches to which they are being sent. The celebrant introduces the intercessions and an assisting minister or one of those present announces the intentions. From the following intentions those best suited to the occasion may be used or adapted, or other intentions that apply to the missionaries and the particular circumstances may be composed.

The celebrant says:

**Let us pray together to God, our merciful Father. He anointed his own Son with the Holy Spirit to preach the Good News to the poor, to heal the brokenhearted, and to comfort the sorrowful. With great confidence we therefore say:**

℟. **Lord, may all your people praise you.**

Assisting minister:

God of everlasting mercy, your will is that all people should be saved and come to the knowledge of the truth; we give you thanks for sending your only Son into the world as our Teacher and Redeemer. ℟.

Assisting minister:

You sent Jesus Christ to preach the Good News to the poor, to proclaim the release of captives, and to announce the age of grace; grant that the embrace of your Church may extend to people of every tongue and every nation. ℟.

Assisting minister:

You call all peoples out of darkness into your marvelous light, so that at the name of Jesus every knee must bend in heaven, on earth, and under the earth; enable us to bear true witness to the Gospel of salvation. ℟.

Assisting minister:

Give us hearts that are upright and simple, so that we will be open to your word; make our lives and all the world rich in works of holiness. ℟.

## PRAYER OF BLESSING

467    The celebrant immediately continues with the prayer of blessing; as circumstances suggest, he may hold his hands outstretched over the departing missionaries, as he says the prayer of blessing.

We bless you, O God, and we praise your name.
In your merciful providence you sent your Son into the world
to free us from the bondage of sin by his own blood
and to enrich us with the gifts of the Holy Spirit.
Before he returned, triumphant over death, to you, Father,
he sent his apostles, the bearers of his love and power,
to proclaim the Gospel of life to all peoples
and in the waters of baptism to cleanse those who believe.

Lord, look kindly on your servants:
we send them forth as messengers of salvation and peace,
marked with the sign of the cross.

Guide their steps with your mighty arm
and with the power of your grace strengthen them in spirit,
so that they will not falter through weariness.

Make their words the echo of Christ's voice,
so that those who hear them
may be drawn to obey the Gospel.

Fill the hearts of your missionaries with the Holy Spirit,
so that, becoming all things to all people,
they may lead many to you, the Father of all,
to sing your praises in your holy Church.

We ask this through Christ our Lord.

℞. Amen.

## Presentation of Crosses to the Missionaries

468    The celebrant blesses the crosses:

Father of holiness,
you willed the cross of your Son
to be the source of all blessings,
the fount of all grace.
Bless these crosses
and grant that those who will preach the crucified Christ
   to others
may themselves strive to be transformed into his image.

We ask this in the name of Jesus the Lord.

℞. Amen.

469    Then one by one the missionaries go to the celebrant, who
gives each one a cross, as he says:

Receive this sign of Christ's love and of our faith.
Preach Christ crucified,
who is the power and wisdom of God.

The missionary replies:

Amen.

Then the missionary takes the crucifix, kisses it, and returns to
his or her place.

470　As circumstances suggest, the celebrant may pronounce the formulary of presentation just once, saying:

**Receive this sign of Christ's love and of our faith.**
**Preach Christ crucified,**
**who is the power and wisdom of God.**

Or:

**Receive this sign of Christ's love**
**and of the mission for which the Church has chosen you.**

The missionaries all reply together:

**Amen.**

Each one then goes to the celebrant and receives a cross.

## CONCLUDING RITE

471　After the invitation, "Bow your heads and pray for God's blessing," or something similar is said, the celebrant faces the missionaries and, with hands outstretched, concludes the rite by saying:

**May God, who in Christ has shown us his truth and love, make you messengers of the Gospel and witnesses to the divine love before all the world.**

R̝. **Amen.**

**May the Lord Jesus Christ, who promised that he would be with his Church until the end of time, guide your steps and fill your words with power.**

R̝. **Amen.**

**May the Spirit of the Lord be upon you, enabling you as you go through the world to bring the Good News to the lowly and to heal the brokenhearted.**

R̝. **Amen.**

Then he blesses all present.

**And may almighty God bless you all,**
**the Father, and the Son, ✠ and the Holy Spirit.**

R̝. **Amen.**

472　It is preferable to end the celebration with a suitable song.

# II. ORDER OF BLESSING WITHIN MASS

**473**    When the celebration of the blessing is joined with the celebration of Mass, the following norms are to be observed in the choice of texts:

**a.** on solemnities and on the Sundays of Advent, Lent, and the Easter season the Mass is the Mass of the day;

**b.** on the Sundays of the Christmas season and in Ordinary Time, on feasts, and on memorials the Mass may be either the Mass of the day or the Mass, "For the Spread of the Gospel."

**474**    When the bishop is the celebrant, everything should be adapted accordingly.

**475**    The liturgy of the word is carried out in the usual manner, with the following exceptions:

**a.** if the rubrics permit, instead of the readings assigned for the day those given in the Lectionary for Mass from Masses for Various Needs and Occasions, "For the Spread of the Gospel," may be used;[16]

**b.** before the proclamation of the gospel reading, it is most fitting that the missionaries be introduced to the congregation in the way described in no. 476.

**476**    The assisting deacon announces to the faithful the names of those departing for the missions and, as circumstances suggest, he may indicate the rank or office the missionaries hold within the people of God, as well as the Churches to which they are being sent. Thus, for example:

Deacon:

**These are the names of those who, in keeping with the Lord's command, are being sent by our Church of N. to preach the Gospel, accompanied by our prayers:**

**N.N., priest, to the Church in N.**
**N.N., deacon, to the Church in N.**
**N.N., religious of (N.), to the Church in N.**
**N.N., layman/laywoman, to the Church in N.**

---

[16] See Lectionary for Mass (2nd ed., 1981), nos. 872–876 (Masses for Various Needs and Occasions, I. For the Church, 11. For the Spread of the Gospel).

**477**　But when the group of departing missionaries includes men religious or women religious, the superior of the order or congregation to which they belong, rather than the assisting deacon, announces their names, charges, and destinations. Thus, for example:

Superior:

**From our institute, inspired by charity and strengthened by obedience, these members are going forth to proclaim the Gospel:**

**Brother N., (*for example*, teacher,) to N.**
**Sister N., (*for example*, catechist,) to N.**

**478**　When their name is called, the missionaries respond either by word, for example, by saying, "Present," or by a gesture, for example, by standing.

**479**　A deacon or a priest from among the departing missionaries proclaims the gospel reading.

During the singing of the verse before the gospel, the celebrant puts incense into the censer, then, omitting the usual blessing of the deacon, in a clear voice addresses the following or other suitable words to the deacon and to all the missionaries.

**By your words and your lives proclaim to all peoples the Gospel that is proclaimed in this house of God, so that the mystery of Christ and the Church may be revealed to all.**

The deacon and the departing missionaries reply:

**Amen.**

**480**　After the gospel reading, the celebrant in the homily explains both the biblical readings and the meaning of the rite.

## Prayer of Blessing

**481**　After the homily, all stand. The departing missionaries take places near the celebrant, but in such a way as not to obstruct the people's view of the rite. With hands outstretched over the missionaries as a group, the celebrant says the prayer of blessing.

We bless you, O God, and we praise your name.
In your merciful providence you sent your Son into the world
to free us from the bondage of sin by his own blood
and to enrich us with the gifts of the Holy Spirit.

Before he returned, triumphant over death, to you, Father,
he sent his apostles, the bearers of his love and power,
to proclaim the Gospel of life to all peoples
and in the waters of baptism to cleanse those who believe.

Lord, look kindly on your servants:
we send them forth as messengers of salvation and peace,
marked with the sign of the cross.

Guide their steps with your mighty arm
and with the power of your grace strengthen them in spirit,
so that they will not falter through weariness.

Make their words the echo of Christ's voice,
so that those who hear them
may be drawn to obey the Gospel.

Fill the hearts of your missionaries with the Holy Spirit,
so that, becoming all things to all people,
they may lead many to you, the Father of all,
to sing your praises in your holy Church.

We ask this through Christ our Lord.

R̷. Amen.


## PRESENTATION OF CROSSES TO THE MISSIONARIES

482    The celebrant blesses the crosses:

Father of holiness,
you willed the cross of your Son
to be the source of all blessings,
the fount of all grace.
Bless these crosses
and grant that those who will preach the crucified Christ
   to others
may themselves strive to be transformed into his image.

We ask this in the name of Jesus the Lord.

R̷. Amen.

**483**    Then one by one the missionaries go to the celebrant, who gives each one a cross, as he says:

**Receive this sign of Christ's love and of our faith.**
**Preach Christ crucified,**
**who is the power and wisdom of God.**

The missionary replies:

**Amen.**

Then the missionary takes the crucifix, kisses it, and returns to his or her place.

**484**    As circumstances suggest, the celebrant may pronounce the formulary of presentation just once, saying:

**Receive this sign of Christ's love and of our faith.**
**Preach Christ crucified,**
**who is the power and wisdom of God.**

Or:

**Receive this sign of Christ's love**
**and of the mission for which the Church has chosen you.**

The missionaries all reply together:

**Amen.**

Each one then goes to the celebrant and receives a cross.

**485**    The presentation is accompanied by the singing of either the following antiphon with Psalm 96 or some other suitable song.

Ant.    **Day after day, proclaim the salvation of the Lord.**

**486**    The general intercessions follow, with intentions included both for the departing missionaries and for the Churches to which they are being sent.

**487**    During the song for the presentation of the gifts, the bread and wine for the eucharistic celebration should be brought to the altar by some of the departing missionaries.

**488**    After the celebrant has said: "The peace of the Lord be with you always," the missionaries, as circumstances suggest, may go one by one to the altar to receive the sign of peace from the celebrant.

**489**   After the celebrant has received the Lord's body and blood, the missionaries go to the altar to receive communion under both kinds.

## CONCLUDING RITE

**490**   Except when the Mass has its own proper solemn blessing, the following formulary may be used. The celebrant says:

**The Lord be with you.**

All reply:

**And also with you.**

In the following or similar words, the assisting deacon may then invite the people to receive the blessing.

**Bow your heads and pray for God's blessing.**

Then, with hands outstretched over the missionaries, the celebrant says:

**May God, who in Christ has shown us his truth and love, make you messengers of the Gospel and witnesses to the divine love before all the world.**

R̲7̲. **Amen.**

**May the Lord Jesus Christ, who promised that he would be with his Church until the end of time, guide your steps and fill your words with power.**

R̲7̲. **Amen.**

**May the Spirit of the Lord be upon you, enabling you as you go through the world to bring the Good News to the lowly and to heal the brokenhearted.**

R̲7̲. **Amen.**

Then he blesses all present.

**And may almighty God bless you all,**
**the Father, and the Son, ✝ and the Holy Spirit.**

R̲7̲. **Amen.**

## CHAPTER 4

# ORDERS FOR BLESSINGS THAT PERTAIN TO CATECHESIS AND TO COMMUNAL PRAYER

## I. ORDER FOR THE BLESSING OF THOSE APPOINTED AS CATECHISTS

### INTRODUCTION

491    A suitable celebration of the word of God or a eucharistic celebration, as provided in this chapter, is the preferable occasion for celebrating the rite for the blessing of those who are appointed to serve the local Church as catechists.

492    The present order may be used by a priest or deacon. While maintaining the structure and chief elements of the rite, the celebrant should adapt the celebration to the circumstances of the place and the people involved.

# A. ORDER OF BLESSING WITHIN A CELEBRATION OF THE WORD OF GOD

## INTRODUCTORY RITES

493  When the community has gathered, a suitable song may be sung. After the singing, the celebrant says:

**In the name of the Father, and of the Son, and of the Holy Spirit.**

All make the sign of the cross and reply:

**Amen.**

494  The celebrant greets those present in the following or other suitable words, taken mainly from sacred Scripture.

**May God the Father of mercies, who wills that all be saved, be with you.**

All make the following or some other suitable reply.

**And also with you.**

495  In the following or similar words, the celebrant briefly addresses those present, in order to prepare them for the celebration and explain the rite.

**For the pastoral activity of the Church the cooperation of a great many people is needed, so that communities as well as individuals may advance to full maturity in faith and continually show forth their faith through the celebration of the liturgy, through study, and through their manner of life.**

**This cooperation is provided by those who devote themselves to catechesis. Enlightened by God's word and the teaching of the Church, catechists impart to others an initiation or a deeper formation in those realities that they themselves have learned as truths to be followed in living and to be celebrated in liturgy.**

**In this celebration we will bless the name of the Lord for giving us such co-workers and pray that through the Holy Spirit they will receive the grace they need in their service to the Church.**

# READING OF THE WORD OF GOD

496 A reader, another person present, or the celebrant reads either the following text of sacred Scripture or one taken preferably from the readings given in the Lectionary for Mass in Masses for Various Needs and Occasions, "For the Spread of the Gospel"[17] or "For the Ministers of the Church."[18]

**Brothers and sisters, listen to the words of the apostle Paul to the Romans:**                                                        10:9-15

*How beautiful are the feet of those who bring tidings of peace, joy, and salvation.*

**If you confess with your mouth that Jesus is Lord and believe in your heart that God raised him from the dead, you will be saved. For one believes with the heart and so is justified, and one confesses with the mouth and so is saved. For the scripture says, "No one who believes in him will be put to shame." For there is no distinction between Jew and Greek; the same Lord is Lord of all, enriching all who call upon him. For "everyone who calls on the name of the Lord will be saved."**

**But how can they call on him in whom they have not believed? And how can they believe in him of whom they have not heard? And how can they hear without someone to preach? And how can people preach unless they are sent? As it is written, "How beautiful are the feet of those who bring the good news!"**

497  As circumstances suggest, the following responsorial psalm may be sung or said, or some other suitable song.

℟. **Proclaim his marvelous deeds to all the nations.**

Psalm 96

**Sing to the LORD a new song;
sing to the LORD, all you lands.
Sing to the LORD, bless his name. ℟.**

**Announce his salvation, day after day.
Tell his glory among the nations;
among all peoples, his wondrous deeds. ℟.**

---

[17] See Lectionary for Mass (2nd ed., 1981), nos. 872–876 (Masses for Various Needs and Occasions, I. For the Church, 11. For the Spread of the Gospel).

[18] See ibid., nos. 848–851 (6. For the Ministers of the Church).

Give to the LORD, you families of nations,
give to the LORD glory and praise;
give to the LORD the glory due his name! R̸.

Say among the nations: The LORD is king.
He has made the world firm, not to be moved;
he governs the people with equity. R̸.

498    As circumstances suggest, the celebrant may give those
present a brief explanation of the biblical text, so that they may
understand through faith the meaning of the celebration.

## INTERCESSIONS

499    The intercessions are then said. The celebrant introduces
them and an assisting minister or one of those present announces
the intentions. From the following intentions those best suited
to the occasion may be used or adapted, or other intentions that
apply to the particular circumstances may be composed.

The celebrant says:

**Since God wills the salvation of all, let us pray to him in these
words:**

R̸. **Lord, draw all people to yourself.**

Or:

R̸. **Lord, hear our prayer.**

Assisting minister:

**Father, grant that all people will come to know you, the one
true God, and Jesus Christ, whom you have sent. (For this we
pray:)** R̸.

Assisting minister:

**Send workers into your harvest, so that your name will be glori-
fied among the nations. (For this we pray:)** R̸.

Assisting minister:

**You sent the disciples of Jesus to preach the Gospel; help us
to spread the victory of his cross. (For this we pray:)** R̸.

*Assisting minister:*

**Make us docile to the teaching of the apostles and our lives consistent with the truths we believe. (For this we pray:)** ℟.

*Assisting minister:*

**As you call us to serve you in our brothers and sisters, make us the ministers of your truth. (For this we pray:)** ℟.

*Assisting minister:*

**Keep us as faithful ministers of your Church, so that, having taught others, we ourselves may be found faithful in your service. (For this we pray:)** ℟.

*Assisting minister:*

**May the grace of the Holy Spirit guide our hearts and our lips, so that we may remain constant in loving and praising you. (For this we pray:)** ℟.

## PRAYER OF BLESSING

500    With hands outstretched, the celebrant says the prayer of blessing.

**With your fatherly blessing, Lord,
strengthen these servants of yours
in their resolve to dedicate themselves as catechists.
Grant that they will strive to share with others
what they themselves derive from pondering your word
and studying the Church's teaching.
And let them gladly join those they teach
in honoring and serving your name.**

**We ask this through Christ our Lord.**

℟. **Amen.**

501    Or:

**Lord God,
source of all wisdom and knowledge,
you sent your Son, Jesus Christ, to live among us
and to proclaim his message of faith, hope, and love to
   all nations.**

USA

In your goodness
bless our brothers and sisters
who have offered themselves as catechists for your Church.
Strengthen them with your gifts
that they may teach by word and example
the truth which comes from you.

We ask this through Christ our Lord.

All reply:

Amen.


# CONCLUDING RITE

502    Facing the catechists, the celebrant concludes the rite by saying:

In Christ God has revealed his love and his truth.
May he make you witnesses to the Gospel and to the divine love.

Ŗ. Amen.

The Lord Jesus promised to be with his Church until the end of the world.

May he give power to your actions and your words.

Ŗ. Amen.

May the Spirit of the Lord be with you,
so that you may help the ministers of his word.

Ŗ. Amen.

Then he blesses all present.

And may almighty God bless you all,
the Father, and the Son ✝ and the Holy Spirit.

Ŗ. Amen.

503    It is preferable to end the celebration with a suitable song.

# B. ORDER OF BLESSING WITHIN MASS

504    If the rubrics permit, the Mass, "For the Laity," provided in the Roman Missal in Masses and Prayers for Various Needs and Occasions, may be used, as circumstances suggest, with the readings that are provided in the Lectionary for Mass.[19]

505    The homily follows the gospel reading. In it the celebrant, basing himself on the sacred text, gives an explanation of the celebration pertinent to the particular place and the people involved.

## GENERAL INTERCESSIONS

506    The general intercessions follow, either in the form usual at Mass or in the form given here. The celebrant concludes the general intercessions with the prayer of blessing, unless it is thought better to have the prayer of blessing at the end of Mass as a prayer over the people. From the following intentions those best suited to the occasion may be used or adapted, or other intentions that apply to the particular circumstances may be composed.

The celebrant says:

**Since God wills the salvation of all, let us pray to him in these words:**

℞. **Lord, draw all people to yourself.**

Or:

℞. **Lord, hear our prayer.**

Assisting minister:

**Father, grant that all people will come to know you, the one true God, and Jesus Christ, whom you have sent. (For this we pray:)** ℞.

Assisting minister:

**Send workers into your harvest, so that your name will be glorified among the nations. (For this we pray:)** ℞.

---

[19] See Lectionary for Mass (2nd ed., 1981), nos. 862–866 (Masses for Various Needs and Occasions, I. For the Church, 9. For the Laity).

Assisting minister:

**You sent the disciples of Jesus to preach the Gospel; help us to spread the victory of his cross. (For this we pray:)** ℟.

Assisting minister:

**Make us docile to the teaching of the apostles and our lives consistent with the truths we believe. (For this we pray:)** ℟.

Assisting minister:

**As you call us to serve you in our brothers and sisters, make us the ministers of your truth. (For this we pray:)** ℟.

Assisting minister:

**Keep us as faithful ministers of your Church, so that, having taught others, we ourselves may be found faithful in your service. (For this we pray:)** ℟.

Assisting minister:

**May the grace of the Holy Spirit guide our hearts and our lips, so that we may remain constant in loving and praising you. (For this we pray:)** ℟.

## Prayer of Blessing

507    With hands outstretched, the celebrant says the prayer of blessing.

**With your fatherly blessing, Lord,**
**strengthen these servants of yours**
**in their resolve to dedicate themselves as catechists.**
**Grant that they will strive to share with others**
**what they themselves derive from pondering your word**
**and studying the Church's teaching.**
**And let them gladly join those they teach**
**in honoring and serving your name.**

**We ask this through Christ our Lord.**

℟. **Amen.**

Or:

**Lord God,**
**source of all wisdom and knowledge,**
**you sent your Son, Jesus Christ, to live among us**
**and to proclaim his message of faith, hope, and love to**
**    all nations.**
**In your goodness**
**bless our brothers and sisters**
**who have offered themselves as catechists for your Church.**
**Strengthen them with your gifts**
**that they may teach by word and example**
**the truth which comes from you.**

**We ask this through Christ our Lord.**

All reply:

**Amen.**

508    But as an alternative, if this seems more opportune, the prayer of blessing may be used at the end of Mass after the following or some other invitation.

**Bow your heads and pray for God's blessing.**

After the prayer of blessing, the celebrant always adds:

**And may almighty God bless you,**
**the Father, the Son,  ✝ and the Holy Spirit.**

R̸. **Amen.**

# II. ORDER OF BLESSING FOR A CATECHETICAL OR PRAYER MEETING

## INTRODUCTION

509    Whenever Christians or catechumens come together in the name of Christ, he himself, as he has said, is present in their midst. It is therefore entirely natural that those taking part in the meeting should wish to offer prayers in praise of Christ and in petition for the divine help needed to achieve the purpose for which they have gathered. This is particularly the case in meetings held for the purpose of catechesis or communal prayer, but it is also proper that other meetings be planned in such a way that a period of time is set aside so that the meeting begins with liturgical prayer.

This is the reason why the General Instruction of the Liturgy of the Hours (see no. 27) encourages lay groups that gather for any reason (prayer, apostolic work, etc.) to fulfill the Church's duty by celebrating part of the liturgy of the hours. ''The laity must learn above all how in the liturgy they are adoring God the Father in spirit and in truth (see John 4:23); they should bear in mind that through public worship and prayer they reach all humanity and can contribute significantly to the salvation of the whole world.''

But in some circumstances a celebration of the liturgy of the hours may not be possible. In this case the meeting should begin with an invocation of the Holy Spirit and of the divine blessing in the hymn *Veni, creator*, or the antiphon *Veni, Sancte Spiritus*, or some other suitable song; then there is a short, well-chosen reading from sacred Scripture, followed by an opening prayer from the Roman Missal: from the Proper of Seasons, ''Pentecost''; from Votive Masses: ''7. Holy Spirit''; from the Proper of Seasons, one of the Masses in the seventh week of the Easter season; or from Masses and Prayers for Various Needs and Occasions: ''16. For Pastoral or Spiritual Meetings.''

510    At the end of a meeting a blessing may be celebrated by use of the prayer of blessing provided in no. 516.

511    This prayer of blessing is not to be used when celebration of the eucharist immediately follows the meeting.

512    The present order may be used by a priest or deacon. It may also be used by a layperson, who follows the rites and prayers designated for a lay minister. While maintaining the structure and chief elements of the rite, the minister should adapt the celebration to the circumstances of the place and the people involved.

# ORDER OF BLESSING

513    In the following or similar words, the minister prepares those present for the blessing.

**Through this meeting Jesus himself has spoken to us. We should now, therefore, give thanks to him who has revealed to us the mysterious design that for ages was hidden in God. Since our task is to conform our lives to the word we have heard, before leaving let us raise our minds and hearts to God, praying that he may guide us through the Holy Spirit to a fuller possession of the truth and give us the power always to do what is pleasing to him.**

## INTERCESSIONS

514    As circumstances suggest, the prayer of blessing may be preceded by the intercessions. The minister introduces them and an assisting minister or one of those present announces the intentions. From the following intentions those best suited to the occasion may be used or adapted, or other intentions that apply to the particular circumstances may be composed. The intentions are followed immediately by the prayer of blessing, no. 516.

The minister says:

**The words of the Lord are spirit and life. Let us pray then to him, who has the words of eternal life, that we may be not only hearers of the word of God but doers, and workers with him in bearing witness to the truth.**

R℣. **Speak, Lord, for you have the words of eternal life.**

Or:

R℣. **Lord, hear our prayer.**

Assisting minister:

**Christ, Son of God, you came into the world to proclaim the Gospel of the Father's love; increase our faith, so that we will receive your word as the sign of his love. (For this we pray:)** R℣.

Assisting minister:

**Christ, Son of God, the Father's favor rested on you and he commanded us to listen to you; give us the gift of understanding, so that we may contemplate your word and experience its gentle power. (For this we pray:)** R̶⁊.

Assisting minister:

**Christ, Son of God, you said: "Blest are they who hear the word of God and keep it"; grant that with Mary we may keep your word in our hearts and dwell upon it. (For this we pray:)** R̶⁊.

Assisting minister:

**Christ, Son of God, your word lights up the darkness of our minds and gives understanding to the lowly; help us to listen to your word with simplicity and to treasure the mysteries of your kingdom. (For this we pray:)** R̶⁊.

Assisting minister:

**Christ, Son of God, you continually proclaim your word in the Church, so that the one faith may enlighten all who hear it and the one charity may bind them together; make us grow as lovers and doers of your word, so that as Christians we may all be of one mind and one heart. (For this we pray:)** R̶⁊.

Assisting minister:

**Christ, Son of God, your word is a lamp to our feet, showing us the way through life; become our companion on the road, making our hearts burn within, so that we may run in the way of your commands. (For this we pray:)** R̶⁊.

Assisting minister:

**Christ, Son of God, you gave us your word to hasten our salvation for your greater glory; fill our minds and hearts with that word to make us heralds and witnesses of the Gospel. (For this we pray:)** R̶⁊.

515 When there are no intercessions, the minister, before the prayer of blessing, invites those present to ask for God's help in these or similar words.

**My brothers and sisters, let us ask God, our all-powerful Father, to keep our steps always in the way of his commandments.**

As circumstances suggest, all may then pray for a moment in silence before the prayer of blessing.

## Prayer of Blessing

516 A minister who is a priest or deacon says the prayer of blessing with hands outstretched; a lay minister says the prayer with hands joined.

**We thank you and bless you, Lord our God.**
**In times past you spoke in many varied ways through the prophets,**
**but in this, the final age, you have spoken through your Son**
**to reveal to all nations the riches of your grace.**
**May we who have met to ponder the Scriptures**
**be filled with the knowledge of your will**
**in all wisdom and spiritual understanding,**
**and, pleasing you as we should in all things,**
**may we bear fruit in every good work.**

**We ask this through Christ our Lord.**

℟. **Amen.**

## Concluding Rite

517 The minister concludes the rite by saying:

**God, the Father of mercies, has sent his Son into the world.**
**Through the Holy Spirit, who will teach us all truth,**
**may he make us messengers of the Gospel**
**and witnesses of his love to the world.**

℟. **Amen.**

518 It is preferable to end the celebration with a suitable song.

# III. BLESSINGS OF CATECHUMENS[20]

USA

## INTRODUCTION

519    The blessings of the catechumens are a sign of God's love and of the Church's tender care. They are bestowed on the catechumens so that, even though they do not as yet have the grace of the sacraments, they may still receive from the Church courage, joy, and peace as they proceed along the difficult journey they have begun.[21]

520    The blessings may be given by a priest, a deacon, or a qualified catechist appointed by the bishop. The blessings are usually given at the end of a celebration of the word; they may also be given at the end of a meeting for catechesis. When there is some special need, the blessings may be given privately to individual catechumens.[22]

## PRAYERS OF BLESSING

521    The minister, with hands outstretched over the catechumens, says one of the following prayers. After the prayer of blessing, if this can be done conveniently, the catechumens come before the minister, who lays hands on them individually. Then the catechumens leave.[23]

**Let us pray.**

A    **Lord,
form these catechumens by the mysteries of the faith,
that they may be brought to rebirth in baptism
and be counted among the members of your Church.**

**We ask this through Christ our Lord.**

R̸. **Amen.**

B    **Father,
through your holy prophets**

---

[20] The blessings of catechumens are taken from the *Rite of Christian Initiation of Adults* (hereafter RCIA), Part I, Period of the Catechumenate.

[21] RCIA, no. 95.

[22] RCIA, no. 96.

[23] RCIA, no. 97.

you proclaimed to all who draw near you,
"Wash and be cleansed,"
and through Christ you have granted us rebirth in the Spirit.

Bless these your servants
as they earnestly prepare for baptism.

Fulfill your promise:
sanctify them in preparation for your gifts,
that they may come to be reborn as your children
and enter the community of your Church.

We ask this through Christ our Lord.

R̸. **Amen.**

C    God of power,
look upon these your servants
as they deepen their understanding of the Gospel.

Grant that they may come to know and love you
and always heed your will
with receptive minds and generous hearts.

Teach them through this time of preparation
and enfold them within your Church,
so that they may share your holy mysteries
both on earth and in heaven.

We ask this through Christ our Lord.

R̸. **Amen.**

D    God our Father,
you sent your only Son, Jesus Christ,
to free the world from falsehood.

Give to your catechumens fullness of understanding,
unwavering faith,
and a firm grasp of your truth.

Let them grow even stronger,
that they may receive in due time the new birth of baptism
that gives pardon of sins,
and join with us in praising your name.

We ask this through Christ our Lord.

R̸. **Amen.**

E      Almighty and eternal God,
you dwell on high yet look on the lowly;
to bring us your gift of salvation
you sent Jesus your Son,
our Lord and God.

Look kindly on these catechumens,
who bow before you in worship;
prepare them for their rebirth in baptism,
the forgiveness of their sins,
and the garment of incorruptible life.

Enfold them in your holy, catholic, and apostolic Church,
that they may join with us
in giving glory to your name.

We ask this through Christ our Lord.

℟. Amen.


F      Lord of all,
through your only begotten Son
you cast down Satan
and broke the chains that held us captive.

We thank you for these catechumens
whom you have called.

Strengthen them in faith,
that they may know you, the one true God,
and Jesus Christ, whom you have sent.

Keep them clean of heart and make them grow in virtue,
that they may be worthy to receive baptism
and enter into the holy mysteries.

We ask this through Christ our Lord.

℟. Amen.


G      Lord God,
you desire that all be saved
and come to the knowledge of truth.

Enliven with faith those who are preparing for baptism;
bring them into the fold of your Church,
there to receive the gift of eternal life.

We ask this through Christ our Lord.

R̶. Amen.


H God of power and Father of our Savior Jesus Christ,
look kindly upon these your servants.

Drive from their minds all taint of false worship
and stamp your law and commands on their hearts.

Lead them to full knowledge of the truth
and prepare them to be the temple of the Holy Spirit
through their rebirth in baptism.

Grant this through Christ our Lord.

R̶. Amen.


I Lord,
look with love on your servants,
who commit themselves to your name
and bow before you in worship.

Help them to accomplish what is good;
arouse their hearts,
that they may always remember your works and your
  commands
and eagerly embrace all that is yours.

Grant this through Christ our Lord.

R̶. Amen.

# CHAPTER 5

# ORDER FOR THE BLESSING OF STUDENTS AND TEACHERS

USA

## INTRODUCTION

522　It is appropriate that students and teachers alike acknowledge that all human wisdom and knowledge have God as their source. Accordingly, this order may be used for blessing both students and teachers at the beginning of the school year or on other occasions.

523　Although both students and teachers are usually blessed at the same time, the prayers should be adapted when either students or teachers alone are blessed.

524　The blessing may be given during Mass or at a celebration of the word of God. If this blessing is given during Mass on Sunday, the Mass of the day is celebrated.

525　The blessing may be given by a priest, deacon, or a lay minister.

# I. ORDER OF BLESSING WITHIN MASS

526     After the gospel reading, the celebrant in the homily, based on the sacred text and pertinent to the particular place and the people involved, explains the meaning of the celebration.

## GENERAL INTERCESSIONS

527     The general intercessions follow, either in the form usual at Mass or in the form provided here. The celebrant concludes the intercessions with the prayer of blessing. From the following intentions those best for the occasion may be used or adapted, or other intentions that apply to the particular circumstances may be composed.

The celebrant says:

**God is the source of all wisdom and knowledge.**
**Let us ask him to bless those who seek to learn and their teachers.**

R̷. **Lord, hear our prayer.**

Or:

R̷. **Fill us with your wisdom, Lord.**

Assisting minister:

**For students (as they begin this new school year), that the Spirit of God may grant them the gifts of wisdom and understanding, let us pray to the Lord.** R̷.

Assisting minister:

**For teachers, that they may share their knowledge with gentleness, patience, and concern for their students, let us pray to the Lord.** R̷.

Assisting minister:

**For those who seek knowledge of the things of this world, that they may always pursue God's wisdom, let us pray to the Lord.** R̷.

Assisting minister:

**For parents, the first teachers of their children, that their faith and love may be an example to us always, let us pray to the Lord.** R̶⁊.

## PRAYER OF BLESSING

528    With hands extended over the students and teachers, the celebrant says immediately:

**Lord our God,
in your wisdom and love
you surround us with the mysteries of the universe.
In times long past you sent us your prophets
to teach your laws
and to bear witness to your undying love.
You sent us your Son
to teach us by word and example
that true wisdom comes from you alone.**

**Send your Spirit upon these students and their teachers
and fill them with your wisdom and blessings.
Grant that during this academic year
they may devote themselves to their studies
and share what they have learned from others.**

**Grant this through Christ our Lord.**

**R̶⁊. Amen.**

529    Or:

**Lord God,
your Spirit of wisdom fills the earth
and teaches us your ways.**

**Look upon these students.
Let them enjoy their learning
and take delight in new discoveries.
Help them to persevere in their studies
and give them the desire to learn all things well.**

**Look upon these teachers.**
**Let them strive to share their knowledge**
    **with gentle patience**
**and endeavor always to bring the truth to eager minds.**

**Grant that students and teachers alike may follow**
    **Jesus Christ,**
**the way, the truth, and the life,**
**for ever and ever.**

R̓. **Amen.**

# II. ORDER OF BLESSING WITHIN A CELEBRATION OF THE WORD OF GOD

530    The present order may be used by a priest or a deacon, and also by a layperson, who follows the rites and prayers designated for a lay minister.

## INTRODUCTORY RITES

531    When the community has gathered, a suitable song may be sung. After the singing, the minister says:

**In the name of the Father, and of the Son, and of the Holy Spirit.**

All make the sign of the cross and reply:

**Amen.**

532    A minister who is a priest or deacon greets those present in the following or other suitable words, taken mainly from sacred Scripture.

**May the God of wisdom, knowledge, and grace be with you always.**

And all reply:

**And also with you.**

**533**   A lay minister greets those present in the following words:

**Let us praise the God of wisdom, knowledge, and grace. Blessed be God for ever.**

℟. **Blessed be God for ever.**

**534**   In the following or similar words, the minister prepares those present for the blessing.

**We gather here today to ask God's blessing on these students and their teachers (as they begin the new academic year). Studies are hard, yet the reward is great. They lead to a knowledge of the world and of God. May God enlighten our hearts and minds as we listen now to the word of God.**

## READING OF THE WORD OF GOD

**535**   A reader, another person present, or the minister reads a text of sacred Scripture.

**Brothers and sisters, listen to the words of the book of Sirach:**

6:32-37

*If you are willing to listen you will learn.*

**If you wish, you can be taught;**
**if you apply yourself, you will be shrewd.**
**If you are willing to listen, you will learn;**
**if you give heed, you will be wise.**
**Frequent the company of the elders;**
**whoever is wise, stay close to him.**
**Be eager to hear every godly discourse;**
**let no wise saying escape you.**
**If you see a man of prudence, seek him out;**
**let your feet wear away his doorstep!**
**Reflect on the precepts of the LORD,**
**let his commandments be your constant meditation;**
**Then he will enlighten your mind,**
**and the wisdom you desire he will grant.**

536    Or:

Wisdom 7:9-21—*Learn wisdom.*

Sirach 4:11-18—*The rewards of wisdom.*

1 Corinthians 15:1-11—*This is the gospel I preached to you.*

537    As circumstances suggest, the following responsorial psalm may be sung, or some other suitable song.

R̸. **Great are the works of the Lord.**

Psalm 111

**I will give thanks to the Lord with all my heart
in the company and assembly of the just.** R̸.

**Great are the works of the Lord,
exquisite in all their delights.
Majesty and glory are his work,
and his justice endures forever.** R̸.

**He has won renown for his wondrous deeds;
gracious and merciful is the Lord.
He has given food to those who fear him;
he will forever be mindful of his covenant.** R̸.

**He has made known to his people the power of his works,
giving them the inheritance of the nations.** R̸.

**The works of his hands are faithful and just;
sure are all his precepts,
Reliable forever and ever,
wrought in truth and equity.** R̸.

**He has sent deliverance to his people;
he has ratified his covenant forever;
holy and awesome is his name.** R̸.

**The fear of the Lord is the beginning of wisdom;
prudent are all who live by it.
His praise endures forever.** R̸.

538    As circumstances suggest, the minister may give those present a brief explanation of the biblical text, so that they may understand through faith the meaning of the celebration.

# INTERCESSIONS

539    The intercessions are then said. The minister introduces them and an assisting minister or one of those present announces the intentions. From the following those best suited to the occasion may be used or adapted, or other intentions that apply to the particular circumstances may be composed.

The minister says:

**God is the source of all wisdom and knowledge. Let us ask him to bless those who seek to learn and their teachers.**

R⁊. **Fill us with your wisdom, Lord.**

Assisting minister:

**For students (as they begin this new school year), that the Spirit of God may grant them the gifts of wisdom and understanding, let us pray to the Lord.** R⁊.

Assisting minister:

**For teachers, that they may share their knowledge with gentleness, patience, and concern for their students, let us pray to the Lord.** R⁊.

Assisting minister:

**For those who seek knowledge of the things of this world, that they may always pursue God's wisdom, let us pray to the Lord.** R⁊.

Assisting minister:

**For parents, the first teachers of their children, that their faith and love may be an example to us always, let us pray to the Lord.** R⁊.

540    After the intercessions the minister, in the following or similar words, invites all present to sing or say the Lord's Prayer.

**Taught by our Savior's command and formed by the word of God, we pray:**

All:

**Our Father . . .**

# PRAYER OF BLESSING

541 A minister who is a priest or deacon says the prayer of blessing with hands outstretched over the students and teachers; a lay minister says the prayer with hands joined.

Lord our God,
in your wisdom and love
you surround us with the mysteries of the universe.
In times long past you sent us your prophets
to teach your laws
and to bear witness to your undying love.
You sent us your Son
to teach us by word and example
that true wisdom comes from you alone.

Send your Spirit upon these students and their teachers
and fill them with your wisdom and blessings.
Grant that during this academic year
they may devote themselves to their studies
and share what they have learned from others.

Grant this through Christ our Lord.

R∕. Amen.

542   Or:

Lord God,
your Spirit of wisdom fills the earth
and teaches us your ways.

Look upon these students.
Let them enjoy their learning
and take delight in new discoveries.
Help them to persevere in their studies
and give them the desire to learn all things well.

Look upon these teachers.
Let them strive to share their knowledge
   with gentle patience
and endeavor always to bring the truth to eager minds.

**Grant that students and teachers alike may follow
  Jesus Christ,
the way, the truth, and the life,
for ever and ever.**

R̷. **Amen.**

## Concluding Rite

543    A minister who is a priest or deacon concludes the rite by saying:

**May God teach you his ways
and lead you to the joys of his kingdom,
now and for ever.**

R̷. **Amen.**

Then he blesses all present.

**And may almighty God bless you all,
the Father, and the Son, ✝ and the Holy Spirit.**

R̷. **Amen.**

544    A lay minister concludes the rite by signing himself or herself with the sign of the cross and saying:

**May God teach us his ways
and lead us to the joys of his kingdom,
now and for ever.**

R̷. **Amen.**

545    It is preferable to end the celebration with a suitable song.

# III. SHORTER RITE

**546**    All make the sign of the cross as the minister says:

**Blessed be the name of the Lord.**

All reply:

**Now and for ever.**

**547**    One of those present or the minister reads a text of sacred
Scripture, for example:

**Brothers and sisters, listen to the words of the book of Sirach:**

6:32-37

*If you are willing to listen you will learn.*

**If you wish, you can be taught;**
**if you apply yourself, you will be shrewd.**
**If you are willing to listen, you will learn;**
**if you give heed, you will be wise.**
**Frequent the company of the elders;**
**whoever is wise, stay close to him.**
**Be eager to hear every godly discourse;**
**let no wise saying escape you.**
**If you see a man of prudence, seek him out;**
**let your feet wear away his doorstep!**
**Reflect on the precepts of the LORD,**
**let his commandments be your constant meditation;**
**Then he will enlighten your mind,**
**and the wisdom you desire he will grant.**

**548**    Or:

Wisdom 7:9-21—*Learn wisdom.*

Sirach 4:11-18—*The rewards of wisdom.*

1 Corinthians 15:1-11—*This is the gospel I preached to you.*

**549**    A minister who is a priest or deacon says the prayer of
blessing with hands outstretched over the students and teachers;
a lay minister says the prayer with hands joined.

**Lord our God,**
**in your wisdom and love**
**you surround us with the mysteries of the universe.**

In times long past you sent us your prophets
to teach your laws
and to bear witness to your undying love.
You sent us your Son
to teach us by word and example
that true wisdom comes from you alone.

Send your Spirit upon these students and their teachers
and fill them with your wisdom and blessings.
Grant that during this academic year
they may devote themselves to their studies
and share what they have learned from others.

Grant this through Christ our Lord.

R̶/. **Amen.**

550   Or:

Lord God,
your Spirit of wisdom fills the earth
and teaches us your ways.

Look upon these students.
Let them enjoy their learning
and take delight in new discoveries.
Help them to persevere in their studies
and give them the desire to learn all things well.

Look upon these teachers.
Let them strive to share their knowledge
   with gentle patience;
and endeavor always to bring the truth to eager minds.

Grant that students and teachers alike may follow
   Jesus Christ,
the way, the truth, and the life,
for ever and ever.

R̶/. **Amen.**

# CHAPTER 6

# ORDERS FOR THE BLESSING OF THOSE GATHERED AT A MEETING

## I. PRAYERS FOR MEETINGS

### INTRODUCTION

551    The following prayers may be used to begin meetings.

552    The leader of prayer may choose other prayers or, if desired, pray in his or her own words.

A          (A prayer used before every session of the Second Vatican Council)

> **We stand before you, Holy Spirit,**
> **conscious of our sinfulness,**
> **but aware that we gather in your name.**
>
> **Come to us, remain with us,**
> **and enlighten our hearts.**
>
> **Give us light and strength**
> **to know your will,**
> **to make it our own,**
> **and to live it in our lives.**
>
> **Guide us by your wisdom,**
> **support us by your power,**
> **for you are God,**
> **sharing the glory of Father and Son.**
>
> **You desire justice for all:**
> **enable us to uphold the rights of others;**
> **do not allow us to be misled by ignorance**
> **or corrupted by fear or favor.**
>
> **Unite us to yourself in the bond of love**
> **and keep us faithful to all that is true.**

As we gather in your name
may we temper justice with love,
so that all our decisions
may be pleasing to you,
and earn the reward
promised to good and faithful servants.

You live and reign with the Father and the Son,
one God, for ever and ever.

℟. Amen.


B    Lord,
may everything we do
begin with your inspiration
and continue with your help,
so that all our prayers and works
may begin in you
and by you be happily ended.

We ask this through Christ our Lord.

℟. Amen.


C    ℣. Come, Holy Spirit, fill the hearts of your faithful.
℟. And kindle in them the fire of your love.

℣. Send forth your Spirit and they shall be created.
℟. And you will renew the face of the earth.

Let us pray.

After a brief pause for silent prayer, the leader continues:

Lord,
by the light of the Holy Spirit
you have taught the hearts of your faithful.
In the same Spirit
help us to relish what is right
and always rejoice in your consolation.

We ask this through Christ our Lord.

℟. Amen.

# II. ORDER FOR THE BLESSING OF ECUMENICAL GROUPS

## INTRODUCTION

553    At the Last Supper Christ prayed for the unity of his Church. The desire for greater Christian unity and prayer that the divisions among Christians may be healed should be a part of every ecumenical endeavor. This blessing is appropriate for use on the occasion of the first meeting of an ecumenical discussion group or an ecumenical group gathered for some other occasion.

554    If a minister of another Church is present, it is appropriate that he or she be invited to take a ministerial role in the service. The manner in which this is to be done should be agreed upon by the ministers involved.

555    The present order may be used by a priest, deacon, minister of another Church, and also by a layperson, who follows the rites and prayers designated for a lay minister.

## ORDER OF BLESSING

### INTRODUCTORY RITES

556    When the community has gathered, a suitable song may be sung. After the singing, the minister says:

**In the name of the Father, and of the Son, and of the Holy Spirit.**

All reply:

**Amen.**

557    A priest, deacon, or minister of another Church greets those present in the following or other suitable words, taken mainly from sacred Scripture.

**The grace of our Lord Jesus Christ, the love of God, and the fellowship of the Holy Spirit be with you all.**

And all reply:

**And also with you.**

558    A lay minister greets those present in the following words:

**The grace and peace of God our Father and Christ Jesus our Savior be with us for ever.**

**R7. Amen.**

559    In the following or similar words, the minister prepares those present for the blessing.

**Brothers and sisters in Christ, we come together in prayer and praise, as people who believe in the one Lord and Savior, Jesus Christ, and share in one baptism for the forgiveness of sins. We also acknowledge that our unity in faith needs to be nourished and deepened. Through our prayer, work and study together may unity among Christians become ever more perfect.**

## READING OF THE WORD OF GOD

560    A reader or another person present reads a text of sacred Scripture.

**Brothers and sisters, listen to the words of the apostle Paul to the Ephesians:**                                                             4:1-6

*There is one Lord, one faith, one baptism.*

**I, then, a prisoner for the Lord, urge you to live in a manner worthy of the call you have received, with all humility and gentleness, with patience, bearing with one another through love, striving to preserve the unity of the spirit through the bond of peace: one body and one Spirit, as you were also called to the one hope of your call; one Lord, one faith, one baptism; one God and Father of all, who is over all and through all and in all.**

561    Or:

Philippians 2:1-11—*Your attitude must be that of Christ.*

Ephesians 2:19-22—*You are strangers and aliens no longer.*

Colossians 3:12-17—*Do everything in the name of the Lord Jesus.*

Matthew 18:19-22—*Where two or three meet in my name, I shall be there with them.*

John 17:11-19—*May these people be one as we are one!*

John 17:20-26—*May these be completely one!*

562    As circumstances suggest, one of the following responsorial psalms may be sung, or some other suitable song.

R̸. **We are his people: the sheep of his flock.**

Psalm 100

**Sing joyfully to the LORD, all you lands;**
**serve the LORD with gladness;**
**come before him with joyful song.** R̸.

**Know that the LORD is God;**
**he made us, his we are;**
**his people, the flock he tends.** R̸.

**Enter his gates with thanksgiving,**
**his courts with praise;**
**Give thanks to him; bless his name.** R̸.

**For he is good:**
**the LORD, whose kindness endures forever,**
**and his faithfulness to all generations.** R̸.

Psalm 23:1-3, 3-4, 5, 6

R̸. **(v. 1) The Lord is my shepherd, there is nothing I shall want.**

563    As circumstances suggest, the minister may give those present a brief explanation of the biblical text, so that they may understand through faith the meaning of the celebration.

# INTERCESSIONS

564    The intercessions are then said. The minister introduces them and an assisting minister or one of those present announces the intentions. From the following those best suited to the occasion may be used or adapted, or other intentions that apply to the particular circumstances may be composed.

The minister says:

**United in Christ, let us pray for all our brothers and sisters in the Lord.**

**R̸. Lord, hear our prayer.**

Assisting minister:

**For the holy people of God: may the Lord guide and protect us, we pray to the Lord. R̸.**

Assisting minister:

**For the unity of the Church of God: may we grow in faith, hope, and love, we pray to the Lord. R̸.**

Assisting minister:

**For all the peoples of the world: may the Lord unite us in peace and harmony, we pray to the Lord. R̸.**

Assisting minister:

**For all those in need: may we be attentive to their call for help, we pray to the Lord. R̸.**

Assisting minister:

**For ourselves and for our communities: may our lives be an acceptable sacrifice to God, we pray to the Lord. R̸.**

565   After the intercessions the minister, in the following or similar words, invites all present to sing or say the Lord's Prayer.

**Let us pray with confidence to the Father in the words our Savior gave us:**

All:

**Our Father . . .**

## PRAYER OF BLESSING

566   A priest, deacon, or minister of another Church says the prayer of blessing with hands outstretched; a lay minister says the prayer with hands joined.

**Lord God,**
**whose blessings reach to the ends of the earth,**
**you show us your love in the life, death, and**
**resurrection of Jesus,**
**whom we call Savior and Lord.**

**Confirm us in our common faith**
**that we may walk together with you and one another.**
**Send your blessing upon your Church**
**that what we have begun in the Spirit**
**may be brought to completion by your power.**

**To you be glory and honor,**
**now and for ever.**

R℣. **Amen.**

## CONCLUDING RITE

567. A priest, deacon, or minister of another Church concludes the rite by saying:

**May the gifts of God unite us in faith, hope, and love,**
**now and for ever.**

R℣. **Amen.**

Then the priest, deacon, or minister of another Church blesses all present.

**And may almighty God bless you all,**
**the Father, and the Son, ✝ and the Holy Spirit.**

R℣. **Amen.**

---

568    A lay minister concludes the rite by saying:

**May the gifts of God, Father, Son and Holy Spirit, unite us**
**in faith, hope, and love, now and for ever.**

R℣. **Amen.**

---

569    It is preferable to end the celebration with a suitable song.

# III. PRAYERS FOR INTERFAITH GATHERINGS

## INTRODUCTION

570    These prayers may be used to begin and conclude gatherings of Christians and those of other religious traditions.

571    Other prayers may also be used. However, care should be taken to see that prayers which are used do not offend the religious sensibilities of those who are present.

### 572    Prayers of invocation

A    **Blessed are you, Lord, God of all creation,**
**whose goodness fills our hearts with joy.**
**Blessed are you,**
**who have brought us together this day**
**to work in harmony and peace.**
**Strengthen us with your grace and wisdom**
**for you are God for ever and ever.**

R̸. **Amen.**

B    **In you, Lord our God,**
**all things have their beginning, continuation,**
    **and end.**
**Grace us with your saving presence,**
**aid us with your constant help**
**and let us glorify you,**
**now and for ever.**

R̸. **Amen.**

C    **Lord,**
**may everything we do**
**begin with your inspiration**
**and continue with your help,**
**so that all our prayers and works**
**may begin in you**
**and by you be happily ended.**
**Glory and praise to you,**
**for ever and ever.**

R̸. **Amen.**

A   **May the God of every grace and blessing**
    **grant you joy and peace.**
    **May you rejoice in God's protection,**
    **now and for ever.**

    ℟. **Amen.**

B   **May God strengthen you and bring your work to completion.**
    **May hope accompany your journey through the days to come.**
    **May God's abiding presence be with you**
    **all the days of your life.**

    ℟. **Amen.**

C   **May the Lord bless you and keep you.**
    **May his face shine upon you and be gracious to you.**
    **May he look upon you with kindness and give you his peace.**

    ℟. **Amen.**

CHAPTER 7

# ORDER FOR THE BLESSING OF ORGANIZATIONS CONCERNED WITH PUBLIC NEED

## INTRODUCTION

574    Faithful to the Gospel, the Church actively encourages and supports every good endeavor of the human community.

All the people of God have the duty of devoting their efforts to relieving the sufferings of others in cases of public need or danger. But particular recognition and support are due to those associations that by their concentration of resources are able more effectively to serve public need and that also enlist others to assist in providing proper help in emergencies.

575    The name "Organizations Concerned with Public Need" refers here to such groups as ambulance companies, fire departments, those concerned with flood control, etc. The term includes those that come under the jurisdiction of a civil government.

576    The present order may be used by a priest or deacon. While maintaining the structure and chief elements of the rite, the celebrant should adapt the celebration to the circumstances of the place and the people involved.

# ORDER OF BLESSING

## INTRODUCTORY RITES

577   When the community has gathered, a suitable song may be sung. After the singing, the celebrant says:

**In the name of the Father, and of the Son, and of the Holy Spirit.**

All make the sign of the cross and reply:

**Amen.**

578   The celebrant greets those present in the following or other suitable words, taken mainly from sacred Scripture.

**May the Lord, who went about doing good, be with you.**

All make the following or some other suitable reply.

**And also with you.**

579   In the following or similar words, the celebrant prepares those present for the blessing.

**God is love. In the desire to make us share in this love, he sent his Son into the world to come to our aid and in gentle kindness to help those who were weak, sick, or unfortunate. In his great love for all of us, Christ said that whatever we do for the least among us we do for him. He called those who show mercy "blessed of his Father" and promised them eternal life.**

**Let us then pray for the Lord's richest blessings on the members of this organization, who are devoted to helping their brothers and sisters.**

## READING OF THE WORD OF GOD

580   A reader, another person present, or the celebrant reads a text of sacred Scripture. The reading chosen should be one that best applies to the aims of the organization.

**Brothers and sisters, listen to the words of the holy gospel according to Matthew:**                                          25:31-46

*As often as you did it for the least among you, you did it for me.*

Jesus said to his disciples: "When the Son of Man comes in his glory, and all the angels with him, he will sit upon his glorious throne, and all the nations will be assembled before him. And he will separate them one from another, as a shepherd separates the sheep from the goats. He will place the sheep on his right and the goats on his left. Then the king will say to those on his right, 'Come, you who are blessed by my Father. Inherit the kingdom prepared for you from the foundation of the world. For I was hungry and you gave me food, I was thirsty and you gave me drink, a stranger and you welcomed me, naked and you clothed me, ill and you cared for me, in prison and you visited me.' Then the righteous will answer him and say, 'Lord, when did we see you hungry and feed you, or thirsty and give you drink? When did we see you a stranger and welcome you, or naked and clothe you? When did we see you ill or in prison, and visit you?' And the king will say to them in reply, 'Amen, I say to you, whatever you did for one of these least brothers of mine, you did for me.' Then he will say to those on his left, 'Depart from me, you accursed, into the eternal fire prepared for the devil and his angels. For I was hungry and you gave me no food, I was thirsty and you gave me no drink, a stranger and you gave me no welcome, naked and you gave me no clothing, ill and in prison, and you did not care for me.' Then they will answer and say, 'Lord, when did we see you hungry or thirsty or a stranger or naked or ill or in prison, and not minister to your needs?' He will answer them, 'Amen, I say to you, what you did not do for one of these least ones, you did not do for me.' And these will go off to eternal punishment, but the righteous to eternal life."

581  Or:

**Brothers and sisters, listen to the words of the prophet Isaiah:**
58:1ab, 5-11

*Share your bread with the hungry.*

**Cry out full-throated and unsparingly,**
**lift up your voice like a trumpet blast;**
**Is this the manner of fasting I wish,**

of keeping a day of penance:
That a man bow his head like a reed,
and lie in sackcloth and ashes?
Do you call this a fast,
a day acceptable to the LORD?
This, rather, is the fasting I wish,
releasing those bound unjustly,
untying the thongs of the yoke;
Setting free the oppressed,
breaking every yoke;
Sharing your bread with the hungry,
sheltering the oppressed and the homeless;
Clothing the naked when you see them,
and not turning your back on your own.
Then your light shall break forth like the dawn,
and your wound shall quickly be healed;
Your vindication shall go before you,
and the glory of the LORD shall be your rear guard.
Then you shall call, and the LORD will answer,
you shall cry for help, and he will say: Here I am!
If you remove from your midst oppression,
false accusation and malicious speech;
If you bestow your bread on the hungry
and satisfy the afflicted;
Then light shall rise for you in the darkness,
and the gloom shall become for you like midday;
Then the LORD will guide you always
and give you plenty even on the parched land.

582　Or:

Tobit 12:6-13—*Do good, and evil will not find its way to you.*

Sirach 3:33—4:11—*Do not grieve the one who is hungry.*

Sirach 7:36-39 (Greek, 7:32-35)—*Avoid not those who weep.*

Mark 2:1-12—*Four people arrived carrying a paralyzed man to him.*

Luke 10:25-37—*Who is my neighbor?*

John 13:12-17—*You must wash each other's feet.*

583　As circumstances suggest, one of the following responsorial psalms may be sung or said, or some other suitable song.

℟. **Taste and see the goodness of the Lord.**

Psalm 34

**I will bless the LORD at all times;**
**his praise shall be ever in my mouth.**
**Let my soul glory in the LORD:**
**the lowly will hear me and be glad.** R̰.

**Glorify the LORD with me,**
**let us together extol his name.**
**I sought the LORD and he answered me**
**and delivered me from all my fears.** R̰.

**Look to him that you may be radiant with joy,**
**and your faces may not blush with shame.**
**When the afflicted man called out, the LORD heard,**
**and from all his distress he saved him.** R̰.

**Fear the LORD, you his holy ones,**
**for nought is lacking to those who fear him.**
**The great grow poor and hungry;**
**but those who seek the LORD want for no good thing.** R̰.

**Come, children, hear me;**
**I will teach you the fear of the LORD.**
**Which of you desires life,**
**and takes delight in prosperous days?** R̰.

Psalm 103:1-2, 3-4, 11-12, 13-14, 17-18

R̰. **(v. 8) The Lord is kind and merciful, slow to anger and rich**
**in compassion.**

584    As circumstances suggest, the celebrant may give those
present a brief explanation of the biblical text, so that they may
understand through faith the meaning of the celebration.

## INTERCESSIONS

585    As circumstances suggest, the prayer of blessing may be
preceded by the intercessions. The celebrant introduces them and
an assisting minister or one of those present announces the intentions. From the following intentions those best suited to the
occasion may be used or adapted, or other intentions that apply
to the particular circumstances may be composed. The intentions
are followed immediately by the prayer of blessing, no. 587.

The celebrant says:

**Christ the Lord bore our infirmities and endured our sufferings. He went about doing good, leaving us an example to follow. Having Christ's charity as the foundation of all we do, let us pray to him, saying:**

℟. **Lord, teach us to serve our sisters and brothers.**

Or:

℟. **Lord, hear our prayer.**

Assisting minister:

**Lord, for our sake you were poor and came not to be served but to serve; grant that we too may love our brothers and sisters and help them in their need. (For this we pray:)** ℟.

Assisting minister:

**By your redeeming work you made a new world where we have become neighbors to each other and are enabled to love one another; grant that we too may strive toward a way of life in keeping with the Gospel. (For this we pray:)** ℟.

Assisting minister:

**You want all people to share in the blessings you have brought; stir the hearts of many among your people, so that, moved by your love, they may gladly devote themselves to assisting those in need and in misfortune. (For this we pray:)** ℟.

Assisting minister:

**You willed that your Mother should also be our Mother; grant that, whenever we turn to her for protection, we will find in her a helper sent to us from heaven. (For this we pray:)** ℟.

586　When there are no intercessions, the celebrant, before the prayer of blessing and using the following or other similar words, invites those present to ask for God's help.

**My brothers and sisters, let us pray that God who is love will enkindle our hearts with the fire of the Holy Spirit, to give us an ardent love for others, like Christ's love for us.**

As circumstances suggest, all may then pray for a moment in silence before the prayer of blessing.

## PRAYER OF BLESSING

587   With hands outstretched, the celebrant continues with the prayer of blessing.

**Blessed are you, Lord, God of mercy,
who through your Son gave us a marvelous example of charity
and the great commandment of love for one another.
Send down your blessings on these your servants,
who so generously devote themselves to helping others.
When they are called on in times of need,
let them faithfully serve you in their neighbor.**

**We ask this through Christ our Lord.**

**R⁊. Amen.**

## CONCLUDING RITE

588   The prayer of blessing may be followed by one of the following antiphons or some other suitable song.

**R⁊. If there is love among you,
all will know that you are my disciples.**

**Jesus said to his disciples. R⁊.**

589   Or:

Ant. **Where charity and love are found, there is God.**

**The love of Christ has gathered us together into one.
Let us rejoice and be glad in him.
Let us fear and love the living God,
and love each other from the depths of our heart.** Ant.

**Therefore when we are together,
let us take heed not to be divided in mind.
Let there be an end to bitterness and quarrels, an
  end to strife,
and in our midst be Christ our God.** Ant.

**And in company with the blessed, may we see
your face in glory, Christ our God,
pure and unbounded joy
for ever and for ever.** Ant.

# CHAPTER 8

# ORDERS FOR THE BLESSING OF PILGRIMS

## INTRODUCTION

590    Whether in a traditional or a modern form, a pilgrimage to a holy place, to the tomb of a saint, or to a shrine should be regarded as having pastoral value. Pilgrimages are occasions for conversion, spiritual growth, and the advance of the apostolate.

591    The proper, that is, spiritual, character of the Christian pilgrimage must be carefully explained and inculcated ahead of time, so that the pilgrims will truly be "traveling heralds of Christ"[24] and will experience fully the good effects of their pilgrimage.

592    For such pastoral purposes it will often be useful to arrange a special celebration for the blessing of the pilgrims at their departure or on their return.

593    When, instead, the celebration of Mass, the liturgy of the hours, or some other liturgical service is preferred as the beginning or end of a pilgrimage, the celebration may be concluded with a blessing of the pilgrims taken from the orders in this chapter.

594    The present order may be used by a priest or deacon. While maintaining the structure and chief elements of the rite, the celebrant should adapt the celebration to the circumstances of the place and the people involved.

---

[24] Vatican Council II, Decree on the Apostolate of the Laity *Apostolicam actuositatem*, no. 14.

# I. ORDER FOR THE BLESSING OF PILGRIMS ON THEIR DEPARTURE

## INTRODUCTORY RITES

595   When the group of pilgrims has gathered, Psalm 122 or some other suitable song may be sung. After the singing, the celebrant says:

**In the name of the Father, and of the Son, and of the Holy Spirit.**

All make the sign of the cross and reply:

**Amen.**

596   The celebrant greets those present in the following or other suitable words, taken mainly from sacred Scripture.

**May God, our strength and salvation, be with you all.**

All make the following or some other suitable reply.

**And also with you.**

597   In the following or similar words, the celebrant prepares those present for the blessing.

**Brothers and sisters, as we set out, we should remind ourselves of the reasons for our resolve to go on this holy pilgrimage. The place we intend to visit is a monument to the devotion of the people of God. They have gone there in great numbers to be strengthened in the Christian way of life and to become more determined to devote themselves to the works of charity. We must also try to bring something to the faithful who live there: our example of faith, hope, and love. In this way both they and we will be enriched by the help we give each other.**

## READING OF THE WORD OF GOD

598   A reader, another person present, or the celebrant reads a text of sacred Scripture.

**Brothers and sisters, listen to the words of the second letter of Paul to the Corinthians:** 5:6-10

*We are away from the Lord.*

**So we are always courageous, although we know that while we are at home in the body we are away from the Lord, for we walk by faith, not by sight. Yet we are courageous, and we would rather leave the body and go home to the Lord. Therefore, we aspire to please him, whether we are at home or away. For we must all appear before the judgment seat of Christ, so that each one may receive recompense, according to what he did in the body, whether good or evil.**

**599** Or:

Isaiah 2:2-5—*Let us walk in the light of the Lord.*

Luke 2:41-51—*They went up to Jerusalem for the celebration as was their custom.*

Luke 24:13-35—*Jesus approached and began to walk along with them.*

Hebrews 10:19-25—*Let us draw near in utter sincerity and absolute confidence.*

1 Peter 2:4-12—*As strangers and in exile.*

**600** As circumstances suggest, one of the following responsorial psalms may be sung or said, or some other suitable song.

℟. **Lord, this is the people that longs to see your face.**

Psalm 24

**The LORD's are the earth and its fullness;
the world and those who dwell in it.
For he founded it upon the seas
and established it upon the rivers.** ℟.

**Who can ascend the mountain of the LORD
or who may stand in his holy place?
He whose hands are sinless, whose heart is clean,
who desires not what is vain.** ℟.

**He shall receive a blessing from the LORD,
a reward from God his savior.
Such is the race that seeks for him,
that seeks the face of the God of Jacob.** ℟.

Psalm 27:1, 4, 13-14

℟. (see v. 4) **One thing I seek: to dwell in the house of the Lord.**

601    As circumstances suggest, the celebrant may give those present a brief explanation of the biblical text, so that they may understand through faith the meaning of the celebration.

## INTERCESSIONS

602    The intercessions are then said. The celebrant introduces them and an assisting minister or one of those present announces the intentions. From the following intentions those best suited to the occasion may be used or adapted, or other intentions that apply to the particular circumstances may be composed.

The celebrant says:

**God is the beginning and the end of life's pilgrimage. Let us call on him with confidence, saying:**

℟. **Lord, be the companion of our journey.**

Or:

℟. **Lord, hear our prayer.**

Assisting minister:

**Father all-holy, of old you made yourself the guide and the way for your people as they wandered in the desert; be our protection as we begin this journey, so that we may return home again in safety. (For this we pray:)** ℟.

Assisting minister:

**You have given us your only Son to be our way to you; make us follow him faithfully and unswervingly. (For this we pray:)** ℟.

Assisting minister:

**You gave us Mary as the image and model for following Christ; grant that through her example we may live a new life. (For this we pray:)** ℟.

**You guide your pilgrim Church on earth through the Holy Spirit; may we seek you in all things and walk always in the way of your commandments. (For this we pray:) R℣.**

Assisting minister:

**You lead us along right and peaceful paths; grant that we may one day see you face to face in heaven. (For this we pray:) R℣.**

## PRAYER OF BLESSING

603    With hands outstretched, the celebrant continues with the prayer of blessing.

**All-powerful God,**
**you always show mercy toward those who love you**
**and you are never far away for those who seek you.**
**Remain with your servants on this holy pilgrimage**
**and guide their way in accord with your will.**
**Shelter them with your protection by day,**
**give them the light of your grace by night,**
**and, as their companion on the journey,**
**bring them to their destination in safety.**

**We ask this through Christ our Lord.**

**R℣. Amen.**

## CONCLUDING RITE

604    The celebrant concludes the rite by saying:

**May the Lord guide us and direct our journey in safety.**

**R℣. Amen.**

**May the Lord be our companion along the way.**

**R℣. Amen.**

**May the Lord grant that the journey**
**we begin, relying on him,**
**will end happily through his protection.**

**R℣. Amen.**

605    It is preferable to end the celebration with a suitable song.

# II. ORDER FOR THE BLESSING OF PILGRIMS BEFORE OR AFTER THEIR RETURN

## INTRODUCTORY RITES

606   When the group of pilgrims has gathered, a suitable song may be sung, for example, *Urbs Jerusalem beata*, or some other song related to the place and circumstances of the pilgrimage. After the singing, the celebrant says:

**In the name of the Father, and of the Son, and of the Holy Spirit.**

All make the sign of the cross and reply:

**Amen.**

607   The celebrant greets those present in the following or other suitable words, taken mainly from sacred Scripture.

**May God, our hope and our strength, fill you with peace and with joy in the Holy Spirit. Glory to God now and for ever.**

All make one of the following or some other suitable reply.

**Amen.**

Or:

**Glory to God now and for ever.**

608   In the following or similar words, the celebrant prepares those present for the blessing.

**Our pilgrimage has been a privileged period of grace given us by God. We who have come in trust to this holy place are moved with a new resolve to be renewed in heart.**

**The sanctuaries that we have visited are a sign of that house not built with hands, namely, the Body of Christ, in which we are the living stones built upon Christ, the cornerstone. As we return home, let us live up to the vocation God has given us: to be a chosen race, a royal priesthood, a holy nation, a people God claims for his own, so that we may everywhere proclaim the goodness of him who called us from darkness into his marvelous light.**

609    A reader, another person present, or the celebrant reads
a text of sacred Scripture.

## Brothers and sisters, listen to the words of the first book of Chronicles:

29:9-18

*We stand before you as aliens, we are only your guests.*

**The people rejoiced over these free-will offerings, which had been contributed to the LORD wholeheartedly. King David also rejoiced greatly.**

**Then David blessed the LORD in the presence of the whole assembly, praying in these words:**

**"Blessed may you be, O LORD,
God of Israel our father,
from eternity to eternity.**

**"Yours, O LORD, are grandeur and power,
majesty, splendor, and glory.
For all in heaven and on earth is yours;
yours, O LORD, is the sovereignty;
you are exalted as head over all.**

**"Riches and honor are from you,
and you have dominion over all.
In your right hand are power and might;
it is yours to give grandeur and strength to all.**

**"Therefore, our God, we give you thanks
and we praise the majesty of your name.**

**"But who am I, and who are my people, that we should have the means to contribute so freely? For everything is from you, and we only give you what we have received from you. For we stand before you as aliens: we are only your guests, like all our fathers. Our life on earth is like a shadow that does not abide. O LORD our God, all this wealth that we have brought together to build you a house in honor of your holy name comes from you and is entirely yours. I know, O my God, that you put hearts to the test and that you take pleasure in uprightness. With a sincere heart I have willingly given all these things, and now with joy I have seen your people here**

present also giving to you generously. O LORD, God of our fathers Abraham, Isaac, and Israel, keep such thoughts in the hearts and minds of your people forever, and direct their hearts toward you.''

610    Or:

Luke 24:28-35—*They recounted what had happened on the road.*

John 5:1-15—*Pick up your mat and walk.*

John 9:1-38—*I left, and washed, and returned able to see.*

Acts 8:26-35—*He had come on a pilgrimage to Jerusalem and was returning home.*

Hebrews 13:12-21—*Here we have no lasting city; we are seeking one which is to come.*

611    As circumstances suggest, one of the following responsorial psalms may be sung or said, or some other suitable song.

R℟. **How lovely is your dwelling place, Lord mighty God!**

Psalm 84

**My soul yearns and pines
for the courts of the LORD.
My heart and my flesh
cry out for the living God.** R℟.

**Even the sparrow finds a home,
and the swallow a nest
in which she puts her young—
Your altars, O LORD of hosts,
my king and my God!** R℟.

**Happy they who dwell in your house!
continually they praise you.
Happy the men whose strength you are!
their hearts are set upon the pilgrimage.** R℟.

**When they pass through the valley of the mastic trees,
they make a spring of it;
the early rain clothes it with generous growth.
They go from strength to strength;
they shall see the God of gods in Zion.** R℟.

Psalm 122:1-2, 4-5, 6-7, 8-9

R⁊. (see v. 1) **Let us go rejoicing to the house of the Lord.**

612    As circumstances suggest, the celebrant may give those present a brief explanation of the biblical text, so that they may understand through faith the meaning of the celebration.

## INTERCESSIONS

613    The intercessions are then said. The celebrant introduces them and an assisting minister or one of those present announces the intentions. From the following intentions those best suited to the occasion may be used or adapted, or other intentions that apply to the particular circumstances may be composed.

The celebrant says:

**The Lord of heaven willed that in Christ's humanity the fullness of divinity should dwell as in its temple. Let us pray to him, saying:**

R⊱. **Look down from heaven, O Lord, and bless your people.**

Or:

R⊱. **Lord, hear our prayer.**

Assisting minister:

**Father all-holy, in the Passover exodus you prefigured the blessed road of your people toward salvation; grant that in all the paths we follow we may remain wholeheartedly faithful to you. (For this we pray:)** R⊱.

Assisting minister:

**You set your Church in this world as a sanctuary from which the true light would shine for all to see; grant that many people will enter this sanctuary and walk in your ways. (For this we pray:)** R⊱.

Assisting minister:

**You have told us that here we have no lasting city; grant that we may always seek the city that is to come. (For this we pray:)** R⊱.

Assisting minister:

**You teach all the faithful to perceive the signs of your presence along all the pathways of life; grant that like the disciples**

of Emmaus we may come to recognize Christ as the companion of our journey and know him in the breaking of the bread. (For this we pray:) ℟.

## PRAYER OF BLESSING

614    With hands outstretched, the celebrant continues with the prayer of blessing.

**Blessed are you, O God,**
**Father of our Lord Jesus Christ.**
**From all races of the earth**
**you have chosen a people dedicated to you,**
**eager to do what is right.**
**Your grace has moved the hearts of these, your friends,**
**to love you more deeply and to serve you more generously.**
**We ask you to bless them,**
**so that they may tell of your wonderful deeds**
**and give proof of them in their lives.**

**We ask this through Christ our Lord.**

℟. **Amen.**

## CONCLUDING RITE

615    The celebrant concludes the rite by saying:

**May God, the Lord of heaven and earth,**
**who so graciously has accompanied you on this pilgrimage,**
**continue to keep you under his protection.**

℟. **Amen.**

**May God, who gathered all his scattered children in**
  **Christ Jesus,**
**grant that you will be of one heart**
**and one mind in Christ.**

℟. **Amen.**

**May God, whose goodness inspires in you**
**all that you desire and achieve,**
**strengthen your devotion by his blessing.**

℟. **Amen.**

616    It is preferable to end the celebration with a suitable song.

# CHAPTER 9

# ORDER FOR THE BLESSING OF TRAVELERS

## INTRODUCTION

617    The practice of having special prayers to ask for God's protection upon travelers, a custom often mentioned in the Bible, should be respected. The order of blessing presented in this chapter provides a model for such prayers, in order that this devout practice will continue to be observed.

This order may be used especially in the case of those who leave their country or home, even if only temporarily, to seek employment or for others who travel, for example, on holiday.

618    The present order may be used by a priest, a deacon, or a lay minister. While maintaining the structure and chief elements of the rite, the minister should adapt the celebration to the circumstances of the place and the people involved.

619    If just one traveler is to be blessed or a small group, the shorter rite provided in nos. 635–638 may be used.

# I. ORDER OF BLESSING

## INTRODUCTORY RITES

620    When the community has gathered, the minister says:

**In the name of the Father, and of the Son, and of the Holy Spirit.**

All make the sign of the cross and reply:

**Amen.**

621    A minister who is a priest or deacon greets those present in the following or other suitable words, taken mainly from sacred Scripture.

**May the Lord, the dawn from on high who breaks upon us to guide our feet into the way of peace, be with you all.**

All make the following or some other suitable reply.

**And also with you.**

622    A lay minister greets those present in the following words.

**May the Lord turn his face toward us and guide our feet into the way of peace, now and for ever.**

R⁊. **Amen.**

623    In the following or similar words, the minister prepares those present for the blessing.

**Let us entrust those who are leaving to the hands of the Lord. Let us pray that he will give them a prosperous journey and that as they travel they will praise him in all his creatures; that they will experience God's own goodness in the hospitality they receive and bring the Good News of salvation to all those they meet; that they will be courteous toward all; that they will greet the poor and afflicted with kindness and know how to comfort and help them.**

# READING OF THE WORD OF GOD

**624**  A reader, another person present, or the minister reads a text of sacred Scripture.

## Brothers and sisters, listen to the words of the holy gospel according to Luke:
3:3-6

*Make straight the path of the Lord.*

**John the Baptist went throughout the whole region of the Jordan, proclaiming a baptism of repentance for the forgiveness of sins, as it is written in the book of the words of the prophet Isaiah:**

**"A voice of one crying out in the desert:**
**'Prepare the way of the Lord,**
  **make straight his paths.**
**Every valley shall be filled**
  **and every mountain and hill shall be made low.**
**The winding roads shall be made straight,**
  **and the rough ways made smooth,**
**and all flesh shall see the salvation of God.' "**

**625**  Or:

## Brothers and sisters, listen to the words of the book of Deuteronomy:
6:4-9

*Take to heart these words at home and abroad.*

**"Hear, O Israel! The LORD is our God, the LORD alone! Therefore, you shall love the LORD, your God, with all your heart, and with all your soul, and with all your strength. Take to heart these words which I enjoin on you today. Drill them into your children. Speak of them at home and abroad, whether you are busy or at rest. Bind them at your wrist as a sign and let them be as a pendant on your forehead. Write them on the doorposts of your houses and on your gates."**

**626**  Or:

Genesis 12:1-9—*Go forth to a land I will show you.*

Genesis 28:10-16—*I am with you, I will protect you wherever you go.*

Tobit 5:17-22—*May God in heaven protect you on the way and bring you back safe and sound.*

Luke 24:13-35—*Jesus approached and began to walk with them.*

John 14:1-11—*I am the way, the truth, and the life.*

627    As circumstances suggest, one of the following responsorial psalms may be sung or said, or some other suitable song.

℟. **The Lord is my shepherd; there is nothing I shall want.**

Psalm 23

**The LORD is my shepherd; I shall not want.
In verdant pastures he gives me repose;
Beside restful waters he leads me;
he refreshes my soul.
He guides me in right paths
for his name's sake.** ℟.

**Even though I walk in the dark valley
I fear no evil; for you are at my side
With your rod and your staff
that give me courage.** ℟.

**You spread the table before me
in the sight of my foes;
You anoint my head with oil;
my cup overflows.** ℟.

**Only goodness and kindness follow me
all the days of my life;
And I shall dwell in the house of the LORD
for years to come.** ℟.

Psalm 25:5-6, 9-10, 12-13

℟. **(v. 4) Teach me your ways, O Lord.**

Psalm 91:1-2, 10-11, 12-13, 14-15

℟. **(see v. 11) He has put his angels in charge of you, to guard you in all your ways.**

628    As circumstances suggest, the minister may give those present a brief explanation of the biblical text, so that they may understand through faith the meaning of the celebration.

# INTERCESSIONS

629    As circumstances suggest, the prayer of blessing may be preceded by the intercessions. The minister introduces them and

an assisting minister or one of those present announces the intentions. From the following intentions those best suited to the occasion may be used or adapted, or other intentions that apply to the particular circumstances may be composed. The intentions are followed immediately by the prayer of blessing, no. 631.

The minister says:

**God is the beginning and the end of every road we take. In confidence we call upon him, saying:**

R̸. **Lord, watch over our every step.**

Or:

R̸. **Lord, hear our prayer.**

Assisting minister:

**Father all-holy, you gave us your only Son as our way to you; make us follow without faltering wherever he may lead. (For this we pray:) R̸.**

Assisting minister:

**At every moment and in every place you are near to those who serve you; keep our brothers and sisters in your fatherly care, so that they will find that you are with them on their journey, even as they hope to live with you in heaven. (For this we pray:) R̸.**

Assisting minister:

**Of old you made yourself the guide and the way for your people as they wandered in the desert; be our protector as we set out on this journey, so that we may return home safely. (For this we pray:) R̸.**

Assisting minister:

**You made hospitality to strangers one of the signs of your coming kingdom; grant that all those who are homeless may find a permanent place to live. (For this we pray:) R̸.**

630   When there are no intercessions, the minister, before the prayer of blessing and using the following or other similar words, invites those present to ask for God's help.

**Lord, teach us your ways: Lord, have mercy.**

**R̷. Lord, have mercy.**

Minister:

**Lord, send help from your sanctuary: Lord, have mercy. R̷.**

Minister:

**Lord, be our tower of strength: Lord, have mercy. R̷.**

Minister:

**Lord, save your servants, for they hope in you: Lord, have mercy. R̷.**

As circumstances suggest, all may then pray for a moment in silence before the prayer of blessing.

## PRAYER OF BLESSING

631    A minister who is a priest or deacon says the prayer of blessing with hands outstretched; a lay minister says the prayer with hands joined.

A minister who is not going to accompany the travelers says the following prayer.

**All-powerful and merciful God,**
**you led the children of Israel on dry land,**
**    parting the waters of the sea;**
**you guided the Magi to your Son by a star.**
**Help these our brothers and sisters and give them**
**    a safe journey.**
**Under your protection let them reach their destination**
**and come at last to the eternal haven of salvation.**

**We ask this through Christ our Lord.**

**R̷. Amen.**

632    A minister who is to accompany the travelers says the following prayer.

All-powerful and ever-living God,
when Abraham left his own land
and departed from his own people,
you kept him safe all through his journey.
Protect us, who also are your servants:
walk by our side to help us;
be our companion and our strength on the road
and our refuge in every adversity.
Lead us, O Lord,
so that we will reach our destination in safety
and happily return to our homes.

We ask this through Christ our Lord.

℞. Amen.


## CONCLUDING RITE

633    A minister who is a priest or deacon concludes the rite by saying:

May the Lord remain constantly at your (our) side
and in his mercy guide your (our) journey
in ways that are pleasing to him.

We ask this though Christ our Lord.

℞. Amen.

Then he blesses all present.

And may almighty God bless you,
the Father, and the Son, ✛ and the Holy Spirit.

℞. Amen.

---

634    A lay minister invokes God's blessing on the travelers and all present by signing himself or herself with the sign of the cross and saying:

May almighty God bless us
and hear our prayers for a safe journey.

℞. Amen.

---

# II. SHORTER RITE

635 The minister says:

**Our help is in the name of the Lord.**

All reply:

**Who made heaven and earth.**

636 One of those present or the minister reads a text of sacred Scripture, for example:

Tobit 4:19a

**At all times bless the Lord God, and ask him to make all your paths straight and to grant success to all your endeavors and plans.**

John 14:6

**Jesus said: "I am the way and the truth and the life. No one comes to the Father except through me."**

637 Then the minister says the prayer of blessing.

**All-powerful and ever-living God,
when Abraham left his own land
and departed from his own people,
you kept him safe all through his journey.
Protect us, who also are your servants:
walk by our side to help us;
be our companion and our strength on the road
and our refuge in every adversity.
Lead us, O Lord,
so that we will reach our destination in safety
and happily return to our homes.**

**We ask this through Christ our Lord.**

R︕. **Amen.**

638 Or:

**May God bless you with every heavenly blessing
and give you a safe journey;
wherever life leads you,
may you may find him there to protect you.**

**We ask this through Christ our Lord.**

R︕. **Amen.**

# Part II
# BLESSINGS RELATED TO
# BUILDINGS AND TO VARIOUS
# FORMS OF HUMAN ACTIVITY

Part II

# BLESSINGS RELATED TO BUILDINGS AND TO VARIOUS FORMS OF HUMAN ACTIVITY

## INTRODUCTION

639    Through the guidance of faith, the assurance of hope, and the inspiration of charity the faithful are enabled to discern with wisdom the reflections of God's goodness not only in all the elements of creation but also in all the events of human life. They see all of these as signs of that fatherly providence by which God guides and governs all things. Christians therefore always and everywhere have occasions for praying to God, for expressing their reliance on his help, and for giving him the thanks they owe him.

640    It is altogether right that the vision of faith, which sees God's hand in all the happenings of life, be expressed by means of rites that are carried out on the occasion of inaugurating the use of new materials or buildings. In this way we bless God, thank him for these new signs of his favor, and above all ask for his blessing on those who will make use of them.

641    The orders of blessing contained in Part II are provided for the buildings, materials, and other major resources involved in the various activities and pursuits of the faithful.

# CHAPTER 10

# ORDER FOR THE BLESSING OF A NEW BUILDING SITE

## INTRODUCTION

642    The following rite is used when ground is broken or the cornerstone laid for an important new building, especially one to be erected for a particular community. In the case of a church, the groundbreaking or cornerstone-laying is carried out according to the rite provided in the *Dedication of a Church and an Altar*.[1]

643    The present order may be used by a priest or deacon. While maintaining the structure and chief elements of the rite, the celebrant should adapt the celebration to the circumstances of the place and the people involved and to the kind of building being blessed.

644    The present celebration has reference to the community for which the new building is intended, but it can take on fuller meaning when the workers who will actually put up the building are also present.

---

[1] See The Roman Pontifical, *Dedication of a Church and an Altar*, ch. 1.

# ORDER OF BLESSING

## Introductory Rites

645   When the assembly has gathered at the construction site,
a suitable song may be sung, for example, Psalm 127:1-2.

646   After the singing, the celebrant says:

**In the name of the Father, and of the Son, and of the Holy Spirit.**

All make the sign of the cross and reply:

**Amen.**

647   The celebrant greets those present in the following or other
suitable words, taken mainly from sacred Scripture.

**May the grace and peace of God our Father, the source of all blessings, be with you all.**

All make the following or some other suitable reply.

**And also with you.**

648   In keeping with local custom, representatives of those in
charge of the construction may then make some introductory remarks about the work.

649   In the following or similar words, the celebrant prepares
those present for the blessing.

**The work we are beginning today should enliven our faith and make us grateful. We know the familiar words of the psalm: ''If the Lord does not build the house, in vain do its builders labor.'' Whenever we look to the interests of our neighbor or the community and serve them, we are, in a sense, God's own co-workers. Let us pray for his help through this celebration, my brothers and sisters, that God will bring this construction to successful completion and that his protection will keep those who work on it safe from injury.**

## Reading of the Word of God

650   A reader, another person present, or the celebrant reads
a text of sacred Scripture.

**Brothers and sisters, listen to the words of the first letter of Paul to the Corinthians:** 3:9-11

*You are God's building.*

**For we are God's co-workers; you are God's field, God's building.**

**According to the grace of God given to me, like a wise master builder I laid a foundation, and another is building upon it. But each one must be careful how he builds upon it, for no one can lay a foundation other than the one that is there, namely, Jesus Christ.**

651   Or:

Isaiah 28:16-17b—*I am laying a stone in Zion.*

1 Peter 2:4-10—*As you are living stones, you will be built into a spiritual temple.*

Luke 6:47-49—*A house with its foundation on a rock.*

652   As circumstances suggest, one of the following responsorial psalms may be sung or said, or some other suitable song.

℟. **Our help is from the Lord.**

Psalm 121

**I lift up my eyes toward the mountains;
whence shall help come to me?
My help is from the LORD,
who made heaven and earth.** ℟.

**May he not suffer your foot to slip;
may he slumber not who guards you:
Indeed he neither slumbers nor sleeps,
the guardian of Israel.** ℟.

**The LORD is your guardian; the LORD is your shade;
he is beside you at your right hand.
The sun shall not harm you by day,
nor the moon by night.** ℟.

**The LORD will guard you from all evil;
he will guard your life.
The LORD will guard your coming and your going,
both now and forever.** ℟.

Psalm 90:12-14, 16-17

R︎. (see v. 17c) **Lord, give success to the work of our hands.**

654 As circumstances suggest, the celebrant may give those present a brief explanation of the biblical text, so that they may understand through faith the meaning of the celebration.

## INTERCESSIONS

654 The intercessions are then said. The celebrant introduces them and an assisting minister or one of those present announces the intentions. From the following intentions those best suited to the occasion may be used or adapted, or other intentions that apply to the particular circumstances may be composed.

The celebrant says:

**Brothers and sisters, let us ask God, our all-powerful Father, that the work we begin today will contribute to the building up of his kingdom and join us in faith and love to Christ, who is the cornerstone.**

R︎. **Blessed be God for ever.**

Assisting minister:

**Lord God, you have given us the knowledge and power to become your co-workers. (Let us bless the Lord:)** R︎.

Assisting minister:

**Through your Son you have chosen to build your Church upon solid rock. (Let us bless the Lord:)** R︎.

Assisting minister:

**Through the Spirit of your Son you form us into a spiritual house where you make your dwelling place. (Let us bless the Lord:)** R︎.

Assisting minister:

**You inspire in us the firm hope that the building we begin today with your blessing will be brought to completion with your protection. (Let us bless the Lord:)** R︎.

Assisting minister:

**With much labor you shape and polish us into living stones until you make us worthy to be built up into a new and holy Jerusalem. (Let us bless the Lord:) R̶.**

## PRAYER OF BLESSING

655    With hands outstretched, the celebrant continues with the prayer of blessing.

**All-powerful and all-merciful Father,
you have created all things through your Son
and have made him the unshakable foundation of your
   kingdom.
Through the gift of your eternal wisdom,
grant that the undertaking we begin today
for your glory and our own well-being
may progress day by day to its successful completion.**

**We ask this through Christ our Lord.**

**R̶. Amen.**

656    Or:

**O God, the builder of all things,
you have placed on us the obligation of toil.
Grant that the work we begin
may serve to better our lives
and through your goodness contribute
to the spread of the kingdom of Christ,
who lives and reigns with you and the Holy Spirit,
one God, for ever and ever.**

**R̶. Amen.**

657    As circumstances suggest, the celebrant may sprinkle the construction site and the cornerstone with holy water. The laying of the cornerstone then takes place, as the people sing a suitable song.

# CONCLUDING RITE

658 With hands outstretched over those present, the celebrant concludes the rite by saying:

**May the Lord almighty bless you**
**and kindly receive the desires of your hearts.**

R̿. **Amen.**

**May the Lord give you trust in him,**
**so that you will do all things in his name.**

R̿. **Amen.**

**May the Lord regard your work with kindness**
**and watch over your lives.**

R̿. **Amen.**

659 It is preferable to end the celebration with a suitable song.

## CHAPTER 11

# ORDER FOR THE BLESSING
# OF A NEW HOME

## INTRODUCTION

660    When any of the faithful wish to mark their moving into a new home with a religious celebration, the parish priest (pastor) and his associates should gladly cooperate. The occasion provides a special opportunity for a gathering of the members of the community to mark the joyful event and to thank God, from whom all blessings come, for the gift of a new home.

661    The present order may be used by a priest or deacon. It may also be used by a layperson, who follows the rites and prayers designated for a lay minister.

662    While maintaining the structure and chief elements of the rite, the minister should adapt the celebration to the circumstances of the place and the people involved.

663    There is to be no blessing of a new home unless those who will live in it are present.

# ORDER OF BLESSING

## Introductory Rites

664    When the family members and their relatives and friends have gathered in a convenient place, the minister says:

**In the name of the Father, and of the Son, and of the Holy Spirit.**

All make the sign of the cross and reply:

**Amen.**

665    A minister who is a priest or deacon greets those present in the following or other suitable words, taken mainly from sacred Scripture.

**Peace be with this house and with all who live here.**

All make the following or some other suitable reply.

**And also with you.**

---

666    A lay minister greets those present in the following words.

**May the God whom we glorify with one heart and voice enable us, through the Spirit, to live in harmony as followers of Christ Jesus, now and for ever.**

**R̸. Amen.**

---

667    In the following or similar words, the minister prepares those present for the blessing.

**When Christ took flesh through the Blessed Virgin Mary, he made his home with us. Let us now pray that he will enter this home and bless it with his presence. May he always be here among you; may he nurture your love for each other, share in your joys, comfort you in your sorrows. Inspired by his teachings and example, seek to make your new home before all else a dwelling place of love, diffusing far and wide the goodness of Christ.**

**668**    A reader, another person present, or the minister reads a text of sacred Scripture.

**Brothers and sisters, listen to the words of the holy gospel according to Luke:**                                                    10:5-9

*Peace to this house.*

**The Lord said to the seventy-two: "Into whatever house you enter, first say, 'Peace to this household.' If a peaceful person lives there, your peace will rest on him; but if not, it will return to you. Stay in the same house and eat and drink what is offered to you, for the laborer deserves his payment. Do not move about from one house to another. Whatever town you enter and they welcome you, eat what is set before you, cure the sick in it and say to them, 'The kingdom of God is at hand for you.'"**

**669**    Or:

Genesis 18:1-10a—*Lord, do not pass your servant by.*

Mark 1:29-30—*Jesus went straight to Simon's house.*

Luke 10:38-42—*Martha welcomed Jesus into her house.*

Luke 19:1-9—*Today salvation has come to this house.*

Luke 24:28-32—*Stay with us.*

**670**    As circumstances suggest, the following responsorial psalm may be sung or said, or some other suitable song.

℟. **Happy are those who fear the Lord.**

Psalm 112

**Happy the man who fears the LORD,**
**who greatly delights in his commands.**
**His posterity shall be mighty upon the earth;**
**the upright generation shall be blessed.** ℟.

**Wealth and riches shall be in his house;**
**his generosity shall endure forever.**
**He dawns through the darkness, a light for the upright;**
**he is gracious and merciful and just.** ℟.

**Well for the man who is gracious and lends,**
**who conducts his affairs with justice;**
**He shall never be moved;**
**the just man shall be in everlasting remembrance.** ℟.

**An evil report he shall not fear;**
**his heart is firm, trusting in the LORD.**
**His heart is steadfast; he shall not fear**
**till he looks down upon his foes.** ℟.

**Lavishly he gives to the poor;**
**his generosity shall endure forever;**
**his horn shall be exalted in glory.** ℟.

Psalm 127:1, 2, 3-4, 5

℟. (see v. 1) **The Lord will build a house for us.**

Psalm 128:1-2, 3, 4-6a

℟. (v. 4) **See how the Lord blesses those who fear him.**

**671**   As circumstances suggest, the minister may give those present a brief explanation of the biblical text, so that they may understand through faith the meaning of the celebration.


# INTERCESSIONS

**672**   The intercessions are then said. The minister introduces them and an assisting minister or one of those present announces the intentions. From the following intentions those best suited to the occasion may be used or adapted, or other intentions that apply to the particular circumstances may be composed.

The minister says:

**The Son of God, Lord of heaven and earth, made his home among us. With thankfulness and gladness let us call upon him, saying:**

℟. **Stay with us, Lord.**

Or:

℟. **Lord, hear our prayer.**

Lord Jesus Christ, by your life with Mary and Joseph you sanctified the life of the home; dwell with us in our home, so that we may have you as our guest and honor you as our Head. (For this we pray:) R℣.

In you every dwelling grows into a holy temple; grant that those who live in this house may be built up together into the dwelling place of God in the Holy Spirit. (For this we pray:) R℣.

You taught your followers to build their houses upon solid rock; grant that the members of this family may hold fast to your teachings and, free of all discord, serve you with their whole heart. (For this we pray:) R℣.

You had no place to lay your head, but in uncomplaining poverty you accepted the hospitality of your friends; grant that through our help people who are homeless may obtain decent housing. (For this we pray:) R℣.

## PRAYER OF BLESSING

673    A minister who is a priest or deacon says the prayer of blessing with hands outstretched; a lay minister says the prayer with hands joined.

Lord,
be close to your servants
who move into this home (today)
and ask for your blessing.
Be their shelter when they are at home,
their companion when they are away,
and their welcome guest when they return.
And at last receive them
into the dwelling place you have prepared for them
in your Father's house,
where you live for ever and ever.

R℣. Amen.

674    A minister who is a priest or deacon may also use the prayers of blessing already given in Chapter 1, nos. 85–86 for the annual blessing of family members in their homes, outside the Easter season.

675    After the prayer of blessing, the minister sprinkles those present and the new home with holy water and, as circumstances suggest, during the sprinkling may say:

**Let this water call to mind our baptism into Christ, who has redeemed us by his death and resurrection.**

℟. **Amen.**


## Concluding Rite

676    The minister concludes the rite by saying:

**May the peace of Christ rule in our hearts, and may the word of Christ in all its richness dwell in us, so that whatever we do in word and in work, we will do in the name of the Lord.**

℟. **Amen.**

677    It is preferable to end the celebration with a suitable song.

CHAPTER 12

# ORDER FOR THE BLESSING
# OF A NEW SEMINARY

## INTRODUCTION

678    The opening of a new seminary, that is, a house where candidates for sacred orders will receive their formation, should be marked by a special rite of blessing.

679    Since the opening of a new seminary affects the Christian life of the faithful in the entire diocese, they should be notified ahead of time about the date for the blessing, so that they may attend in large numbers or at least join the celebration through their prayers. To encourage attendance and in keeping with the proper character of the rite, the day chosen for the celebration should be a festive day, preferably a Sunday.

680    When the rite of dedication or blessing of a church belonging to a seminary is celebrated, invocations should be added to the Litany of the Saints and intentions to the general intercessions that are pertinent to the circumstances of the house and the formation of the seminarians.

681    The present order may be used by a bishop and also by a priest. While maintaining the structure and chief elements of the rite, the celebrant should adapt the celebration to the circumstances of the place and the people involved.[2]

682    In regions where it is customary to have an annual blessing of the seminary during the Easter season or at some other set time, celebration of such a blessing should be arranged by use of the elements of the present order, so that the celebration will be of spiritual benefit to the seminarians who take part.

---

[2] This rite may be adapted for use in the blessing of seminaries other than that of a diocese, for example, a regional seminary or the houses of formation of a religious institute. In the case of the houses of formation of a religious institute, see Chapter 13, no. 702.

# ORDER OF BLESSING

## INTRODUCTORY RITES

683    When the seminarians and the faithful have gathered at the site of the new seminary, a suitable song may be sung.

684    After the singing, the celebrant says:

**In the name of the Father, and of the Son, and of the Holy Spirit.**

All make the sign of the cross and reply:

**Amen.**

685    The celebrant greets those present in the following or other suitable words, taken mainly from sacred Scripture.

**The grace of our Lord Jesus Christ, who is eternal Wisdom and our only Teacher, be with you all.**

All reply:

**And also with you.**

Or:

**To him be glory for ever.**

686    In the following or similar words, the celebrant briefly addresses those present, in order to prepare them for the celebration and explain the rite.

**My dear friends, God's kindness has brought us together to bless this new seminary, the gift of his generosity. Its very name tells us that a seminary is like a seedbed where the Church's ministers are nurtured for the work of a diocese. Let us therefore ask the Lord that this new seminary may be a school of prayer and a center of divine teaching, so that the students it receives may return to you as devoted pastors and as our colleagues and co-workers in the sacred ministry.**

687    All pray briefly in silence; then the celebrant continues:

**Watch over your Church of N., O Lord,
which has built this new seminary
to gather the future ministers of Christ**

in community life and the study of your holy teaching,
and so, by your grace,
to form them for so great a service.

**We ask this through Christ our Lord.**

℞. **Amen.**

## READING OF THE WORD OF GOD

688    Readers (or the assisting deacon) proclaim one or more texts
of sacred Scripture, taken preferably from the texts given here or
from the Lectionary for Mass in Ritual Masses, "Holy Orders."[3]
Between the readings there is a responsorial psalm, related to the
reading that preceded it, or an interval of silence. The gospel reading always holds the place of honor.

689    For the first reading the following text may be proclaimed.

**Brothers and sisters, listen to the words of the first letter of
Paul to the Corinthians:**                                    1:26—2:5

*You are among those called.*

**Consider your own calling, brothers and sisters. Not many of
you were wise by human standards, not many were powerful, not many were of noble birth. Rather, God chose the fool-
ish of the world to shame the wise, and God chose the weak
of the world to shame the strong, and God chose the lowly
and despised of the world, those who count for nothing, to
reduce to nothing those who are something, so that no human
being might boast before God. It is due to him that you are
in Christ Jesus who became for us wisdom from God, as well
as righteousness, sanctification, and redemption, so that, as
it is written, "Whoever boasts, should boast in the Lord."**

**When I came to you, brothers and sisters, proclaiming the mys-
tery of God, I did not come with sublimity of words or of wisdom. For I resolved to know nothing while I was with you
except Jesus Christ, and him crucified. I came to you in weakness and fear and much trembling, and my message and my
proclamation were not with persuasive words of wisdom, but
with a demonstration of spirit and power, so that your faith
might rest not on human wisdom but on the power of God.**

---

[3] See Lectionary for Mass (2nd ed., 1981), nos. 770–774 (Ritual Masses, II. Holy Orders).

690    Or:

1 Samuel 3:1-10—*Speak, O Lord, your servant is listening.*

Wisdom 9:1-6, 10-18—*Send me wisdom, O Lord, that she may be with me and work with me.*

1 Corinthians 9:7-27—*Punishment will come to me if I do not preach the Gospel.*

691    If a responsorial psalm is sung, one of the following may be chosen:

R℣. **You are my inheritance, O Lord.**

Psalm 16

**Keep me, O God, for in you I take refuge;
I say to the LORD, "My Lord are you.
Apart from you I have no good."
O LORD, my allotted portion and my cup,
you it is who hold fast my lot.** R℣.

**I bless the LORD who counsels me;
even in the night my heart exhorts me.
I set the LORD ever before me;
with him at my right hand I shall not be disturbed.** R℣.

**You will show me the path to life,
fullness of joys in your presence,
the delights at your right hand forever.** R℣.

Psalm 23:1-3, 4, 5, 6

R℣. **(v. 1) The Lord is my shepherd; there is nothing I shall want.**

Psalm 84:3-4, 5 and 11

R℣. **(v. 5) Blessed are they who dwell in your house, O Lord.**

Psalm 100:2, 3, 4, 5

R℣. **(John 15:14) You are my friends, if you do what I command you.**

692    For the gospel reading the following text may be proclaimed.

**Brothers and sisters, listen to the words of the holy gospel according to Matthew:**                    9:35-38

*The harvest is rich but the laborers are few.*

Jesus went around to all the towns and villages, teaching in their synagogues, proclaiming the gospel of the kingdom, and curing every disease and illness. At the sight of the crowds, his heart was moved with pity for them because they were troubled and abandoned, like sheep without a shepherd. Then he said to his disciples, "The harvest is abundant but the laborers are few; so ask the master of the harvest to send out laborers for his harvest."

693    Or:

Matthew 13:44-46—*The reign of God is like a buried treasure.*

Mark 4:1-2, 26b-34—*When he was away from the crowd Jesus taught his disciples all things.*

Luke 24:44-48—*He opened their minds to the understanding of the Scriptures.*

John 1:35-42—*They went to see where he lodged and stayed with him.*

John 20:19-23—*As the Father sent me, so I send you.*

694    In the homily the celebrant explains both the biblical readings and the meaning of the celebration.

## INTERCESSIONS

695    The intercessions are then said. The celebrant introduces them and an assisting deacon or other minister announces the intentions. From the following intentions those best suited to the occasion may be used or adapted, or other intentions that apply to the particular circumstances may be composed.

The celebrant says:

All grace and wisdom are found in Christ, the perfect image of the Father. Let us then go to Christ in trust and call upon him, saying:

R̿. Grant, O Lord, that where you have gone we may follow.

Or:

R̿. Look, Lord, upon those you have chosen.

Or:

R̿. You, O Lord, have the words of eternal life.

Or:

R̿. Lord, hear our prayer.

Assisting minister:

**Lord Jesus Christ, you have brought these disciples together, so that by learning from you they may share in the ministry of your kingdom; grant that we may become like you and dedicate ourselves to serving the people of God. (For this we pray:) ℟.**

Assisting minister:

**You prayed that the Father would sanctify your disciples in the truth; send us the Holy Spirit so that, abiding in you, we may produce abundant and lasting fruit. (For this we pray:) ℟.**

Assisting minister:

**You, our high priest, taken from among us, have made the people you redeemed a kingdom and priests for God the Father; make us show in word and life the things we have believed as we meditated on the law of God. (For this we pray:) ℟.**

Assisting minister:

**In complete conformity to your Father's will, you chose a life of virginity and poverty; grant that, in complete dedication to loving God above all, we may stay close to you and endeavor to please you and to live for you alone. (For this we pray:) ℟.**

Assisting minister:

**God has made you our wisdom; grant that, learning the wisdom of the cross, we may speak and live as examples of your spirit and power. (For this we pray:) ℟.**

Assisting minister:

**You prayed that your Father would send laborers to gather in his harvest; hear our prayers that, as the harvest increases, the number of laborers may also increase. (For this we pray:) ℟.**

## PRAYER OF BLESSING

696    With hands outstretched, the celebrant says the prayer of blessing.

O Lord, we bless you and praise you.
In your mysterious and merciful providence
you have established Christ as the one eternal high priest,
whose unseen power always sustains your Church
through visible ministers.
When the preachers of the Gospel proclaim the word
  of salvation,
your Son reveals to all peoples the mystery of your love.
When the voice of the priest is raised in prayer,
Christ prays with us at your right hand in glory.
When priests celebrate his sacred sacrifice at the altar,
Christ again presents to you his own self-offering.
When pastors feed and guide the flock entrusted to them,
Christ shepherds and guides his Church.


Watch over, O Lord, your Church of N.,
which has built this new seminary
to ensure that the future ministers of Christ,
gathered in common life and the study of your holy teaching,
will be rightly formed for so great a service.


Father of all holiness, we pray:
that those you have chosen to be messengers of the Gospel
  and ministers of the altar
will learn through prayer
the truths they must some day teach
and will grasp with the conviction of faith
the mysteries their lives must exemplify;
that here they will grow accustomed to offering
  spiritual sacrifices
and by celebrating the liturgy
experience the saving power of the sacraments;
that their obedience will lead them to follow the
  Good Shepherd,
so that as pastors of the Lord's flock,
they will be ready even to lay down their lives
  for their sheep.

We ask this through Christ our Lord.

R∕. Amen.

After the prayer of blessing, the celebrant sprinkles those present and the building with holy water, as the following antiphon or some other suitable song is sung.

Ant. **Where charity and love are found, there is God.**

**The love of Christ has gathered us together into one.
Let us rejoice and be glad with him.
Let us fear and love the living God,
and love each other from the depths of our heart.** Ant.

**Therefore when we are together,
let us take heed not to be divided in mind.
Let there be an end to bitterness and quarrels,
  an end to strife,
and in our midst be Christ our God.** Ant.

**And, in company with the blessed, may we see
your face in glory, Christ our God,
pure and unbounded joy
for ever and ever.** Ant.


## CONCLUDING RITE

698    As circumstances suggest, in the following or similar words, the assisting deacon may invite those present to receive the final blessing.

**Bow your heads and pray for God's blessing.**

With hands outstretched over those present, the celebrant concludes the rite by saying:

**God never fails to provide his people with pastors.
May he pour forth on his Church
the spirit of reverence and courage,
so that those who at his call accept the priesthood
may by the grace of the Holy Spirit
strive to live up to its demands.**

**We ask this through Christ our Lord.**

R̚. **Amen.**

**And may almighty God bless you all,
the Father, and the Son, ✝ and the Holy Spirit.**

R̚. **Amen.**

699 Or:

May God, whose call you have generously answered
and who is your firm hope,
pour forth his blessings upon you,
so that you may one day be his good and faithful servants
in the sacred ministry.

R̿. Amen.

You intend to share in the hierarchic priesthood of Christ:
may the Holy Spirit fill you with his gifts,
so that your lives may be true images
of the life lived by Christ's apostles.

R̿. Amen.

May God shape your days and your deeds by his love,
so that you will carry on Christ's saving mission to humanity
and offer dedicated, unfailing service to the Church.

R̿. Amen.

Then he blesses all present.

And may almighty God bless you all,
the Father, and the Son, ✝ and the Holy Spirit.

R̿. Amen.

700    It is preferable to end the celebration with a suitable song.

CHAPTER 13

# ORDER FOR THE BLESSING OF A NEW RELIGIOUS HOUSE

## INTRODUCTION

701    A new religious house should receive a special blessing, since it is to be the residence of those who, professing the evangelical counsels, come together out of the resolve to follow and imitate Christ more closely.

702    In the present order the term "religious house" includes a convent or a monastery. While maintaining the structure and chief elements of the rite, ministers should adapt the celebration to the circumstances of the place and the people involved.

Due attention should be given to the proper character of the religious institute or to its apostolic charge. In the case of the blessing of a house for the formation of religious, some of the elements in Chapter 12 for the blessing of a seminary may be used.

703    The celebration primarily concerns the religious themselves, but it would be well to choose a day on which the community of the faithful in whose interest the religious house has been established may take part in the celebration.

704    The present order may be used by a priest. The blessing of a new religious house belongs to the Ordinary entrusted with its care, but if he cannot preside, he assigns this duty to the superior of the community. When a bishop or a priest who is not a member of the religious community involved presides, everything should be adapted accordingly.

705    When the rite of dedication or blessing of a church belonging to a religious house is celebrated, as circumstances suggest, invocations may be added in the Litany of the Saints and intentions in the general intercessions that are relevant to the house and the form of religious life lived by its members.

706    In regions where it is customary to have an annual blessing of religious houses during the Easter season or at some other set time, the celebrant, after consultation with the members of the community, should arrange the elements of the present order in such a way that the celebration will be of spiritual benefit to the participants.

# ORDER OF BLESSING

## INTRODUCTORY RITES

707     When the religious and the faithful have gathered at the new religious house, a suitable song may be sung.

708     After the singing, the celebrant says:

**In the name of the Father, and of the Son, and of the Holy Spirit.**

All make the sign of the cross and reply:

**Amen.**

709     The celebrant greets those present in the following or other suitable words, taken mainly from sacred Scripture.

**May God, the source of all holiness, who never ceases to call us to follow Christ, be with you all.**

All make one of the following or some other suitable reply.

**And also with you.**

Or:

**To God be glory for ever.**

710     In the following or similar words, the celebrant prepares those present for the blessing.

**Where two or three are gathered in Christ's name, he is there in their midst. We have gathered here to bless a house where the love of Christ will bring together those who in charity and virginity, in poverty and obedience desire to follow him more faithfully and closely. Relying on the goodness of God, from whom all blessings flow, we pray that those who live here will conform their way of life to what they have promised. We ask that with Jesus they will seek the Father's glory in all things; that, praying together without ceasing, they will be a sign that the Church is a praying community. We ask that, led by the Spirit, they will continually fulfill their vocation, so that Christ may always dwell in us.**

711     After his introductory remarks, the celebrant says:

**Let us pray.**

---

All pray briefly in silence; then the celebrant continues:

**O God,**
**your continuous work begets in us**
**every measure of desire and achievement.**
**We bless you for setting our hearts on heaven**
**during our pilgrim days on earth.**

**Grant to your servants who will live in this house**
**these blessings:**
**to listen to you in faith,**
**to speak to you in prayer,**
**to seek only you in their work,**
**to find you in all they do,**
**to become witnesses to the Gospel.**
**Through them spread the good aroma of Christ everywhere,**
**until the day they rejoice in the revelation of his glory,**
**who lives and reigns with you for ever and ever.**

R⁄. **Amen.**

## READING OF THE WORD OF GOD

712    Readers (or the assisting deacon) proclaim one or more texts of sacred Scripture, taken from those given in the Lectionary for Mass in Masses for Various Needs and Occasions, "For Religious"[4] or in Ritual Masses, "Consecration to a Life of Virginity and Religious Profession."[5] Between the readings there is a responsorial psalm, related to the reading that preceded it, or an interval of silence. The gospel reading always holds the place of honor.

713    The following texts may also be chosen.

**Brothers and sisters, listen to the words of the letter to the Hebrews:**                              13:1-3, 5-7, 14-17

*Here we have no lasting city.*

**Let mutual love continue. Do not neglect hospitality, for through it some have unknowingly entertained angels. Be mindful of prisoners as if sharing their imprisonment, and of the ill-treated as of yourselves, for you also are in the body.**

---

[4] See Lectionary for Mass (2nd ed., 1981), nos. 852–856 (Masses and Prayers for Various Needs and Occasions, I. For the Church, 7. For Religious).

[5] See ibid., nos. 811–815 (Ritual Masses, VIII. Consecration to a Life of Virginity and Religious Profession).

Let your life be free from love of money but be content with what you have, for he has said, "I will never forsake you or abandon you." Thus we may say with confidence:

"The Lord is my helper,
and I will not be afraid.
What can anyone do to me?"

Remember your leaders who spoke the word of God to you. Consider the outcome of their way of life and imitate their faith. For here we have no lasting city, but we seek the one that is to come. Through him [then] let us continually offer God a sacrifice of praise, that is, the fruit of lips that confess his name. Do not neglect to do good and to share what you have; God is pleased by sacrifices of that kind.

Obey your leaders and defer to them, for they keep watch over you and will have to give an account, that they may fulfill their task with joy and not with sorrow, for that would be of no advantage to you.

714    Or:

Brothers and sisters, listen to the words of the holy gospel according to John:                                             1:35-42

*They stayed with Jesus that day.*

The next day John was there again with two of his disciples, and as he watched Jesus walk by, he said, "Behold, the Lamb of God." The two disciples heard what he said and followed Jesus. Jesus turned and saw them following him and said to them, "What are you looking for?" They said to him, "Rabbi" (which translated means Teacher), "where are you staying?" He said to them, "Come, and you will see." So they went and saw where he was staying, and they stayed with him that day. It was about four in the afternoon. Andrew, the brother of Simon Peter, was one of the two who heard John and followed Jesus. He first found his own brother Simon and told him, "We have found the Messiah" (which is translated Anointed). Then he brought him to Jesus.

715    As circumstances suggest, one of the following responsorial psalms may be sung or said, or some other suitable song.

R℣. **These are the people that long to see your face, O Lord.**

Psalm 24

**The LORD's are the earth and its fullness;**
**the world and those who dwell in it.**
**For he founded it upon the seas**
**and established it upon the rivers.** R℣.

**Who can ascend the mountain of the LORD?**
**or who may stand in his holy place?**
**He whose hands are sinless, whose heart is clean,**
**who desires not what is vain,**
**nor swears deceitfully to his neighbor.** R℣.

**He shall receive a blessing from the LORD,**
**a reward from God his savior.**
**Such is the race that seeks for him,**
**that seeks the face of the God of Jacob.** R℣.

Psalm 45:11-12, 14-15, 16-17

R℣. **(see Matthew 25:6) The bridegroom is here; let us go out to meet Christ the Lord.**

Psalm 84:3, 4, 5, 11, 12

R℣. **(2) How lovely is your dwelling place, Lord, mighty God!**

Psalm 133:2, 3

R℣. **(1) See how good it is, how pleasant, that all live together in unity.**

**716**   In the homily the celebrant explains both the biblical readings and the meaning of the celebration.

## INTERCESSIONS

**717**   The intercessions are then said. The celebrant introduces them and an assisting minister or one of those present announces the intentions. From the following intentions those best suited to the occasion may be used or adapted, or other intentions that apply to the particular circumstances may be composed.

The celebrant says:

**Christ the Lord has promised to be with his followers always, until the end of the world. Let us pray to him in simple and trusting love, as we say:**

**R̸. Stay with us, Lord.**

Assisting minister:

**Lord Jesus, you took flesh from the Virgin Mary by the power of the Holy Spirit and willed to make your home with us; we receive you gratefully into this home. R̸.**

Assisting minister:

**You loved your home with Mary and Joseph in Nazareth; make this home the place of your dwelling. R̸.**

Assisting minister:

**You promised to be in the midst of those who gather in your name; look kindly on us who are brought together by our love for you. R̸.**

Assisting minister:

**On earth you once had no place to lay your head; accept our welcome to this house so lovingly made ready for you. R̸.**

Assisting minister:

**You promised to receive into the everlasting kingdom those who welcomed you in the person of strangers; teach us to see you in all our neighbors and to serve them gladly in your name. R̸.**

## Prayer of Blessing

718    With hands outstretched, the celebrant continues with the prayer of blessing.

**O God,**
**inspirer and author of every holy resolve,**
**hear our prayer that you will bestow the kindness**
**    of your grace**
**on the religious who live in this house.**

Make it a place of continuous meditation on your word,
of mutual love, and of tireless service to others.
Grant that those who here loyally follow Christ
may together become an eloquent witness
of their consecration to you.

We ask this through Christ our Lord.

℟. **Amen.**

719    Or:

**Lord Jesus Christ,
you promised to prepare a home in heaven
for those who follow the evangelical counsels.
Surround this residence with the wall of your protection.
Grant that all who live here
may preserve the bond of mutual love.
Make them generous servants to you and to their neighbor,
living signs and messengers of the Gospel,
who will spread the Christian way of life.
For you live and reign for ever and ever.**

℟. **Amen.**

720    After the prayer of blessing, the celebrant sprinkles those
present and the building with holy water, as the following antiphon or some other suitable song is sung.

Ant. **Where charity and love are found, there is God.**

**The love of Christ has gathered us together into one.
Let us rejoice and be glad with him.
Let us fear and love the living God,
and love each other from the depths of our heart.** Ant.

**Therefore when we are together,
let us take heed not to be divided in mind.
Let there be an end to bitterness and quarrels,
  an end to strife,
and in our midst be Christ our God.** Ant.

**And, in company with the blessed, may we see
your face in glory, Christ our God,
pure and unbounded joy
for ever and ever.** Ant.

## CONCLUDING RITE

721    As circumstances suggest, the assisting deacon may then invite those present to receive the final blessing in the following or similar words:

**Bow your heads and pray for God's blessing.**

Then, with hands outstretched over those present, the celebrant concludes the rite by saying:

**May God, who brings us together to live in this house,**
**keep us safe within and without from all distress,**
**give us the Holy Spirit as our strength,**
**and make us steadfast and faithful**
**in the religious commitment**
**by which we have bound ourselves to God.**

R̷. **Amen.**

Then he blesses all present.

**And may almighty God bless you all,**
**the Father, and the Son, ✛ and the Holy Spirit.**

R̷. **Amen.**

722    Or, with hands outstretched, the celebrant may say:

**May God the Father bless you,**
**so that this may be a holy dwelling**
**where you serve in his presence.**

R̷. **Amen.**

**May Christ the Lord dwell by faith in your hearts**
**and prepare a kingdom for you**
**in the house of his Father.**

R̷. **Amen.**

**May the Holy Spirit abide with you and be in you,**
**so that through his power**
**you may fulfill the promise**
**of those gifts you so joyfully receive today.**

R̷. **Amen.**

Then he blesses all present.

**And may almighty God bless you all,
the Father, and the Son, ✛ and the Holy Spirit.**

℞. **Amen.**

**723** It is preferable to end the celebration with a suitable song.

## Chapter 14

# ORDER FOR THE BLESSING OF
# A NEW SCHOOL OR UNIVERSITY

## Introduction

724    Since the school is the gateway to the mental and moral development of students, the Church maintains a constant concern for schools at every level of education. This concern centers especially upon Catholic institutions, where children and young people are able not only to pursue human learning and culture but also to intensify the influence of the spirit of the Gospel on their Christian lives.

725    The order of blessing is provided in consideration of the teachers, the students, persons with any sort of responsibility for the school or university, and the members of the community it is to serve. All such persons should, as far as possible, take part in the celebration of the blessing.

726    The present order may be used by a priest or deacon. While maintaining the structure and chief elements of the rite, the celebrant should adapt the celebration to the circumstances of the place and the people involved.

727    In regions where it is customary to have an annual blessing of schools or universities during the Easter season or at some other set time, celebration of such a blessing should be arranged by use of the elements of the present order and also those elements in the Order for the Blessing of Children, Chapter 1, nos. 135–155, so that the celebration will be suited to both teachers and students.

728    The blessing may also be celebrated within Mass. When the rite of dedication or blessing of a church belonging to a school or university is celebrated, invocations may be added in the Litany of the Saints and intentions in the general intercessions that are relevant to the character and programs of the school or university.

# I. ORDER OF BLESSING

## INTRODUCTORY RITES

729    When the community has gathered at a convenient place, Psalm 67 or some other suitable song may be sung. After the singing, the celebrant says:

**In the name of the Father, and of the Son, and of the Holy Spirit.**

All make the sign of the cross and reply:

**Amen.**

730    The celebrant greets those present in the following or other suitable words, taken mainly from sacred Scripture.

**May God, the source of all wisdom, Christ the Lord, his Word incarnate, and the Holy Spirit, the Spirit of truth, be with you all.**

All make the following or some other suitable reply.

**And also with you.**

731    In the following or similar words, the celebrant prepares those present for the blessing.

**The all-knowing God, who is Lord, moves us in many ways to deepen that knowledge of him which he revealed completely when for our sake the Word was made flesh. All disciplines, sciences, and teaching about the world and about human life that we pursue must have as their final purpose to bring us to a knowledge of the truth and to the worship of the true God. Today we ask God's blessing on this center of seeking, learning, and teaching what is true. We ask that those entrusted with the education of children or young people in this institution may teach their students how to join the discoveries of human wisdom with the truth of the Gospel, so that they will be able to keep the true faith and to live up to it in their lives. We also ask the Lord that the students will find in their teachers the image of Christ, so that, enriched with both human and divine learning, they will in turn be able and ready to enlighten and assist others.**

# READING OF THE WORD OF GOD

732  A reader, another person present, or the celebrant reads a text of sacred Scripture.

**Brothers and sisters, listen to the words of the holy gospel according to Matthew:** 5:1b-2, 13-16

*You are the light of the world.*

**Jesus went up the mountain, and after he had sat down, his disciples came to him. He began to teach them, saying: "You are the salt of the earth. But if salt loses its taste, with what can it be seasoned? It is no longer good for anything but to be thrown out and trampled underfoot. You are the light of the world. A city set on a mountain cannot be hidden. Nor do they light a lamp and then put it under a bushel basket; it is set on a lampstand, where it gives light to all in the house. Just so, your light must shine before others, that they may see your good deeds and glorify your heavenly Father."**

733  Or:

Proverbs 1:1-7—*The fear of the Lord is the beginning of knowledge.*

Wisdom 7:7-20—*All good things together came to me in the company of wisdom.*

Wisdom 9:1-6, 10-18—*Give me wisdom, the attendant at your throne.*

Sirach 1:1-5, 22-25 (Greek, 1:1-5, 18-20)—*All wisdom is from the Lord.*

Sirach 51:18-29 (Greek, 51:13-21)—*Glory be to him who has given me wisdom.*

Ephesians 4:11-24—*Living by the truth and in love.*

Matthew 11:25-30—*You have hidden these things from the learned and the clever and revealed them to children.*

734  As circumstances suggest, one of the following responsorial psalms may be sung or said, or some other suitable song.

R̄. **Lord, you have the words of everlasting life.**

Psalm 19B

**The law of the LORD is perfect,
refreshing the soul;
The decree of the LORD is trustworthy,
giving wisdom to the simple.** R̄.

The precepts of the LORD are right,
rejoicing the heart;
The command of the LORD is clear,
enlightening the eye. R℟.

The fear of the LORD is pure,
enduring forever;
The ordinances of the LORD are true,
all of them just. R℟.

Though your servant is careful of them,
very diligent in keeping them,
Yet who can detect failings? R℟.

Psalm 78:1-2, 3-4, 5 and 7

R℟. (1 Corinthians 1:30) **God has made Christ Jesus our wisdom.**

Psalm 119:97-98, 99-100, 124-125

R℟. (see v. 105) **Your word, O Lord, is a lamp for my feet.**

Psalm 139:1-2, 3-4, 5-6, 17-18

R℟. (see v. 10) **Your hand will lead me, O Lord.**

735    As circumstances suggest, the celebrant may give those
present a brief explanation of the biblical text, so that they may
understand through faith the meaning of the celebration.

## INTERCESSIONS

736    The intercessions are then said. The celebrant introduces
them and an assisting minister or one of those present announces
the intentions. From the following intentions those best suited
to the occasion may be used or adapted, or other intentions that
apply to the particular circumstances may be composed.

The celebrant says:

**The fear of the Lord is the beginning of knowledge. Let us
then call on God's blessing, so that we may come to know and
to follow in our lives all that is true, all that is right. Let us pray:**

R℟. **Lord, give us the Spirit of wisdom.**

Or:

R℟. **Lord, hear our prayer.**

A　　　　Blessing of a school

Assisting minister:

**Lord our God, you have showered us with such great love that we are called and truly are your children; help us to use what we learn in order to perceive our Christian calling more clearly and to live it more fully. (For this we pray:) R⁷.**

Assisting minister:

**In Christ your Son you gave us the model of your new creation, as he advanced in wisdom, age, and grace; grant that as we advance in our courses of study we may also grow through your grace. (For this we pray:) R⁷.**

Assisting minister:

**In your providence you made mutual cooperation the means of human development; grant that all those charged with our instruction may also teach us to work for the common good. (For this we pray:) R⁷.**

Assisting minister:

**You are the author and the guardian of human dignity; grant that the benefits of a sound education may quickly be extended to all the peoples of the world. (For this we pray:) R⁷.**

B　　　　Blessing of a university

Assisting minister:

**Lord our God, you have made us sharers in your own wisdom; grant that, avoiding a merely secular ideal of learning, we may rightly pursue the integral perfection of the human person. (For this we pray:) R⁷.**

Assisting minister:

**You sent your Son, the true Light for all peoples, to give witness to the truth; grant that we may eagerly seek all that is true and devote our efforts to the betterment of human society. (For this we pray:) R⁷.**

Assisting minister:

In your wisdom and plan the unity of the human community enters into the mystery of salvation; grant that scientific and cultural progress may truly contribute to unity between peoples. (For this we pray:) R⁊.

Assisting minister:

In the Gospel you enjoined upon us the mandate of serving one another; grant that we may unceasingly work together to proclaim human rights. (For this we pray:) R⁊.

## PRAYER OF BLESSING

737   With hands outstretched, the celebrant says the prayer of blessing.

Lord God almighty,
in your kindness hear our prayers.
We dedicate this building to the education of youth,
to the progress of the sciences,
and to learning.
Make it become a center where students and teachers,
imbued with the words of truth,
will search for the wisdom that guides the Christian life
and strive wholeheartedly
to stand by Christ as their teacher,
who lives and reigns for ever and ever.

R⁊. Amen.

738   Or:

O God,
it is by your gracious favor
that today we inaugurate this work,
dedicated to education.
Grant that those who will come here as teachers
  or as students
may always pursue the truth

and learn to know you,
the source of all truth.

We ask this through Christ our Lord.

R̸. Amen.

739     After the prayer of blessing, the celebrant sprinkles those
present and the building with holy water, as a suitable song is
sung.

## CONCLUDING RITE

740     With hands outstretched over those present, the celebrant
concludes the rite by saying:

May the all-knowing God, who is Lord,
show us his ways;
may Christ, eternal Wisdom,
teach us the words of truth;
may the Holy Spirit, the blessed light,
always enlighten our minds,
so that we may learn what is right and good
and in our actions carry out what we have learned.

R̸. Amen.

Then he blesses all present.

And may the blessing of almighty God,
the Father, and the Son, ✝ and the Holy Spirit,
come upon you and remain with you for ever.

R̸. Amen.

741     Or, as circumstances suggest, in the following or similar
words, the celebrant or an assisting deacon may invite those present to receive the final blessing.

Bow your heads and pray for God's blessing.

With hands outstretched over those present, the celebrant concludes the rite by saying:

May the all-knowing God, who is Lord,
strengthen you with his blessing.

R̸. Amen.

**May Christ, our only Teacher,**
**teach you the words of eternal life.**

R̸. **Amen.**

**May the Holy Spirit, the Paraclete,**
**bring you to the knowledge of all truth.**

R̸. **Amen.**

Then he blesses all present.

**And may the blessing of almighty God,**
**the Father, and the Son, ✝ and the Holy Spirit,**
**come upon you and remain with you for ever.**

R̸. **Amen.**

742    It is preferable to end the celebration with a suitable song.

# II. ORDER OF BLESSING WITHIN MASS

**743**   When liturgical norms permit, the prayers and readings for the celebration of Mass may appropriately be taken from one of the Masses of the Holy Spirit.[6]

**744**   The homily follows the gospel reading. In it the celebrant, basing himself on the sacred text, gives an explanation of the celebration pertinent to the particular place and the people involved. As circumstances suggest, the homily may be followed by the profession of faith.

**745**   The general intercessions are then said, in the form usual at Mass or in the form provided in no. 736.

**746**   After the prayer after communion, the celebrant prepares those present for the blessing in these or similar words:

**My dear friends, let us pray to the all-knowing God, who is Lord, that all who enter here seeking instruction and right moral guidance may hear Christ, their Teacher, in his Gospel and receive the inner instruction of the Holy Spirit.**

All pray briefly in silence; then, with hands outstretched, the celebrant says:

**Lord God almighty,**
**in your kindness hear our prayers.**
**We dedicate this building to the education of youth,**
**to the progress of the sciences,**
**and to learning.**
**Make it become a center where students and teachers,**
**imbued with the words of truth,**
**will search for the wisdom that guides the Christian life**
**and strive wholeheartedly**
**to stand by Christ as their teacher,**
**who lives and reigns for ever and ever.**

R℣. **Amen.**

---

[6] See Lectionary for Mass (2nd ed., 1981), nos. 62–63 (Proper of Seasons, Pentecost), nos. 764–768 (Ritual Masses, I. Christian Initiation, 4. Confirmation).

747 Or:

**O God,**
**it is by your gracious favor**
**that today we inaugurate this work,**
**dedicated to education.**
**Grant that those who will come here as teachers**
  **or as students**
**may always pursue the truth**
**and learn to know you,**
**the source of all truth.**

**We ask this through Christ our Lord.**

**R̶⁊. Amen.**

748 As circumstances suggest, in the following or similar words, the celebrant or an assisting deacon may invite those present to receive the final blessing.

**Bow your heads, and pray for God's blessing.**

Then, with hands outstretched over those present, the celebrant concludes the rite by saying:

**May the all-knowing God, who is Lord,**
**strengthen you with his blessing.**

**R̶⁊. Amen.**

**May Christ, our only Teacher,**
**teach you the words of eternal life.**

**R̶⁊. Amen.**

**May the Holy Spirit, the Paraclete,**
**bring you to the knowledge of all truth.**

**R̶⁊. Amen.**

Then he blesses all present.

**And may the blessing of almighty God,**
**the Father, and the Son, ✝ and the Holy Spirit,**
**come upon you and remain with you for ever.**

**R̶⁊. Amen.**

749 It is preferable to end the celebration with a suitable song.

CHAPTER 15

# ORDER FOR THE BLESSING OF A NEW LIBRARY

## INTRODUCTION

750    The opening of a new library, particularly one intended for the use of the community, is a valuable pastoral opportunity for blessing the library and reminding the faithful of its religious significance.

751    The present order may be used by a priest or a deacon. While maintaining the structure and chief elements of the rite, the celebrant should adapt the celebration to the circumstances of the place and the people involved.

752    In regions where it is customary to have an annual blessing of libraries and other buildings during the Easter season or at some other set time, the celebration of such a blessing should be arranged by use of the elements of the present order, so that the celebration will be suited to the participants.

753    The community the library will serve, or at least representatives of that community, should always take part in the rite of blessing.

# ORDER OF BLESSING

## Introductory Rites

754    When the community has gathered, a suitable song may be sung. After the singing, the celebrant says:

**In the name of the Father, and of the Son, and of the Holy Spirit.**

All make the sign of the cross and reply:

**Amen.**

755    The celebrant greets those present in the following or other suitable words, taken mainly from sacred Scripture.

**May the Lord Jesus, who is the way, the truth, and the life, be with you all.**

All make the following or some other suitable reply.

**And also with you.**

756    In the following or similar words, the celebrant prepares those present for the blessing.

**The word of God, which comes from and leads back to him who is truth itself, is living and effective. His word runs swiftly and its clear truth is received when it is heard in preaching or read in books, or when it reaches us through the other media of communication.**

**It is God who inspires in the human spirit the desire to record and preserve through books and other means the discoveries of the human mind that open the way to truth. The books of the Bible contain the truth in a unique way, because they are inspired by the Holy Spirit. But other books, as well, contribute to human thought and discourse. If written and conserved in order to spread genuine culture, to investigate the truth, and to provide honest diversion and relaxation, these books also derive the good they contain from God's goodness and the ideas they express from his wisdom. Through reading, truth becomes the guide for living, wisdom nourishes humility, and people are more easily led to mutual understanding.**

It is therefore fitting that your work of conserving and circulating books, as a form of spreading divine truth, should have the support of God's blessing.

## READING OF THE WORD OF GOD

757    A reader, another person present, or the celebrant reads a text of sacred Scripture.

**Brothers and sisters, listen to the words of the apostle Paul to the Colossians:**                                                          3:16-17

*Never say or do anything except in the name of the Lord Jesus, giving thanks to God the Father through him.*

**Let the word of Christ dwell in you richly, as in all wisdom you teach and admonish one another, singing psalms, hymns, and spiritual songs with gratitude in your hearts to God. And whatever you do, in word or in deed, do everything in the name of the Lord Jesus, giving thanks to God the Father through him.**

758    As circumstances suggest, there may be a lecture on one of the biblical books, particularly one of the four Gospels, or a longer reading from Scripture. But a homily before the prayer of blessing is not to be omitted from the celebration.

759    Among the readings from Scripture that may also be chosen are the following.

Luke 1:1-4—*That you may know how well founded is the teaching you have received.*

Luke 4:16-22a—*The book of the prophet Isaiah was handed to him.*

John 21:24-25—*I doubt there would be room enough in the entire world to hold the books to record them.*

760    As circumstances suggest, one of the following responsorial psalms may be sung or said, or some other suitable song.

℞. **Your words, Lord, are spirit and life.**

Psalm 19B

**The law of the LORD is perfect,
refreshing the soul;
The decree of the LORD is trustworthy,
giving wisdom to the simple.** ℞.

The precepts of the L**ORD** are right,
rejoicing the heart;
The command of the L**ORD** is clear,
enlightening the eye. ℟.

The fear of the L**ORD** is pure,
enduring forever;
The ordinances of the L**ORD** are true,
all of them just. ℟.

Though your servant is careful of them,
very diligent in keeping them,
Yet who can detect failings? ℟.

Psalm 77:12-13, 14-15, 16

℟. (v. 15) You are the God who works wonders.

761    The celebrant gives those present a brief explanation of the
biblical text, so that they may understand through faith the meaning of the celebration.

## INTERCESSIONS

762    As circumstances suggest, the prayer of blessing may be
preceded by intercessions. The celebrant introduces them and an
assisting minister or one of those present announces the intentions. From the following intentions those best suited to the occasion may be used or adapted, or other intentions that apply
to the particular circumstances may be composed. The intentions
are followed immediately by the prayer of blessing, no. 764.

The celebrant says:

The words, miracles, and wonders of the Lord are open for
all to behold in the world of nature and are recorded in writing for those who read the sacred books with faith. With one
mind and spirit therefore let us pray to him, saying:

℟. Lord, grant that we may always search for you and find you.

Or:

℟. Lord, hear our prayer.

Assisting minister:

**Christ our Redeemer, the Word and Wisdom of the Father, you are the true light that gives light to every one; show us the way of truth. (For this we pray:)** R⁊.

Assisting minister:

**You promised your followers the Holy Spirit to teach them all truth, so that they would see more deeply into the divine mysteries; grant that, inspired and empowered by that same Spirit, we may be equipped and ready for every good work. (For this we pray:)** R⁊.

Assisting minister:

**At Nazareth you unrolled the scroll and explained the text you read to those who were listening; grant that we may always search for the truth and profess it in love. (For this we pray:)** R⁊.

Assisting minister:

**You willed that many of your deeds should be handed down in writing, so that we might believe and believing have life in your name; grant that, strong in faith, we may be eager to open up for others the path of truth and salvation. (For this we pray:)** R⁊.

Assisting minister:

**You are worthy to receive the scroll and open its seals; grant that our names may be among those written in the book of life. (For this we pray:)** R⁊.

763    When there are no intercessions, the celebrant, before the prayer of blessing and using the following or other similar words, invites those present to ask for God's help.

**O God, you are the source of all human learning; guide us in your truth: Lord, have mercy.**

R⁊. **Lord, have mercy.**

Celebrant:

**Lord, you know all things; show us your ways: Lord, have mercy.** R⁊.

Celebrant:

**You have created the universe with wisdom, O Lord; make clear to us what is pleasing to you: Lord, have mercy. R℣.**

Celebrant:

**Lord, to those who come here to read or study, impart wisdom, the attendant at your throne: Lord, have mercy. R℣.**

Celebrant:

**Grant that all who come here may make progress in both divine and human science and grow in their love for you: Lord, have mercy. R℣.**

## PRAYER OF BLESSING

764    With hands outstretched, the celebrant says the prayer of blessing.

**Lord, our God,**
**we proclaim your majesty.**
**In many and varied ways**
**you continuously reveal yourself to us**
**and in the Bible you have handed down your inspired word.**
**Listen to our prayers,**
**that all who come to this library**
**in pursuit of the arts and sciences**
**may always be docile to the wisdom of your Word.**
**Grant that, imbued with true learning,**
**they will strive to create a more civilized world.**

**We ask this through Christ our Lord.**

**R℣. Amen.**

765    After the prayer of blessing, the celebrant sprinkles those present and the library with holy water.

## CONCLUDING RITE

766    With hands outstretched over those present, the celebrant concludes the rite by saying:

May the all-knowing God and Lord
show us his ways;
may Christ, the Wisdom of the Father,
teach us the words of truth;
may the Holy Spirit, most blessed Light divine,
ever enlighten our minds,
so that we may learn and put into practice
all that is right and good.

R̸. **Amen.**

Then he blesses all present.

**And may the blessing of almighty God,
the Father, and the Son, ✝ and the Holy Spirit,
come upon you and remain with you for ever.**

R̸. **Amen.**

767    It is preferable to end the celebration with a suitable song.

# Chapter 16

# ORDER FOR THE BLESSING OF A PARISH HALL OR CATECHETICAL CENTER

USA

## Introduction

768 In addition to the parish church, the buildings in which social activities and religious education take place are significant for the parish community. This order is intended for the blessing of a parish hall or catechetical center and recognizes the importance that such a building has in the life of a parish.

769 The blessing may be given by the pastor or by another priest or deacon delegated by him.

## ORDER OF BLESSING

### Introductory Rites

770 When the community has gathered, a suitable song may be sung. After the singing, the minister says:

**In the name of the Father, and of the Son, and of the Holy Spirit.**

All make the sign of the cross and reply:

**Amen.**

771 The minister greets those present in the following or other suitable words, taken mainly from sacred Scripture.

**The grace and peace of Christ be with you all.**

And all reply:

**And also with you.**

772 In the following or similar words, the minister prepares those present for the blessing.

A        For a parish hall

**After much work and prayer by so many members of our parish, we gather now to bless and dedicate this new parish hall. It will be a center for our parish activities and a place where we may come to know one another and give witness to our faith in Christ.**

B        For a catechetical center

**After much work and prayer by so many members of our parish, we gather now to bless and dedicate this new catechetical center. Here the young will learn of their Catholic faith and adults will deepen their commitment to live as Christ has taught us. We pray that the word of God may always echo from its walls.**

## READING OF THE WORD OF GOD

**773**    A reader, another person present, or the minister reads a text of sacred Scripture.

**Brothers and sisters, listen to the words of the apostle Paul to the Ephesians:**                                                   2:19-22

*Through the Lord, the whole building is bound together as one holy temple.*

**So then you are no longer strangers and sojourners, but you are fellow citizens with the holy ones and members of the household of God, built upon the foundation of the apostles and prophets, with Christ Jesus himself as the capstone. Through him the whole structure is held together and grows into a temple sacred in the Lord; in him you also are being built together into a dwelling place of God in the Spirit.**

**774**    Or:

1 Corinthians 3:9-13, 16-17—*You are the temple of God.*

1 Peter 2:4-9—*As living stones, you will be built into a spiritual temple.*

775    As circumstances suggest, one of the following responsorial psalms may be sung, or some other suitable song.

℟. **We praise your glorious name, O mighty God.**

1 Chronicles 29

**Blessed may you be, O LORD,**
**God of Israel our father,**
**from eternity to eternity.** ℟.

**Yours, O LORD, are grandeur and power,**
**majesty, splendor, and glory.**
**For all in heaven and on earth is yours;**
**yours, O LORD, is the sovereignty;**
**you are exalted as head over all.** ℟.

**Riches and honor are from you,**
**and you have dominion over all.**
**In your hand are power and might;**
**it is yours to give grandeur and strength to all.** ℟.

Psalm 95:1-2, 3-5, 6-7

℟. **(v. 2) Let us come before the Lord with songs of praise.**

776    As circumstances suggest, the minister may give those present a brief explanation of the biblical text, so that they may understand through faith the meaning of the celebration.

## INTERCESSIONS

777    The intercessions are then said. The minister introduces them and an assisting minister or one of those present announces the intentions. From the following those best suited to the occasion may be used or adapted, or other intentions that apply to the particular circumstances may be composed.

The minister says:

**With praise and thanksgiving, let us ask God, through whom all things are accomplished, to bless this new parish hall (or catechetical center).**

℟. **Hear us, O Lord.**

Assisting minister:

**For the Church, that all who are baptized may renew their commitment to Christ, we pray to the Lord.** ℟.

Assisting minister:

**For our parish, that God may continue to bless all our works, we pray to the Lord.** ℟.

Assisting minister:

**For those who, by their work and contributions, helped to build this hall (*or* center), we pray to the Lord.** ℟.

Assisting minister:

For a parish hall

**For those who will use this parish hall, that they may deepen their participation in parish life, we pray to the Lord.** ℟.

Assisting minister:

For a catechetical center

**For all those who will use this catechetical center, that they may grow in faith and love for God and the Church, we pray to the Lord.** ℟.

778    After the intercessions the minister, in the following or similar words, invites all present to sing or say the Lord's Prayer.

**Jesus gathers us in faith and calls us to pray:**

All:

**Our Father . . .**

## PRAYER OF BLESSING

779    The minister says the prayer of blessing with hands outstretched.

**God of mercy and truth,**
**you sent your only Son**
**to be our Savior and Lord.**

---

He calls us together as his Church
to carry on the work of salvation.

We ask you now to bless us
and all who will use this parish hall (catechetical center).
May all who come here know the presence of Christ,
experience the joy of his friendship,
and grow in his love.

Grant this through Christ our Lord.

R̸. Amen.


## CONCLUDING RITE

780    The minister concludes the rite by saying:

May the peace of Christ rule in your hearts,
and may the word of Christ dwell in you,
so that all that you do in word and in work,
you will do in the name of the Lord.

R̸. Amen.

Then he blesses all present.

And may almighty God bless you all,
the Father, and the Son, ✛ and the Holy Spirit.

R̸. Amen.

781    It is preferable to end the celebration with a suitable song.

# CHAPTER 17

# ORDER FOR THE BLESSING OF A NEW HOSPITAL OR OTHER FACILITY FOR THE CARE OF THE SICK

## INTRODUCTION

782 Any building erected for the care of the sick may rightly be seen as a sign of the fidelity of Christ's followers to his command, recorded in the gospels, that they heal the sick.

The dedication of such a building is an ideal pastoral opportunity for gathering the Christian community, in order that all the faithful may more deeply grasp the meaning of illness and the important place of the medical arts in the working out of God's providence.

783 The celebration of this blessing does not have immediate reference to the sick but rather to those who help and minister to the sick in any way. Accordingly, the blessing of a hospital or other health-care facility is never to take place without the participation of the physicians and of the other personnel who devote their work and efforts to caring for the patients.

784 The present order may be used by a priest or deacon. While maintaining the structure and chief elements of the rite, the celebrant should adapt the celebration to the circumstances of the place and the people involved.

785 In regions where it is customary to have an annual blessing of hospitals and other similar places during the Easter season or at some other set time, the celebration of such a blessing should be arranged by use of the chief elements in the present order and in the Order for the Blessing of the Sick, Chapter 2, nos. 380–402, so that the celebration has relevance for both the patients and the doctors and nurses.

# ORDER OF BLESSING

## Introductory Rites

786 When the community has gathered in a convenient place, a suitable song may be sung. After the singing, the celebrant says:

**In the name of the Father, and of the Son, and of the Holy Spirit.**

All make the sign of the cross and reply:

**Amen.**

787 The celebrant greets those present in the following or other suitable words, taken mainly from sacred Scripture.

**May the Lord Jesus, who commanded his disciples to heal the sick and bring them relief, be with you all.**

All make the following or some other suitable reply.

**And also with you.**

788 In the following or similar words, the celebrant prepares those present for the blessing.

**The Father of mercies and God of all consolation, who strengthens us through his Son in the Holy Spirit, showers his love and blessing in a particular way on those who are in distress, on the sick, and on those who assist and minister to the sick in any way.**

**Not only do the sick fill up in their flesh what is lacking in the suffering of Christ for the sake of his Body, the Church, but in addition they are a special reflection of Christ himself. Did he not say that whatsoever we do to one of them, we do to him?**

**In this realization, then, let us ask for God's blessing on all those who are (will be) patients here or who devote (will devote) themselves to caring for the sick; and let us ask the divine blessing on this building, erected for the care of the sick.**

**789**  A reader, another person present, or the celebrant reads a text of sacred Scripture.

**Brothers and sisters, listen to the words of the holy gospel according to Matthew:**                                   4:23-25

*They carried to Jesus all the afflicted and he cured them.*

**Jesus went around all of Galilee, teaching in their synagogues, proclaiming the gospel of the kingdom, and curing every disease and illness among the people. His fame spread to all of Syria, and they brought to him all who were sick with various diseases and racked with pain, those who were possessed, lunatics, and paralytics, and he cured them. And great crowds from Galilee, the Decapolis, Jerusalem, and Judea, and from beyond the Jordan followed him.**

**790**  Or:

Sirach 38:1-14—*God it was who established the profession of the physician.*

2 Corinthians 1:3-7—*The God of all consolation.*

Matthew 25:31-46—*I was ill and you comforted me.*

Luke 10:30-37—*He was moved to pity at the sight of him.*

**791**  As circumstances suggest, one of the following responsorial psalms may be sung or said, or some other suitable song.

R℣. **You saved my life, O Lord, I shall not die.**

Isaiah 38

**Once I said,
"In the noontime of life I must depart!
To the gates of the nether world I shall be consigned
for the rest of my years."** R℣.

**I said, "I shall see the LORD no more
in the land of the living.
No longer shall I behold my fellow men
among those who dwell in the world."** R℣.

**My dwelling, like a shepherd's tent,
is struck down and borne away from me;
You have folded up my life,
like a weaver who severs the last thread.** R℣.

Those live whom the LORD protects;
yours . . . the life of my spirit.
You have given me health and life. ℟.

Psalm 102:2-3, 24-25

℟. (v. 2) O Lord, hear my prayer, and let my cry come to you.

792    As circumstances suggest, the celebrant may give those
present a brief explanation of the biblical text, so that they may
understand through faith the meaning of the celebration.

## INTERCESSIONS

793    The intercessions are then said. The celebrant introduces
them and an assisting minister or one of those present announces
the intentions. From the following intentions those best suited
to the occasion may be used or adapted, or other intentions that
apply to the particular circumstances may be composed.

The celebrant says:

Christ the Lord came into the world to heal the sick and comfort the afflicted. Let us pray to him in humility, saying:

℟. Lord, bless those who put their trust in you.

Or:

℟. Lord, hear our prayer.

Assisting minister:

Lord Jesus, you came to cure the sick and heal the brokenhearted; come into this place, prepared for the care of the sick.
(For this we pray:) ℟.

Assisting minister:

As you preached the Gospel of the kingdom, you healed every
kind of illness; show your compassion and goodness to all.
(For this we pray:) ℟.

Assisting minister:

You touched the sick and they were healed; by the gift of your
grace lift up the hearts of the afflicted who have (will) come
to this place. (For this we pray:) ℟.

**You commanded the apostles to heal the sick; hear the prayers of your Church for the speedy recovery of the sick. (For this we pray:) R℣.**

Assisting minister:

**You promised an everlasting reward to those who in your name would visit and comfort the sick; deepen our compassion, so that we may always see and love you in our brothers and sisters who are suffering. (For this we pray:) R℣.**

## PRAYER OF BLESSING

794    With hands outstretched, the celebrant says the prayer of blessing.

**Lord our God,**
**through the power of the Holy Spirit**
**your Son healed our infirmities and diseases.**
**When he sent forth his disciples to preach the Gospel,**
**he commanded them to visit and heal the sick.**
**Grant that in this hospital the physicians and staff**
**will receive with kindness**
**all the patients who are (will be) confined here**
**and will tend to them with skill and care,**
**so that those who come here sick**
**will leave restored in spirit and in body**
**and for ever praise your mercy.**

**We ask this through Christ our Lord.**

**R℣. Amen.**

795    Or:

**Blessed are you, O God, our Father.**
**Through your Son you commanded your people**
**who walk in newness of life**
**to care compassionately for the sick.**
**Attend to the desires of your children.**
**By the grace of your Holy Spirit**
**make this place a house of blessing and a center of love,**

where physicians practice the art of healing wisely,
where nurses and aides serve the sick with care,
where the faithful come to visit Christ
in the person of their brothers and sisters.
Grant that, comforted in their illness,
the patients will quickly regain their health
and joyfully thank you
for the favors they have received.

**We ask this through Christ our Lord.**

℟. **Amen.**

796     After the prayer of blessing, the celebrant sprinkles those present and the building with holy water, as a suitable song is sung.

## CONCLUDING RITE

797     With hands outstretched over those present, the celebrant concludes the rite by saying:

**God, the comforter of the afflicted and the strength
  of the weak,
has brought you together for the dedication
  of this building,
established for the care of the sick.
May he strengthen you by his grace,
so that, in serving the sick with tender charity,
you may serve Christ himself.**

**Who lives and reigns for ever.**

℟. **Amen.**

**And may the blessing of almighty God,
the Father, and the Son, ✝ and the Holy Spirit,
come upon you and remain with you for ever.**

℟. **Amen.**

798     It is preferable to end the celebration with a suitable song.

CHAPTER 18

# ORDER FOR THE BLESSING OF AN OFFICE, SHOP, OR FACTORY

## INTRODUCTION

799 Through the labor of our hands we continually seek to be the stewards over God's creation. Similarly, "progress in the means of production and in the exchange of goods and services make business economy an effective means of more perfectly providing for the needs of the human family."[7] It is therefore altogether fitting to celebrate a special blessing of the centers of the various occupations by which we seek to benefit ourselves and others.

800 The present celebration has reference both to the community whose interests the new factory, shop, or office will serve and to those who will work or conduct business there. The blessing is therefore not to be celebrated without the presence both of the community involved, or at least a group of its representatives, and of those who in any capacity will work in the place to be blessed.

801 The present order may be used by a priest or deacon. While maintaining the structure and chief elements of the rite, the celebrant should adapt the celebration to the circumstances of the place and the people involved.

802 In regions where it is customary to have an annual blessing of factories, offices, and shops during the Easter season or at some other set time, the celebration of such a blessing should be arranged by use of the chief elements of the present order.

---

[7] Vatican Council II, Pastoral Constitution on the Church in the Modern World *Gaudium et spes*, no. 63.

# ORDER OF BLESSING

## INTRODUCTORY RITES

803 When the community has gathered in a convenient place,
a suitable song is sung. After the singing, the celebrant says:

**In the name of the Father, and of the Son, and of the Holy Spirit.**

All make the sign of the cross and reply:

**Amen.**

804 The celebrant greets those present in the following or other
suitable words, taken mainly from sacred Scripture.

**May God, who has given us power over the works of his hands, be with you all.**

All make the following or some other suitable reply.

**And also with you.**

805 In the following or similar words, the celebrant prepares
those present for the blessing.

**In his own life Christ Jesus clearly showed us the dignity of labor. When he became incarnate, the Word of the Father was known as the carpenter's son and willingly worked with the tools of his trade. By working with his own hands he transformed toil from being an inherited curse for sin into a source of blessings.**

**If we do our work well, whatever it may be, and offer it to God, we purify ourselves and through the labor of our hands and minds we build up God's creation. Our work enables us to practice charity and to help the less fortunate, so that, joined to Christ the Redeemer, we grow in his love.**

**Let us bless the Lord, then, and pray that he will shower his blessings on all who will work in this place.**

## READING OF THE WORD OF GOD

806 A reader, another person present, or the celebrant reads
a text of sacred Scripture.

---

**Brothers and sisters, listen to the words of the book of Genesis:**
1:27-31a

*Fill the earth and subdue it.*

**God created man in his image;
in the divine image he created him;
male and female he created them.**

**God blessed them, saying: "Be fertile and multiply; fill the earth and subdue it. Have dominion over the fish of the sea, the birds of the air, and all the living things that move on the earth." God also said: "See, I give you every seed-bearing plant all over the earth and every tree that has seed-bearing fruit on it to be your food; and to all the animals of the land, all the birds of the air, and all the living creatures that crawl on the ground, I give all the green plants for food." And so it happened. God looked at everything he had made, and he found it very good.**

808    Or:

**Brothers and sisters, listen to the words of the holy gospel according to Mark:**
6:1-3

*Is this not the carpenter, the son of Mary?*

**Jesus departed from the house of Jairus and came to his native place, accompanied by his disciples. When the sabbath came he began to teach in the synagogue, and many who heard him were astonished. They said, "Where did this man get all this? What kind of wisdom has been given him? What mighty deeds are wrought by his hands! Is he not the carpenter, the son of Mary, and the brother of James and Joses and Judas and Simon? And are not his sisters here with us?" And they took offense at him.**

808    Or:

Sirach 38:25-39 (Greek, 38:24-34)—*His care is to finish the work.*

1 Thessalonians 4:9-12—*Work with your hands as we directed you to do.*

2 Thessalonians 3:6-13—*We did not depend on anyone for food. Rather, we worked day and night, laboring to the point of exhaustion.*

Matthew 6:25-34—*Your heavenly Father knows all that you need.*

Matthew 25:14-29—*He went to invest it and made another five talents.*

Luke 16:9-12—*Those you can trust in little things, you can also trust in greater.*

809     As circumstances suggest, one of the following responsorial psalms may be sung or said, or some other suitable song.

R℣. **Lord, give success to the work of our hands.**

Psalm 90

**Before the mountains were begotten
and the earth and the world were brought forth,
from everlasting to everlasting you are God.** R℣.

**You turn man back to dust,
saying, "Return, O children of men."
For a thousand years in your sight
are as yesterday, now that it is past,
or as a watch of the night.** R℣.

**Teach us to number our days aright,
that we may gain wisdom of heart.
Return, O LORD! How long?
Have pity on your servants!** R℣.

**Fill us at daybreak with your kindness,
that we may shout for joy and gladness all our days.
Let your work be seen by your servants
and your glory by their children.** R℣.

Psalm 104:1ab and 5, 14-15, 23-24

R℣. **(v. 31) May the glory of the Lord last for ever; may the Lord be glad in his works.**

810     As circumstances suggest, the celebrant may give those present a brief explanation of the biblical text, so that they may understand through faith the meaning of the celebration.

## INTERCESSIONS

811     As circumstances suggest, the prayer of blessing may be preceded by the intercessions. The celebrant introduces them and an assisting minister or one of those present announces the intentions. From the following intentions those best suited to the

occasion may be used or adapted, or other intentions that apply to the particular circumstances may be composed. The intentions are followed immediately by the prayer of blessing, no. 613.

The celebrant says:

**Our God created the world and filled it with marvelous signs of his power. He also blessed human toil from the very beginning, so that in modest imitation of the Creator's own goodness we might diligently devote ourselves to bringing creation to its perfection. Let us, then, offer our prayers to God, saying:**

℟. **Lord, graciously guide the work of our hands.**

Assisting minister:

**Blessed are you, O Lord, who gave us the command to work, so that by relying on our minds and our hands we might devote ourselves to perfecting creation.** ℟.

Assisting minister:

**Blessed are you, O Lord, who willed that your Son made flesh for us should practice the carpenter's trade.** ℟.

Assisting minister:

**Blessed are you, O Lord, who in Christ made the yoke of toil sweet and its burden light.** ℟.

Assisting minister:

**Blessed are you, O Lord, who in your providence move us always to strive to do our best.** ℟.

Assisting minister:

**Blessed are you, O Lord, who receive with favor the offering of our labor, so that it becomes an offering of penance, brings joy to our brothers and sisters, and helps the poor.** ℟.

Assisting minister:

**Blessed are you, O Lord, who graciously chose bread and wine, the work of human hands, as the sacramental signs of the eucharist.** ℟.

**812**  When there are no intercessions, the celebrant, before the prayer of blessing, says:

**Let us pray.**

As circumstances suggest, all may then pray for a moment in silence before the prayer of blessing.

## PRAYER OF BLESSING

**813**  With hands outstretched, the celebrant says the prayer of blessing.

A  Blessing of an office

**O God,**
**in your wise providence**
**you are glad to bless all human labor,**
**the work of our hands and of our minds.**
**Grant that all who plan and conduct business in this office**
**may through your guidance and support**
**come to right decisions and carry them out fairly.**

**We ask this through Christ our Lord.**

**R7. Amen.**

B  Blessing of a factory

**O God,**
**by working as a carpenter**
**your Son enhanced the dignity of human labor**
**and in a wonderful way joined us**
**through our own toil to the work of redemption.**
**Through the blessing they seek,**
**strengthen your faithful.**
**Give to those who are employed in skillfully transforming**
**the things you have created**
**a sense of their own dignity.**
**Make them content in their dedication**
**to bettering the human family**
**in praise of your name.**

**We ask this through Christ our Lord.**

**R7. Amen.**

C     Blessing of a shop

**God, our all-provident Father,**
**you have placed the earth and its fruits under our care,**
**so that by our labor we will endeavor**
**to ensure that all share in the benefits of your creation.**
**Bless all those who will use this building**
**either as buyers or sellers,**
**so that by respecting justice and charity**
**they will see themselves as working for the common good**
**and find joy in contributing to the progress**
  **of the earthly city.**

**We ask this through Christ our Lord.**

**R̸. Amen.**

814    After the prayer of blessing, the celebrant sprinkles those
present and the place with holy water, as a suitable song is sung.


## CONCLUDING RITE

815    With hands outstretched over those present, the celebrant
concludes the rite by saying:

**May God, the Father of goodness,**
**who commanded us to help one another as brothers**
    **and sisters,** _Rɛs̄_
**bless this new ~~building~~ with his presence**
**and look kindly on all who enter here.**

**R̸. Amen.**

Then he blesses all present.

**And may almighty God bless you all,**
**the Father, and the Son, ✝ and the Holy Spirit.**

**R̸. Amen.**

816    It is preferable to end the celebration with a suitable song.

# CHAPTER 19

# ORDER FOR THE BLESSING OF CENTERS OF SOCIAL COMMUNICATION

## INTRODUCTION

817    The Church pays particularly attentive care to the technological developments that have an important influence on the human spirit. Preeminent among these are those organs of communication that have the power to affect not only individuals but whole populations, even all of human society. These include the press, the cinema, radio, television, and the like and are designated by the general term ''media of social communication.'' The provision of a blessing for the buildings and equipment for these media is one way in which the Church exercises its vigilance for the right use of the media.

818    The present celebration has reference both to the community whose interests the new building and media will serve and particularly to those who will work in the building and use the media to communicate news, ideas, and other forms of information. The blessing is therefore not to be celebrated without the presence both of the community involved, or at least a group of its representatives, and of the management and staff of the facilities to be blessed.

819    The present order may be used by a priest or deacon. While maintaining the structure and chief elements of the rite, the celebrant should adapt the celebration to the circumstances of the place and the people involved.

820    In regions where it is customary to have an annual blessing of centers of communication during the Easter season or at some other set time, celebration of such a blessing should be arranged by use of the chief elements in this present order.

# ORDER OF BLESSING

## INTRODUCTORY RITES

821    When the community has gathered, a suitable song may be sung. After the singing, the celebrant says:

**In the name of the Father, and of the Son, and of the Holy Spirit.**

All make the sign of the cross and reply:

**Amen.**

822    The celebrant greets those present in the following or other suitable words, taken mainly from sacred Scripture.

**May God, who sent us his Son as the herald of salvation and who continually pours the Holy Spirit of truth into our hearts, be with you all.**

All make the following or some other suitable reply.

**And also with you.**

823    In the following or similar words, the celebrant prepares those present for the blessing.

**The wisdom of God is beyond imagining and his goodness, a boundless treasure. He unfailingly enlightens our minds to open up new and better means of sharing with each other all kinds of information, ideas, and aspirations. The discoveries of technology, if used properly, can be of great service to the human family, not only to bring help in times of need, but also as resources for education and entertainment and even for spreading and building up the kingdom of God.**

## READING OF THE WORD OF GOD

824    A reader, another person present, or the celebrant reads a text of sacred Scripture.

**Brothers and sisters, listen to the words of the holy gospel according to Mark:**                          16:14a, 15-20

*Preach the Gospel to every creature.*

But later, as the eleven were at table, Jesus appeared to them and said, "Go into the whole world and proclaim the gospel to every creature. Whoever believes and is baptized will be saved; whoever does not believe will be condemned. These signs will accompany those who believe: in my name they will drive out demons, they will speak new languages. They will pick up serpents with their hands, and if they drink any deadly thing, it will not harm them. They will lay hands on the sick, and they will recover."

So then the Lord Jesus, after he spoke to them, was taken up into heaven and took his seat at the right hand of God. But they went forth and preached everywhere, while he Lord worked with them and confirmed the word through accompanying signs.

825   Or:

Baruch 3:29-36—*God who knows all things knows wisdom.*

Philippians 4:8-9—*Your thoughts shall be wholly directed to all that is true, all that deserves respect, all that is honest, pure, admirable, decent, virtuous, and worthy of praise.*

Hebrews 4:12-16—*Everything is open and uncovered to the eyes of God.*

Matthew 5:1b, 2, 13-16—*You are the salt of the earth; you are the light of the world.*

826   As circumstances suggest, one of the following responsorial psalms may be sung or said, or some other suitable song.

℟. O Lord, our God, how wonderful your name in all the earth!

Psalm 8

When I behold your heavens, the work of your fingers,
the moon and the stars which you set in place—
What is man that you should be mindful of him,
or the son of man that you should care for him? ℟.

You have made him little less than the angels,
and crowned him with glory and honor.
You have given him rule over the works of your hands,
putting all things under his feet: ℟.

All sheep and oxen,
yes, and the beasts of the field,
The birds of the air, the fishes of the sea,
and whatever swims the paths of the seas. ℞.

Psalm 19A:2-3, 4-5

℞. (v. 5) **Their message goes out through all the world; their news to the ends of the earth.**

Psalm 104:24, 31-32, 33-34

℞. (v. 24c) **The earth is full of your creatures, O Lord.**

827    As circumstances suggest, the celebrant may give those present a brief explanation of the biblical text, so that they may understand through faith the meaning of the celebration.

# INTERCESSIONS

828    As circumstances suggest, the prayer of blessing may be preceded by the intercessions. The celebrant introduces them and an assisting minister or one of those present announces the intentions. From the following intentions those best suited to the occasion may be used or adapted, or other intentions that apply to the particular circumstances may be composed. The intentions are followed immediately by the prayer of blessing, no. 830.

The celebrant says:

**A proper use of the available communications media contributes greatly to the progress of the human family. It is also in complete accord with the plan of God, who wants us all to be bound closely together in a union of truth and freedom. Let every tongue, then, proclaim God's wonders, saying:**

℞. **How wonderful are your works, O Lord!**

Or:

℞. **Blessed be God for ever.**

Assisting minister:

**Blessed are you, O Lord, eternal Wisdom, who enlighten our minds and support our endeavors by your blessing. (Let us bless the Lord:)** ℞.

Assisting minister:

**Blessed are you, O Lord, who move us to continue to seek the things that are unseen through those that are seen. (Let us bless the Lord:)** R̷.

Assisting minister:

**Blessed are you, O Lord, who never cease to reveal the secrets of your power to those who search for you. (Let us bless the Lord:)** R̷.

Assisting minister:

**Blessed are you, O Lord, who urge those who search the mysteries of nature to discover you and to praise you as the author of nature. (Let us bless the Lord:)** R̷.

Assisting minister:

**Blessed are you, O Lord, who chose to reunite in Christ your children whom sin had driven apart and to make them one family throughout the world. (Let us bless the Lord:)** R̷.

Assisting minister:

**Blessed are you, O Lord, who wish the Gospel of the kingdom to be preached to all peoples, so that all might know you, the only true God, and him whom you have sent, Jesus Christ, your Son and our Lord. (Let us bless the Lord:)** R̷.

829    When there are no intercessions, the celebrant, before the prayer of blessing, says:

**Let us pray.**

As circumstances suggest, all may then pray for a moment in silence before the prayer of blessing.

# Prayer of Blessing

830    With hands outstretched, the celebrant says the prayer of blessing.

Lord God almighty,
we humbly praise you,
for you enlighten and inspire
those who by probing the powers implanted in creation
develop the work of your hands in wonderful ways.
Look with favor on your servants
who use the technology discovered by long research.
Enable them to communicate truth,
to foster love, to uphold justice and right,
and to provide enjoyment.
Let them promote and support
that peace between peoples
which Christ the Lord brought from heaven,
for he lives and reigns with you for ever and ever.

℟. Amen.

831    After the prayer of blessing, the celebrant sprinkles those present and the place with holy water, as a suitable song is sung.

## CONCLUDING RITE

832    With hands outstretched over those present, the celebrant concludes the rite by saying:

May God, the Creator of all things,
who never ceases to work his wonders among us
enlighten our minds,
so that we may know him more deeply
and strive always to spread his truth and his peace.

℟. Amen.

Then he blesses all present.

And may almighty God bless you all,
the Father, and the Son, ✝ and the Holy Spirit.

℟. Amen.

833    It is preferable to end the celebration with a suitable song.

CHAPTER 20

# ORDER FOR THE BLESSING OF A GYMNASIUM OR A FIELD FOR ATHLETICS

## INTRODUCTION

834    Physical exercise and athletic contests have as their purpose the health and psychological well-being of the individual as well as friendly relations between people, whatever their status, nationality, or race. The celebration of a blessing may serve to emphasize these aims, whenever a new gymnasium or other sports center is inaugurated, and particularly when the facility is for use by the faithful.

835    The present celebration has reference both to those in whose interest the new facility has been erected and those who will manage or staff it. Therefore the blessing is not to be celebrated without the presence of such persons.

836    The present order may be used by a priest or deacon. While maintaining the structure and chief elements of the rite, the celebrant should adapt the celebration to the circumstances of the place and the people involved.

837    In regions where an annual blessing of centers for athletics is customary during the Easter season or at some other set time, celebration of such a blessing should be arranged by use of the chief elements in this present order.

# ORDER OF BLESSING

## INTRODUCTORY RITES

838   When the community has gathered, a suitable song may be sung. After the singing, the celebrant says:

**In the name of the Father, and of the Son, and of the Holy Spirit.**

All make the sign of the cross and reply:

**Amen.**

839   The celebrant greets those present in the following or other suitable words, taken mainly from sacred Scripture.

**May God, the source and origin of all, from whom every good thing comes to us, be with you all.**

All make the following or some other suitable reply.

**And also with you.**

840   In the following or similar words, the celebrant prepares those present for the blessing.

**God has given us our physical powers in order that we may serve him joyously, help one another, and, by discipline in accord with the law of God, make our body fit for every good work. God therefore approves of recreation for the relaxation of the mind and the exercise of the body. Care of our bodies fosters mental well-being, and we more readily establish friendly and affable relations with other people.**

## READING OF THE WORD OF GOD

841   A reader, another person present, or the celebrant reads a text of sacred Scripture.

**Brothers and sisters, listen to the words of the first letter of Paul to the Corinthians:**      9:24-27

*Run so as to win.*

**Do you not know that the runners in the stadium all run in the race, but only one wins the prize? Run so as to win. Every athlete exercises discipline in every way. They do it to win a perishable crown, but we an imperishable one. Thus I do not run aimlessly; I do not fight as if I were shadowboxing. No, I drive my body and train it, for fear that, after having preached to others, I myself should be disqualified.**

842   Or:

1 Corinthians 3:16-17—*You are the temple of God.*

1 Corinthians 6:19-20—*Glorify God in your body.*

Philippians 3:12-15—*I am racing for the finish.*

843   As circumstances suggest, one of the following responsorial psalms may be sung or said, or some other suitable song.

R̸. **We are his people: the sheep of his flock.**

Psalm 100

**Sing joyfully to the LORD, all you lands;
serve the LORD with gladness;
come before him with joyful song.** R̸.

**Know that the LORD is God,
he made us, his we are;
his people, the flock he tends.** R̸.

**Enter his gates with thanksgiving,
his courts with praise;
Give thanks to him; bless his name.** R̸.

**For he is good:
the LORD, whose kindness endures forever,
and his faithfulness, to all generations.** R̸.

Psalm 148:5-6, 11-13b, 13c-14

R̸. **Heaven and earth are full of your glory.**

844   As circumstances suggest, the celebrant may give those present a brief explanation of the biblical text, so that they may understand through faith the meaning of the celebration.

# INTERCESSIONS

845    As circumstances suggest, the prayer of blessing may be preceded by the intercessions. The celebrant introduces them and an assisting minister or one of those present announces the intentions. From the following intentions those best suited to the occasion may be used or adapted, or other intentions that apply to the particular circumstances may be composed. The intentions are followed immediately by the prayer of blessing, no. 847.

The celebrant says:

**The Lord Jesus, our strength and our joy, calls all human beings to himself, so that all who are weary and find life burdensome may be refreshed by walking in his love. Therefore let us call on him with trust, saying:**

℟. **Lord Jesus, draw us to yourself.**

Assisting minister:

**You are the life of all those you redeemed by your blood.** ℟.

Assisting minister:

**You are the strength of the weak and the prize of the strong.** ℟.

Assisting minister:

**You went about doing good and healing all ills.** ℟.

Assisting minister:

**You sent your Spirit to be the Comforter who sustains us.** ℟.

Assisting minister:

**You have made love for you and for one another the source of true joy.** ℟.

Assisting minister:

**You heed our prayer that our joy may be full.** ℟.

Assisting minister:

**You want us to be of one heart and one mind in you.** ℟.

**846** When there are no intercessions, the celebrant, before the prayer of blessing, says:

**Let us pray.**

As circumstances suggest, all may then pray for a moment in silence before the prayer of blessing.

## Prayer of Blessing

**847** With hands outstretched, the celebrant says the prayer of blessing.

**Lord,**
**we sing your praises without ceasing.**
**You rule over all things with wonderful order,**
**you temper the cares and burdens of our toil,**
**and, by giving us rest and healthy recreation,**
**you refresh our weary bodies and minds.**

**We entreat your kindness,**
**that this place and its facilities**
**will contribute to leisure activities**
**that renew the spirit and strengthen mind and body.**
**Grant that all who meet here may find**
**the enrichment of companionship**
**and together offer you the praise that is your due.**

**We ask this through Christ our Lord.**

**R⁊. Amen.**

**848** After the prayer of blessing, the celebrant sprinkles those present and the site with holy water, as a suitable song is sung.

## Concluding Rite

**849** With hands outstretched over those present, the celebrant concludes the rite by saying:

**May God who brings light to our minds and strength**
**  to our bodies**
**guide us in all we do,**
**so that each day we may find gladness and friendship.**

**R⁊. Amen.**

Then he blesses all present.

**And may almighty God bless you,
the Father, and the Son, ✝ and the Holy Spirit.**

℟. **Amen.**

850    It is preferable to end the celebration with a suitable song.

## CHAPTER 21

# ORDER FOR THE BLESSING OF THE VARIOUS MEANS OF TRANSPORTATION

## INTRODUCTION

851    The quality of life is enhanced by the various means of overcoming distance and of making it possible for people to come together for meetings, visits, and other forms of social contact. These resources for transportation include highways, streets, bridges, railroads, harbors, all types of motor vehicles, ships, and aircraft.

Since all of them require respect for social responsibility, a blessing provides an opportunity to praise God for giving us such benefits and to pray for the safety of those who will use them.

852    The order provided in this chapter may be used on the occasion of the blessing of any means of transportation. Also, with elements provided here a special celebration can be arranged wherever it is the custom on certain fixed days to present automobiles or other means of transportation at a church, in order to ask for a blessing as a pledge of God's protection during travel.

853    The blessing of a highway, bridge, street, or railroad has reference to the community in whose interest it has been provided. Therefore the blessing is not to be celebrated without the presence of the community or at least of its representatives.

854    The present order may be used by a priest or deacon. It may also be used by a layperson, who follows the rites and prayers designated for a lay minister.

855    While maintaining the structure and chief elements of the rite, the minister should adapt the celebration to the circumstances of the place and the people involved.

856    Whenever just one vehicle is to be blessed, the shorter rite provided in nos. 873–877 may be used.

# I. ORDER OF BLESSING

## INTRODUCTORY RITES

857    When the community has gathered, a suitable song may be sung. After the singing, the minister says:

**In the name of the Father, and of the Son, and of the Holy Spirit.**

All make the sign of the cross and reply:

**Amen.**

858    A minister who is a priest or deacon greets those present in the following or other suitable words, taken mainly from sacred Scripture.

**May the Lord Jesus Christ, who is the way, the truth, and the life, be with you all.**

All make the following or some other suitable reply.

**And also with you.**

---

859    A lay minister greets those present in the following words.

**With one heart and one mind let us bless the Lord Jesus Christ, who is the way, the truth, and the life. Blessed be God now and for ever.**

**R̦. Amen.**

---

860    In the following or similar words, the minister prepares those present for the blessing.

**Christ, the Son of God, came into the world to gather those who were scattered. Whatever contributes to bringing us closer together therefore is in accord with God's plan. Thus those who are separated from each other by mountains, oceans, or great distances are brought nearer to each other whenever new highways are built or other means of transportation developed.**

**Let us, then, call on God to bless those who have worked on this project and to protect with his gracious help those who will make use of it.**

861   A reader, another person present, or the minister reads a text of sacred Scripture, which should be chosen for its relevance to the circumstances.

**Brothers and sisters, listen to the words of the holy gospel according to John:**                                                     14:6-7

*I am the way, the truth, and the life.*

**Jesus said to Thomas, "I am the way and the truth and the life. No one comes to the Father except through me. If you know me, then you will also know my Father. From now on you do know him and have seen him."**

862   Or:

**Brothers and sisters, listen to the words of the Acts of the Apostles:**                                                             17:22-28

*In him we live and move and have our being.*

**Then Paul stood up at the Areopagus and said: "You Athenians, I see that in every respect you are very religious. For as I walked around looking carefully at your shrines, I even discovered an altar inscribed, 'To an Unknown God.' What therefore you unknowingly worship, I proclaim to you. The God who made the world and all that is in it, the Lord of heaven and earth, does not dwell in sanctuaries made by human hands, nor is he served by human hands because he needs anything. Rather it is he who gives to everyone life and breath and everything. He made from one the whole human race to dwell on the entire surface of the earth, and he fixed the ordered seasons and the boundaries of their regions, so that people might seek God, even perhaps grope for him and find him, though indeed he is not far from any one of us. For 'In him we live and move and have our being,' as even some of your poets have said, 'For we too are his offspring.'"**

863   Or:

Isaiah 40:1a, 3-5—*The crooked made straight and the rough places plain.*

Acts 8:26-39—*He had come on a pilgrimage to Jerusalem to worship and was returning home. He was sitting on his carriage.*

Mark 4:35-41—*The wind fell off and everything grew calm.*

Luke 3:3-6—*Make ready the way of the Lord.*

John 1:47-51—*You shall see the angels of God ascending and descending.*

John 14:1-7—*I am the way, the truth, and the life.*

**864**    As circumstances suggest, one of the following responsorial psalms may be sung or said, or some other suitable song.

℞. **Guide me, O Lord, in right paths.**

Psalm 23

**The LORD is my shepherd; I shall not want.**
**In verdant pastures he gives me repose;**
**Beside restful waters he leads me;**
**he refreshes my soul. ℞.**

**Even though I walk in the dark valley**
**I fear no evil; for you are at my side**
**With your rod and your staff**
**that give me courage. ℞.**

**You spread the table before me**
**in the sight of my foes;**
**You anoint my head with oil;**
**my cup overflows. ℞.**

**Only goodness and kindness follow me**
**all the days of my life;**
**And I shall dwell in the house of the LORD**
**for years to come. ℞.**

Psalm 25:4-5, 9-10, 12-13

℞. **(v. 2a) My God, I place my trust in you.**

Psalm 150:1-2, 3-4, 5

℞. **(v. 2b) Praise the Lord for his abundant greatness.**

**865**    As circumstances suggest, the minister may give those present a brief explanation of the biblical text, so that they may understand through faith the meaning of the celebration.

# INTERCESSIONS

866    As circumstances suggest, the prayer of blessing may be
preceded by the intercessions. The minister introduces them and
an assisting minister or one of those present announces the intentions. From the following intentions those best suited to the
occasion may be used or adapted, or other intentions that apply
to the particular circumstances may be composed. The intentions
are followed immediately by the prayer of blessing, no. 868.

The minister says:

**Let us join together in prayer to the Lord Jesus Christ, who
is the way for us to reach our eternal homeland, saying:**

R∕. **Guide our steps along your way, O Lord.**

Or:

R∕. **Lord, hear our prayer.**

Assisting minister:

**Lord Jesus, you became one of us and willed to live like us;
grant that with you always at our side, we may walk gladly
along the paths of your love. (For this we pray:)** R∕.

Assisting minister:

**Lord Jesus, you went from town to town preaching your Gospel
and healing the sick; may you still pass along our streets and
highways and with your compassion give us strength. (For this
we pray:)** R∕.

Assisting minister:

**Lord Jesus, when your disciples were on the waters of the lake,
you were there to rescue them from every peril; be with us amid
the storms of this world. (For this we pray:)** R∕.

Assisting minister:

**Lord Jesus, you became a companion to your disciples on the
road to Emmaus; bless us on our journeys and warm our hearts
by your words. (For this we pray:)** R∕.

**Lord Jesus, when you ascended into heaven, you showed the way for us; bear us up in our earthly pilgrimage, so that we may have a dwelling place in your Father's house. (For this we pray:) ℟.**

Assisting minister:

**Lord Jesus, you gave us to your Mother to be her children; through her intercession make our journey safe, so that some day we may see you and for ever rejoice with you. (For this we pray:) ℟.**

867    When there are no intercessions, the minister, before the prayer, says:

**Let us pray.**

As circumstances suggest, all may then pray for a moment in silence before the prayer of blessing.

## Prayer of Blessing

868    A minister who is a priest or deacon says the prayer of blessing with hands outstretched; a lay minister says the prayer with hands joined.

A          Blessing of a bridge, highway, street, railway, or airport

**O God,
you are never far off
from those who serve you;
with fatherly protection you always guard
those who trust in you.
By your grace be the guide
going before those who use this
   (bridge, highway, street, railway, airport)
and be the companion to sustain them on their way.
By your favor protect them from adversity,
so that they may arrive safely at their destination
and accomplish what they set out to do.**

**We ask this through Christ our Lord.**

**℟. Amen.**

B       Blessing of a bridge, highway, street, railway, or airport

**O God of boundless mercy and majesty,**
**neither distance nor time separates you from those**
   **you watch over.**
**In every place stay close to your servants who trust in you,**
**and wherever they go**
**be their leader and companion.**
**Let no adversity harm them**
**nor any obstacle hinder them on their way.**
**Make all things work for their well-being and true benefit,**
**so that whatever they rightly desire**
**they may successfully achieve.**

**We ask this through Christ our Lord.**

**R⁊. Amen.**

C       Blessing of a motor vehicle

**All-powerful God,**
**Creator of heaven and earth,**
**in the rich depths of your wisdom**
**you have empowered us to produce great and beautiful works.**
**Grant, we pray, that those who use this vehicle**
**may travel safely, with care for the safety of others.**
**Whether they travel for business or pleasure,**
**let them always find Christ to be the companion**
   **of their journey,**
**who lives and reigns for ever and ever.**

**R⁊. Amen.**

D       Blessing of an airplane

**Lord our God,**
**you make the clouds your chariot and walk on the wings**
   **of the wind.**
**Grant that this airplane,**
**built by human skill and talent,**
**may make its flights in calm weather.**
**Keep those who travel on it unharmed**
**and bring them safely to their destination.**

**We ask this through Christ our Lord.**

**R⁊. Amen.**

E        Blessing of an airplane

**Lord our God,**
**you walk on the wings of the wind**
**and the heavens declare your glory.**
**We bless you and proclaim your greatness in all your works.**
**In the richness of your wisdom**
**you have empowered us to create great and beautiful works.**
**Grant, we pray, that this airplane will serve to spread**
    **your praises**
**and contribute to the well-being of those who fly in it.**
**Through your blessing may its pilots and crew**
**operate it with prudence,**
**so that its passengers may reach their destination**
    **happily and safely.**

**We ask this through Christ our Lord.**

℟. **Amen.**

F        Blessing of a boat

**Listen kindly to our prayers, O Lord,**
**as we ask that you turn aside every unfavorable wind**
    **from this boat**
**and by your unsurpassed power calm the seas around it.**
**Under your protection let those who sail it**
**realize their just desires and arrive safely in harbor.**

**We ask this through Christ our Lord.**

℟. **Amen.**

G        Blessing of a ship

**O God,**
**you pilot your Church through the stormy seas of this world.**
**Prosper the voyages of this vessel**
**and all who go down to the seas in it.**
**Grant that those who sail in this ship**
**may have you as their steersman,**
**so that they may be blessed with all good things**
**and some day reach the safe and joyous harbor of eternity.**

**We ask this through Christ our Lord.**

℟. **Amen.**

869    As circumstances suggest, after the prayer of blessing, the
minister may sprinkle those present and the site or the vehicle
blessed with holy water, as a suitable song is sung.

## CONCLUDING RITE

870    A minister who is a priest or deacon concludes the rite by
saying:

**May the Lord be the guide on your journeys,
so that you may travel in peace and reach eternal life.**

**R̷. Amen.**

Then he blesses all present.

**And may almighty God bless you,
the Father, and the Son, ✝ and the Holy Spirit.**

**R̷. Amen.**

871    A lay minister concludes the rite by saying:

**May the Lord be the guide on our journeys,
so that we may travel in peace and reach eternal life.**

**R̷. Amen.**

872    It is preferable to end the celebration with a suitable song.

# II. SHORTER RITE

873    At the beginning of the celebration, the minister says:
**Our help is in the name of the Lord.**

All reply:
**Who made heaven and earth.**

**874** One of those present or the minister reads a short text from sacred Scripture, for example:

John 14:6

**Jesus said to Thomas, "I am the way and the truth and the life. No one comes to the Father except through me."**

Matthew 22:37a, 39b-40

**He said to the Pharisee: "You shall love the Lord, your God, with all your heart. You shall love your neighbor as yourself. The whole law and the prophets depend on these two commandments."**

**875** A minister who is a priest or deacon says the prayer of blessing with hands outstretched; a lay minister says the prayer with hands joined.

**All-powerful God,**
**Creator of heaven and earth,**
**in the rich depths of your wisdom**
**you have empowered us to produce great and beautiful works.**
**Grant, we pray, that those who use this vehicle**
**may travel safely, with care for the safety of others.**
**Whether they travel for business or pleasure,**
**let them always find Christ to be the companion**
**of their journey,**
**who lives and reigns with you for ever and ever.**

℞. **Amen.**

**876** Or, for a boat:

**Listen kindly to our prayers, O Lord,**
**as we ask that you turn aside every unfavorable wind**
**from this boat**
**and by your unsurpassed power calm the seas around it.**
**Under your protection let those who sail it**
**realize their just desires and arrive safely in harbor.**

**We ask this through Christ our Lord.**

℞. **Amen.**

**877** As circumstances suggest, the minister may sprinkle those present and the vehicle with holy water.

# CHAPTER 22

# ORDER FOR THE BLESSING OF BOATS AND FISHING GEAR

USA

## INTRODUCTION

878    Boats are an important means of transportation and are essential to the livelihood of fishermen. It is customary that God's blessing be sought for the protection of those who sail them.

879    This order may be used for the blessing of boats, fishing fleets, and fishing gear.

880    These orders may be used by a priest or a deacon, and also by a layperson, who follows the rites and prayers designated for a lay minister.

# I. ORDER OF BLESSING

## INTRODUCTORY RITES

881 When the community has gathered, a suitable song may be sung.

The minister says:

**In the name of the Father, and of the Son, and of the Holy Spirit.**

All make the sign of the cross and reply:

**Amen.**

882 A minister who is a priest or deacon greets those present in the following or other suitable words, taken mainly from sacred Scripture.

**The grace and peace of God our Father and the Lord Jesus Christ be with you.**

And all reply:

**And also with you.**

---

883 A lay minister greets those present in the following words:

**Let us praise and glorify God the Father and the Lord Jesus Christ, now and for ever.**

R̸. **Amen.**

---

884 In the following or similar words, the minister prepares those present for the blessing.

**Today we gather to bless this boat (this fishing equipment) and those who will use it for work or pleasure. The Lord calmed the Sea of Galilee and brought his disciples to safety. We commend those who sail this craft into his care.**

## READING OF THE WORD OF GOD

885 A reader, another person present, or the minister reads a text of sacred Scripture.

**Brothers and sisters, listen to the words of the holy gospel according to Matthew:** 8:23-27

*Jesus calms the storm.*

**Jesus got into a boat and his disciples followed him. Suddenly a violent storm came up on the sea, so that the boat was being swamped by waves; but Jesus was asleep. The disciples came and woke him, saying, "Lord, save us! We are perishing!" Jesus said to them, "Why are you terrified, O you of little faith?" Then he got up, rebuked the winds and the sea, and there was great calm. The men were amazed and said, "What sort of man is this, whom even the winds and the sea obey?"**

886    Or:

Genesis 1:26-28, 31a—*God gives us dominion over the fish of the sea.*

Matthew 4:18-22—*Call of the first disciples.*

Matthew 14:22-33—*Jesus walks on the water.*

Mark 6:45-51a—*Jesus walks on the water.*

Luke 5:1-11—*The call of the disciples.*

John 21:1-24—*Appearance of Jesus at the Sea of Tiberias.*

887    As circumstances suggest, one of the following responsorial psalms may be sung, or some other suitable song.

R̷. **O Lord, our God, how wonderful your name in all the earth!**

Psalm 8

**O LORD, our Lord,
how glorious is your name over all the earth!
You have exalted your majesty above the heavens.** R̷.

**When I behold your heavens, the work of your fingers,
the moon and the stars which you set in place—** R̷.

**What is man that you should be mindful of him,
or the son of man that you should care for him?** R̷.

**You have given him rule over the works of your hands,
putting all things under his feet:** R̷.

**All sheep and oxen,
yes, and the beasts of the field,** R̷.

**The birds of the air, the fishes of the sea,
and whatever swims the paths of the seas.** R̷.

Psalm 148:1, 2, 3, 4, 5, 6

℟. (v. 13) **Praise the name of the Lord, whose name alone is exalted.**

**888**    As circumstances suggest, the minister may give those present a brief explanation of the biblical text, so that they may understand through faith the meaning of the celebration.

## LITANY

**889**    The litany is then said. The minister introduces the invocations and an assisting minister or one of those present announces them. From the following those best suited to the occasion may be used or adapted, or other invocations that apply to the particular circumstances may be composed.

The minister says:

**At the command of the Son of God the sea was calmed and the nets were filled to overflowing. Let us call upon Christ with faith:**

℟. **Guide us safely, Lord.**

Assisting minister:

**In the face of wind and rain, we pray:** ℟.

Assisting minister:

**In the stillness and calm of the sea, we pray:** ℟.

Assisting minister:

**In our respect for the world's natural resources, we pray:** ℟.

Assisting minister:

**In remembrance of those who labored at sea and have gone to their rest, we pray:** ℟.

**890**    After the litany the minister, in the following or similar words, invites all present to sing or say the Lord's Prayer.

**Christ taught us to call upon the Father, and so we pray:**

All:

**Our Father . . .**

## PRAYER OF BLESSING

891   A minister who is a priest or deacon says the prayer of blessing with hands outstretched; a lay minister says the prayer with hands joined.

**God of boundless love,
at the beginning of creation
your Spirit hovered over the deep.
You called forth every creature,
and the seas teemed with life.**

**Through your Son, Jesus Christ,
you have given us the rich harvest of salvation.**

**Bless this boat, its equipment and all who will use it.
Protect them from the dangers of wind and rain
and all the perils of the deep.
May Christ, who calmed the storm
and filled the nets of his disciples,
bring us all to the harbor of light and peace.**

**Grant this through Christ our Lord.**

℟. **Amen.**

## CONCLUDING RITE

892   A minister who is a priest or deacon concludes the rite by saying:

**May the saving power of our Lord guide and protect you, now and for ever.**

℟. **Amen.**

Then he blesses all present.

**And may almighty God bless you all,
the Father, and the Son, ✝ and the Holy Spirit.**

℟. **Amen.**

893　　A lay minister concludes the rite by signing himself or herself with the sign of the cross and saying:

**May the saving power of our Lord guide and protect us, now and for ever.**

℟. **Amen.**

894　　It is preferable to end the celebration with a suitable song.

# II. SHORTER RITE

895　　All make the sign of the cross as the minister says:

**Blessed be the name of the Lord.**

All reply:

**Now and for ever.**

896　　One of those present or the minister reads a text of sacred Scripture, for example:

**Brothers and sisters, listen to the words of the holy gospel according to Matthew:**　　　　　　　　　　　　　8:23-27

*Jesus calms the storm.*

**Jesus got into a boat and his disciples followed him. Suddenly a violent storm came up on the sea, so that the boat was being swamped by waves; but Jesus was asleep. The disciples came and woke him, saying, "Lord, save us! We are perishing!" Jesus said to them, "Why are you terrified, O you of little faith?" Then he got up, rebuked the winds and the sea, and there was great calm. The men were amazed and said, "What sort of man is this, whom even the winds and the sea obey?"**

897　　Or:

Genesis 1:26-28, 31a—*God gives us dominion over the fish of the sea.*

Matthew 4:18-22—*Call of the first disciples.*

Matthew 14:22-33—*Jesus walks on the water.*

Mark 6:45-51a—*Jesus walks on the water.*

Luke 5:1-11—*The call of the disciples.*

John 21:1-24—*Appearance of Jesus at the Sea of Tiberias.*

898 A minister who is a priest or deacon says the prayer of blessing with hands outstretched; a lay minister says the prayer with hands joined.

**God of boundless love,**
**at the beginning of creation**
**your Spirit hovered over the deep.**
**You called forth every creature,**
**and the seas teemed with life.**

**Through your Son, Jesus Christ,**
**you have given us the rich harvest of salvation.**

**Bless this boat, its equipment and all who will use it.**
**Protect them from the dangers of wind and rain**
**and all the perils of the deep.**
**May Christ, who calmed the storm**
**and filled the nets of his disciples,**
**bring us all to the harbor of light and peace.**

**Grant this through Christ our Lord.**

℟. **Amen.**

# CHAPTER 23

# ORDER FOR THE BLESSING OF TECHNICAL INSTALLATIONS OR EQUIPMENT

## INTRODUCTION

899    Through labor and intelligence, and especially by using science and technology, the human race continually extends its mastery over nature, with resultant benefits that improve human life for both individuals and peoples. The inauguration therefore of technical installations or equipment is an opportune occasion for the celebration of a blessing, in order to make it clear that the message of the Gospel is not inimical to the building up of this world.[8]

900    The order of blessing provided here has reference to the community in whose interest the technical equipment or installation (for example, a central energy source or power house, a reservoir or water system, a seismograph) has been established and to the managers and staff. Therefore the blessing is not to be celebrated without the presence at least of representatives of such groups.

901    The present order may be used by a priest or deacon. It may also be used by a layperson, who follows the rites and prayers designated for a lay minister.

902    While maintaining the structure and chief elements of the rite, the minister should adapt the celebration to the circumstances of the place and the people involved.

---

[8] See Vatican Council II, Pastoral Constitution on the Church in the Modern World *Gaudium et spes*, nos. 33–34.

# ORDER OF BLESSING

## Introductory Rites

903    When the community has gathered, a suitable song may
be sung. After the singing, the minister says:

**In the name of the Father, and of the Son, and of the Holy
Spirit.**

All make the sign of the cross and reply:

**Amen.**

904    A minister who is a priest or deacon greets those present
in the following or other suitable words, taken mainly from sacred
Scripture.

**May God, who has set us over the works of his hands, be with
you all.**

All make the following or some other suitable reply.

**And also with you.**

---

905    A lay minister greets those present in the following words.

**Let us give praise to God, who has set us over the works of
his hands. Blessed be God now and for ever.**

R̷. **Amen.**

---

906    In the following or similar words, the minister prepares
those present for the blessing.

**Through the work of our hands and the help of technology
we cooperate with the Creator to improve the earth as the dwelling place of the human family. By our efforts to bring the work
of creation to perfection, we contribute to the advancement of
society and carry out Christ's mandate to follow him in serving one another in love. Let us, then, bless God as we use these
products of technology for our advantage and never forget to
offer praise to him, who is the true light and the fount of that
water which springs up to eternal life.**

# Reading of the Word of God

907    A reader, another person present, or the minister reads a text of sacred Scripture.

**Brothers and sisters, listen to the words of the book of Genesis:**
1:1-5a, 14-18

*God said: Let there be light, and there was light.*

**In the beginning, when God created the heavens and the earth, the earth was a formless wasteland, and darkness covered the abyss, while a mighty wind swept over the waters. Then God said, "Let there be light," and there was light. God saw how good the light was. God then separated the light from the darkness. God called the light "day," and the darkness he called "night."**

**Then God said: "Let there be lights in the dome of the sky, to separate day from night. Let them mark the fixed times, the days and the years, and serve as luminaries in the dome of the sky, to shed light upon the earth." And so it happened: God made the two great lights, the greater one to govern the day, and the lesser one to govern the night; and he made the stars. God set them in the dome of the sky, to shed light upon the earth, to govern the day and the night, and to separate the light from the darkness. God saw how good it was.**

908    Or:

**Brothers and sisters, listen to the words of the holy gospel according to John:**
4:5-14

*Whoever drinks the water I give will never be thirsty.*

**Jesus came to a town of Samaria called Sychar, near the plot of land that Jacob had given to his son Joseph. Jacob's well was there. Jesus, tired from his journey, sat down there at the well. It was about noon.**

**A woman of Samaria came to draw water. Jesus said to her, "Give me a drink." His disciples had gone into the town to buy food. The Samaritan woman said to him, "How can you, a Jew, ask me, a Samaritan woman, for a drink?" (For Jews use nothing in common with Samaritans.) Jesus answered and said to her, "If you knew the gift of God and who is saying to you, 'Give me a drink,' you would have asked him and he**

would have given you living water." The woman said to him, "Sir, you do not even have a bucket and the cistern is deep; where then can you get this living water? Are you greater than our father Jacob, who gave us this cistern and drank from it himself with his children and his flocks?" Jesus answered and said to her, "Everyone who drinks this water will be thirsty again; but whoever drinks the water I shall give will never thirst; the water I shall give will become in him a spring of water welling up to eternal life."

909    Or:

Numbers 20:2-11—*Water gushed out in abundance.*

Isaiah 55:1-11—*All you who are thirsty, come to the water.*

Sirach 17:1-6 (Greek, 17:1-7)—*He gave them authority over everything on earth.*

910    As circumstances suggest, one of the following responsorial psalms may be sung or said, or some other suitable song.

R̸. **My God, you are always there to help me; I place my trust in you.**

Psalm 18

**And he made darkness the cloak about him;
dark, misty rain-clouds his wrap.
From the brightness of his presence
coals were kindled to flame.** R̸.

**And the LORD thundered from heaven,
the Most High gave forth his voice;
He sent forth his arrows to put them to flight,
with frequent lightnings he routed them.** R̸.

**Then the bed of the sea appeared,
and the foundations of the world were laid bare,
At the rebuke of the LORD,
at the blast of the wind of his wrath.** R̸.

**He reached out from on high and grasped me;
he drew me out of the deep waters.
He set me free in the open,
and he rescued me, because he loves me.** R̸.

Psalm 29:1-2, 3-4, 7-9, 10-11

℟. (v. 2) **Give to the Lord the glory due his name.**

Psalm 148:1-2, 3-4, 5-6

℟. (v. 13c) **His glory is above earth and heaven.**

**911**  As circumstances suggest, the minister may give those present a brief explanation of the biblical text, so that they may understand through faith the meaning of the celebration.

# INTERCESSIONS

**912**  As circumstances suggest, the prayer of blessing may be preceded by the intercessions. The minister introduces them and an assisting minister or one of those present announces the intentions. From the following intentions those best suited to the occasion may be used or adapted, or other intentions that apply to the particular circumstances may be composed. The intentions are followed immediately by the prayer of blessing, no. 914.

The minister says:

**In human works and the inventions of human genius we must recognize the continuing activity of God the Creator. Rightly, then, we offer praise to God with grateful hearts and call on him with confidence, saying:**

℟. **Lord, sustain the work of our hands.**

Or:

℟. **Lord, hear our prayer.**

Assisting minister:

**Eternal God, you made all things good and gave them into our care; grant that we may use the forces of nature wisely for your glory and our own well-being. (For this we pray:)** ℟.

Assisting minister:

**You continually give us your Holy Spirit; grant that we may cooperate with the same Spirit for the renewal of the face of the earth, not merely through technology but through justice and charity. (For this we pray:)** ℟.

Assisting minister:

**You know what lies in our hearts; grant that a desire for what is right and good will guide the use of scientific knowledge. (For this we pray:)** ℟.

Assisting minister:

**Your wish is that all should call you Father; grant that those people who suffer discrimination may be helped by all of us to gain the rights and advantages that belong to every human being. (For this we pray:)** ℟.

913 When there are no intercessions, the minister, before the prayer of blessing, says:

**Let us pray.**

As circumstances suggest, all may then pray for a moment in silence before the prayer of blessing.

## PRAYER OF BLESSING

914 A minister who is a priest or deacon says the prayer of blessing with hands outstretched; a lay minister says the prayer with hands joined.

A Blessing of any kind of technical equipment

**Blessed are you, Lord our God,
and worthy of all praise,
for you have provided for the perfecting of your creation
through human labor and intelligence,
and you show your own power and goodness
in the inventions of the human race.
Grant that all those who will use this equipment
  to improve their lives
may recognize that you are wonderful in your works
and may learn to carry out your will more readily.**

**We ask this through Christ our Lord.**

**℟. Amen.**

B       Blessing of a central energy source or power house

**Lord God,**
**all-powerful Creator of light,**
**source and origin of us all,**
**look with kindness upon your servants**
**who will use this equipment to produce (electricity,**
    **atomic power).**

**Grant that by continuing to seek your face**
**they may, after the darkness of this world,**
**find you, the unfailing light,**
**in whom we live and move and have our being.**

**We ask this through Christ our Lord.**

℞. **Amen.**

C       Blessing of a reservoir or water system

**Blessed are you, Lord our God,**
**and worthy of all praise,**
**for you have provided for the perfecting of your creation**
**through human labor and intelligence,**
**and you show your own power and goodness**
**in the inventions of the human race.**

**Grant that all those who will use this supply of water**
    **for their needs**
**may recognize that you are their living fountain,**
**the source of the water that springs up to eternal life.**

**We ask this through Christ our Lord.**

℞. **Amen.**

915     After the prayer of blessing, the new equipment is turned on for the first time and a suitable song may be sung.

## CONCLUDING RITE

916     A minister who is a priest or deacon concludes the rite by saying:

**May God, from whom every good gift comes,
make his countenance to shine upon you
and guide you into the way of peace,
now and for ever.**

℟. **Amen.**

Then he blesses all present.

**And may almighty God bless you,
the Father, and the Son, ✝ and the Holy Spirit.**

℟. **Amen.**

917    A lay minister concludes the rite by signing himself or herself with the sign of the cross and saying:

**May God, from whom every good gift comes,
make his countenance to shine upon us
and guide us into the way of peace,
now and for ever.**

℟. **Amen.**

918    It is preferable to end the celebration with a suitable song.

## CHAPTER 24

# ORDER FOR THE BLESSING OF TOOLS OR OTHER EQUIPMENT FOR WORK

## INTRODUCTION

919    It is appropriate to bless tools or even larger implements or equipment (for example, trucks, tractors, fishing boats) that people use in their work. Such a blessing enables us to realize that our work forms a bond and a channel of mutual service and charity between the members of the human family; that by our labor we can share in the work of perfecting God's creation. Such a blessing may be celebrated on special occasions, for example, the feast of Saint Joseph the Worker or a patron saint, or during a convention of workers, who gather and present the tools of their trade to be blessed.

920    The celebration of this blessing has reference not so much to the objects but to the people who will use them in their work. Therefore the blessing is not to be celebrated without their presence or at least the presence of representatives.

921    The present order may be used by a priest or deacon. It may also be used by a layperson, who follows the rites and prayers designated for a lay minister.

922    While maintaining the structure and chief elements of the rite, the minister should adapt the celebration to the circumstances of the place and the people involved.

923    Whenever just a single tool or piece of equipment is to be blessed, the shorter rite provided in nos. 939–941 may be used.

# I. ORDER OF BLESSING

## INTRODUCTORY RITES

924   When the community has gathered, a suitable song may be sung. After the singing, the minister says:

**In the name of the Father, and of the Son, and of the Holy Spirit.**

All make the sign of the cross and reply:

**Amen.**

925   A minister who is a priest or deacon greets those present in the following or other suitable words, taken mainly from sacred Scripture.

**May Christ, the Son of God, who was pleased to be known as the carpenter's son, be with you all.**

All make the following or some other suitable reply.

**And also with you.**

---

926   A lay minister greets those present in the following words.

**With glad hearts let us praise and bless Christ, the Son of God, who was pleased to be known as the carpenter's son. Praised be the Lord now and for ever.**

**℟. Amen.**

---

927   In the following or similar words, the minister prepares those present for the blessing.

**God commanded us to inhabit the earth and care for it, until a new heaven and a new earth come to be. As Saint Paul said: "All these things are yours, and you are Christ's, and Christ is God's" (1 Corinthians 3:22-23). To accomplish God's purpose, we use suitable tools and so in some way cooperate with him and share in the good of redemption. Let us therefore bless God from our hearts for his wonderful plan and pray that his help will protect and sustain us as we work.**

# READING OF THE WORD OF GOD

**928**   A reader, another person present, or the minister reads a text of sacred Scripture.

**Brothers and sisters, listen to the words of the first letter of Paul to the Thessalonians:**                     4:9, 10b-12

*Work with your hands.*

**On the subject of mutual charity you have no need for anyone to write you, for you yourselves have been taught by God to love one another. Nevertheless we urge you, brothers and sisters, to progress even more, and to aspire to live a tranquil life, to mind your own affairs, and to work with your own hands, as we instructed you, that you may conduct yourselves properly toward outsiders and not depend on anyone.**

**929**   Or:

Exodus 35:30—36:1—*God filled them with the skill and perception to carry out all that was required.*

Job 28:1-28—*Iron is extracted from the earth; the smelted rocks yield copper.*

Proverbs 31:10-31—*She sets her hands to the distaff, her fingers grasp the spindle.*

Sirach 38:25-39 (Greek, 38:24-34)—*They are skilled at their own crafts.*

Isaiah 28:23-29—*Does the plowman do nothing but plow and turn the soil and harrow it?*

Acts 18:1-5—*Paul was a tentmaker and worked at his trade.*

Matthew 13:1-9—*A sower went out to sow.*

Luke 5:3-11—*If you say so, I will lower the nets.*

**930**   As circumstances suggest, one of the following responsorial psalms may be sung or said, or some other suitable song.

℞. **You answer us, O God our Savior.**

Psalm 65

**You have visited the land and watered it;
greatly have you enriched it.
God's watercourses are filled;
you have prepared the grain.** ℞.

Thus have you prepared the land:
drenching its furrows,
breaking up its clods,
Softening it with showers,
blessing its yield.
You have crowned the year with your bounty,
and your paths overflow with a rich harvest. ℟.

The untilled meadows overflow with it,
and rejoicing clothes the hills.
The fields are garmented with flocks
and the valleys blanketed with grain.
They shout and sing for joy. ℟.

Psalm 90:2, 3-4, 12-13, 14 and 16

℟. (v. 17c) **Lord, give success to the work of our hands.**

Psalm 107:35-36, 37-38, 41-42

℟. (v. 1b) **Give thanks to the Lord, for he is good.**

Psalm 127:1, 2

℟. (see v. 1) **May the Lord build our house and guard our city.**

931    As circumstances suggest, the minister may give those present a brief explanation of the biblical text, so that they may understand through faith the meaning of the celebration.

## INTERCESSIONS

932    As circumstances suggest, the prayer of blessing may be preceded by the intercessions. The minister introduces them and an assisting minister or one of those present announces the intentions. From the following intentions those best suited to the occasion may be used or adapted, or other intentions that apply to the particular circumstances may be composed. The intentions are followed immediately by the prayer of blessing, no. 934 or no. 935.

The minister says:

**God put us into the world to perfect and preserve it. He continually inspires us to apply our talents and efforts to the progress of creation. Let us together, then, praise God, saying:**

R7. **Blessed are you, O Lord, Creator of the universe.**

Or:

R7. **Blessed be God for ever.**

Assisting minister:

**In commanding us to work, you entrust us with building up the world you created. (Let us bless the Lord:) R7.**

Assisting minister:

**In entrusting to us the dignity of work, you make us your own co-workers in the world. (Let us bless the Lord:) R7.**

Assisting minister:

**You continually enlighten us with the vision to build new things that glorify your name and make all the earth resound with your praises. (Let us bless the Lord:) R7.**

Assisting minister:

**You sent your Son into the world to be for us a model of untiring toil, as he sanctified and exalted manual labor by the sweat of his own brow. (Let us bless the Lord:) R7.**

Assisting minister:

**You direct all our actions by your holy inspiration and you carry them on with your gracious help. (Let us bless the Lord:) R7.**

**933**   When there are no intercessions, the minister, before the prayer of blessing, says:

**Let us pray.**

As circumstances suggest, all may then pray for a moment in silence before the prayer of blessing.

## PRAYER OF BLESSING

**934**   A minister who is a priest or deacon says the prayer of blessing with hands outstretched; a lay minister says the prayer with hands joined.

O God,
the fullness of blessing comes down from you,
to you our prayers of blessing rise up.
In your kindness protect your servants,
who stand before you devout and faithful,
bearing the tools of their trade.

Grant that their hard work may contribute
to the perfecting of your creation
and provide a decent life for themselves and their families.
Help them to strive for a better society
and to praise and glorify your holy name always.

We ask this through Christ our Lord.

R̶. Amen.

935     Or:

In your loving providence, O God,
you have made the forces of nature
subject to the work of our hands.
Grant that by devotion to our own work
we may gladly cooperate with you
in the building up of creation.

We ask this through Christ our Lord.

R̶. Amen.

936     As circumstances suggest, after the prayer of blessing, the
minister may sprinkle those present and the implements with
holy water.


## Concluding Rite

937     The minister concludes the rite by saying:

May Christ the Lord,
who for our salvation took on the burden of human toil,
continue now to strengthen us with his help
and give us his peace,
now and for ever.

R̶. Amen.

938     It is preferable to end the celebration with a suitable song.

# II. SHORTER RITE

**939**   At the beginning of the celebration, the minister says:

**Our help is in the name of the Lord.**

All reply:

**Who made heaven and earth.**

**940**   One of those present or the minister reads a short text of sacred Scripture, for example:

Sirach 38:31 and 34

**All these men are skilled with their hands,**
**each one an expert at his own task;**
**Yet they maintain God's ancient handiwork,**
**and their concern is for exercise of their skill.**

2 Thessalonians 3:7-8

**For you know how one must imitate us. For we did not act in a disorderly way among you, nor did we eat food received free from anyone. On the contrary, in toil and drudgery, night and day we worked, so as not to burden any of you.**

**941**   With hands joined, the minister says the prayer of blessing. After the prayer of blessing, as circumstances suggest, the minister may sprinkle those present and the implements with holy water.

**In your loving providence, O God,**
**you have made the forces of nature**
**subject to the work of our hands.**
**Grant that by devotion to our own work**
**we may gladly cooperate with you**
**in the building up of creation.**

**We ask this through Christ our Lord.**

℟. **Amen.**

## CHAPTER 25

# ORDER FOR THE BLESSING OF ANIMALS

### INTRODUCTION

942    According to the providence of the Creator, many animals have a certain role to play in human existence by helping with work or providing food and clothing. Thus when the occasion arises, for example, the feast of some saint, the custom of invoking God's blessing on animals may be continued.

943    The present order may be used by a priest or deacon. It may also be used by a layperson, who follows the rites and prayers designated for a lay minister.

944    While maintaining the structure and chief elements of the rite, the minister should adapt the celebration to the circumstances of the place and the people involved.

945    Whenever just one or a few animals are to be blessed or the blessing of animals is to be included in some other celebration, the shorter rite provided in nos. 962–965 may be used.

# I. ORDER OF BLESSING

## INTRODUCTORY RITES

946    When the community has gathered, a suitable song may be sung. After the singing, the minister says:

**In the name of the Father, and of the Son, and of the Holy Spirit.**

All make the sign of the cross and reply:

**Amen.**

947    A minister who is a priest or deacon greets those present in the following or other suitable words, taken mainly from sacred Scripture.

**May God, who is wonderful in all his works, be with you all.**

All make the following or some other suitable reply.

**And also with you.**

---

948    A lay minister greets those present in the following words.

**God has done all things wisely, let us praise his name, now and for ever.**

℟. **Amen.**

---

949    In the following or similar words, the minister prepares those present for the blessing.

**The animals of God's creation inhabit the skies, the earth, and the sea. They share in the fortunes of human existence and have a part in human life. God, who confers his gifts on all living things, has often used the service of animals or made them symbolic reminders of the gifts of salvation. Animals were saved from the flood and afterwards made a part of the covenant with Noah (Genesis 9:9-10). The paschal lamb brings to mind the passover sacrifice and the deliverance from the bondage of Egypt (Exodus 12:3-14); a giant fish saved Jonah (Jonah 2:1-11); ravens brought bread to Elijah (1 Kings 17:6); animals were included in the repentance enjoined on humans (Jonah 3:7).**

And animals share in Christ's redemption of all of God's creation. We therefore invoke the divine blessing on these animals (through the intercession of Saint N.). As we do so, let us praise the Creator and thank him for setting us over other creatures of the earth. Let us also ask him that, remembering our human dignity, we may walk always in his law.

## READING OF THE WORD OF GOD

950    A reader, another person present, or the minister reads a text of sacred Scripture.

**Brothers and sisters, listen to the words of the book of Genesis:**
1:1, 20-28

*Have dominion over all living things that move on the earth.*

In the beginning, when God created the heavens and the earth, God said, "Let the water teem with an abundance of living creatures, and on the earth let birds fly beneath the dome of the sky." And so it happened: God created the great sea monsters and all kinds of swimming creatures with which the water teems, and all kinds of winged birds. God saw how good it was and God blessed them, saying, "Be fertile, multiply, and fill the water of the seas; and let the birds multiply on the earth." Evening came, and morning followed—the fifth day.

Then God said, "Let the earth bring forth all kinds of living creatures: cattle, creeping things, and wild animals of all kinds." And so it happened: God made all kinds of wild animals, all kinds of cattle, and all kinds of creeping things of the earth. God saw how good it was. Then God said, "Let us make man in our image, after our likeness. Let them have dominion over the fish of the sea, the birds of the air, and the cattle, and over all the wild animals and all the creatures that crawl on the ground."

God created man in his image;
in the divine image he created him;
male and female he created them.

God blessed them, saying: "Be fertile and multiply; fill the earth and subdue it. Have dominion over the fish of the sea, the birds of the air, and all the living things that move on the earth."

951   Or:

**Brothers and sisters, listen to the words of the book of Genesis:**

2:19-20a

*The man gave names to all the animals.*

**So the LORD God formed out of the ground various wild animals and various birds of the air, and he brought them to the man to see what he would call them; whatever the man called each of them would be its name. The man gave names to all the cattle, all the birds of the air, and all the wild animals.**

952   Or:

*Genesis 6:17-23—Of all other living creatures you shall bring two into the ark to live there with you.*

*Isaiah 11:6-10—Animals will be tame and there shall be no harm or ruin on all my holy mountain.*

953   As circumstances suggest, one of the following responsorial psalms may be sung or said, or some other suitable song.

R̠. **O Lord, our God, how wonderful your name in all the earth!**

Psalm 8

**O LORD, our Lord,**
**how glorious is your name over all the earth!**
**You have exalted your majesty above the heavens.** R̠.

**When I behold your heavens, the work of your fingers,**
**the moon and the stars which you set in place—**
**What is man that you should be mindful of him**
**or the son of man that you should care for him?** R̠.

**You have given him rule over the works of your hands,**
**putting all things under his feet:**
**All sheep and oxen,**
**yes, and beasts of the field,**
**The birds of the air, the fishes of the sea,**
**and whatever swims the paths of the seas.** R̠.

Psalm 104:1-2a, 10-12, 25, 27-28

R̠. **(v. 27) All look to you to give them their food in due season.**

Psalm 147:5-6, 7-8, 9-11

R℣. (v. 1a) **O praise the Lord! How good to sing praise to our God.**

**954** As circumstances suggest, the minister may give those present a brief explanation of the biblical text, so that they may understand through faith the meaning of the celebration.

## INTERCESSIONS

**955** As circumstances suggest, the prayer of blessing may be preceded by the intercessions. The minister introduces them and an assisting minister or one of those present announces the intentions. From the following intentions those best suited to the occasion may be used or adapted, or other intentions that apply to the particular circumstances may be composed. The intentions are followed immediately by the prayer of blessing, no. 957 or no. 958.

The minister says:

**God created us and placed us on this earth to be the stewards of all living things and so to proclaim the glory of their Creator. Let us, then, praise God, saying:**

R℣. **How wonderful are the works of your hands, O Lord!**

Or:

R℣. **Blessed be God for ever.**

Assisting minister:

**Blessed are you, O Lord, who created the animals and gave us the ability to train them to help us in our work. (Let us bless the Lord:)** R℣.

Assisting minister:

**Blessed are you, O Lord, who gave us food from animals to replenish our energies. (Let us bless the Lord:)** R℣.

Assisting minister:

**Blessed are you, O Lord, who for the sake of our comfort give us domestic animals as companions. (Let us bless the Lord:)** R℣.

Assisting minister:

**Blessed are you, O Lord, who show us a sign of your providence, as your Son told us, by caring for the birds of the air. (Let us bless the Lord:)** R℣.

Assisting minister:

**Blessed are you, O Lord, who offered your Son to us as the paschal lamb and in him willed that we should be called and should truly be your children. (Let us bless the Lord:)** R℣.

Assisting minister:

**Blessed are you, O Lord, who through your lowliest creatures never cease to draw us toward your love. (Let us bless the Lord:)** R℣.

956    When there are no intercessions, the minister, before the prayer of blessing, says:

**Let us pray.**

As circumstances suggest, all may then pray for a moment in silence before the prayer of blessing.

## PRAYER OF BLESSING

957    A minister who is a priest or deacon says the prayer of blessing with hands outstretched; a lay minister says the prayer with hands joined.

**O God,**
**the author and giver of every gift,**
**animals also are part of the way you provide help**
**for our needs and labors.**
**We pray (through the intercession of Saint N.)**
**that you will make available for our use**
**the things we need to maintain a decent human life.**

**We ask this through Christ our Lord.**

R℣. **Amen.**

**O God,**
**you have done all things wisely;**
**in your goodness you have made us in your image**
**and given us care over other living things.**

**Reach out with your right hand**
**and grant that these animals may serve our needs**
**and that your bounty in the resources of this life**
**may move us to seek more confidently**
**the goal of eternal life.**

**We ask this through Christ our Lord.**

℞. **Amen.**

959    After the prayer of blessing, as circumstances suggest, the minister may sprinkle those present and the animals with holy water.

## CONCLUDING RITE

960    The minister concludes the rite by saying:

**May God, who created the animals of this earth as a help**
  **to us,**
**continue to protect and sustain us**
**with the grace his blessing brings,**
**now and for ever.**

℞. **Amen.**

961    It is preferable to end the celebration with a suitable song.

# II. SHORTER RITE

962    At the beginning of the celebration, the minister says:

**Our help is in the name of the Lord.**

All reply:

**Who made heaven and earth.**

963 One of those present or the minister reads a short text of sacred Scripture, for example:

Genesis 2:20a

**The man gave names to all the cattle, all the birds of the air, and all the wild animals.**

See Psalm 8:7-9a

**You have given him rule over the works of your hands,**
**putting all things under his feet:**
**All sheep and oxen,**
**yes, and the beasts of the field,**
**the birds of the air, the fishes of the sea.**

964 With hands joined, the minister says the prayer of blessing.

**O God,**
**you have done all things wisely;**
**in your goodness you have made us in your image**
**and given us care over other living things.**

**Reach out with your right hand**
**and grant that these animals may serve our needs**
**and that your bounty in the resources of this life**
**may move us to seek more confidently**
**the goal of eternal life.**

**We ask this through Christ our Lord.**

℟. **Amen.**

965 After the prayer of blessing, as circumstances suggest, the minister may sprinkle those present and the animals with holy water.

CHAPTER 26

# ORDER FOR THE BLESSING OF FIELDS AND FLOCKS

## INTRODUCTION

966 Through this rite the faithful express their grateful recognition of the blessings of God, who created the universe out of his inexpressible love and entrusted its care to human labor as the way of providing for common human needs.

967 The present order may be used on suitable occasions in rural life to sanctify the work of the farm through prayer and to mark through God's blessing the changes of the seasons and the labor each season brings.

968 The present order may be used by a priest or deacon. It may also be used by a layperson, who follows the rites and prayers designated for a lay minister.

969 While maintaining the structure and chief elements of the rite, the minister should adapt the celebration to the circumstances of the place and the people involved.

# ORDER OF BLESSING

## INTRODUCTORY RITES

970    When the community has gathered, a suitable song may
be sung. After the singing, the minister says:

**In the name of the Father, and of the Son, and of the Holy
Spirit.**

All make the sign of the cross and reply:

**Amen.**

971    A minister who is a priest or deacon greets those present
in the following or other suitable words, taken mainly from sacred
Scripture.

**May God, who is wonderful in all his works, be with you all.**

All make the following or some other suitable reply.

**And also with you.**

972    A lay minister greets those present in the following words.

**Let us together praise the Lord, from whom we have rain from
the heavens and abundance from the earth. Blessed be God
now and for ever.**

**R̷. Amen.**

973    In the following or similar words, the minister prepares
those present for the blessing.

**Let us bless God, whose might has created the earth and whose
providence has enriched it. He has given us the earth to cultivate, so that we may gather its fruits to sustain life.**

**But as we thank God for his bounteousness, let us learn also,
as the Gospel teaches, to seek first his kingship over us, his
way of holiness. Then all our needs will be given us besides.**

# Reading of the Word of God

**974**    A reader, another person present, or the minister reads a text of sacred Scripture.

## Brothers and sisters, listen to the words of the book of Genesis:

1:1, 11-12, 29-31a

*God looked at everything he had made, and he found it very good.*

**In the beginning, when God created the heavens and the earth, God said, "Let the earth bring forth vegetation: every kind of plant that bears seed and every kind of fruit tree on earth that bears fruit with its seed in it." And so it happened: the earth brought forth every kind of plant that bears seed and every kind of fruit tree on earth that bears fruit with its seed in it. God saw how good it was.**

**God also said: "See, I give you every seed-bearing plant all over the earth and every tree that has seed-bearing fruit on it to be your food; and to all the animals of the land, all the birds of the air, and all the living creatures that crawl on the ground, I give all the green plants for food." And so it happened. God looked at everything he had made, and he found it very good.**

**975**    Or:

## Brothers and sisters, listen to the words of the book of Deuteronomy:

32:10c-14

*God had them ride triumphant over the summits of the land and live off the products of its fields.*

**The LORD shielded them and cared for them,
guarding them as the apple of his eye.
As an eagle incites its nestlings forth
by hovering over its brood,
So he spread his wings to receive them
and bore them up on his pinions.
The LORD alone was their leader,
no strange god was with him.
He had them ride triumphant over the summits of the land
and live off the products of its fields,
Giving them honey to suck from its rocks
and olive oil from its hard, stony ground;**

**Butter from its cows and milk from its sheep;**
**with the fat of its lambs and rams;**
**Its Bashan bulls and its goats,**
**with the cream of its finest wheat;**
**and the foaming blood of its grapes you drank.**

976    Or:

Matthew 6:25-34—*Learn a lesson from the way the wild flowers grow.*

Mark 4:26-29—*The seed sprouts and grows without the man's knowing what happens.*

977    As circumstances suggest, one of the following responsorial psalms may be sung or said, or some other suitable song.

℞. **You answer us, O God our Savior.**

Psalm 65

**You have visited the land and watered it;**
**greatly have you enriched it.**
**God's watercourses are filled;**
**you have prepared the grain.** ℞.

**Thus have you prepared the land: drenching its furrows,**
**breaking up its clods,**
**Softening it with showers,**
**blessing its yield.**
**You have crowned the year with your bounty,**
**and your paths overflow with a rich harvest.** ℞.

**The untilled meadows overflow with it,**
**and rejoicing clothes the hills.**
**The fields are garmented with flocks**
**and the valleys blanketed with grain.**
**They shout and sing for joy.** ℞.

Psalm 104:1-2a, 14-15, 24, 27-28

℞. **(v. 24c) The earth is full of your creatures, O Lord.**

Psalm 107:35-36, 37-38, 41-42

℞. **(v. 1b) Give thanks to the Lord, for he is good.**

978    As circumstances suggest, the minister may give those present a brief explanation of the biblical text, so that they may understand through faith the meaning of the celebration.

---

# INTERCESSIONS

979 As circumstances suggest, the prayer of blessing may be preceded by the intercessions. The minister introduces them and an assisting minister or one of those present announces the intentions. From the following intentions those best suited to the occasion may be used or adapted, or other intentions that apply to the particular circumstances may be composed. The intentions are followed immediately by the prayer of blessing, no. 981 or no. 982.

The minister says:

**The Lord and Father of us all, looking with benign providence on his children, gives them nourishment and growth by blessing the earth with the fruitfulness that sustains human life. As children of this Father, let us pray to him, saying:**

℟. **Lord, hear our prayer.**

Assisting minister:

**You have called us, as Saint Paul says, a field under your cultivation; grant that by doing your will in all things we may remain always close to you. (For this we pray:)** ℟.

Assisting minister:

**You have told us that Christ is the vine and we are the branches; grant that by living in your Son we may produce much good fruit. (For this we pray:)** ℟.

Assisting minister:

**You bless the earth and abundance flows in its pastures; grant that by your blessing our fields may yield the food we need. (For this we pray:)** ℟.

Assisting minister:

**You make the wheat grow that provides our daily bread and the gift of the eucharist; give us a crop made rich by abundant rain and fertile soil. (For this we pray:)** ℟.

Assisting minister:

**You feed the birds of the air and clothe the lilies of the field; teach us not to worry about what we are to eat or drink or wear, but to seek first your kingship over us and your way of holiness. (For this we pray:)** ℟.

980     When there are no intercessions, the minister, before the prayer of blessing, says:

**Let us pray.**

As circumstances suggest, all may then pray for a moment in silence before the prayer of blessing.

## PRAYER OF BLESSING

981     A minister who is a priest or deacon says the prayer of blessing with hands outstretched; a lay minister says the prayer with hands joined.

**All-holy Lord and Father,**
**you have commanded us**
**to work the land and cultivate it.**
**Your devoted people now pray that you will grant us**
**an abundant harvest from our fields, vineyards,**
  **and orchards.**
**In your goodness protect our lands from wind and hail**
**and let a rich crop grow**
**from the seeds we plant (today).**

**We ask this through Christ our Lord.**

**R̰. Amen.**

982    Or:

**O God,**
**from the very beginning of time**
**you commanded the earth to bring forth vegetation**
**and fruit of every kind.**
**You provide the sower with seed and give bread to eat.**
**Grant, we pray, that this land,**
**enriched by your bounty and cultivated by human hands,**
**may be fertile with abundant crops.**
**Then your people, enriched by the gifts of your goodness,**
**will praise you unceasingly now and for ages unending.**

**We ask this through Christ our Lord.**

**R̰. Amen.**

# CONCLUDING RITE

**983** A minister who is a priest or deacon concludes the rite by saying:

**May God, the source of every good,**
**bless ✝ you and give success to your work,**
**so that you may receive the joy of his gifts**
**and praise his name now and for ever.**

℟. **Amen.**

**984** A lay minister concludes the rite by signing himself or herself with the sign of the cross and saying:

**May God, the source of every good,**
**bless us and give success to our work,**
**so that we may receive the joy of his gifts**
**and praise his name now and for ever.**

℟. **Amen.**

**985** It is preferable to end the celebration with a suitable song.

# CHAPTER 27

# ORDER FOR THE BLESSING OF SEEDS AT PLANTING TIME

## INTRODUCTION

986    At the beginning of the planting season it is customary for farmers to seek God's blessing on their crops. As the seeds are planted, God is asked to protect them from disease and destruction and to bring forth from them an abundant yield.

987    This order may be used for the blessing of seeds or for young plants before planting.

988    These orders may be used by a priest or a deacon, and also by a layperson, who follows the rites and prayers designated for a lay minister.

# I. ORDER OF BLESSING

## INTRODUCTORY RITES

989    When the community has gathered, a suitable song may
be sung. After the singing, the minister says:

**In the name of the Father, and of the Son, and of the Holy
Spirit.**

All make the sign of the cross and reply:

**Amen.**

990    A minister who is a priest or deacon greets those present
in the following or other suitable words, taken mainly from sacred
Scripture.

**The grace, the love, and the mercy of God be with you all.**

And all reply:

**And also with you.**

991    A lay minister greets those present in the following words:

**Let us praise God, who plants the seeds and reaps the harvest.
Blessed be God for ever.**

℞. **Blessed be God for ever.**

992    In the following or similar words, the minister prepares
those present for the blessing.

**Today we seek God's blessing on these seeds and the crops
they will produce. Christ reminds us that, unless the seed is
planted in the earth and dies, it will not yield fruit. As these
seeds grow and are cared for, may they be signs of the new
life that comes from God.**

## READING OF THE WORD OF GOD

993    A reader, another person present, or the minister reads a
text of sacred Scripture.

**Brothers and sisters, listen to the words of the first letter of Paul to the Corinthians:** 15:35-39

*The seed you sow does not germinate unless it dies.*

**But someone may say, "How are the dead raised? With what kind of body will they come back?"**

**You fool! What you sow is not brought to life unless it dies. And what you sow is not the body that is to be but a bare kernel of wheat, perhaps, or of some other kind; but God gives it a body as he chooses, and to each of the seeds its own body. Not all flesh is the same, but there is one kind for human beings, another kind of flesh for animals, another kind of flesh for birds, and another for fish.**

994    Or:

Genesis: 1:27-31—*Creation.*

Isaiah 55:10-13—*God gives seed to the one who sows.*

2 Corinthians 9:6-10—*God will increase the harvest.*

Matthew 13:31-32—*Parable of the mustard seed.*

Mark 4:26-29—*The seed and the kingdom of God.*

Luke 12:16-21—*Be rich in what matters to God.*

John 12:23-25—*Unless the grain of wheat falls to the earth and dies.*

995    As circumstances suggest, one of the following responsorial psalms may be sung, or some other suitable song.

℟. **Those that sow in tears shall reap rejoicing.**

Psalm 126

**When the LORD brought back the captives of Zion,
we were like men dreaming.
Then our mouth was filled with laughter,
and our tongue with rejoicing.** ℟.

**Then they said among the nations,
"The LORD has done great things for them."
The LORD has done great things for us;
we are glad indeed.** ℟.

**Restore our fortunes, O LORD,
like the torrents in the southern desert.
Those that sow in tears
shall reap rejoicing.** ℟.

**Although they go forth weeping,
carrying the seed to be sown,
They shall come back rejoicing,
carrying their sheaves.** R̞.

Psalm 65:1-2, 9-10, 11-12, 13

R̞. **(v. 2) To you we owe our hymn of praise, O God, in Zion.**

**996** As circumstances suggest, the minister may give those present a brief explanation of the biblical text, so that they may understand through faith the meaning of the celebration.

## LITANY

**997** The litany is then said. The minister introduces the invocations and an assisting minister or one of those present announces them. From the following those best suited to the occasion may be used or adapted, or other invocations that apply to the particular circumstances may be composed.

The minister says:

**The Lord of the harvest sustains us, let us call upon him:**

R̞. **Deliver us, O Lord.**

Assisting minister:

**From despair in times of drought:** R̞.

Assisting minister:

**From wastefulness in times of plenty:** R̞.

Assisting minister:

**From neglect of those in need:** R̞.

Assisting minister:

**From blindness to your presence in our work:** R̞.

Assisting minister:

**From hunger and thirst:** R̞.

**998** After the litany the minister, in the following or similar words, invites all present to sing or say the Lord's Prayer.

**Remember us, Lord, in your kingdom, and teach us to pray:**

All:

**Our Father . . .**

## PRAYER OF BLESSING

999   A minister who is a priest or deacon says the prayer of blessing with hands outstretched; a lay minister says the prayer with hands joined.

**Lord of the harvest,**
**you placed the gifts of creation in our hands**
**and called us to till the earth and make it fruitful.**

**We ask your blessing**
**as we prepare to place these seeds (seedlings) in the earth.**
**May the care we show these seeds (seedlings)**
**remind us of your tender love for your people.**

**We ask this through Christ our Lord.**

℞. **Amen.**

## CONCLUDING RITE

1000   A minister who is a priest or deacon concludes the rite by saying:

**May God nourish you and care for you, now and for ever.**

℞. **Amen.**

Then he blesses all present.

**And may almighty God bless you all,**
**the Father, and the Son, ✝ and the Holy Spirit.**

℞. **Amen.**

---

1001   A lay minister concludes the rite by signing himself or herself with the sign of the cross and saying:

**May God nourish us and care for us, now and for ever.**

℞. **Amen.**

---

1002   It is preferable to end the celebration with a suitable song.

# II. SHORTER RITE

1003    All make the sign of the cross as the minister says:

**Our help is in the name of the Lord.**

All reply:

**Who made heaven and earth.**

1004    One of those present or the minister reads a text of sacred Scripture, for example:

**Brothers and sisters, listen to the words of the first letter of Paul to the Corinthians:**                    15:35-39

*The seed you sow does not germinate unless it dies.*

**But someone may say, "How are the dead raised? With what kind of body will they come back?"**

**You fool! What you sow is not brought to life unless it dies. And what you sow is not the body that is to be but a bare kernel of wheat, perhaps, or of some other kind; but God gives it a body as he chooses, and to each of the seeds its own body. Not all flesh is the same, but there is one kind for human beings, another kind of flesh for animals, another kind of flesh for birds, and another for fish.**

1005    Or:

Genesis: 1:27-31—*Creation.*

Matthew 13:31-32—*Parable of the mustard seed.*

Mark 4:26-29—*The seed and the kingdom of God.*

John 12:23-25—*Unless the grain of wheat falls to the earth and dies.*

1006    A minister who is a priest or deacon says the prayer of blessing with hands outstretched; a lay minister says the prayer with hands joined.

**Lord of the harvest,**
**you placed the gifts of creation in our hands**
**and called us to till the earth and make it fruitful.**

**We ask your blessing**
**as we prepare to place these seeds (seedlings) in the earth.**
**May the care we show these seeds (seedlings)**
**remind us of your tender love for your people.**

**We ask this through Christ our Lord.**

R̸. **Amen.**

CHAPTER 28

# ORDER FOR A BLESSING ON THE OCCASION OF THANKSGIVING FOR THE HARVEST

## INTRODUCTION

1007 The symbolic offering of firstfruits of the harvest to God, in order to praise him for this gift, is a custom that should be maintained. It is a reminder of the debt of gratitude owed to God for all his favors and it continues a tradition that is mentioned in the Old Testament.

1008 The present order may be used by a priest or deacon. It may also be used by a layperson, who follows the rites and prayers designated for a lay minister.

1009 While maintaining the structure and chief elements of the rite, the minister should adapt the celebration to the circumstances of the place and the people involved.

# ORDER OF BLESSING

## INTRODUCTORY RITES

1010  When the community has gathered, a suitable song may be sung. After the singing, the minister says:

**In the name of the Father, and of the Son, and of the Holy Spirit.**

All make the sign of the cross and reply:

**Amen.**

1011  A minister who is a priest or deacon greets those present in the following or other suitable words, taken mainly from sacred Scripture.

**May God, the Most High, who created heaven and earth, be with you all.**

All make the following or some other suitable reply.

**And also with you.**

---

1012  A lay minister greets those present in the following words.

**Let us for ever praise and extol God, who in his all-embracing providence gives us food from the fruits of the earth. Blessed be God now and for ever.**

**R⁷. Amen.**

---

1013  In the following or similar words, the minister prepares those present for the blessing.

**The Church's supreme thanksgiving for blessings received is the offering of the eucharistic sacrifice, and in the Church's liturgy of the hours this eucharistic praise of God continues through the different parts of the day. In this way the Church teaches us to maintain and live in an attitude of gratitude to God. Therefore let us now bless the Lord, who has once again bestowed on us the fruits of the earth. Abel offered his firstfruits to God; let us also learn to share our blessings for the good of those in need, so that we may be true children of the Father, who bestows his gifts for the benefit of all the peoples of the earth.**

# READING OF THE WORD OF GOD

**1014**   A reader, another person present, or the minister reads a text of sacred Scripture.

**Brothers and sisters, listen to the words of the Acts of the Apostles:**                14:15b-17

*God fills your spirits with food and delight.*

**Paul shouted to the crowd: "We proclaim to you good news that you should turn from these idols to the living God, 'who made heaven and earth and sea and all that is in them.' In past generations he allowed all Gentiles to go their own ways; yet, in bestowing his goodness, he did not leave himself without witness, for he gave you rains from heaven and fruitful seasons, and filled you with nourishment and gladness for your hearts."**

**1015**   Or:

Deuteronomy 27:1a; 28:1-12b—*Blessed be the produce of your soil.*

Joel 2:21-24, 26-27—*The threshing floors will be full of grain.*

1 Timothy 6:6-11, 17-19—*Warn the rich not to set their hopes on money, which is untrustworthy.*

Luke 12:15-21—*Your life is not made secure by what you own, even when you have more than you need.*

**1016**   As circumstances suggest, one of the following responsorial psalms may be sung or said, or some other suitable song.

**℞. The earth has yielded its fruit, the Lord our God has blessed us.**

Psalm 67

**May God have pity on us and bless us;
may he let his face shine upon us.
So may your way be known upon earth;
among all nations your salvation. ℞.**

**May the nations be glad and exult
because you rule the peoples in equity;
the nations on earth you guide. ℞.**

**The earth has yielded its fruits;
God, our God, has blessed us.
May God bless us,
and may all the ends of the earth fear him! ℞.**

Psalm 126:4-5, 6

R℣. (v. 3) **The Lord has done great things for us.**

Psalm 147:7, 8-9, 10-11

R℣. (v. 5) **Mighty and great is our Lord, his wisdom is without measure.**

1017    As circumstances suggest, the minister may give those present a brief explanation of the biblical text, so that they may understand through faith the meaning of the celebration.

# INTERCESSIONS

1018    As circumstances suggest, the prayer of blessing may be preceded by the intercessions. The minister introduces them and an assisting minister or one of those present announces the intentions. From the following intentions those best suited to the occasion may be used or adapted, or other intentions that apply to the particular circumstances may be composed. The intentions are followed immediately by the prayer of blessing, no. 1020 or no. 1021.

The minister says:

**As we pray in gratitude for God's blessing upon the work of our hands, let us not forget that we must do the works of holiness in our lives. Let us, then, pray to God, saying:**

R℣. **Lord, bless the fruits of our labor.**

Or:

R℣. **Lord, hear our prayer.**

Assisting minister:

**All-provident God, your care has given us food from the earth; grant that these crops we have harvested in the sweat of our brow may sustain us in body and help us to grow in spirit. (For this we pray:)** R℣.

Assisting minister:

**Through Jesus Christ you have made the world abound in the works of holiness; grant that, living in him, we may share in his fullness of life and bear much fruit. (For this we pray:)** R℣.

Assisting minister:

**In the eucharist you have taken up the fruits of our hands as signs of the mystery of faith; grant that the gifts we bring to be consecrated at your Son's table may work for the continuing good of the Church's life. (For this we pray:)** ℟.

Assisting minister:

**You planned that all your children should share in the goods you have provided; grant that all those who are in need may come to enjoy an untroubled life and to glorify you and together praise your name. (For this we pray:)** ℟.

1019   When there are no intercessions, the minister, before the prayer of blessing, says:

**Let us pray.**

As circumstances suggest, all may then pray for a moment in silence before the prayer of blessing.

## PRAYER OF BLESSING

1020   A minister who is a priest or deacon says the prayer of blessing with hands outstretched; a lay minister says the prayer with hands joined.

**God our Creator,**
**who never cease to bestow your bounteous fruits**
**from the rains of the heavens and the riches of the soil,**
**we thank your loving majesty for this year's harvest.**
**Through these blessings of your generosity**
**you have fulfilled the hopes of your children.**
**Grant that together they may praise your mercy without end**
**and in their life amid the good things of this world**
**strive also after the blessings of the world to come.**

**We ask this through Christ our Lord.**

℟. **Amen.**

1021  Or:

**All-powerful God,
we appeal to your tender care
that even as you temper the winds and rains
to nurture the fruits of the earth
you will also send upon them
the gentle shower of your blessing.
Fill the hearts of your people with gratitude,
that from the earth's fertility
the hungry may be filled with good things
and the poor and needy proclaim the glory of your name.**

**We ask this through Christ our Lord.**

R℣. **Amen.**


## Concluding Rite

1022  Facing those present, the minister concludes the rite by
saying:

**Let us bless God,
for ever let us praise and extol the name
of Father, Son, and Holy Spirit.**

R℣. **Amen.**

1023  It is preferable to end the celebration with a suitable song.

# CHAPTER 29

# ORDER FOR THE BLESSING OF AN ATHLETIC EVENT

## INTRODUCTION

1024   This blessing is intended for those who participate in an athletic event. The blessing asks that God may protect the athletes from injury and that throughout the event they may show respect for one another.

1025   The blessing may be given by a priest, deacon, or a lay minister.

## ORDER OF BLESSING

1026   All make the sign of the cross as the minister says:

**Blessed be the name of the Lord.**

All reply:

**Now and for ever.**

1027   One of those present or the minister reads a text of sacred Scripture, for example:

**Brothers and sisters, listen to the words of the second letter of Paul to Timothy:**                          4:6-8

*I have fought the good fight.*

**For I am already being poured out like a libation, and the time of my departure is at hand. I have competed well; I have finished the race; I have kept the faith. From now on the crown of righteousness awaits me, which the Lord, the just judge, will award to me on that day, and not only to me, but to all who have longed for his appearance.**

1028   Or:

1 Corinthians 9:24-27—*We win a crown that is imperishable.*

## Prayer of Blessing

1029   A minister who is a priest or deacon says the prayer of blessing with hands outstretched over the athletes; a lay minister says the prayer with hands joined.

**Strong and faithful God,
as we come together for this contest,
we ask you to bless these athletes.**

**Keep them safe from injury and harm,
instill in them respect for each other,
and reward them for their perseverance.**

**Lead us all to the rewards of your kingdom
where you live and reign for ever and ever.**

R̸. **Amen.**

CHAPTER 30

# ORDER FOR THE BLESSING
# BEFORE AND AFTER MEALS

## INTRODUCTION

1030   Christians, whether alone or with companions at table, say grace before and after meals to thank God for his goodness in providing their daily food. This practice is also a reminder that the Lord Jesus combined the sacrament of the eucharist with the ritual of a family meal and showed himself to his disciples as their risen Lord in the breaking of the bread.

1031   As they gather at table and see in the food they share a sign of God's blessings on them, Christians should be mindful of the poor, who lack even the bare minimum of food that those at table may have in abundance. By their moderation they will therefore try to provide help for the hungry and as a sign of Christ's love will on occasion invite the poor to their own table, in keeping with the words of Christ recorded in the Gospel (see Luke 14:13-14).

1032   The plans, texts, and formularies provided in the present chapter are to be regarded as models for the use of families or of any type of community. But the blessing at table should be given a tone that is in keeping with the festive or penitential character of the various days and seasons of the liturgical year.

# FIRST PLAN

## Before the Principal Meal

1033 The person who is presiding at table says:

**In the name of the Father, and of the Son, and of the Holy Spirit.**

All make the sign of the cross and reply:

**Amen.**

Then:

**The eyes of all creatures look to you
to give them food in due time.**

R⁷. **You give it to them, they gather it up;
you open your hand, they have their fill.**

**Let us call on the name of the Father,
who always takes care of his children.**

R⁷. **Our Father . . . but deliver us from evil.
For the kingdom, the power, and the glory are yours, now and
for ever. Amen.**

The one presiding then signs himself or herself with the sign of
the cross (a priest or a deacon also makes the sign of the cross
over the food) and says:

**Bless ✝ us, O Lord, and these your gifts
which we are about to receive from your goodness.
Through Christ our Lord.**

R⁷. **Amen.**

## After the Principal Meal

1034

**Let all your works praise you, O Lord.**

R⁷. **Let all your people bless you.**

---

We give you thanks for all your gifts, almighty God,
living and reigning now and for ever.

R̷. Amen.

For the sake of your name, O Lord,
reward those who have been good to us
and give them eternal life.

R̷. Amen.

Or:

Lord, give all people the food they need,
so that they may join us in giving you thanks.

R̷. Amen.

## BEFORE A LIGHT MEAL

1035  The person who is presiding at table says:

In the name of the Father, and of the Son, and of the Holy
Spirit.

All make the sign of the cross and reply:

Amen.

Then:

The poor shall eat and have their fill.
Those who long for the Lord shall give him praise.

R̷. May their hearts live for ever.

Let us call on the name of the Lord,
who gives us our daily bread.

R̷. Our Father . . . but deliver us from evil.
For the kingdom, the power and the glory are yours now and
for ever. Amen.

Protect us, O Lord our God,
and give us the help we need in our frailty.
Through Christ our Lord.

R̷. Amen.

## After a Light Meal

1036

Our compassionate Lord has left us a memorial of his wonderful works.

℟. He has given food to those who fear him.

Lord, you have fed us from your gifts and favors;
fill us with your mercy,
for you live and reign for ever and ever.

℟. Amen.

Or:

God is blessed in all his gifts
and holy in all his works,
who lives and reigns for ever and ever.

℟. Amen.

For the sake of your name, O Lord,
reward those who have been good to us
and give them eternal life.

℟. Amen.

Or:

Lord, give all people the food they need,
so that they may join us in giving you thanks.

℟. Amen.

1037 The foregoing manner of blessing before and after meals
is for use in any liturgical season, except on the days indicated
here; even on such days only the verses are changed.

# Advent

## Before Meals

Give ear, O Lord and shepherd of your people.

℟. Stir up your power and come.

## After Meals

Let us live soberly, justly, and devoutly in this world.

℟. As we wait in joyful hope for the coming of our Savior, Jesus Christ.

# Christmas Season

## Before Meals

The Word became flesh, alleluia.

℟. And dwelt among us, alleluia.

## After Meals

The Lord has made known, alleluia.

℟. His saving power, alleluia.

# Lent

## Before Meals

No one lives on bread alone.

℟. But on every word that comes from the mouth of God.

## After Meals

A time of penance has been granted us.

℟. To atone for our sins and heal our souls.

# Holy Thursday, Good Friday, Holy Saturday

## Before and after Meals

For our sake Christ was obedient, accepting even death.

℟. Death on a cross.

## Easter Week

BEFORE AND AFTER MEALS

This is the day the Lord has made, alleluia.

R̶7. Let us rejoice and be glad, alleluia.

## Easter Season

BEFORE MEALS

With glad and generous hearts all who believed took their meals in common, alleluia.

R̶7. Praising God, alleluia.

AFTER MEALS

The disciples recognized the Lord, alleluia.

R̶7. In the breaking of the bread, alleluia.

# SECOND PLAN

## I. Advent

BEFORE MEALS

1038  The person who is presiding at table says:

In the name of the Father, and of the Son, and of the Holy Spirit.

All make the sign of the cross and reply:

Amen.

**1039**  Then one of those present reads a brief text from sacred Scripture.

### Brothers and sisters, listen to the words of the prophet Isaiah:

58:10-11a

If you bestow your bread on the hungry
and satisfy the afflicted;
Then light shall rise for you in the darkness,
and the gloom shall become for you like midday;
Then the LORD will guide you always
and give you plenty even on the parched land.

**1040**  Or:

### Brothers and sisters, listen to the words of the Acts of the Apostles:

2:42-47a

The believers devoted themselves to the teaching of the apostles and to the communal life, to the breaking of the bread and to the prayers. Awe came upon everyone, and many wonders and signs were done through the apostles. All who believed were together and had all things in common; they would sell their property and possessions and divide them among all according to each one's need. Every day they devoted themselves to meeting together in the temple area and to breaking bread in their homes. They ate their meals with exultation and sincerity of heart, praising God and enjoying favor with all the people.

**1041**  Or:

### Brothers and sisters, listen to the words of the second letter of Paul to the Corinthians:

9:8-10

God is able to make every grace abundant for you, so that in all things, always having all you need, you may have an abundance for every good work. As it is written:

"He scatters abroad, he gives to the poor;
his righteousness endures forever."

The one who supplies seed to the sower and bread for food will supply and multiply your seed and increase the harvest of your righteousness.

1042   Or:

**Brothers and sisters, listen to the words of the apostle Paul to the Ephesians:**                               5:19-20

**Address one another in psalms and hymns and spiritual songs, singing and playing to the Lord in your hearts, giving thanks always and for everything in the name of our Lord Jesus Christ to God the Father.**

1043   Or:

**Brothers and sisters, listen to the words of the first letter of Paul to the Thessalonians:**                    5:16-18

**Rejoice always. Pray without ceasing. In all circumstances give thanks, for this is the will of God for you in Christ Jesus.**

1044   Or:

**Brothers and sisters, listen to the words of the letter to the Hebrews:**                                    13:1-2

**Let mutual love continue. Do not neglect hospitality, for through it some have unknowingly entertained angels.**

1045   Or:

**Brothers and sisters, listen to the words of the holy gospel according to Matthew:**                         6:25ab, 32b-33

**Jesus said to the crowds: "Therefore I tell you, do not worry about your life, what you will eat or drink. Your heavenly Father knows that you need them all. But seek first the kingdom of God and his righteousness, and all these things will be given you besides."**

1046   After the reading, the one presiding says the following prayer (a priest or a deacon makes the sign of the cross).

**Let us pray.**

**God, the Father of mercies,**
**you willed your Son to take flesh,**
**in order to give life back to us.**

**Bless ✝ these your gifts**
**with which we are about to nourish our bodies,**
**so that, receiving new strength, we may wait in watchfulness**
**for the glorious coming of Christ.**

**We ask this through the same Christ our Lord.**

**R̸. Amen.**

## AFTER MEALS

1047

**Let us live soberly, justly, and devoutly in this world.**

**R̸. As we wait in joyful hope for the coming of our Savior,**
**Jesus Christ.**

The one presiding adds:

**Let us pray.**

**We thank you, all-powerful God,**
**for your kindness in refreshing our bodies**
**by these gifts from your providence.**
**Strengthen us, we pray,**
**not only in body, but also in spirit.**

**We ask this through Christ our Lord.**

**R̸. Amen.**

# II. Christmas Season

## BEFORE MEALS

1048   Everything is as in Advent, except for the following.

**Let us pray.**

**Blessed are you, Lord God.**
**Through the fruitful virginity of Mary**
**you fulfilled the long expectation of the poor**
**    and oppressed.**

Grant that with the same faith with which Mary
awaited the birth of her Son,
we may look for him in our brothers and sisters in need.

We ask this through Christ our Lord.

R̸. Amen.

## AFTER MEALS

1049   The one presiding says:

The Word became flesh, alleluia.

R̸. And dwelt among us, alleluia.

Let us pray.

All-holy Father,
your Word made flesh is the Son who is born to us,
the child who is given to us.
Grant that we who are committed to serving him
   in our brothers and sisters
may satisfy their needs of body and soul.

We ask this through Christ our Lord.

R̸. Amen.

# III. Lent

## BEFORE MEALS

1050   Everything is as in Advent, except for the following.

Let us pray.

We thank you, O Lord,
who give us this food to eat.
We pray that you may also provide food
for those who are hungry
and gather all of us together
at the table of your heavenly kingdom.

We ask this through Christ our Lord.

R̸. Amen.

## AFTER MEALS

1051 The one presiding says:

**No one lives on bread alone.**

R⁊. **But on every word that comes from the mouth of God.**

**Let us pray.**

**O God,
by his forty days of fasting
your Son has taught us
that we do not live on bread alone,
but on every word that comes from your mouth.
Help us to lift up our hearts,
so that, strengthened by your power,
we may truly love you in our brothers and sisters.**

**We ask this through Christ our Lord.**

R⁊. **Amen.**

## IV. Holy Thursday, Good Friday, Holy Saturday

### BEFORE MEALS

1052 Everything is as in Advent, except for the following.

**Let us pray.**

**Lord Jesus Christ,
who in fulfilling your Father's will
became obedient unto death,
bless us who are gathered as a family at this table.
May our spiritual food be like yours:
always to do God's good and gracious will,
for you live and reign for ever and ever.**

R⁊. **Amen.**

### AFTER MEALS

1053 The one presiding says:

**For our sake Christ was obedient, accepting even death.**

R⁊. **Death on a cross.**

Let us pray.

Father of all peoples,
look kindly upon this family, which belongs to you.
Grant that we who rejoice to be together at this table,
may one day also be numbered among those
who share the surpassing joys of your heavenly kingdom.

We ask this through Christ our Lord.

℟. Amen.

## V. Easter Season

### Before Meals

1054  Everything is as in Advent, except for the following.

Let us pray.

We joyfully sing your praises, Lord Jesus Christ,
who on the day of your resurrection
were recognized by your disciples in the breaking of the bread.

Remain here with us
as we gratefully partake of these gifts,
and at the banquet table in heaven welcome us,
who have welcomed you in our brothers and sisters,
for you live and reign for ever and ever.

℟. Amen.

### After Meals

1055  The one presiding says:

The disciples recognized the Lord, alleluia.

℟. In the breaking of the bread, alleluia.

Let us pray.

O God, source of life,
fill our hearts with the joys of Easter.

In your goodness you have given us food to eat;
grant also that we may continue to live that new life
which the risen Christ has won for us
and graciously bestowed on us,
for he lives and reigns with you for ever and ever.

R̖. **Amen.**

# VI. Ordinary Time

## BEFORE MEALS

1056    Everything is as in Advent, except for the following.

**Let us pray.**

**Lord, our God,
with fatherly love you come to the aid of your children.
Bless us and these your gifts
which we are about to receive from your goodness.
Grant that all peoples may be gladdened
by the favors of your providence.**

**We ask this through Christ our Lord.**

R̖. **Amen.**

1057    Or:

**Let us pray.**

**Lord God,
you sustain all creatures
and never cease to give your children the food they need.
We bless you for bringing us together
in the love that unites us around this table
where the food we take strengthens our bodies.
We pray that, nourished by your word,
we may grow ever stronger in faith
as we strive for the coming of your kingdom.**

**We ask this through Christ our Lord.**

R̖. **Amen.**

1058    Or:

Let us pray.

Lord, the lover of life,
you feed the birds of the skies
and array the lilies of the field.
We bless you for all your creatures
and for the food we are about to receive.
We humbly pray that in your goodness
you will provide for our brothers and sisters
   who are hungry.

We ask this through Christ our Lord.

R̞. Amen.

1059   Or (a priest or a deacon makes the sign of the cross):

Let us pray.

God of all goodness,
through the breaking of bread together
you strengthen the bonds that unite us in love.
Bless ✛ us and these your gifts.
Grant that as we sit down together at table
in joy and sincerity,
we may grow always closer in the bonds of love.

We ask this through Christ our Lord.

R̞. Amen.

## AFTER MEALS

1060   The one presiding says:

I will bless the Lord at all times.

R̞. His praise shall be ever on my lips.

Let us pray.

We thank you, O Lord, the giver of all good gifts,
who have kindly brought us together at this table.
Refreshed in body, may we make our earthly journey in joy
and one day arrive at the banquet table of heaven.

We ask this through Christ our Lord.

R̞. Amen.

1061 Or:

**Let us pray.**

**Lord, you feed every living thing.**
**We have eaten together at this table; keep us in your love.**
**Give us true concern for the least of our sisters and brothers,**
**so that, as we gladly share our food with them,**
**we may also sit down together with them**
**at the table of the kingdom of heaven.**

**We ask this through Christ our Lord.**

**R̸. Amen.**

1062 Or:

**Let us pray.**

**We thank you, O Lord,**
**for graciously giving us food at this table.**
**Grant that the nourishment of our bodies**
**may also serve our growth in spirit.**

**We ask this through Christ our Lord.**

**R̸. Amen.**

# THIRD PLAN

## Before Meals

1063 When the community has gathered, the one presiding at table says:

**Let us bless the Lord for his gifts.**

**R̸. We thank him at all times.**

**Let his praise be ever on our lips.**

**R̸. We thank him at all times.**

(A priest or a deacon makes the sign of the cross.)

**We praise you, O Lord, from whom all good things come.**
**Bless ✢ this food we are about to receive.**
**Grant that in the spirit of genuine love for one another**
**we may always remain one in you.**

**We ask this through Christ our Lord.**

**R℣. Amen.**


## AFTER MEALS

1064

**Blessed be the name of the Lord.**

**R℣. Now and for ever.**

**Glory to the Father, and to the Son, and to the Holy Spirit.**

**R℣. Now and for ever.**

**God our Father,**
**we thank you for the food your bounty has given us,**
**your gathered family.**
**Grant that we also may freely give to others**
**what you have so generously given to us,**
**and that we may all share**
**in the banquet of heaven.**

**We ask this through Christ our Lord.**

**R℣. Amen.**


# FOURTH PLAN


## BEFORE MEALS

1065 When the community has gathered, all make the sign of
the cross and the one presiding says the following (a priest or
a deacon makes the sign of the cross).

Bless ✝ us, O Lord, and these your gifts
which we are about to receive from your goodness.
Through Christ our Lord.

℟. Amen.

1066   Or:

Protect us, O Lord our God,
and give us the help we need in our frailty.
Through Christ our Lord.

℟. Amen.

1067   Or:

May your gifts refresh us, O Lord,
and your grace give us strength.

℟. Amen.

1068   Or:

Every good and perfect gift comes from you, O Lord.
We ask you to bless ✝ this food,
which we wish to receive with grateful hearts.

℟. Amen.

1069   Or:

Blessed are you, almighty Father,
who give us our daily bread.
Blessed is your only begotten Son,
who continually feeds us with the word of life.
Blessed is the Holy Spirit,
who brings us together at this table of love.
Blessed be God now and for ever.

℟. Amen.

## AFTER MEALS

1070   The one presiding says:

We give you thanks for all your gifts, almighty God,
living and reigning now and for ever.

℟. Amen.

1071  Or:

Lord, you have fed us from your gifts and favors;
fill us with your mercy,
for you live and reign for ever and ever.

R7. Amen.

1072  Or:

God is blessed in all his gifts
and holy in all his works,
who lives and reigns for ever and ever.

R7. Amen.

1073  Or:

We give you thanks, holy Lord, our Father,
for your loving gifts of our food and drink.
Grant that some day we may sit
at the table of your heavenly kingdom
and there sing a hymn of praise to you for ever.

R7. Amen.

1074  Or:

For the sake of your name, O Lord,
reward those who have been good to us
and give them eternal life.

R7. Amen.

1075  Or:

Lord, give all people the food they need,
so that they may join us in giving you thanks.

R7. Amen.

# Part III
# BLESSINGS OF OBJECTS THAT ARE DESIGNED OR ERECTED FOR USE IN CHURCHES, EITHER IN THE LITURGY OR IN POPULAR DEVOTIONS

# BLESSINGS OF OBJECTS THAT ARE DESIGNED OR ERECTED FOR USE IN CHURCHES, EITHER IN THE LITURGY OR IN POPULAR DEVOTIONS

## INTRODUCTION

1076    The Church has always sought to ensure that all those things that are involved in any way in divine worship should be worthy, becoming, and beautiful; that they first be blessed, and then kept exclusively for sacred celebrations, and never turned to commonplace uses. It is the Church's intention to maintain this practice.

Consequently, those objects that through a blessing are set aside for divine worship are to be treated with reverence by all and to be put only to their proper use, never profaned.

1077    To complement the celebrations provided in other liturgical books, further orders of blessing are provided here in Part III for church objects that are designed or erected for liturgical use or for popular devotion.

1078    When a church is to be consecrated to God or is to be blessed by use of the rite for the dedication of a church, everything in the church, except the altar, is regarded as blessed and erected in virtue of the rite of dedication or blessing, so that no further rite is needed.

1079    There are certain blessings that have particular significance and importance in the life of the ecclesial community: for example, the blessing of a crucifix or image that is to be offered for public veneration, the blessing of bells, an organ, church doors, the erection of stations of the cross. Such blessings should by right be carried out by the bishop or by the priest who is the rector of the church involved, but in particular circumstances, when no priest is available, these blessings can be assigned to a deacon.

# CHAPTER 31

# ORDER FOR THE BLESSING OF A BAPTISTERY OR OF A NEW BAPTISMAL FONT

## INTRODUCTION

1080   The baptistery or site of the baptismal font is rightly considered to be one of the most important parts of a church. For it is the place for celebrating baptism, the first sacrament of the New Law, through which those who firmly accept Christ in faith and receive the Spirit of adoption[1] become in name and in fact God's adopted children.[2] Joined with Christ in a death and resurrection like his,[3] they become part of his Body.[4] Filled with the anointing of the Spirit, they become God's holy temple[5] and members of the Church, "a chosen race, a royal priesthood, a holy nation, God's own people."[6]

1081   Because baptism is the beginning of the entire Christian life, every cathedral and parish church ought to have its own baptistery or a special place where the baptismal font flows or is situated. For pastoral reasons and with the consent of the local Ordinary,[7] other churches or chapels may have a baptistery or baptismal font.

1082   In the building of a baptistery or in the setting up of a baptismal font the primary consideration must be the proper and worthy celebration of the rites of baptism, as these are set out in the *Rite of Baptism for Children* and in the *Rite of Christian Initiation of Adults*.

1083   In the case both of a baptistery that is erected apart from the main body of the church for the celebration of the entire baptismal rite and of a font that is set up within the church itself, everything must be arranged in such a way as to bring out the connection of baptism with the word of God and with the eucharist, the high point of Christian initiation.

---

[1] See Romans 8:15.

[2] See 1 John 3:1; John 1:12; Romans 9:8.

[3] See Romans 6:5.

[4] See Ephesians 5:30; 1 Corinthians 12:27; Romans 12:5.

[5] See 1 Corinthians 3:16-17 and 6:19; 2 Corinthians 6:16; Ephesians 2:21-22.

[6] 1 Peter 2:9.

[7] See Roman Ritual, *Rite of Baptism for Children*, Introduction, no. 11.

1084   A baptistery separated from the body of the church is to be worthy of the sacrament celebrated there and is to be set aside exclusively for baptism,[8] as befits the place where, from the womb of the Church, so to speak, Christians are reborn through water and the Holy Spirit.

1085   The baptismal font, particularly one in a baptistery, should be stationary, gracefully constructed out of a suitable material, of splendid beauty and spotless cleanliness; it should permit baptism by immersion, wherever this is the usage.[9] In order to enhance its force as a sign, the font should be designed in such a way that it functions as a fountain of running water; where the climate requires, provision should be made for heating the water.[10]

## Rite of Blessing

1086   When a new baptistery has been erected or a new font installed, it is opportune to celebrate a special rite of blessing. But in the case simply of a portable vessel "in which on occasion the water is prepared for celebration of the sacrament in the sanctuary," this special rite is not celebrated.[11]

## Minister of the Rite

1087   The reception of baptism stands as the beginning of the faithful's life in Christ that in some way derives from and depends on their high priest, the bishop.[12] In his own diocese the bishop himself, then, should dedicate a new baptistery or new baptismal font. But he may entrust this duty to another bishop or a priest, especially to one who is his associate and assistant in the pastoral care of the faithful for whom the new baptistery or font is intended. When a bishop is the celebrant, everything in the rite should be adapted accordingly.

## Choice of Day

1088   As a rule the day designated for the celebration of the blessing should be a Sunday, especially a Sunday of the Easter season or the Sunday or feast of the Baptism of the Lord, in order to bring out more clearly the paschal character of baptism and to make possible a large attendance of the faithful.

   The rite of blessing may not be celebrated on Ash Wednesday, during Holy Week, or on All Souls Day.

---

[8] Roman Ritual, *Rite of Baptism for Children:* Christian Initiation, General Introduction, no. 25.

[9] See ibid., no. 22.

[10] Ibid., no. 20.

[11] Ibid., no. 19.

[12] See SC, art. 41.

*Pastoral Preparation*

1089   The erection of a new baptistery or baptismal font is an important event in the life of a Christian community. The celebration of the blessing should therefore be announced to the faithful well ahead of time and they should be properly prepared to take an active part in the rite. They should be particularly well instructed about the significance of the baptismal font and its sign value, so that they will be inspired with a renewed reverence and appreciation toward baptism and toward the font as a symbol of baptism.

*Requisites*

1090   The following are to be prepared for the rite of blessing a baptistery or a new baptismal font:
>   —the font filled with water;
>   —the Easter candle for the procession;
>   —candlestand for the Easter candle;
>   —Roman Ritual;
>   —Lectionary for Mass;
>   —censer and boat containing incense;
>   —container to receive the newly blessed water and sprinkler;
>   —chairs for the celebrant and other ministers.

When baptism is to be celebrated, all the requisites for celebrating the sacrament are also to be made ready.

1091   The color of the vestments for the rite is white or another festive color. The following are to be prepared:
>   (—for a bishop: alb, pectoral cross, stole, cope or, if he is to celebrate Mass, chasuble, miter, and pastoral staff;)
>   —for priests: alb and stole, or Mass vestments;
>   —for deacons: alb, stole (dalmatic);
>   —for other ministers: alb or other lawfully approved liturgical vesture.

# I. ORDER OF BLESSING OF A NEW BAPTISMAL FONT JOINED WITH THE CELEBRATION OF BAPTISM

## INTRODUCTORY RITES

1092    When the community has gathered, the celebrant, priests, deacons, and ministers, all with their proper vestments, proceed from the sacristy through the body of the church to the baptistery; they are led by a censer bearer carrying a censer with lighted charcoal; they are followed by an acolyte bearing the Easter candle and by other persons in the procession.

The candidates for baptism together with their sponsors may properly form part of the procession; otherwise they assemble at a convenient place inside the baptistery.

1093    During the procession the Litany of the Saints is sung.

| | |
|---|---|
| **Lord, have mercy** | **Lord, have mercy** |
| **Christ, have mercy** | **Christ, have mercy** |
| **Lord, have mercy** | **Lord, have mercy** |
| **Holy Mary, Mother of God** | **pray for us** |
| **Saint Michael** | **pray for us** |
| **Holy angels of God** | **pray for us** |
| **Saint John the Baptist** | **pray for us** |
| **Saint Joseph** | **pray for us** |
| **Saint Peter and Saint Paul** | **pray for us** |
| **Saint Andrew** | **pray for us** |
| **Saint John** | **pray for us** |
| **Saint Mary Magdalene** | **pray for us** |
| **Saint Stephen** | **pray for us** |
| **Saint Ignatius** | **pray for us** |
| **Saint Lawrence** | **pray for us** |
| **Saint Perpetua and** | |
| **Saint Felicity** | **pray for us** |
| **Saint Agnes** | **pray for us** |
| **Saint Gregory** | **pray for us** |
| **Saint Augustine** | **pray for us** |
| **Saint Athanasius** | **pray for us** |
| **Saint Basil** | **pray for us** |
| **Saint Martin** | **pray for us** |

| | |
|---|---|
| Saint Benedict | pray for us |
| Saint Francis and<br>    Saint Dominic | pray for us |
| Saint Francis Xavier | pray for us |
| Saint John Vianney | pray for us |
| Saint Catherine of Siena | pray for us |
| Saint Teresa of Jesus | pray for us |
| All holy men and women | pray for us |
| | |
| Lord, be merciful | Lord, save your people |
| From all evil | Lord, save your people |
| From every sin | Lord, save your people |
| From everlasting death | Lord, save your people |
| By your coming as man | Lord, save your people |
| By your death and rising<br>    to new life | Lord, save your people |
| By your gift of the Holy<br>    Spirit | Lord, save your people |
| | |
| Be merciful to us sinners | Lord, hear our prayer |
| Give new life to these<br>    chosen ones by the grace<br>    of baptism | Lord, hear our prayer |
| Jesus, Son of the living<br>    God | Lord, hear our prayer |
| Christ, hear us | Christ, hear us |
| Lord Jesus, hear our prayer | Lord Jesus, hear our prayer |

1094 When the procession reaches the baptistery, all go and stand in their assigned places. The Easter candle is placed on the candlestand prepared for it at the center of the baptistery or near the font. When the Litany of the Saints has ended, the celebrant greets the people in the following or other suitable words, taken mainly from sacred Scripture.

**The grace of our Lord Jesus Christ and the love of God and the fellowship of the Holy Spirit be with you all.**

All make the following or some other suitable reply.

**And also with you.**

1095　In the following or similar words, the celebrant prepares those present for the blessing.

**My dear brothers and sisters, we have come together to carry out a joyous celebration. We are about to bless a new baptismal font and to bestow on these elect the sacrament of their rebirth. Receiving God's mercy, they will, as a result of their baptism, become members of a people set apart, the Church; they will be joined to Christ, the firstborn of many brothers and sisters, and, having received the Holy Spirit of adoption, they will dare to call upon God as Father in virtue of being his children.**

1096　After his introductory remarks, the celebrant, with hands joined, says:

**Let us pray.**

All pray briefly in silence; then, with hands outstretched, the celebrant continues:

**O God,
by the sacrament of rebirth
you continually increase the number of your children.
Grant that all who will come forth reborn from
　this saving font
may by their way of life give glory to your name
and add to the holiness of the Church, their mother.**

**We ask this through Christ our Lord.**

**R̸. Amen.**

## RECEPTION OF THOSE TO BE BAPTIZED

1097　This opening prayer is followed by the rite of welcoming those to be baptized. Depending on whether the elect are infants or adults, the rites to be used, with the requisite adaptations, are: in the case of children, *Rite of Baptism for Children* (nos. 36–43); in the case of adults, *Rite of Christian Initiation of Adults* (nos. 341–345), unless this rite has already been carried out as the second step of Christian initiation (nos. 129–137).

## Liturgy of the Word

1098 For the liturgy of the word, everything takes place as in the *Rite of Christian Initiation of Adults* (nos. 346–347) or the *Rite of Baptism for Children* (nos. 44, 81, 112), and suitable readings are chosen from the Lectionary for Mass.[13]

1099 After the reading of the gospel, the celebrant in the homily explains the biblical texts, so that those present may better understand the importance of baptism and the symbolism of the font.

1100 The rites that precede baptism are carried out in the way indicated in the *Rite of Christian Initiation of Adults* (nos. 351–352) or in the *Rite of Baptism for Children* (nos. 49–52).

## Blessing of the New Font

1101 The candidates gather around the font, the infants held by their mothers and the adults standing with their godparents. Then in the following or similar words the celebrant invites the faithful to prayer.

**My dear brothers and sisters, the time has come to bless this font through the prayer of the Church, that the gift of the Holy Spirit will endow its waters with the power to sanctify. But we should first offer prayers to God our Father for his servants, N. and N., who are asking to be baptized. He has called them and brought them to this moment of rebirth. Let us pray that he will give them light and strength, so that, holding fast to Christ, they may reach the fullness of life.**

All pray briefly in silence; then, turning to the font, the celebrant, with hands outstretched, says:

**Lord God,**
**Creator of the world**
**and Father of all who are born into it,**
**it is right that we should give you praise**
**for allowing us to open this saving font**
**through the liturgy of your Church.**
**Here the door is reopened to the life of the spirit**
**and the gateway to the Church is swung wide**
**to those against whom the gates of paradise were shut.**

---

[13] See Lectionary for Mass (2nd ed., 1981), nos. 751–760 (Ritual Masses, I. Christian Initiation, 1. Order of Catechumens and Christian Initiation of Adults, Celebration of the Sacraments of Initiation apart from the Easter Vigil; 2. Christian Initiation of Children).

This pool is opened and in it the newness of its pure waters
will again make clean and spotless
those who were stained by the old ways of sin.
A new torrent is released
whose gushing waters sweep away sin
and bring new virtue to life.
A stream of living water, coming from Christ's side,
   now flows
and those who drink this water will be brought
   to eternal life.
Over this font the lamp of faith spreads the holy light
that banishes darkness from the mind
and fills those who are reborn here with heavenly gifts.
Those who profess their faith at this font
are plunged beneath the waters and joined to Christ's death,
so that they may rise with him to newness of life.

Lord,
we ask you to send the life-giving presence of your
   Spirit upon this font,
placed here as the source of new life for your people.
The power of the Spirit made the Virgin Mary the mother
   of your Son;
send forth the power of the same Spirit,
so that your Church may present you
with countless new sons and daughters
and bring forth new citizens of heaven.

Grant, O Lord, that the people who are reborn from this font
may fulfill in their actions
what they pledge by their faith
and show by their lives
what they begin by the power of your grace.
Let the people of different nations and conditions
who come forth as one from these waters of rebirth
show by their love that they are brothers and sisters
and by their concord that they are citizens of the
   one kingdom.
Make them into true sons and daughters
who reflect their Father's goodness,
disciples who are faithful to the teaching of their
   one Master,

temples in whom the voice of the Spirit resounds.
Grant that they may be witnesses to the Gospel,
doers of the works of holiness.
Enable them to fill with the Spirit of Christ
the earthly city where they live,
until they are welcomed home in the heavenly Jerusalem.

We ask this through Christ our Lord.

R⁄. **Amen.**

1102 The celebrant places incense in the censer and incenses the font.

1103 The blessing of the font is followed by the celebration of baptism: of children, as indicated in the *Rite of Baptism for Children* (nos. 56–66); of adults, as indicated in the *Rite of Christian Initiation of Adults* (nos. 223–243 or nos. 355–369).

## CONCLUDING RITE

1104 In the case of the baptism of infants, the rite is concluded in the way indicated either in the *Rite for the Baptism of Children* (nos. 67–71) or in the way given in the following paragraphs.

1105 The celebrant then blesses the fathers, the mothers, the children in their mothers' arms, and all present:

**May the Creator of all, who shares with human beings the mystery of his own fatherhood, lead the fathers of these children to be teachers and witnesses of the Gospel.**

R⁄. **Amen.**

**May Christ, the Son of God, who became the Son of the Virgin Mary, give these mothers joy in their children, who have been reborn to eternal life.**

R⁄. **Amen.**

**May the Holy Spirit, the Paraclete, who has sanctified these children, live always in their hearts.**

R⁄. **Amen.**

Then he blesses all present.

**And may almighty God bless you all,**
**the Father, and the Son, ✝ and the Holy Spirit.**

R̥. **Amen.**

1106 After the blessing, a song expressing paschal joy and thanksgiving or the Canticle of Mary may be sung.

1107 The assisting deacon then dismisses the people in the usual way.

1108 In accord with ancient tradition, at the Christian initiation of adults, after baptism, the newly baptized receive the sacrament of confirmation and for the first time participate in the eucharist. Thus after baptism, everything is done as in the *Rite of Christian Initiation of Adults* (nos. 231–243 or 363–369).

# II. ORDER OF BLESSING OF A NEW BAPTISMAL FONT WITHOUT THE CELEBRATION OF BAPTISM

## INTRODUCTORY RITES

**1109**   In the way indicated in no. 1092, when the community has gathered, the celebrant and ministers proceed from the sacristy through the body of the church to the baptistery.

**1110**   During this procession one of the following antiphons with Psalm 36 and the doxology is sung, or some other suitable song.

Ant. **You will drink of the Lord's waters of delight, of the fountains of salvation.**

Or:

Ant. **Lord, you are the source of life, and in the light of your glory we see light.**

Psalm 36

**O LORD, your kindness reaches to heaven,**
**your faithfulness, to the clouds.**
**Your justice is like the mountains of God;**
**your judgments, like the mighty deep;**
**man and beast you save, O LORD.** ℟.

**How precious is your kindness, O God!**
**The children of men take refuge in the shadow of your wings.**
**They have their fill of the prime gifts of your house;**
**from your delightful stream you give them to drink.** ℟.

**For with you is the fountain of life,**
**and in your light we see light.**
**Keep up your kindness toward your friends,**
**your just defense of the upright of heart.** ℟.

**Glory to the Father, and to the Son, and to the Holy Spirit:**
**as it was in the beginning, is now, and will be for ever.**
**Amen.** ℟.

1111   When the procession reaches the baptistery, all go and stand in their assigned places. The Easter candle is placed on the candlestand prepared for it at the center of the baptistery or near the font. When the singing has ended, the celebrant greets those present in the following or other suitable words, taken mainly from sacred Scripture.

**The grace of our Lord Jesus Christ and the love of God and the fellowship of the Holy Spirit be with you all.**

All make the following or some other suitable reply.

**And also with you.**

1112   In the following or similar words, the celebrant prepares those present for the blessing.

**My dear brothers and sisters, we have come together to carry out a joyous celebration. We are about to bless a new baptismal font for all who will come forth reborn from it. Receiving God's mercy, they will, as a result of their baptism, become members of a people set apart, the Church; they will be joined to Christ, the firstborn of many brothers and sisters, and, having received the Holy Spirit of adoption, they will dare to call upon God as Father in virtue of being his children.**

1113   After his introductory remarks, the celebrant, with hands joined, says:

**Let us pray.**

All pray briefly in silence; then, with hands outstretched, the celebrant continues:

**O God,
by the sacrament of rebirth
you continually increase the number of your children.
Grant that all who will come forth reborn from this
   saving font
may by their way of life give glory to your name
and add to the holiness of the Church, their mother.**

**We ask this through Christ our Lord.**

**R∕. Amen.**

# READING OF THE WORD OF GOD

**1114**  After the introductory rites, the celebrant sits. Then one or more texts of sacred Scripture are read, taken from those provided in the Lectionary for Mass for use in the celebration of Christian initiation apart from the Easter Vigil[14] or for use in the celebration of baptism of children.[15] Between the readings there is a responsorial psalm, related to the reading that preceded it, or an interval of silence. The gospel reading always holds the place of honor.

**1115**  After the reading of the word of God, the celebrant in the homily explains the biblical texts, so that those present may better understand the importance of baptism and the symbolism of the font.

# BLESSING OF THE NEW FONT

**1116**  In the following or similar words, the celebrant invites the faithful to prayer.

**My dear brothers and sisters, the time has come to bless this font through the prayer of the Church, that the gift of the Holy Spirit will endow its waters with the power to sanctify. But we should first pray to God our Father that he will keep the faith alive in our community and increase the bonds of love between us. For the font of baptism is truly opened when our ears are heedful of God's word; when our minds are brightened with Christ's light and closed to the darkness of sin; when our hearts are bound closely to the Lord and renounce Satan and all his works.**

**1117**  All pray briefly in silence; then, turning to the font, the celebrant, with hands outstretched, says:

**Lord God,**
**Creator of the world**
**and Father of all who are born into it,**
**it is right that we should give you praise**
**for allowing us to open this saving font**
**through the liturgy of your Church.**

---

[14] See Lectionary for Mass (2nd ed., 1981), nos. 751–755 (Ritual Masses, I. Christian Initiation, 1. Order of Catechumens and Christian Initiation of Adults, Celebration of the Sacraments of Initiation apart from the Easter Vigil).

[15] See ibid., nos. 756–760 (2. Christian Initiation of Children).

Here the door is reopened to the life of the spirit
and the gateway to the Church is swung wide
to those against whom the gates of paradise were shut.
This pool is opened and in it the newness of its pure waters
will again make clean and spotless
those who were stained by the old ways of sin.
A new torrent is released
whose gushing waters sweep away sin
and bring new virtue to life.
A stream of living water, coming from Christ's side,
    now flows
and those who drink this water will be brought
    to eternal life.
Over this font the lamp of faith spreads the holy light
that banishes darkness from the mind
and fills those who are reborn here with heavenly gifts.
Those who profess their faith at this font
are plunged beneath the waters and joined to Christ's death,
so that they may rise with him to newness of life.

Lord,
we ask you to send the life-giving presence of your
    Spirit upon this font,
placed here as the source of new life for your people.
The power of the Spirit made the Virgin Mary the mother
    of your Son;
send forth the power of the same Spirit,
so that your Church may present you
with countless new sons and daughters
and bring forth new citizens of heaven.

Grant, O Lord, that the people who are reborn from this font
may fulfill in their actions
what they pledge by their faith
and show by their lives
what they begin by the power of your grace.
Let the people of different nations and conditions
who come forth as one from these waters of rebirth
show by their love that they are brothers and sisters
and by their concord that they are citizens of the
    one kingdom.
Make them into true sons and daughters
who reflect their Father's goodness,

disciples who are faithful to the teaching of their
   one Master,
temples in whom the voice of the Spirit resounds.
Grant that they may be witnesses to the Gospel,
doers of the works of holiness.
Enable them to fill with the Spirit of Christ
the earthly city where they live,
until they are welcomed home in the heavenly Jerusalem.

We ask this through Christ our Lord.

℟. Amen.

1118   After the invocation over the font, the celebrant places incense in the censer and incenses the font; during this time, a baptismal song may be sung, for example, one of the following
antiphons.

Ant. **The Lord's voice resounding over the waters, the Lord
over the vastness of the waters.**

Or:

Ant. **The Father's voice calls us above the waters, the glory
of the Son shines on us, the love of the Spirit fills us with life.**

Or:

Ant. **This is the fountain of life, the water made holy by the
suffering of Christ, washing all the world.**

1119   As circumstances suggest, when the baptismal song is over,
all may renew their profession of baptismal faith. The celebrant
addresses the faithful in these or similar words.

**Brothers and sisters, call to mind at this moment the faith you
professed when you received the sacraments of Christian initiation, so that, led by the grace of the Holy Spirit, you may
have the power to live up to it more fully each day.**

The celebrant then asks all present:

**Do you believe in God, the Father almighty,
   creator of heaven and earth?**

All:

**I do.**

Celebrant:

**Do you believe in Jesus Christ, his only Son, our Lord,
who was born of the Virgin Mary,
was crucified, died, and was buried,
rose from the dead,
and is now seated at the right hand of the Father?**

All:

**I do.**

Celebrant:

**Do you believe in the Holy Spirit,
the holy Catholic Church, the communion of saints,
the forgiveness of sins, the resurrection of the body,
and the life everlasting?**

All:

**I do.**

The celebrant expresses his own assent to the profession of faith by proclaiming the faith of the Church in the following formulary. But, as occasion suggests, another formulary may be substituted or a song that allows all in the assembly to proclaim their faith together.

**This is our faith. This is the faith of the Church.
We are proud to profess it in Christ Jesus our Lord.**

℟. **Amen.**

1120 Then the celebrant takes the sprinkler and sprinkles the assembly with water from the newly blessed font, as all sing an antiphon, for example:

Ant. **I saw water flowing from the right side of the temple, alleluia. It brought God's life and his salvation, and the people sang in joyful praise: alleluia, alleluia** (See Ezekiel 47:1-2).

Or:

Ant. **I will pour clean water over you and wash away all your defilement.**

# Concluding Rite

1121 As circumstances suggest, the intercessions may be said. The celebrant introduces them and an assisting minister or one of those present announces the intentions. From the following intentions those best suited to the occasion may be used or adapted, or other intentions that apply to the particular circumstances may be composed.

The celebrant says:

**Through the paschal mystery our loving Father has given us rebirth from water and the Holy Spirit into a new life as his own children. With hearts united let us pray to him, saying:**

℟. **Lord, renew in us the wonders of your power.**

Or:

℟. **Lord, hear our prayer.**

Assisting minister:

**Father of mercies, you have created us in your own image and sanctified us through baptism; make us always and everywhere conscious of your gift and of our Christian dignity. (For this we pray:) ℟.**

Assisting minister:

**From the side of Christ you brought forth the waters of the Holy Spirit; make this life-giving water that we receive become for us a fountain of living water leaping up to provide eternal life. (For this we pray:) ℟.**

Assisting minister:

**In the waters of baptism you have made us a chosen race, a royal priesthood, a holy people; grant that we will fulfill our Christian responsibilities by proclaiming your goodness to all. (For this we pray:) ℟.**

Assisting minister:

**You constantly increase your Church with new members; grant that all those reborn in the water of this font will live up to what they have acknowledged in faith. (For this we pray:) ℟.**

**In your kindness you have permitted us to erect this new baptismal font; grant that for catechumens it will become the pool of new life and for all of us a reminder of constant renewal of life. (For this we pray:)** ℟.

1122  The celebrant then introduces the Lord's Prayer in these or similar words.

**Remembering that our baptism gave us the spirit of adopted children and mindful of our Savior's command, let us pray to our heavenly Father, saying:**

All:

**Our Father . . .**

The celebrant continues immediately:

**O God,
who endowed these waters with the power of death and life,
grant that those who are buried with Christ in this font
may put aside all sin
and rise again with him,
clothed in the radiant garment of immortality.**

**We ask this through Christ our Lord.**

℟. **Amen.**

1123  After the blessing, a song expressing paschal joy and thanksgiving or the Canticle of Mary may be sung.

1124  The assisting deacon then dismisses the people in the usual way.

CHAPTER 32

# ORDER FOR THE BLESSING OF
# A REPOSITORY FOR THE HOLY OILS

## INTRODUCTION

1125   The oils used for the celebration of the sacraments of initiation, holy orders, and the anointing of the sick according to ancient tradition are reverently reserved in a special place in the church. This repository should be secure and be protected by a lock.

1126   The vessels used to hold the holy oils should be worthy of their function and be closed in such a way as to prevent the oils from being spilled and to insure that they remain fresh.

1127   Each year when the bishop blesses the oils and consecrates the chrism, the pastor should see that the old oils are properly disposed of by burning and that they are replaced by the newly blessed oils.

1128   This order may be used for blessing a repository for the holy oils or blessing the vessels in which the oils are stored. The celebration may take place during Mass or a celebration of the word of God.

1129   The blessing may be given by a priest or deacon.

# I. ORDER OF BLESSING WITHIN MASS

**1130**   After the gospel reading, the celebrant in the homily, based on the sacred text and pertinent to the particular place and the people involved, explains the meaning of the celebration.

## General Intercessions

**1131**   The general intercessions follow, either in the form usual at Mass or in the form provided here. The celebrant concludes the intercessions with the prayer of blessing. From the following intentions those best for the occasion may be used or adapted, or other intentions that apply to the particular circumstances may be composed.

The celebrant says:

**The Holy Spirit has poured out God's love upon us and enables us to call upon the Father as we pray:**

℞. **Lord, hear our prayer.**

Or:

℞. **Hear us, O Lord.**

Assisting minister:

**That the Church may be filled with the transforming power of the Holy Spirit, let us pray to the Lord.** ℞.

Assisting minister:

**That those who are anointed with the oil of catechumens may resist sin and temptation and embrace Christ wholeheartedly, let us pray to the Lord.** ℞.

Assisting minister:

**That those who are sealed with holy chrism in baptism and confirmation may live their faith with confidence, let us pray to the Lord.** ℞.

**That those who are ordained to the service of God and the Church may be ministers of mercy, compassion, and love, let us pray to the Lord.** R⁷.

Assisting minister:

**That those who are anointed with the oil of the sick may be strengthened, comforted, and healed by the grace of the Holy Spirit, let us pray to the Lord.** R⁷.

## PRAYER OF BLESSING

1132  With hands outstretched, the celebrant says the prayer of blessing:

**Gracious and loving God,**
**you anointed priests, prophets, and kings of old**
  **with the oil of gladness.**
**You infuse your Church with the gifts of the Holy Spirit,**
**and heal, comfort, and sanctify**
**those anointed with oil in your name.**

**Let this repository (these vessels)**
**remind us always of your sacramental mysteries.**

**May the holy oils kept here,**
**the oil of the sick, the oil of catechumens, and holy chrism,**
**confirm our unity in faith and prayer with our bishop**
**and with all the members of your Church,**
**and be effective signs of the love**
**that you pour forth into our hearts.**

**We ask this through Christ our Lord.**

R⁷. **Amen.**

The holy oils are then placed in the repository.

# II. ORDER OF BLESSING WITHIN
# A CELEBRATION OF THE WORD OF GOD

1133　The present order may be used by a priest or a deacon.

## INTRODUCTORY RITES

1134　When the community has gathered, a suitable song may be sung. After the singing, the minister says:

**In the name of the Father, and of the Son, and of the Holy Spirit.**

All make the sign of the cross and reply:

**Amen.**

1135　The minister greets those present in the following or other suitable words, taken mainly from sacred Scripture.

**May the grace and love of God be with you always.**

And all reply:

**And also with you.**

1136　In the following or similar words, the minister prepares those present for the blessing.

**God manifests his grace through the sacramental signs he has entrusted to his Church. By the anointing with oil, the sick are strengthened and healed, the catechumens are empowered to resist Satan and to reject sin and evil, the baptized are sealed with the gifts of the Spirit, and the ministers of the Church are sanctified in God's service. Through the use of these holy oils may God's grace be poured forth always upon the Church.**

## READING OF THE WORD OF GOD

1137　A reader, another person present, or the minister reads a text of sacred Scripture.

**Brothers and sisters, listen to the words of the book of Leviticus:**
8:10-12

---

*Moses anointed and consecrated the Dwelling and all that was in it.*

**Taking the anointing oil, Moses anointed and consecrated the Dwelling, with all that was in it. Then he sprinkled some of this oil seven times on the altar, and anointed the altar, with all its appurtenances, and the laver, with its base, thus consecrating them. He also poured some of the anointing oil on Aaron's head, thus consecrating him.**

1138 Or:

Isaiah 61:1-3, 6, 8-9—*The Lord has anointed me to give them the oil of gladness.*

Revelation 1:5-8—*Christ has made us a line of kings, priests to serve his God and Father.*

Luke 4:16-21—*The spirit of the Lord has been given to me, for he has anointed me.*

1139 As circumstances suggest, the following responsorial psalm may be sung or some other suitable song.

R̥. **For ever I will sing the goodness of the Lord.**

Psalm 89

**"I have found David, my servant;
with my holy oil I have anointed him,
That my hand may be always with him,
and that my arm may make him strong.** R̥.

**"My faithfulness and my kindness shall be with him,
and through my name shall his horn be exalted.** R̥.

**"He shall say of me, 'You are my father,
my God, the Rock, my savior.'"** R̥.

1140 As circumstances suggest, the minister may give those present a brief explanation of the biblical text, so that they may understand through faith the meaning of the celebration.

## INTERCESSIONS

1141 The intercessions are then said. The minister introduces them and an assisting minister or one of those present announces the intentions. From the following those best suited to the occasion may be used or adapted, or other intentions that apply to the particular circumstances may be composed.

The minister says:

**The Holy Spirit has poured out God's love upon us and enables us to call upon the Father as we pray:**

**R̸. Hear us, O Lord.**

Assisting minister:

**That the Church may be filled with the transforming power of the Holy Spirit, let us pray to the Lord. R̸.**

Assisting minister:

**That those who are anointed with the oil of catechumens may resist sin and temptation and embrace Christ wholeheartedly, let us pray to the Lord. R̸.**

Assisting minister:

**That those who are sealed with holy chrism in baptism and confirmation may live their faith with confidence, let us pray to the Lord. R̸.**

Assisting minister:

**That those who are ordained to the service of God and the Church may be ministers of mercy, compassion, and love, let us pray to the Lord. R̸.**

Assisting minister:

**That those who are anointed with the oil of the sick may be strengthened, comforted, and healed by the grace of the Holy Spirit, let us pray to the Lord. R̸.**

1142 After the intercessions the minister, in the following or similar words, invites all present to sing or say the Lord's Prayer.

**The Spirit dwelling within us cries out and we dare to say:**

All:

**Our Father . . .**

## Prayer of Blessing

1143 The minister says the prayer of blessing with hands outstretched.

**Gracious and loving God,**
**you anointed priests, prophets, and kings of old**
**  with the oil of gladness.**
**You infuse your Church with the gifts of the Holy Spirit,**
**and heal, comfort, and sanctify**
**those anointed with oil in your name.**

**Let this repository (these vessels)**
**remind us always of your sacramental mysteries.**

**May the holy oils kept here,**
**the oil of the sick, the oil of catechumens, and holy chrism,**
**confirm our unity in faith and prayer with our bishop**
**and all the members of your Church,**
**and be effective signs of the love**
**that you pour forth into our hearts.**
**We ask this through Christ our Lord.**

R̷. **Amen.**

The holy oils are then placed in the repository.

## Concluding Rite

1144 The minister concludes the rite by saying:

**May the peace of God**
**which is beyond all understanding**
**keep your hearts and minds**
**in the knowledge and love of God**
**and of his Son, our Lord Jesus Christ.**

R̷. **Amen.**

Then he blesses all present.

**And may almighty God bless you all,**
**the Father, and the Son, ☩ and the Holy Spirit.**

R̷. **Amen.**

1145 It is preferable to end the celebration with a suitable song.

# III. SHORTER RITE

**1146**  All make the sign of the cross as the minister says:

**Our help is in the name of the Lord.**

All reply:

**Who made heaven and earth.**

**1147**  One of those present or the minister reads a text of sacred Scripture, for example:

**Brothers and sisters, listen to the words of the book of Leviticus:**                                            8:10-12

*Moses anointed and consecrated the Dwelling and all that was in it.*

**Taking the anointing oil, Moses anointed and consecrated the Dwelling, with all that was in it. Then he sprinkled some of this oil seven times on the altar, and anointed the altar, with all its appurtenances, and the laver, with its base, thus consecrating them. He also poured some of the anointing oil on Aaron's head, thus consecrating him.**

**1148**  Or:

Isaiah 61:1-3, 6, 8-9—*The Lord has anointed me to give them the oil of gladness.*

Revelation 1:5-8—*Christ has made us a line of kings, priests to serve his God and Father.*

Luke 4:16-21—*The spirit of the Lord has been given to me, for he has anointed me.*

**1149**  The minister says the prayer of blessing with hands outstretched.

**Gracious and loving God,**
**you anointed priests, prophets, and kings of old**
**    with the oil of gladness.**
**You infuse your Church with the gifts of the Holy Spirit,**
**and heal, comfort, and sanctify**
**those anointed with oil in your name.**

**Let this repository (these vessels)**
**remind us always of your sacramental mysteries.**

---

May the holy oils kept here,
the oil of the sick, the oil of catechumens, and holy chrism,
confirm our unity in faith and prayer with our bishop
and all the members of your Church,
and be effective signs of the love
that you pour forth into our hearts.

We ask this through Christ our Lord.

R̷. Amen.

The holy oils are then placed in the repository.

# CHAPTER 33

# ORDERS FOR A BLESSING ON THE OCCASION OF THE INSTALLATION OF A NEW EPISCOPAL OR PRESIDENTIAL CHAIR, A NEW LECTERN, A NEW TABERNACLE, OR A NEW CONFESSIONAL

## INTRODUCTION

1150   When a church is dedicated or blessed, all the appointments that are already in place are considered to be blessed along with the church. But when the episcopal chair in the cathedral church and, in other churches, the presidential chair, the tabernacle, the lectern for proclamation of the word, or the confessional are newly installed or renovated, there is an opportunity to teach the faithful the importance of such appointments by means of the celebration of a blessing.

1151   Those principles and rules must be respected that are laid down in the various liturgical books on the construction and design of the appointments for churches.

1152   The present orders may be used by a priest. While maintaining the structure and chief elements of the rite, the celebrant should adapt the celebration to the circumstances of the place and the people involved.

# I. ORDER FOR A BLESSING ON THE OCCASION OF THE INSTALLATION OF A NEW EPISCOPAL OR PRESIDENTIAL CHAIR

## INTRODUCTION

1153   The chair or *cathedra* of the bishop in the cathedral church is a pre-eminent sign of the teaching authority belonging to each bishop in his own Church. Consequently, the rite for the blessing of a new episcopal chair may only be celebrated by the diocesan bishop; but in altogether special circumstances, he may authorize another bishop to celebrate the rite.

1154   The place for the presider, that is, the chair for the priest celebrant, is a symbol of his office of presiding at the liturgical assembly and of guiding the prayer of the people of God.

1155   It is preferable that this rite be joined to the celebration of Mass, but, as occasion may suggest, it may also be joined to a celebration of the word of God.

## A. ORDER OF BLESSING WITHIN MASS

1156   On reaching the altar, the celebrant, with the assisting ministers, makes the customary reverence, kisses the altar, and incenses it. Then before going to the episcopal or presidential chair, he signs himself with the sign of the cross and says:

**In the name of the Father, and of the Son, and of the Holy Spirit.**

All make the sign of the cross and reply:

**Amen.**

1157   Using one of the usual formularies provided in the Sacramentary (Roman Missal), the celebrant greets those present.

1158   In the following or similar words, he then gives a suitable introduction to the Mass, at the same time explaining to the faithful the meaning of the rite being celebrated.

**Today this new (episcopal/presidential) chair is for the first time set aside for liturgical use. Let us together, my dear brothers and sisters, praise our God and Lord. Out of his goodness toward us, he is present through those who are ordained**

to fulfill a sacred ministry, in order that through them he may teach, sanctify, and shepherd the faithful. Let us ask God to make his servants ever more worthy to carry out such a holy ministry.

## PRAYER OF BLESSING

1159 After his introductory remarks, the celebrant, with hands joined, says:

**Let us pray.**

All pray briefly in silence; then, with hands outstretched, the celebrant continues:

**Lord Jesus,**
**with one voice we praise your holy name**
**and raise our hearts to you in prayer.**
**You are the Good Shepherd**
**who came to gather your scattered sheep into one fold.**
**Through those you have chosen as ministers of your truth,**
**feed your faithful;**
**through your chosen shepherds, lead them.**
**Then one day gather both shepherds and flock**
**into the joyous green pastures of eternity,**
**where you live and reign for ever and ever.**

R̰. **Amen.**

1160 The celebrant places incense in the censer and incenses the chair to be blessed, then takes his place at the chair, where he is incensed by a minister. During this time a suitable song is sung.

1161 The Mass, without the penitential rite, continues in the usual manner.

## B. ORDER OF BLESSING WITHIN A CELEBRATION OF THE WORD OF GOD

1162 When the blessing of an episcopal or presidential chair takes place within a celebration of the word of God, the procedure is as follows. After greeting those present and before he takes his seat, the celebrant, in the following or similar words, briefly addresses them, in order to prepare them for the celebration and to explain the meaning of the rite.

Today this new (episcopal/presidential) chair is for the first time set aside for liturgical use. Let us together, my dear brothers and sisters, praise our God and Lord. Out of his goodness toward us, he is present through those who are ordained to fulfill a sacred ministry, in order that through them he may teach, sanctify, and shepherd the faithful. Let us ask God to make his servants ever more worthy to carry out such a holy ministry.

## PRAYER OF BLESSING

1163 After his introductory remarks, the celebrant, with hands joined, says:

**Let us pray.**

All pray briefly in silence; then, with hands outstretched, the celebrant continues:

**Lord Jesus,**
**with one voice we praise your holy name**
**and raise our hearts to you in prayer.**
**You are the Good Shepherd**
**who came to gather your scattered sheep into one fold.**
**Through those you have chosen as ministers of your truth,**
**feed your faithful;**
**through your chosen shepherds, lead them.**
**Then one day gather both shepherds and flock**
**into the joyous green pastures of eternity,**
**where you live and reign for ever and ever.**

R̘. **Amen.**

1164 The celebrant places incense in the censer and incenses the chair to be blessed, then takes his place at the chair, where he is incensed by a minister. During this time a suitable song is sung.

## READING OF THE WORD OF GOD

1165 Texts of sacred Scripture are then read, between which, as circumstances suggest, there is a responsorial psalm or a period of silent reflection. The gospel reading always holds the place of honor.

**1166**  Readings:

Nehemiah 8:1-4a, 5-6, 8-10—*Ezra the scribe stood on a wooden dais erected for the purpose.*

Isaiah 40:9-11—*He is like a shepherd feeding his flock.*

Acts 10:34-48—*Now I and those with me can witness to everything he did.*

Acts 13:15-32—*We have come here to tell you the Good News that God has promised to our ancestors.*

Luke 4:16-22a—*All eyes in the synagogue were fixed on him.*

**1167**  Responsorial psalms:

Psalm 119:129, 130, 133, 135, 144

℞. (v. 105) **Your word, O Lord, is a lamp for my feet.**

Psalm 19B:8-9, 10, 15

℞. (see John 6:63c) **Your words, Lord, are spirit and life.**

**1168**  In the homily the celebrant gives those present an explanation of the biblical text and the truth of Christ's presence in virtue of the fact that ministers act in his name when exercising their office.

## INTERCESSIONS

**1169**  The intercessions are then said. The celebrant introduces them and an assisting minister or one of those present announces the intentions. From the following intentions those best suited to the occasion may be used or adapted, or other intentions that apply to the particular circumstances may be composed.

The celebrant says:

**Our Lord Jesus Christ so loved the Church that through its ministers and pastors it continues along the path of salvation, taught by the word of God and nourished by the sacraments. Let us therefore exalt his name with praise and say:**

℞. **O Lord, we thank you.**

Or:

℞. **Blessed be God for ever.**

Assisting minister:

**Blessed are you, O Lord, who through the teachers of the faith continue to teach us your Gospel. (Let us bless the Lord:) R⁷.**

Assisting minister:

**Blessed are you, O Lord, who through the pastors you have chosen continue to feed and strengthen your flock. (Let us bless the Lord:) R⁷.**

Assisting minister:

**Blessed are you, O Lord, who through the heralds of your word continue to urge and exhort us to sing the praises of the Father. (Let us bless the Lord:) R⁷.**

## PRAYER OF BLESSING

1170 With hands outstretched, the celebrant says the prayer of blessing.

**Lord Jesus Christ,
you taught the pastors of the Church
not to want to be served by others,
but to serve.**

**Grant that those who preside from this chair
will proclaim your word ardently
and celebrate your sacraments rightly,
so that, with the people entrusted to their care,
they may come before the seat of your majesty,
there to praise you without ceasing,
for you live and reign for ever and ever.**

**R⁷. Amen.**

## CONCLUDING RITE

1171 With hands outstretched over those present, the celebrant concludes the rite by saying:

**May God bless you with every heavenly blessing
and keep you holy and pure in his sight.
May he shower you with the riches of his glory,**

instruct you with the word of truth,
form your hearts with the Gospel of salvation,
and enrich you with love for one another,
now and for ever.

R̰. **Amen.**

Then he blesses all present.

**And may almighty God bless you all,
the Father, and the Son, ✛ and the Holy Spirit.**

R̰. **Amen.**

1172  It is preferable to end the celebration with a suitable song.

# II. ORDER FOR THE BLESSING
# OF A NEW LECTERN

## INTRODUCTION

1173 The lectern or ambo must be worthy to serve as the place from which the word of God is proclaimed and must be a striking reminder to the faithful that the table of God's word is always prepared for them. The present blessing may only be imparted to a true lectern, that is, not a simple, movable stand, but a lectern that is fixed and of a design worthy of its function. Because of the architecture of a particular church, a lectern may have to be movable, but if it is truly becoming, worthy of its function, and designed with beauty, such a lectern may be blessed.

1174 The present rite may be joined to the celebration of Mass and, as occasion suggests, may also be joined to a celebration of the word of God.

## A. ORDER OF BLESSING WITHIN MASS

1175 The Book of Gospels is carried in the entrance procession and placed on the altar. Everything proceeds in the usual way up to and including the opening prayer.

It is recommended that the proclamation of the word of God be carried out in this way: two readers, one of whom carries the Lectionary for Mass, and the psalmist (cantor) go to the celebrant. The celebrant stands, takes the Lectionary, holds it up before the assembly, and says the following or other suitable words.

**May the word of God always be heard in this place,
as it unfolds the mystery of Christ before you
and achieves your salvation within the Church.**

All make the following or some other suitable reply.

**Amen.**

1176 The celebrant then hands the Lectionary to the reader of the first reading. The readers and psalmist go to the lectern, carrying the Lectionary so that it is plainly visible to all.

1177 The readings are either those assigned for the Mass of the day, or the following texts may be chosen: first reading: Nehemiah 8:1-4a, 5-6, 8-10, followed by the responsorial psalm: Psalm 19B:8-9, 10, 15, with the response: "Your words, O Lord, are spirit and life''; if there is a second reading: 2 Timothy 3:14—4:5a. The verse before the gospel is ''No one lives on bread alone, but on every word that comes forth from the mouth of God'' with or without the ''alleluia,'' depending on the season; the recommended gospel reading is Luke 4:14-22a.

**1178** After the second reading, the assisting deacon, if one is present, or else the priest takes the Book of Gospels from the altar and, preceded by candlebearers and censer bearer, carries it to the lectern.

**1179** In the homily the celebrant gives those present an explanation of the biblical text and of the truth that Christ is present in the word of God.

**1180** Mass then continues in the usual way; as circumstances suggest, the profession of faith may be included, in order that the faithful may see that they should respond in faith to God, who has spoken to them in the proclamation of his word.

# B. ORDER OF BLESSING WITHIN A CELEBRATION OF THE WORD OF GOD

## INTRODUCTORY RITES

**1181** When the blessing of a lectern takes place within a celebration of the word of God, the procedure is as follows. After greeting those present, the celebrant, in the following or similar words, gives a brief address in order to prepare them for the celebration and to explain the meaning of the rite.

**Brothers and sisters, we have come together to bless this lectern and to begin its sacred use, namely, as the symbol to us all of the table of God's word that provides the first and necessary nourishment for our Christian life. Let us take part in this celebration attentively, listening faithfully to God speaking to us, so that his words may truly become for us spirit and life.**

**1182** After his introductory remarks, the celebrant, with hands joined, says:

**Let us pray.**

All pray briefly in silence; then, with hands outstretched, the celebrant continues:

**O God,**
**you speak to us not as strangers but as friends.**

**In your goodness grant us the grace of the Holy Spirit,**
**so that, in tasting the sweetness of your word,**
**we may be filled with the love of your Son**
**that surpasses all knowledge.**

**We ask this through Christ our Lord.**

R̷. **Amen.**

## READING OF THE WORD OF GOD

**1183**  Texts of sacred Scripture are then read, between which, as circumstances suggest, there is a responsorial psalm or a period of silent reflection. The gospel reading always holds the place of honor.

**1184**  Readings:

Nehemiah 8:1-4a, 5-6, 8-10—*Ezra read from the Law of God, translating and giving the sense so that the people understood what was read.*

2 Timothy 3:14—4:5a—*From the holy Scriptures you can learn the wisdom that leads to salvation through faith in Christ Jesus.*

Luke 4:16-22a—*This text is being fulfilled today even as you listen.*

**1185**  Responsorial psalms:

Psalm 19B:8-9, 10, 15

R̷. **(see John 6:63c) Your words, Lord, are spirit and life.**

Psalm 119:129, 130, 133, 135, 144

R̷. **(v. 105) Your word, O Lord, is a lamp for my feet.**

**1186**  In the homily the celebrant gives those present an explanation of the biblical text and of the truth that Christ is present in the word of God.

**1187**  As circumstances suggest, the profession of faith may be said or sung after the homily.

## INTERCESSIONS

**1188**  The intercessions are then said. The celebrant introduces them and an assisting minister or one of those present announces the intentions. From the following intentions those best suited to the occasion may be used or adapted, or other intentions that apply to the particular circumstances may be composed.

**Brothers and sisters, God the Father has presented us with the Word made flesh, so that hearing him we will be nourished by him and live faithfully for him. Let us then pray together to the Father, saying:**

R̸. **May the Word of Christ dwell in us with all its richness.**

Or:

R̸. **Lord, hear our prayer.**

Assisting minister:

**Lord, give to the followers of Christ your Son a constant hunger for your word, and make them your witnesses before the world. (For this we pray:) R̸.**

Assisting minister:

**Lord, grant that by searching deeply into your word we may remain firmly convinced in faith and resolute in the desire to do what is right and good. (For this we pray:) R̸.**

Assisting minister:

**Lord, in the light of your word give us knowledge of you and of ourselves, so that we will return your love and serve you as we ought. (For this we pray:) R̸.**

Assisting minister:

**Lord, stand by the ministers of your word, so that what they preach they will believe in their hearts and manifest in their actions. (For this we pray:) R̸.**

## PRAYER OF BLESSING

1189　With hands outstretched, the celebrant says the prayer of blessing.

**O God,**
**who have called us out of darkness into your own**
**　wonderful light,**
**we owe you our thanks at all times.**

You satisfy the hunger in our hearts
with the sweet nourishment of your word.
When we gather together in this church
you remind us again and again
of your wondrous words and works.

We pray that in this church
we may listen to the voice of your Son,
so that, responding to the inspiration of the Holy Spirit,
we may not be hearers only but doers of your word.

Grant that those who proclaim your message from this lectern
may show us how to direct our lives,
so that we will walk in the ways of Christ,
following him faithfully
until we reach eternal life.

We ask this though Christ our Lord.

R̶ʒ. **Amen.**

## Concluding Rite

1190 With hands outstretched over those present, the celebrant
concludes the rite by saying:

May God bless you with every heavenly blessing
and keep you holy and pure in his sight.
May he shower you with the riches of his glory,
instruct you with the word of truth,
form your hearts with the Gospel of salvation,
and enrich you with love for one another,
now and for ever.

R̶ʒ. **Amen.**

Then he blesses all present.

And may almighty God bless you all,
the Father, and the Son, ✝ and the Holy Spirit.

R̶ʒ. **Amen.**

1191 It is preferable to end the celebration with a suitable song.

# III. ORDER FOR THE BLESSING OF A NEW TABERNACLE

## INTRODUCTION

1192    The tabernacle for eucharistic reservation is a reminder of Christ's presence that comes about in the sacrifice of the Mass. But it is also a reminder of the brothers and sisters we must cherish in charity, since it was in fulfillment of the sacramental ministry received from Christ that the Church first began to reserve the eucharist for the sake of the sick and the dying.

In our churches adoration has always been offered to the reserved sacrament, the bread which came down from heaven.

## ORDER OF BLESSING

1193    The most fitting manner of celebrating this blessing is in conjunction with the celebration of Mass, in which, if the rubrics permit, the readings and prayers are taken from the Lectionary for Mass, Votive Masses, "Holy Eucharist."[16] In the homily the celebrant explains the word of God and should in some way always bring out for the faithful the meaning of this rite.

1194    After the general intercessions, the celebrant, standing near the tabernacle that is to be blessed and facing the assembly, invites all to pray, saying:

**Let us pray.**

As circumstances suggest, all may then pray for a moment in silence, after which the celebrant, with hands outstretched, says the prayer of blessing.

**Lord and Father of all holiness,**
**from whom the true bread from heaven has come down to us,**
**bless us and the tabernacle we have prepared**
**for the sacrament of Christ's body and blood.**
**Through our adoration of your Son present in the eucharist,**
**lead us to a closer union with the mystery of redemption.**

**We ask this through Christ our Lord.**

℟. **Amen.**

---

[16] See Lectionary for Mass (2nd ed., 1981), nos. 976-981 (Votive Masses, "Holy Eucharist").

**1195** The celebrant places incense in the censer and incenses the tabernacle.

**1196** The Mass proceeds in the usual manner, but after the communion of the faithful a pyx or ciborium containing the blessed sacrament is left on the altar table.

Following the prayer after communion, there may be a procession, suited to the particular circumstances, to the chapel or place where the new tabernacle has been installed.

During the procession, a suitable antiphon and psalm may be sung, for example, "Taste and see the goodness of the Lord" with Psalm 34:2-3, 4-5, 6-7, 8-9, or the antiphon "Body of Jesus, born of the Virgin Mary" (*"Ave, verum Corpus, natum de Maria Virgine"*), or some other suitable song.

**1197** When the procession has reached the place where the tabernacle is, the celebrant places the pyx or ciborium in the tabernacle and leaves the door open. After placing incense in the censer, he kneels and incenses the blessed sacrament. After a suitable pause for all to pray in silence, the celebrant closes the tabernacle door.

**1198** If it can be done conveniently, the assisting deacon, if one is present, or the celebrant may, in the following or similar words, invite those present to receive a blessing.

**Bow your heads and pray for God's blessing.**

Then, with hands outstretched over the people, the celebrant blesses them by saying:

**May the all-powerful and merciful God,**
**whose Son was the true and living temple on earth,**
**bless us and make us holy**
**through Christ's death and resurrection,**
**the mysteries we honor as we adore him.**

**R̲⁷. Amen.**

**May Christ, who before the eyes of his disciples**
**ascended into heaven to prepare a place for us,**
**and who is present here, invisible in the sacrament**
  **of the altar,**
**to bring us the grace that comes from his sacrifice alone,**
**help you and strengthen you always.**

**R̲⁷. Amen.**

**For all who come here to consider prayerfully**
**the work of their salvation,**
**may our Lord present in the eucharist**
**be the inexhaustible fountain of living water,**
**leaping up to provide eternal life.**

℟. **Amen.**

Then he blesses all present.

**And may the blessing of almighty God,**
**the Father, and the Son, ✠ and the Holy Spirit,**
**come upon you and remain with you for ever.**

℟. **Amen.**

1199 Instead of a blessing, the celebrant may say the following as a prayer over the people.

**Lord,**
**grant to your servants**
**a constant deepening in faith and in grace,**
**so that whenever we honor**
**your Son's loving presence among us,**
**we will be led to a more fruitful sharing**
**in the memorial of our redemption.**

**We ask this through Christ our Lord.**

℟. **Amen.**

After the prayer, the celebrant says:

**And may the blessing of almighty God,**
**the Father, and the Son, ✠ and the Holy Spirit,**
**come upon you and remain with you for ever.**

℟. **Amen.**

1200 When there is no procession, once the prayer after communion has been said, the pyx or ciborium is placed in the tabernacle and the door is left open. After placing incense in the censer, the celebrant kneels and incenses the blessed sacrament.

1201 After a suitable pause for all to pray in silence, the celebrant closes the tabernacle door and blesses the people, using one of the formularies given in nos. 1198 and 1199.

1202 The assisting deacon, if one is present, or the celebrant dismisses the people in the usual way.

# IV. ORDER FOR THE BLESSING OF A NEW CONFESSIONAL

## INTRODUCTION

1203 The practice of reserving a special place in churches for the celebration of the sacrament of reconciliation is a clear expression of the truth that sacramental confession and absolution constitute a liturgical action which involves the entire body of the Church and is intended to renew the participation of the faithful in the Church's offering of the sacrifice of Christ.

1204 The celebration of the present blessing is never to be joined to the celebration of Mass, but it may be opportune to join such a celebration to a penitential service.

## ORDER OF BLESSING

### INTRODUCTORY RITES

1205 When the community has gathered, a psalm, antiphon, or some other suitable song may be sung, as circumstances suggest.

1206 After the singing, the priest says:

**In the name of the Father, and of the Son, and of the Holy Spirit.**

All make the sign of the cross and reply:

**Amen.**

1207 The celebrant greets those present in the following or other suitable words, taken mainly from sacred Scripture.

**May grace, peace, and mercy from God the Father, through Jesus Christ, in the Holy Spirit, from whom we have the remission of all our sins, be with you all.**

All make the following or some other suitable reply.

**And also with you.**

1208 In the following or similar words, the priest gives the faithful a brief instruction on the meaning of the rite.

The rite of blessing in which our faith leads us to take part moves us to learn that again and again we should thank God, who shows his almighty power most of all when in mercy he pardons our sins. We come to this confessional as sinners and we leave forgiven and restored to grace, because of the ministry of reconciliation that Christ Jesus has entrusted to his Church. Out of Christ's goodness those who are weighed down by sin are relieved of their burden when they come to the confessional; those who come here with the stains of evil upon them go away cleansed, washed in the blood of the Lamb.

## READING OF THE WORD OF GOD

1209   The celebration of the word of God follows. A reader, another person present, or the celebrant reads one or more texts of sacred Scripture, chosen from those given in the lectionary of the *Rite of Penance*[17] or from those listed here.

2 Samuel 12:1-9, 13—*David said to Nathan: I have sinned against Yahweh.*

Ezekiel 18:20-32—*If the wicked renounce all their sins, they will certainly live; they will not die.*

Romans 5:6-11—*We are filled with joyful trust in God, through our Lord Jesus Christ, through whom we have already gained our reconciliation.*

2 Corinthians 5:17-21—*God in Christ was reconciling the world to himself.*

Matthew 9:1-8—*Courage, my child, your sins are forgiven.*

Luke 7:36-50—*Her many sins must have been forgiven her, or she would not have shown such great love.*

John 8:1-11—*Go away and sin no more.*

1210   As circumstances suggest, one of the following responsorial psalms may be sung or said, or some other suitable song may be sung.

Psalm 32:1-2, 3-4, 5, 6-7

Ry. (v. 5c) **I will confess my sins to the Lord.**

Psalm 51:3-4, 5-6, 7-8, 9-10, 11-12

Ry. (v. 14a) **Give back to me the joy of salvation.**

---

[17] See *Rite of Penance,* ch. IV, nos. 101–201.

Psalm 130:1-2, 3-4, 5-6b, 6c-8

℟. (v. 7bc) **With the Lord there is mercy and fullness of redemption.**

1211   In the homily the celebrant gives those present an explanation of the biblical text and of the ecclesial significance of the sacrament of penance.


## INTERCESSIONS

1212   The intercessions are then said. The celebrant introduces them and an assisting minister or one of those present announces the intentions. From the following intentions those best suited to the occasion may be used or adapted, or other intentions that apply to the particular circumstances may be composed.

The celebrant says:

**Brothers and sisters, let us give thanks to God, the almighty Father, who through the death and resurrection of his Son, in the power of the Holy Spirit, has delivered us from the dominion of darkness and forgiven us all our sins.**

℟. **O Lord, we thank you.**

Or:

℟. **Blessed be God for ever.**

Assisting minister:

**Blessed are you, O Lord, who have given your Son for our sins, so that you might snatch us from the power of darkness and bring us into the light and peace of your kingdom. (Let us bless the Lord:)** ℟.

Assisting minister:

**Blessed are you, O Lord, who through the Holy Spirit rid our conscience of the works of death. (Let us bless the Lord:)** ℟.

Assisting minister:

**Blessed are you, O Lord, who have given your Church the keys of the kingdom, so that the gates of your mercy may open wide to all. (Let us bless the Lord:)** ℟.

Assisting minister:

**Blessed are you, O Lord, who always accomplish great and wonderful deeds in the ministry of reconciliation, so that those whom you pardon may one day reach eternal life. (Let us bless the Lord:) R℟.**

## PRAYER OF BLESSING

1213  With hands outstretched, the celebrant continues:

**All-powerful and ever-living God,
we do well always and everywhere
to give you thanks.
Whether out of justice you correct
or out of compassion forgive,
your ways with us are always marked by mercy:
your chastisement keeps us from perishing for ever
and your forbearance gives us time to correct our ways.**

**We give you praise through Christ our Lord.**

**R℟. Amen.**

## CONCLUDING RITE

1214  With hands outstretched over those present, the celebrant concludes the rite by saying:

**May the Father,
who has called us to adoption as his children,
bless us.**

**R℟. Amen.**

**May the Son,
who has taken us as his brothers and sisters,
help us.**

**R℟. Amen.**

**May the Holy Spirit,
who has chosen us as a dwelling place,
remain with us.**

**R℟. Amen.**

Then he blesses all present.

**And may almighty God bless you all,
the Father, and the Son, ✝ and the Holy Spirit.**

℟. **Amen.**

**1215** It is preferable to end the celebration with a suitable song.

# CHAPTER 34

# ORDER FOR THE BLESSING OF NEW CHURCH DOORS

## INTRODUCTION

1216   In the liturgical celebrations of baptism, marriage, and funerals provision is made for a rite of reception at the doors of the church. On certain days of the liturgical year, the faithful pass through these doors in procession into the body of the church. It is proper, then, that in construction, design, and decoration church doors should stand as a symbol of Christ, who said: "I am the door, whoever enters through me will be safe," and of those who have followed the path of holiness that leads to the dwelling place of God.

1217   The installation of new church doors can be taken as an opportunity to call the attention of the faithful to the happy occasion itself and to the inner significance of the church building, to which the doors provide entrance.

   The blessing of church doors, then, is truly an occasion for offering special prayers to God and for gathering together the faithful to hear the word of God and to give voice to their petitions.

1218   The present order may be used by a priest. While maintaining the structure and chief elements of the rite, the celebrant should adapt the celebration to the circumstances of the place and the people involved.

# ORDER OF BLESSING

## INTRODUCTORY RITES

1219 When the community has gathered outside the doors of the church, a suitable song may be sung, for example, the following antiphon with Psalm 24.

Ant. **Lift up your heads, O gates, be lifted up, O ancient doors.**

After the singing, the celebrant says:

**In the name of the Father, and of the Son, and of the Holy Spirit.**

All make the sign of the cross and reply:

**Amen.**

1220 The celebrant greets those present in the following or other suitable words, taken mainly from sacred Scripture.

**Grace and peace in God's holy Church be with you all.**

All make the following or some other suitable reply.

**And also with you.**

1221 In the following or similar words, the celebrant briefly addresses the faithful, in order to prepare them for the celebration and to explain the rite.

**Brothers and sisters, gathered for the blessing of the new church doors, let us take part in this celebration with reverence and a spirit of devotion. Let us pray fervently to the Lord that all who enter the church through these doors in order to hear the word of God and celebrate the sacraments may heed the voice of Christ: it is Christ who gave himself to us as the true door to eternal life.**

1222 After his introductory remarks, the celebrant says:

**Let us pray.**

All pray briefly in silence; then, with hands outstretched, the celebrant continues:

**O God,**
**you have honored your people**
**with the dignity of being called your Church.**
**Grant that this assembly of your faithful**
**may revere and love you,**
**and with you as their leader**
**reach the promised rewards of heaven.**

**We ask this through Christ our Lord.**

**℞. Amen.**

## READING OF THE WORD OF GOD

**1223**  A reader, another person present, or the celebrant reads a text of sacred Scripture.

**Brothers and sisters, listen to the words of the book of Revelation:**                                          21:2-3, 23-26

*I saw the holy city coming down out of heaven from God.*

**I also saw the holy city, a new Jerusalem, coming down out of heaven from God, prepared as a bride adorned for her husband. I heard a loud voice from the throne saying, ''Behold, God's dwelling is with the human race. He will dwell with them and they will be his people and God himself will always be with them as their God.''**

**The city had no need of sun or moon to shine on it, for the glory of God gave it light, and its lamp was the Lamb. The nations will walk by its light; to it the kings of the earth will bring their treasure. During the day its gates will never be shut, and there will be no night there. The treasure and wealth of the nations will be brought there.**

**1224**  Or:

Isaiah 26:1-9—*Open up the gates to let in a nation that is just.*

Jeremiah 7:1-7—*Stand at the gate of the house of the Lord and there proclaim this message.*

John 10:1-10—*I am the sheepgate.*

**1225**  As circumstances suggest, one of the following responsorial psalms may be sung or said, or some other suitable song.

---

R̶?. **Serve the Lord with gladness.**

Psalm 100

**Sing joyfully to the LORD, all you lands;
serve the LORD with gladness;
come before him with joyful song.** R̶?.

**Know that the LORD is God;
he made us, his we are;
his people, the flock he tends.** R̶?.

**Enter his gates with thanksgiving,
his courts with praise;
Give thanks to him; bless his name.** R̶?.

**For he is good:
the LORD, whose kindness endures forever,
and his faithfulness to all generations.** R̶?.

Psalm 118:1 and 4, 15-16, 19-20, 22-23

R̶?. **(v. 26) Blessed is he who comes in the name of the Lord.**

**1226** As circumstances suggest, the celebrant may give those present a brief explanation of the biblical text, so that they may understand through faith the meaning of the celebration.

# INTERCESSIONS

**1227** As circumstances suggest, the prayer of blessing may be preceded by the intercessions. The celebrant introduces them and an assisting minister or one of those present announces the intentions. From the following intentions those best suited to the occasion may be used or adapted, or other intentions that apply to the particular circumstances may be composed. The intentions are followed immediately by the prayer of blessing, no. 1229.

The celebrant says:

**We are living stones, built upon Christ, who is God's chosen cornerstone. Let us together offer intercession to Christ for the Church, which he loves, and profess our trust in that Church, saying:**

℟. **This is God's house, the gate of heaven.**

Or:

℟. **Lord, hear our prayer.**

Assisting minister:

**Lord Jesus, Good Shepherd and door of the sheepfold, make your flock increase, gather it together in unity, and protect it from harm. (For this we pray:) ℟.**

Assisting minister:

**You built your own house upon rock; strengthen the Church in firm faith and unshakable trust in you. (For this we pray:) ℟.**

Assisting minister:

**From your side flowed water and blood; fill your Church with life through the sacraments of your new and everlasting covenant. (For this we pray:) ℟.**

Assisting minister:

**You promised to be present wherever two or three gather in your name; listen to your Church praying together, one in mind and in heart. (For this we pray:) ℟.**

Assisting minister:

**With the Father and the Holy Spirit you dwell in the hearts of those who love you; bring your Church to perfection in charity. (For this we pray:) ℟.**

Assisting minister:

**You never cast out those who come to you; welcome all sinners into your Father's house. (For this we pray:) ℟.**

1228  When there are no intercessions, the celebrant, before the prayer of blessing and using the following or other similar words, invites those present to ask for God's help.

**My brothers and sisters, we have happily gathered here to bless these new church doors. Let us then lift our voices to pray that God will draw near with his grace.**

As circumstances suggest, all may then pray for a moment in silence before the prayer of blessing.

## Prayer of Blessing

1229 With hands outstretched, the celebrant says the prayer of blessing.

**We praise you, Lord God, Father all-holy.**
**You sent your Son into our world**
**to gather by the shedding of his blood**
**those whom the destructive power of sin had scattered.**
**You sent him to unite us all in the one sheepfold.**
**He is the Good Shepherd;**
**he is the door through which those who follow him**
**enter and are safe, go in and go out, and find pasture.**

**Grant that those who enter this church**
**with confident faith in him**
**may persevere in the teaching of the apostles,**
**in the breaking of the bread,**
**and in unceasing prayer,**
**and so be built into the heavenly Jerusalem.**

**We ask this through Christ our Lord.**

℟. **Amen.**

1230 After the prayer of blessing, as circumstances suggest, the celebrant may sprinkle the new doors with holy water; then he places incense in the censer and incenses the doors.

## Concluding Rite

1231 With hands outstretched over the faithful, the celebrant blesses them.

**The Lord God of heaven and earth**
**has been pleased to bring you together today**
**for the blessing of these doors.**
**May he also welcome you within his gates giving thanks,**
**and allow you to enter his courts singing songs of praise,**
**so that you may share in the inheritance of eternal happiness.**

℟. **Amen.**

Then he blesses all present.

**And may the blessing of almighty God,
the Father, and the Son, ✛ and the Holy Spirit,
come upon you and remain with you for ever.**

℟. **Amen.**

1232   It is preferable to end the celebration with a suitable song.

# Chapter 35

# ORDER FOR THE BLESSING OF A NEW CROSS FOR PUBLIC VENERATION

## Introduction

1233  Of all sacred images the "figure of the precious, life-giving cross of Christ"[18] is preeminent, because it is the symbol of the entire paschal mystery. The cross is the image most cherished by the Christian people and the most ancient; it represents Christ's suffering and victory and at the same time, as the Fathers of the Church have taught, it points to his Second Coming.

1234  On Good Friday the cross is presented to the faithful for their adoration and on the feast of the Triumph of the Cross, 14 September, it is honored as the symbol of Christ's victory and the tree of life. But the cross also is the sign under which the people gather whenever they come to church and in the homes of the baptized it holds a place of honor. When the times and local conditions permit, the faithful erect a cross in a public place as an attestation of their faith and a reminder of the love with which God has loved us.

1235  The image of the cross should preferably be a crucifix, that is, have the corpus attached, especially in the case of a cross that is erected in a place of honor inside a church.

1236  The present order may be used by a priest. While maintaining the structure and chief elements of the rite, the celebrant should adapt the celebration to the circumstances of the place and the people involved.

  When, as is desirable, the bishop is the celebrant, everything should be adapted accordingly.

1237  The blessing of a new cross may be celebrated at any hour and on any day, except Ash Wednesday, the Easter triduum, and All Souls Day. But the preferred day is one that permits a large attendance of the faithful. They should receive proper preparation for their active participation in the rite.

1238  The order presented in this chapter is meant for only two situations:
1      the solemn blessing of a cross erected in a public place, separate from a church;
2      the blessing of the principal cross that occupies a central place in the body of the church where the worshiping community assembles.

---

[18] Council of Nicaea II, Act. 7: Mansi 13, 378; Denzinger-Schoenmetzer, no. 601.

# ORDER OF BLESSING

## INTRODUCTORY RITES

1239  When feasible, it is preferable for the community of the faithful to go in procession from the church or another location to the site where the cross that is to be blessed has been erected. When a procession either is not feasible or seems inadvisable, the faithful simply assemble at the site of the cross.

1240  When the people have gathered, the celebrant greets them in the following or other suitable words, taken mainly from sacred Scripture.

**The grace of Jesus Christ our Lord, who for our sake hung upon the cross, be with you all.**

All make the following or some other suitable reply.

**And also with you.**

1241  In the following or similar words, the celebrant briefly addresses the faithful in order to prepare them for the celebration and to explain the meaning of the rite.

**My dear brothers and sisters, we are here for the blessing of a new cross. Let us venerate in faith the eternal plan by which God has made the cross of Christ the preeminent sign of his mercy.**

**As we look upon the cross, let us call to mind that on it Christ brought to completion the sacrament of his love for the Church.**

**As we bow before the cross, let us remember that in his own blood Christ has removed all divisions and out of the many nations created the one people of God.**

**As we venerate the cross, let us reflect that we are ourselves Christ's disciples and must therefore follow him, willingly taking up our own cross each day.**

**Let us, then, take part with all our hearts in this celebration, so that we may grasp the mystery of the cross more clearly and experience its power more deeply.**

1242  After his introductory remarks, the celebrant says:

**Let us pray.**

All pray briefly in silence; then the celebrant continues:

**Lord,
your Son reconciled us to you
by suffering on the cross
and then returned to you in glory.**

**May your people who have raised this cross as a sign of redemption
find in it protection and strength;
may they shoulder their own crosses
in the spirit of the Gospel
until their journey ends.**

**We ask this through Christ our Lord.**

℟. **Amen.**

1243 When there is to be a procession, the assisting deacon then says:

**Let us proceed in peace.**

1244 The procession to the site of the cross is then formed. During the procession the following antiphon with Psalm 98 and the doxology, or a hymn, or some other suitable song is sung.

Ant. **We should glory in the cross of our Lord Jesus Christ.**

Psalm 98

**Sing to the LORD a new song,
for he has done wondrous deeds.** ℟.

**His right hand has won victory for him, his holy arm.
The LORD has made his salvation known:
in the sight of the nations he has revealed his justice.
He has remembered his kindness and his faithfulness
toward the house of Israel.
All the ends of the earth have seen
the salvation by our God.** ℟.

**Sing joyfully to the LORD, all you lands;
break into song; sing praise.
Sing praise to the LORD with the harp,
with the harp and melodious song.
With trumpets and the sound of the horn
sing joyfully before the King, the LORD.** ℟.

**Let the sea and what fills it resound,**
**the world and those who dwell in it;**
**Let the rivers clap their hands,**
**the mountains shout with them for joy**
**Before the LORD, for he comes,**
**for he comes to rule the earth;**
**He will rule the world with justice**
**and the peoples with equity. R̶7.**

**Glory to the Father, and to the Son, and to the Holy Spirit:**
**as it was in the beginning, is now, and will be for ever. Amen.**
**R̶7.**

> **1245** When there is no procession, the opening prayer is fol-
> lowed immediately by the reading of the word of God.

## READING OF THE WORD OF GOD

> **1246** A reader, another person present, or the minister reads a
> text of sacred Scripture, taken preferably from the texts given in
> the Lectionary for Mass, Votive Masses, "Holy Cross,"[19] or from
> those indicated here. Each reading is followed by a responsorial
> psalm, related to it, or an interval of silence. The gospel reading
> always holds the place of honor. The readings on Christ's pas-
> sion given in the Lectionary for Mass may also be used.[20]

**Brothers and sisters, listen to the words of the apostle Paul to**
**the Philippians:**                                              2:5-11

*He humbled himself, obediently accepting even death, death on a cross.*

**Have among yourselves the same attitude that is also yours**
**in Christ Jesus,**

**Who, though he was in the form of God,**
**did not regard equality with God something to be grasped.**
**Rather, he emptied himself,**
**taking the form of a slave,**
**coming in human likeness;**
**and found human in appearance,**
**he humbled himself,**

---

[19] See Lectionary for Mass (2nd ed., 1981), nos. 969–974 (Votive Masses, "Holy Cross").
[20] See ibid., no. 975 (Readings from the Account of the Lord's Passion).

---

becoming obedient to death,
even death on a cross.

Because of this, God greatly exalted him
and bestowed on him the name
that is above every name,
that at the name of Jesus
every knee should bend,
of those in heaven and on earth and under the earth,
and every tongue confess that
Jesus Christ is Lord,
to the glory of God the Father.

**1247**  Or:

Numbers 21:4-9—*Whoever looks at the fiery serpent shall live.*

1 Corinthians 2:1-5—*I have told you of the witness of the crucified Christ.*

Hebrews 4:12-16—*Let us be confident in approaching the throne of grace.*

John 3:13-17—*The Son of Man must be lifted up.*

John 19:25-27—*Near the cross of Jesus there stood his Mother.*

**1248**  As circumstances suggest, one of the following responsorial psalms may be sung or said, or some other suitable song.

℟. **My God, my God, why have you abandoned me?**

Psalm 22

**All who see me scoff at me;
they mock me with parted lips, they wag their heads:
"He relied on the LORD; let him deliver him,
let him rescue him, if he loves him." ℟.**

**Indeed, many dogs surround me,
a pack of evildoers closes in upon me;
They have pierced my hands and my feet;
I can count all my bones. ℟.**

**I will proclaim your name to my brethren;
in the midst of the assembly I will praise you:
"You who fear the LORD, praise him;
all you descendants of Jacob, give glory to him." ℟.**

Psalm 31:2 and 6, 12-13, 15-16

R/. (Luke 23:46) **Father, I put my life in your hands.**

Psalm 55:5-6, 13, 14-15, 17-18, 23

R/. (v. 23ab) **Throw your cares on the Lord, and he will support you.**

1249   As circumstances suggest, the celebrant may give those present a brief explanation of the biblical text, so that they may understand through faith the meaning of the celebration.

## PRAYER OF BLESSING

1250   After the homily, the celebrant, standing before the cross and with hands outstretched, says the prayer of blessing.

**Blessed are you, Lord God, Father all-holy,
for your boundless love.
The tree, once the source of shame and death for humankind,
has become the cross of our redemption and life.**

**When his hour had come to return to you in glory,
the Lord Jesus,
our King, our Priest, and our Teacher,
freely mounted the scaffold of the cross
and made it his royal throne,
his altar of sacrifice,
his pulpit of truth.**

**On the cross,
lifted above the earth,
he triumphed over our age-old enemy.
Cloaked in his own blood,
he drew all things to himself.**

**On the cross,
he opened out his arms
and offered you his life:
the sacrifice of the New Law
that gives to the sacraments their saving power.**

**On the cross,
he proved what he had prophesied:
the grain of wheat must die
to bring forth an abundant harvest.**

Father,
we honor this cross
as the sign of our redemption.
May we reap the harvest of salvation
planted in pain by Christ Jesus.
May our sins be nailed to his cross,
the power of life released,
pride conquered,
and weakness turned to strength.

May the cross be our comfort in trouble,
our refuge in the face of danger,
our safeguard on life's journey,
until you welcome us to our heavenly home.

Grant this through Christ our Lord.

R⃰. Amen.

1251  Or:

Lord God, Father all-holy,
you will the cross of your Son to be
the fountain of all blessings,
the source of all grace.

In your goodness be near us
who have raised this cross
as a sign of our faith.

May we always hold fast
to the mystery of Christ's suffering
and enter the joy of his risen life,
who is Lord for ever and ever.

R⃰. Amen.

1252  Then the celebrant places incense in the censer and incenses the cross. After this, one of the following antiphons or some other song in honor of the cross is sung.

Ant. **We worship you, Lord, we venerate your cross, we praise your resurrection. Through the cross you brought joy to the world.**

Or:

Ant. **Through the sign of the cross, O saving God, deliver us from those who would do us harm.**

**1253** After the singing, the celebrant, the ministers, and the faithful venerate the new cross, if this can be done conveniently. One by one all go to the cross and offer some sign of reverence in keeping with local custom. But if this procedure is impossible, the celebrant speaks a few words, inviting the people to venerate the cross, either by observing an interval of silent prayer or by some appropriate acclamation, for example:

**This sign of the cross will appear in the heavens, when the Lord comes to judge us.**

## Concluding Rite

**1254** The veneration of the cross is followed by intercessions, either in the form usual at Mass or in the form given here.

The celebrant says:

**Let us pray with confidence to Christ, who has redeemed us by his cross, as we say:**

℟. **By the power of your cross, save us, O Lord.**

Or:

℟. **Lord, hear our prayer.**

Assisting minister:

**Christ Jesus, you emptied yourself, taking the form of a servant and being made like us; grant that your people may follow the example of your humility. (For this we pray:)** ℟.

Assisting minister:

**Christ Jesus, you humbled yourself and became obedient unto death, even death on a cross; grant that your servants may imitate your obedience and patient endurance of trials. (For this we pray:)** ℟.

Assisting minister:

**Christ Jesus, you were raised up by the Father and given the name that is above all names; may your people persevere in your service to the end. (For this we pray:)** ℟.

**Christ Jesus, at your name every knee, in heaven, on earth, and under the earth, will bend in adoration; draw all people to your heart so that they will honor and adore you in faith. (For this we pray:) ℟.**

Assisting minister:

**Christ Jesus, every tongue shall proclaim to the glory of the Father: Jesus Christ is Lord; welcome our brothers and sisters who have died into the unfailing joy of your kingdom. (For this we pray:) ℟.**

1255   In the following or similar words, the celebrant invites all present to sing or say the Lord's Prayer.

**We have remembered the words and example of our Lord in his passion: in faith let us surrender ourselves as he did to the will of the Father, using the words our Savior taught us.**

All:

**Our Father . . .**

The celebrant immediately continues:

**O God,
to save the whole human race
you allowed your Son to undergo the agony of the cross.**

**Listen kindly to our prayer,
that we who on earth confess the mystery of redemption
may in heaven receive the glorious reward won by our
Redeemer.**

**We ask this through Christ our Lord.**

**℟. Amen.**

1256   After the celebrant blesses the people in the usual way, the assisting deacon dismisses them.

CHAPTER 36

# ORDER FOR THE BLESSING OF IMAGES FOR PUBLIC VENERATION BY THE FAITHFUL

## INTRODUCTION

1257    God made us in his own image and likeness,[21] but by sinning we disfigured this image. By dying out of love, Christ, the full and complete "image of the invisible God,"[22] restored in us the divine image. Those who follow Christ become in him a new creation[23] and are being transformed into his image[24] by the working of the Holy Spirit.

1258    The Church encourages the devout veneration of sacred images by the faithful, in order that they may see more deeply into the mystery of God's glory. For that glory has shone in the face of Christ[25] and is reflected in his saints, who have become "light in the Lord."[26]

In many instances sacred images are masterpieces of art, noble in inspiration and resplendent with the beauty that goes out from God and leads back to him. For the faithful such images recall our Lord and the saints whom they depict, but they also in some way lead the faithful back to the Lord and the saints themselves. "The more often we gaze on these images, the quicker we who behold them are led back to their prototypes in memory and in hope."[27]

Accordingly, the veneration of images ranks among the chief and important forms of the *cultus* that is due to the saints.[28] Images are venerated "not because of a belief that these images themselves possess anything of divinity or power, but because the honor shown them is directed to the prototypes they represent."[29]

---

[21] See Genesis 1:26-27.

[22] Colossians 1:15.

[23] See 2 Corinthians 5:17.

[24] See 2 Corinthians 3:18.

[25] See 2 Corinthians 4:6; Matthew 17:2.

[26] Ephesians 5:8.

[27] Council of Nicaea II, Act. 7: Mansi 13, 378; Denzinger-Schoenmetzer, no. 601.

[28] See SC, art. 111.

[29] Council of Trent, sess. 25: Denzinger-Schoenmetzer, no. 1823.

1259　Whenever a new sacred image is first exposed for public veneration by the faithful, particularly in a church, there should be a solemn blessing by use of the special rite given here; but the rite is not to be celebrated within Mass. Images that will be venerated in the homes of the faithful are blessed by use of the rite given in chapter 44.

1260　The present chapter contains rites for the blessing of:
a. an image of our Lord;
b. an image of the blessed Virgin Mary;
c. an image of a saint or of saints.

1261　The present order may be used by a priest. While maintaining the structure and chief elements of the rite, the celebrant should adapt the celebration to the circumstances of the place and the people involved.

When, as is desirable, the bishop is the celebrant, everything should be adapted accordingly.

1262　If celebrated within evening prayer, the blessing takes place on the day requiring or permitting the evening prayer that celebrates the title represented by the image.

Evening prayer is celebrated in the usual way. The psalmody should preferably be followed by a longer reading, taken from those provided in the Lectionary for Mass for celebrations of our Lord, the blessed Virgin Mary, or the saints.

After the reading, the celebrant in the homily explains both the biblical readings and the significance of images in the life of the Church.

As circumstances suggest, the readings or the homily may be followed by an interval of silent reflection on the word of God. A responsory from the liturgy of the hours is then sung or some other song of similar character.

After the singing, the celebrant says the prayer of blessing, which is followed by the singing of the Canticle of Mary with its proper antiphon. During the singing, the altar, the cross, and the new image are incensed. Then the minister and the people may be incensed.

Evening prayer then continues in the usual way.

# I. ORDER FOR THE BLESSING OF AN IMAGE OF OUR LORD JESUS CHRIST

## INTRODUCTORY RITES

**1263** When the community has gathered, a suitable song may be sung. After the singing, the celebrant says:

**In the name of the Father, and of the Son, and of the Holy Spirit.**

All make the sign of the cross and reply:

**Amen.**

**1264** The celebrant greets those present in the following or other suitable words, taken mainly from sacred Scripture.

**The grace and peace of God our Father and our Lord Jesus Christ, the image of the unseen God, be with you all.**

All make the following or some other suitable reply.

**And also with you.**

**1265** In the following or similar words, the celebrant briefly addresses the faithful, in order to prepare them for the celebration and to explain the meaning of the rite.

**Dear brothers and sisters, we have genuine reason to rejoice, because we are about to bless this image of our Lord Jesus Christ (title\*), to be erected for public veneration. This image honors, above all, the truth that Christ is the visible image of the invisible God. The eternal Son of God, who came down to the womb of the Virgin Mary, is the sign and sacrament of God the Father. As Christ himself said: "He who sees me sees the Father." Therefore when we honor this image, let us lift up our eyes to Christ, who reigns for ever with the Father and the Holy Spirit.**

---

\*Insert the title or mystery of the Lord represented by the image.

## READING OF THE WORD OF GOD

**1266** A reader, another person present, or the celebrant reads a text of sacred Scripture, taken preferably from those given in the Lectionary for Mass or in the lectionary of *The Liturgy of the Hours* for the celebration of the particular mystery of our Lord depicted by the image, or from the texts given here. Each reading is followed by a responsorial psalm, related to it, or an interval of silence. The gospel reading always holds the place of honor.

**Brothers and sisters, listen to the words of the apostle Paul to the Colossians:**                                                      1:12-20

*Christ the Lord is the image of the invisible God.*

**Give thanks to the Father, who has made you fit to share in the inheritance of the holy ones in light. He delivered us from the power of darkness and transferred us to the kingdom of his beloved Son, in whom we have redemption, the forgiveness of sins.**

**He is the image of the invisible God,**
**the firstborn of all creation.**
**For in him were created all things in heaven and on earth,**
**the visible and the invisible,**
**whether thrones or dominions or principalities or powers;**
**all things were created through him and for him.**
**He is before all things,**
**and in him all things hold together.**
**He is the head of the body, the church.**
**He is the beginning, the firstborn from the dead,**
**that in all things he himself might be preeminent.**
**For in him all the fullness was pleased to dwell,**
**and through him to reconcile all things for him,**
**making peace by the blood of his cross**
**through him, whether those on earth or those in heaven.**

**1267** Or:

John 14:1-11—*Whoever sees me, sees the Father.*

**1268** As circumstances suggest, one of the following responsorial psalms may be sung or said, or some other suitable song.

℟. O Lord, our God, how wonderful your name in all the earth!

Psalm 8

When I behold your heavens, the work of your fingers,
the moon and the stars which you set in place—
What is man that you should be mindful of him,
or the son of man that you should care for him? ℟.

You have made him little less than the angels,
and crowned him with glory and honor.
You have given him rule over the works of your hands. ℟.

Revelation 15:3, 4

℟. (Revelation 14:7) Fear God and give him glory.

1269 As circumstances suggest, the celebrant may give those present a brief explanation of the biblical text and of the mystery of the Lord represented by the new image, so that they may understand through faith the meaning of the celebration.

## INTERCESSIONS

1270 As circumstances suggest, the prayer of blessing may be preceded by the intercessions. The celebrant introduces them and an assisting minister or one of those present announces the intentions. From the following intentions those best suited to the occasion may be used or adapted, or other intentions that apply to the particular circumstances may be composed. The intentions are followed immediately by the prayer of blessing, no. 1272 or no. 1273.

The celebrant says:

Let us pray to God the Father, who has given us the Word, through whom all things were made and in whom they have their being; he is our Savior and Redeemer.

℟. Lord, make us like your Son.

Or:

℟. Lord, hear our prayer.

Assisting minister:

Father, your Son is boundless wisdom and the truth above all truths; grant that we may grow in our knowledge of him and the desire to remain united to him. (For this we pray:) ℟.

Assisting minister:

**Father, you have sent your Son into the world and raised him up to glory; grant us the joy of having Christ with us all the days of our life. (For this we pray:) R⁊.**

Assisting minister:

**Father, you have anointed Christ as Priest, King, and Prophet; grant that Christ may regard us as pleasing offerings, as faithful subjects, and as attentive listeners. (For this we pray:) R⁊.**

Assisting minister:

**Father, it is your will that in Christ we should have a teacher who is gentle and humble of heart; grant that we may obediently learn from him kindness and goodness. (For this we pray:) R⁊.**

Assisting minister:

**Father, through the blood of Christ's cross you have reconciled all things to yourself; make us instruments of your peace and reconciliation. (For this we pray:) R⁊.**

Assisting minister:

**Father, in the mysterious design of your providence you willed our Savior's death on the cross as the victory over death and hell; grant that we may die with him so that we may also rise with him. (For this we pray:) R⁊.**

1271 When there are no intercessions, the celebrant, before the prayer of blessing and using the following or other similar words, invites those present to ask for God's help.

**Brothers and sisters, let us pray to the all-powerful Father, that as we honor the mystery of Christ we may share in the benefits he has won for our salvation.**

As circumstances suggest, all may then pray for a moment in silence before the prayer of blessing.

# PRAYER OF BLESSING

1272 With hands outstretched, the celebrant says the prayer of blessing.

**Good Father,
lover of the human race,
we praise you for the great love shown us
in the sending of your Word.
Born of the Virgin,
he became our Savior,
our firstborn brother,
like us in all things but sin.**

**You have given us Christ
as the perfect example of holiness:**

**We see him as a child in the manger,
yet acknowledge him God almighty.**

**We see his face
and discern the countenance of your goodness.**

**We hear him speak the words of life
and are filled with your wisdom.**

**We search the deepest reaches of his heart
and our own hearts burn with that fire of the Spirit
which he spread in order to renew the face of the earth.**

**We look on the Bridegroom of the Church,
streaked in his own blood,
but we revere that blood,
which washes our sins away.**

**The Church rejoices in the glory of his resurrection
and shares in the promise it holds.**

**Lord,
listen to our prayer.
As your faithful people honor this image of your Son
may they be of one mind with Christ.
May they exchange the image of the old Adam of earth
by being transformed into Christ, the new Adam from heaven.**

**May Christ be the way that leads them to you,
the truth that shines in their hearts,
the life that animates their actions.**

---

May Christ be a light to their footsteps,
a safe place of rest on their journey,
and the gate that opens to them the city of peace.
For he lives there reigning with you and the Holy Spirit,
one God for ever and ever.

R̸. Amen.

1273 Or:

Lord,
although your glory lies beyond our sight,
out of your great love
you have revealed yourself in the person of Christ.
May those who have crafted
this image of your Son
show him honor by growing in his likeness,
who is Lord for ever and ever.

R̸. Amen.

1274 After the prayer of blessing, the celebrant places incense
in the censer and incenses the image, as an antiphon, psalm,
hymn, or some other song suited to the mystery represented by
the image is sung.

## CONCLUDING RITE

1275 With hands outstretched over the people, the celebrant
blesses them by saying:

May the peace of God, which surpasses all understanding,
keep your minds and hearts
in the knowledge and love of God
and of his Son, our Lord Jesus Christ,
now and for ever.

R̸. Amen.

Then he blesses all present.

And may almighty God bless you all,
the Father, and the Son, ✝ and the Holy Spirit.

R̸. Amen.

1276 It is preferable to end the celebration with a suitable song.

# II. ORDER FOR THE BLESSING OF AN IMAGE OF THE BLESSED VIRGIN MARY

## INTRODUCTORY RITES

1277  When the community has gathered, a suitable song may be sung. After the singing, the celebrant says:

**In the name of the Father, and of the Son, and of the Holy Spirit.**

All make the sign of the cross and reply:

**Amen.**

1278  The celebrant greets those present in the following or other suitable words, taken mainly from sacred Scripture.

**The grace of our Lord Jesus Christ, born of the Virgin Mother, and the love of God and the fellowship of the Holy Spirit be with you all.**

All make the following or some other suitable reply.

**And also with you.**

1279  In the following or similar words, the celebrant briefly addresses the faithful, in order to prepare them for the celebration and to explain the meaning of the rite.

**My dear brothers and sisters, we have gathered here in joy for the solemn blessing of this image of the blessed Virgin Mary. Under the title N., this image will remind us of the close ties of Mary to Christ and his Church. First of all, she is Christ's Mother, the Mother of the visible image of the invisible God. But she is also the image and the model of the Church, and she is its exemplar. In Mary the Church joyously contemplates the image of all that the Church itself desires and hopes wholly to be. The Church recognizes in Mary the model of the path and the practice it must follow to reach complete union with Christ. As the Spouse of Christ, the Church raises its eyes to Mary, the exemplar it must look to in carrying out the work of the apostolate. We should strive to take part in this service with the greatest intensity and reverent devotion.**

# Reading of the Word of God

1280 A reader, another person present, or the celebrant reads a text of sacred Scripture, taken preferably from the texts given either in the Lectionary for Mass or in the lectionary of *The Liturgy of the Hours* for the Common or a proper of the blessed Virgin, or from the texts given here. Each reading is followed by a responsorial psalm, related to it, or an interval of silence. The gospel reading always holds the place of honor.

**Brothers and sisters, listen to the words of the holy gospel according to Luke:** 1:42-50

*All generations shall call me blessed.*

**Elizabeth cried out in a loud voice and said, ''Most blessed are you among women, and blessed is the fruit of your womb. And how does this happen to me, that the mother of my Lord should come to me? For at the moment the sound of your greeting reached my ears, the infant in my womb leaped for joy. Blessed are you who believed that what was spoken to you by the Lord would be fulfilled.''**

**And Mary said:**

**''My soul proclaims the greatness of the Lord;
my spirit rejoices in God my savior.
For he has looked upon his handmaid's lowliness;
behold, from now on will all ages call me blessed.
The Mighty One has done great things for me,
and holy is his name.
His mercy is from age to age
to those who fear him.''**

1281   Or:

Revelation 11:19a and 12:1-6a, 10ab—*A great sign appeared in the heavens.*

Luke 1:26-38—*You are to conceive and bear a son.*

John 19:25-27—*This is your Son. This is your mother.*

1282   As circumstances suggest, one of the following responsorial psalms may be sung or said, or some other suitable song.

R̷. **Blessed be the name of the Lord for ever.**

Psalm 113

**Praise, you servants of the LORD,**
**praise the name of the LORD.**
**Blessed be the name of the LORD**
**both now and forever.** R̷.

**From the rising to the setting of the sun**
**is the name of the LORD to be praised.**
**High above all nations is the LORD,**
**above the heavens is his glory.** R̷.

**Who is like the LORD, our God, who is enthroned on high**
**and looks upon the heavens and the earth below?** R̷.

**He raises up the lowly from the dust;**
**from the dunghill he lifts up the poor**
**To seat them with princes,**
**with the princes of his own people.** R̷.

Luke 1:46-47, 48-49, 50-51, 52-53, 54-55

R̷. **(Luke 1:49) The Almighty has done great things for me, and**
**holy is his Name.**

1283　As circumstances suggest, the celebrant may give a homily, explaining the biblical text and the place of Mary in the history of salvation, so that those present may understand through faith the meaning of the celebration.

# INTERCESSIONS

1284　As circumstances suggest, the prayer of blessing may be preceded by the intercessions. The celebrant introduces them and an assisting minister or one of those present announces the intentions. From the following intentions those best suited to the occasion may be used or adapted, or other intentions that apply to the particular circumstances may be composed. The intentions are followed immediately by the prayer of blessing, no. 1286 or no. 1287.

**Let us glorify our Savior, who chose to be born of the Virgin Mary and let us pray to him, saying:**

℞. **Lord, through your Mother's intercession, hear our prayer.**

Or:

℞. **Lord, hear our prayer.**

Assisting minister:

**Savior of the world, by your redeeming power you preserved your Mother from every stain of sin; keep watch over us that we may not sin. (For this we pray:)** ℞.

Assisting minister:

**Our Lord and Redeemer, you dwelt within the immaculate Virgin Mary and made her the sanctuary of the Holy Spirit; make us temples of the same Spirit for ever. (For this we pray:)** ℞.

Assisting minister:

**Christ our Priest, your Mother stood at the foot of the cross; grant through her intercession that we may rejoice to share in your passion. (For this we pray:)** ℞.

Assisting minister:

**King of Kings, you lifted up your Mother, body and soul, into heaven; help us fix our thoughts and hearts on the things above. (For this we pray:)** ℞.

Assisting minister:

**Lord of heaven and earth, you crowned Mary and set her at your right hand as queen; make us worthy to share also in this glory. (For this we pray:)** ℞.

1285 When there are no intercessions, the celebrant, before the prayer of blessing and using the following or other similar words, invites those present to ask for God's help.

**As we are gathered here together like the apostles with the Mother of Jesus, let us also like them offer our prayers to God.**

As circumstances suggest, all may then pray for a moment in silence before the prayer of blessing.

# PRAYER OF BLESSING

1286 With hands outstretched, the celebrant says the prayer of blessing.

Lord God,
we acknowledge your infinite glory
and the abundance of your gifts.
Before the foundation of the world,
you appointed Christ
the beginning and end of all things.

You chose the blessed Virgin Mary
as the Mother and companion of your Son,
the image and model of your Church,
the Mother and advocate of us all.

She is the new Eve,
through whom you restored
what the first Eve had lost.
She is the daughter of Zion,
who echoed in her heart
the longings of the patriarchs
and the hopes of Israel.

She is the poor and lowly servant,
who trusted solely in her Lord.

In the fullness of time
she was delivered of the Sun of justice,
the dayspring from on high,
your Son, Jesus Christ.

In her flesh she was his Mother,
in her person, his disciple,
in her love, his servant.

Father,
may your children who have provided
this image (statue) of Mary
know her protection
and trace in their hearts the pattern of her holiness.

Bless them with faith and hope, love and humility;
bless them with strength in hardship and self-respect
  in poverty;

bless them with patience in adversity and kindheartedness
in times of plenty.

May they search for peace,
strive for justice,
and realize your love,
as they pursue their journey through life
toward your heavenly city,
where the blessed Virgin Mary
intercedes as Mother and reigns as Queen.

We ask this through Christ our Lord.

R̸. **Amen.**

1287 Or:

**Lord,
in the blessed Virgin
you have given your pilgrim Church
an image of the glory to come.**

**May those who have fashioned this likeness of Mary
look to her as a model of holiness
for all your chosen people.**

**Grant this through Christ our Lord.**

R̸. **Amen.**

1288 After the prayer of blessing, as circumstances suggest, the celebrant may place incense in the censer and incense the image. During this time a psalm, a hymn to Mary under the title represented by the image, or one of the following antiphons may be sung.

Ant. **Blessed are you, O Virgin Mary, for the Lord has exalted you above all other women on the earth.**

Or:

Ant. **We turn to you for protection, holy Mother of God. Listen to our prayers and help us in our needs. Save us from every danger, glorious and blessed Virgin.**

# CONCLUDING RITE

1289 With hands outstretched over the people, the celebrant blesses them by saying:

**Through the motherhood of Mary,**
**God in his goodness has chosen**
**to redeem the human race.**
**May he enrich you with his blessing.**

R̸. **Amen.**

**May you always and everywhere**
**experience the protection of Mary,**
**through whom you have received the author of life.**

R̸. **Amen.**

**May you who have come here today out of devotion**
**take away with you the gift of joy in your hearts**
**and the rewards of heaven.**

R̸. **Amen.**

Then he blesses all present.

**And may almighty God bless you all,**
**the Father, and the Son, ✠ and the Holy Spirit.**

R̸. **Amen.**

1290   It is preferable to end the celebration with a suitable song.

# III. ORDER FOR THE BLESSING OF IMAGES OF THE SAINTS

## INTRODUCTORY RITES

1291   When the community has gathered, a suitable song may be sung. After the singing, the celebrant says:

**In the name of the Father, and of the Son, and of the Holy Spirit.**

All make the sign of the cross and reply:

**Amen.**

1292   The celebrant greets those present in the following or other suitable words, taken mainly from sacred Scripture.

**The grace of our Lord Jesus Christ, who is the crowning glory of all the saints, and the love of God and the fellowship of the Holy Spirit be with you all.**

All make the following or some other suitable reply.

**And also with you.**

1293   In the following or similar words, the celebrant briefly addresses the faithful, in order to prepare them for the celebration and to explain the meaning of the rite.

**My brothers and sisters, as we begin to celebrate this rite in praise of God on the occasion of the unveiling of this beautiful new image of Saint N. for public veneration, we must be properly disposed and have a clear appreciation of the meaning of this celebration. When the Church blesses a picture or statue and presents it for public veneration by the faithful, it does so for the following reasons: that when we look at the representation of those who have followed Christ faithfully, we will be motivated to seek the city that is to come; that we will learn the way that will enable us most surely to attain complete union with Christ; that, as we struggle along with our earthly cares, we will be mindful of the saints, those friends and coheirs of Christ who are also our own brothers and sisters and our special benefactors; that we will remember how they love us, are near us, intercede ceaselessly for us, and are joined to us in a marvelous communion.**

# READING OF THE WORD OF GOD

**1294** A reader, another person present, or the celebrant reads a text of sacred Scripture, taken preferably from the texts given in the Lectionary for Mass or in the lectionary of *The Liturgy of the Hours* for the Commons or a proper of the saints, or from the texts given here. Each reading is followed by a responsorial psalm, related to it, or an interval of silence. The gospel reading always holds the place of honor.

**Brothers and sisters, listen to the words of the holy gospel according to Matthew:**                                                5:1-12a

*Be glad and rejoice, your reward is great in heaven.*

**When Jesus saw the crowds, he went up the mountain, and after he had sat down, his disciples came to him. He began to teach them, saying:**

**"Blessed are the poor in spirit,
for theirs is the kingdom of heaven.
Blessed are they who mourn,
for they will be comforted.
Blessed are the meek,
for they will inherit the land.
Blessed are they who hunger and thirst for righteousness,
for they will be satisfied.
Blessed are the merciful,
for they will be shown mercy.
Blessed are the clean of heart,
for they will see God.
Blessed are the peacemakers,
for they will be called children of God.
Blessed are they who are persecuted for the sake
  of righteousness,
for theirs is the kingdom of heaven.**

**Blessed are you when they insult you and persecute you and utter every kind of evil against you falsely because of me. Rejoice and be glad, for your reward will be great in heaven."**

**1295** Or:

Ephesians 3:14-19—*Knowing the love of Christ, which is beyond all knowing.*

1 Peter 4:7b-11—*Each one of you has received a special grace; put yourself at the service of others.*

1 John 5:1-5—*This is the victory over the world, our faith.*

**1296** As circumstances suggest, one of the following responsorial psalms may be sung or said, or some other suitable song.

R̸. **Blessed are they who delight in the law of the Lord.**

Psalm 1

**Happy the man who follows not
the counsel of the wicked
Nor walks in the way of sinners,
nor sits in the company of the insolent,
But delights in the law of the LORD
and meditates on his law day and night.** R̸.

**Not so the wicked, not so;
they are like chaff which the wind drives away.
For the LORD watches over the way of the just,
but the way of the wicked vanishes.** R̸.

Psalm 15:2-3, 4-5

R̸. **(see v. 1b) The just shall live on your holy mountain, O Lord.**

Psalm 34:2-3, 4-5, 6-7, 8-9, 10-11

R̸. **(v. 2a) I will bless the Lord at all times.**

**1297** As circumstances suggest, the celebrant may give a homily, explaining the biblical text and the place of the saints in the life of the Church, so that those present may understand through faith the meaning of the celebration.

## INTERCESSIONS

**1298** As circumstances suggest, the prayer of blessing may be preceded by the intercessions. The celebrant introduces them and an assisting minister or one of those present announces the intentions. From the following intentions those best suited to the occasion may be used or adapted, or other intentions that apply to the particular circumstances may be composed. The intentions are followed immediately by the prayer of blessing, no. 1300 or no. 1301.

**God our Father makes his saints into the likeness of his Son and by the power of the Holy Spirit continually sanctifies the Church. Let us therefore offer our petitions to him, saying:**

℟. **Through the intercession of Saint N., save us, O Lord.**

Or:

℟. **Lord, hear our prayer.**

Assisting minister:

**O God, source of all holiness, in the saints you have shown the many splendors of your grace; grant that in them we may honor your majesty. (For this we pray:)** ℟.

Assisting minister:

**O God of all wisdom, through your Son Jesus Christ you built your Church on the foundation of the apostles; keep their teaching secure among your faithful people. (For this we pray:)** ℟.

Assisting minister:

**You made the martyrs powerful witnesses even to the point of giving up their lives; help all Christians to bear faithful witness to your Son. (For this we pray:)** ℟.

Assisting minister:

**You gave holy virgins the gift of imitating the virginity of Christ; grant that we may see in consecrated virginity a special sign of the promises of heaven. (For this we pray:)** ℟.

Assisting minister:

**In all your saints you show your presence and make known your countenance and your word; grant to your faithful that when they honor the saints they will find themselves drawn closer to you. (For this we pray:)** ℟.

1299 When there are no intercessions, the celebrant, before the prayer of blessing and using the following or other similar words, invites those present to ask for God's help.

We are a people gathered into one by the power of the Holy Spirit, called to the same holiness. Let us therefore together raise our prayers to our one God and Father.

As circumstances suggest, all may then pray for a moment in silence before the prayer of blessing.

## PRAYER OF BLESSING

1300 With hands outstretched, the celebrant says the prayer of blessing.

Lord,
we bless you for you alone are holy,
and because in your compassion for sinners
you sent into the world your Son, Jesus Christ,
the author and perfecter of holiness.

He sent the Spirit
to sustain his newborn Church,
a voice that teaches us the secrets of holiness,
a breeze that strengthens and refreshes,
a fire that sears our hearts in love,
the seed of God that yields a harvest of grace.

Today we praise you
for the gifts of the Spirit bestowed on Saint N.,
in whose honor we dedicate this image (statue).

May we follow in the footsteps of the Lord,
keeping before us the example of Saint N.,
and grow to a maturity
measured not by nature, but by the fullness of Christ.

May we proclaim his Gospel by word and deed
and, shouldering our crosses daily,
expend ourselves for others in your service.

As we carry out our earthly duties,
may we be filled with the Spirit of Christ
and keep our eyes fixed on the glories of heaven,
where you, Father, receive those who will reign
  with your Son,
for ever and ever.

R̸. Amen.

**1301** Or:

**O God,
source of all grace and holiness,
look kindly on your servants
who have erected this image of Saint N.,
the friend and coheir of Christ.
He/she is for us your witness to the life of the Gospel
and stands in your presence to plead for us.
Grant that we may benefit from his/her intercession.**

**We ask this through Christ our Lord.**

**℟. Amen.**

**1302** After the prayer of blessing, as circumstances suggest, the celebrant may place incense in the censer and incense the image. During this time, a psalm or a hymn in honor of the saint whose image is being blessed or one of the following antiphons may be sung.

Ant. **Sing praise to our God, all you his servants, all who worship him reverently, great and small. The Lord our all-powerful God is King; let us rejoice, sing praise, and give him glory.**

Or:

Ant. **Let the peoples declare the wisdom of the saints and the Church proclaim their praises.**

## CONCLUDING RITE

**1303** With hands outstretched over the people, the celebrant blesses them by saying:

**God, the crowning glory
and the joy of all his saints,
has graciously given you
the gift of their patronage.
May he continue to bestow his blessing upon you.**

**℟. Amen.**

Delivered from present evils
by the intercession of the saints
and guided by the example of their holy lives,
may you be found always ready
to serve God and your neighbor.

R̷. **Amen.**

**The Church rejoices in serenity
that you, sons and daughters of the Church,
are destined to join the saints in heaven
and to share their unending happiness.**

R̷. **Amen.**

Then he blesses all present.

**And may almighty God bless you all,
the Father, and the Son, ✝ and the Holy Spirit.**

R̷. **Amen.**

1304  It is preferable to end the celebration with a suitable song.

# CHAPTER 37

# ORDER FOR THE BLESSING OF BELLS

## INTRODUCTION

1305  It is an ancient practice to summon the Christian people to the liturgical assembly by means of some sign or signal and also to alert them to important happenings in the local community. The peal of bells, then, is in a way the expression of the sentiments of the people of God as they rejoice or grieve, offer thanks or petition, gather together and show outwardly the mystery of their oneness in Christ.

1306  Because bells are so closely involved in the life of the Christian people, the longstanding custom of blessing the bells before they are hung in the belfry or campanile should be continued.

1307  The bells should be hung or set up in the place chosen for the blessing in such a way that it will be easy to walk around the bells or ring them, if this suits the occasion.

1308  Depending on the place and the individual circumstances, the bells are blessed either outside or inside the church and by use of the rite given in nos. 1310–1323. When it is decided that bells should be blessed within Mass, the blessing takes place after the homily and the provisions in no. 1324 are followed.

1309  The present order may be used by a priest. While maintaining the structure and chief elements of the rite, the celebrant should adapt the celebration to the circumstances of the place and the people involved.

When, as is desirable, the bishop is the celebrant, everything should be adapted accordingly.

# ORDER OF BLESSING

## INTRODUCTORY RITES

1310   When the community has gathered, a suitable song may be sung. After the singing, the celebrant says:

**In the name of the Father, and of the Son, and of the Holy Spirit.**

All make the sign of the cross and reply:

**Amen.**

1311   The celebrant greets those present in the following or other suitable words, taken mainly from sacred Scripture.

**The grace of our Lord Jesus Christ and the love of God, who makes us one Church, and the fellowship of the Holy Spirit be with you all.**

All make the following or some other suitable reply.

**And also with you.**

1312   In the following or similar words, the celebrant briefly addresses the faithful, in order to prepare them for the celebration and to explain the meaning of the rite.

**Dear brothers and sisters, today is a joyous and happy day for all of us, as the new bells are installed in our church and we have the opportunity in this celebration to praise God's name. Bells have a special place in the life of God's people: the peal of bells marks the hours for prayer and calls us to the celebration of the liturgy; bells alert us to important events, both happy and sad, in the life of the Church and the community. Let us, then, participate devoutly in this celebration, so that whenever we hear the ringing of the bells we will remember that we are one family, coming together to show our unity in Christ.**

## READING OF THE WORD OF GOD

1313   A reader, another person present, or the celebrant reads a text of sacred Scripture, taken preferably from the texts given here.

---

**Brothers and sisters, listen to the words of the holy gospel according to Mark:** 16:14-16, 20

*Go into the whole world and proclaim the Good News to all creation.*

**Later, as the eleven were at table, Jesus appeared to them and rebuked them for their unbelief and hardness of heart because they had not believed those who saw him after he had been raised. He said to them, "Go into the whole world and proclaim the gospel to every creature. Whoever believes and is baptized will be saved; whoever does not believe will be condemned."**

**They went forth and preached everywhere, while the Lord worked with them and confirmed the word through accompanying signs.**

1314   Or:

Numbers 10:1-8, 10—*Make two trumpets of beaten silver.*

1 Chronicles 15:11-12, 25-28; 16:1-2—*They brought back the ark of the covenant of the Lord with joyful shouting and to the sound of horns, trumpets, and cymbals.*

Isaiah 40:1-5, 9-11—*Cry out at the top of your voice, Jerusalem, herald of good news.*

Acts 2:36-39, 41-42—*To you the promise was made and to all whom the Lord our God calls.*

Matthew 3:1-11—*John the Baptizer came preaching: The reign of God is at hand.*

Mark 1:1-8—*A herald's voice in the desert, crying: Make ready the way of the Lord.*

1315   As circumstances suggest, one of the following responsorial psalms may be sung or said, or some other suitable song.

℟. **The voice of the Lord is mighty, the voice of the Lord is majestic.**

Psalm 29

**Give to the LORD, you sons of God,
give to the LORD glory and praise,
Give to the LORD the glory due his name;
adore the LORD in holy attire. ℟.**

The voice of the LORD is over the waters,
the God of glory thunders,
the LORD, over vast waters.
The voice of the LORD breaks the cedars,
the LORD breaks the cedars of Lebanon. R̸.

The voice of the LORD strikes fiery flames;
the voice of the LORD shakes the desert,
the LORD shakes the wilderness of Kadesh.
The voice of the LORD twists the oaks
and strips the forests,
and in his temple all say, "Glory!" R̸.

The LORD is enthroned above the flood;
the LORD is enthroned as king forever.
May the LORD give strength to his people;
may the LORD bless his people with peace! R̸.


Psalm 150:1-2, 3-4, 5

R̸. (v. 2b) **Praise the Lord for his abundant greatness.**

1316 As circumstances suggest, the celebrant may give those present a brief explanation of the biblical text, so that they may understand through faith the meaning of the celebration.


## INTERCESSIONS

1317 As circumstances suggest, the prayer of blessing may be preceded by the intercessions. The celebrant introduces them and an assisting minister or one of those present announces the intentions. From the following intentions those best suited to the occasion may be used or adapted, or other intentions that apply to the particular circumstances may be composed. The intentions are followed immediately by the prayer of blessing, no. 1319 or no. 1320.

The celebrant says:

**To God our Father, whose will it is to form one Church out of many peoples, let us offer our prayers with one heart, saying:**

R̸. **Gather your Church from all peoples.**

*Assisting minister:*

**Lord God, you never cease to summon us to unity, so that, as we are enlivened by the one Spirit, we may walk together in the one path of salvation.** ℟.

*Assisting minister:*

**Lord God, your will is that we, your people, become a fuller sign of your presence in the world.** ℟.

*Assisting minister:*

**Lord God, you teach us to share in each other's joys and sorrows, so that our mutual love will be increased.** ℟.

*Assisting minister:*

**Lord God, on this day you fill our assembly with the joys of heaven, so that we may proclaim your mysteries to all our brothers and sisters.** ℟.

1318 When there are no intercessions, the celebrant, before the prayer of blessing and using the following or other similar words, invites those present to ask for God's help.

**Let us now reaffirm our praise and petition to the Father, who has gathered us together in one house.**

As circumstances suggest, all may then pray for a moment in silence before the prayer of blessing.

## PRAYER OF BLESSING

1319 With hands outstretched, the celebrant says the prayer of blessing.

**We praise you, Lord, Father all-holy.**
**To a world wounded and divided by sin**
**you sent your only Son.**
**He gave his life for his sheep,**
**to gather them into one fold**
**and to guide and feed them**
**as their one shepherd.**

May your people
hasten to your church
when they hear the call of this bell.

May they persevere in the teaching of the apostles,
in steadfast fellowship, in unceasing prayer,
and in the breaking of the bread.
May they remain ever one in mind and heart
to the glory of your name.

Grant this through Christ our Lord.

℟. Amen.

1320   Or:

Lord,
from the beginning of time
your voice has called to us,
inviting us to communion with you,
teaching us the mysteries of your life,
guiding us on the way to salvation.

With silver trumpets Moses summoned Israel
to gather as your people.
Now you are pleased that in the Church
the sound of bells should summon your people to prayer.

By this blessing ✛ accept
these bells into your service.

May their voice direct our hearts toward you
and prompt us to come gladly to this church,
there to experience the presence of Christ,
listen to your word,
offer you our prayers,
and both in joy and in sorrow
be friends to one another.

We ask this through Christ our Lord.

℟. Amen.

1321   After the prayer of blessing, as circumstances suggest, the
celebrant may sprinkle the bells with holy water and then place
incense in the censer and incense them. During this time the following antiphon with Psalm 149 and the doxology or some other
suitable song may be sung.

Ant. **Sing to the Lord, praise his name, alleluia.**

Psalm 149

**Sing to the LORD a new song
of praise in the assembly of the faithful.
Let Israel be glad in their maker,
let the children of Zion rejoice in their king.** R℣.

**Let them praise his name in the festive dance,
let them sing praise to him with timbrel and harp.
For the LORD loves his people,
and he adorns the lowly with victory.** R℣.

**Let the faithful exult in glory;
let them sing for joy upon their couches.** R℣.

**Glory to the Father, and to the Son, and to the Holy Spirit:
as it was in the beginning, is now, and will be for ever. Amen.**
R℣.

## CONCLUDING RITE

1322 With hands outstretched over the people, the celebrant
blesses them by saying:

**From many peoples,
God has gathered his own people.
In his kindness may he bless you,
who have joined so gladly in the blessing of these new bells.**

R℣. **Amen.**

**In his mercy may he grant
that when he calls you to this church
through the clear voice of these bells
you will listen attentively to his word.**

R℣. **Amen.**

**And may he grant
that you will celebrate the divine mysteries
united in spirit,
putting aside all division
and accepting one another in sincere charity.**

R℣. **Amen.**

Then he blesses all present.

**And may almighty God bless you all,
the Father, and the Son, ✝ and the Holy Spirit.**

℞. **Amen.**

> 1323   As circumstances suggest, the celebrant and the people
> may ring the newly blessed bells in jubilation. It is preferable to
> end the celebration with a suitable song.

1324   If the blessing of bells is to be celebrated within Mass (see no. 1308),
the following provisions are to be observed.

The Mass is the Mass of the day.

Except on solemnities, feasts, and Sundays, the readings may be taken
either from the Mass of the day or from those given in nos. 1313–1315.

The blessing takes place after the homily, according to the rite set
out in nos. 1317–1321.

# CHAPTER 38

# ORDER FOR THE BLESSING OF AN ORGAN

## INTRODUCTION

1325   Music is of the highest importance in the celebration of the divine mysteries, and in the Latin Church among musical instruments the organ has always held a place of honor.* Whether as an accompaniment for singing or as a solo instrument, this instrument adds splendor to sacred celebrations, offers praise to God, fosters a sense of prayer in the faithful, and raises their spirits to God.

Because of its close connection with the music and song for liturgical services and popular devotions, an organ should be blessed before being played for the first time in a liturgical celebration.

1326   The present order may be used by a priest. While maintaining the structure and chief elements of the rite, the celebrant should adapt the celebration to the circumstances of the place and the people involved.

When, as is desirable, the bishop is the celebrant, everything should be adapted accordingly.

1327   The blessing may be celebrated on any day, except in those seasons when liturgical law limits the use of the organ.

---

* SC, art. 120 specifies the pipe organ, *organum tubulatum*.

# ORDER OF BLESSING

## INTRODUCTORY RITES

1328 When the community has gathered, a suitable song may be sung. After the singing, the celebrant says:

**In the name of the Father, and of the Son, and of the Holy Spirit.**

All make the sign of the cross and reply:

**Amen.**

1329 The celebrant greets those present in the following or other suitable words, taken mainly from sacred Scripture.

**The love of God our Father, the peace of our Lord Jesus Christ, and the comfort of the Holy Spirit be with you all.**

Or:

**May the Lord, whose praises are sung by the saints, be with you all.**

All make the following or some other suitable reply.

**And also with you.**

1330 In the following or similar words, the celebrant briefly addresses the faithful, in order to prepare them for the celebration and to explain the meaning of the rite.

**My dear brothers and sisters, we have come together to bless this new organ, installed so that the celebration of the liturgy may become more beautiful and solemn. The purpose of music in the liturgy is above all to give glory to God and to lead us to holiness. Thus the music of the organ wonderfully expresses the new song that Scripture tells us to sing to the Lord. To sing this new song is to live rightly, to follow God's will eagerly and gladly, and, by loving one another, to carry out the new commandment that Jesus gave us.**

## READING OF THE WORD OF GOD

1331 A reader, another person present, or the celebrant reads a text of sacred Scripture, taken preferably from the texts given here.

**Brothers and sisters, listen to the words of the apostle Paul to the Colossians:** 3:12-17

*Sing gratefully to God from your hearts.*

**Put on then, as God's chosen ones, holy and beloved, heartfelt compassion, kindness, humility, gentleness, and patience, bearing with one another and forgiving one another, if one has a grievance against another; as the Lord has forgiven you, so must you also do. And over all these put on love, that is, the bond of perfection. And let the peace of Christ control your hearts, the peace into which you were also called in one body. And be thankful. Let the word of Christ dwell in you richly, as in all wisdom you teach and admonish one another, singing psalms, hymns, and spiritual songs with gratitude in your hearts to God. And whatever you do, in word or in deed, do everything in the name of the Lord Jesus, giving thanks to God the Father through him.**

1332  Or:

Numbers 10:1-10—*You shall blow the trumpets over your holocausts and peace offerings.*

1 Chronicles 15:3, 16, 19-21, 25—*They sounded the trumpets before the ark of the Lord.*

2 Chronicles 5:2-5a, 11-14—*The priests blowing trumpets.*

Ephesians 5:15-20—*Sing praise to the Lord with all your hearts.*

Luke 1:39-47—*My spirit rejoices in God my Savior.*

Luke 10:21-22—*Jesus was filled with joy by the Holy Spirit.*

1333  As circumstances suggest, one of the following responsorial psalms may be sung or said, or some other suitable song.

℟. **Sing to the Lord with shouts of joy, praise him with the blare of trumpets.**

Psalm 47

**All you peoples, clap your hands,**
**shout to God with cries of gladness,**
**For the LORD, the Most High, the awesome,**
**is the great king over all the earth.** ℟.

**Sing praise to God, sing praise;**
**sing praise to our king, sing praise.**
**For king of all the earth is God;**
**sing hymns of praise.** ℟.

Psalm 98:1, 2-3, 4-6

℟. (see vv. 5 and 6) **Sing and shout for joy to the Lord.**

1334 As circumstances suggest, the celebrant may give those present a brief explanation of the biblical text, so that they may understand through faith the meaning of the celebration.

## INTERCESSIONS

1335 As circumstances suggest, the prayer of blessing may be preceded by the intercessions. The celebrant introduces them and an assisting minister or one of those present announces the intentions. From the following intentions those best suited to the occasion may be used or adapted, or other intentions that apply to the particular circumstances may be composed. The intentions are followed immediately by the prayer of blessing, no. 1337.

The celebrant says:

**In exultation, brothers and sisters, let us glorify the all-powerful God for his countless favors and, as Saint Paul counsels, let us give him thanks, singing his praises with hearts and voices.**

℟. **Glory to you, O Lord.**

Or:

℟. **Blessed be God for ever.**

Assisting minister:

**Father, all holy, king of heaven and earth, source of all perfection, inspirer of all sacred music, we praise you for your great glory. (Let us bless the Lord:)** ℟.

Assisting minister:

**Lord Jesus Christ, splendor of the Father's glory, you came among us as one of us to take away sin and to enrich the redeemed with your grace; we give you glory for your great mercy. (Let us bless the Lord:)** ℟.

Assisting minister:

**God the Holy Spirit, you dwell in our hearts and build us up into the one Body of Christ; we honor you for the mystery of your presence in the Church. (Let us bless the Lord:)** ℟.

Assisting minister:

**Holy Trinity, one God, beginning and end of all things, the heavens and the earth sing a new song to you; we adore you for your unsearchable blessedness. (Let us bless the Lord:) R̷.**

1336 When there are no intercessions, the celebrant, before the prayer of blessing and using the following or other similar words, invites those present to ask for God's help.

**We are all members of the one, holy Church; together, then, in voice and in heart, let us call upon God our Father.**

As circumstances suggest, all may then pray for a moment in silence before the prayer of blessing.

## PRAYER OF BLESSING

1337 With hands outstretched, the celebrant says the prayer of blessing.

**Lord God,
your beauty is ancient yet ever new,
your wisdom guides the world in right order,
and your goodness gives the world its variety and splendor.
The choirs of angels join together
to offer their praise by obeying your commands.
The galaxies sing your praises by the pattern
    of their movement
that follows your laws.
The voices of the redeemed join in a chorus of praise
    to your holiness
as they sing to you in mind and heart.
We your people, joyously gathered in this church,
wish to join our voices to the universal hymn of praise.
So that our song may rise more worthily to your majesty,
we present this organ for your blessing:
grant that its music may lead us
to express our prayer and praise
in melodies that are pleasing to you.**

**We ask this through Christ our Lord.**

**R̷. Amen.**

1338 Then the celebrant places incense in the censer and incenses the organ, as the organ is played for the first time.

# CONCLUDING RITE

1339 With hands outstretched over the people, the celebrant blesses them by saying:

**The Lord is worthy of all praise;**
**may he give you the gift of striving to sing a new song**
  **to him**
**with your voices, your hearts, and your lives,**
**so that one day you may sing that song for ever in heaven.**

℞. **Amen.**

Then he blesses all present.

**And may almighty God bless you all,**
**the Father, and the Son, ✝ and the Holy Spirit.**

℞. **Amen.**

1340   It is preferable to end the celebration with a suitable song.

CHAPTER 39

# ORDER FOR THE BLESSING OF ARTICLES FOR LITURGICAL USE

## INTRODUCTION

1341    Certain objects that are used in divine worship are deserving of special respect and therefore should be blessed before being used.

1342    Chalices and patens are blessed in the rite provided for this in The Roman Pontifical.[30]

1343    It is proper to bless other articles used for liturgical celebration: the ciborium or pyx, the monstrance, the vestments worn by ordained ministers, such linens as the corporal and altar cloths, and hymnals and service books (*Sacramentary, Lectionary for Mass,* etc.).

1344    Anything that is to be blessed for liturgical use must meet the standards set by lawful authority; it must be beautiful and finely made, but mere lavishness and ostentation must be avoided.

1345    It is preferable that several such items be blessed in the one rite, either within Mass or in a separate celebration, in which the faithful should take part. But for the blessing of a single item the shorter rite may be used outside Mass.

1346    A deacon may be the celebrant for the shorter rite outside Mass.

---

[30] See The Roman Pontifical, *Dedication of a Church and an Altar,* ch. 7, Blessing of a Chalice and Paten.

# I. ORDER OF BLESSING WITHIN MASS

1347 An occasion in which the articles to be blessed are used in the celebration of the same Mass will contribute to the instructive character of the liturgy and to the faithful's understanding of the rites. Thus the vestments the priest will wear in the celebration of the Mass and the cloths that will cover the altar may be blessed in the presence of the congregation before the introductory rites of the Mass. But when the blessing does not take place before Mass, the rite proceeds as follows.

1348 In the homily after the reading of the word of God, the celebrant explains both the biblical readings and the meaning of the blessing.

1349 After the general intercessions, assisting ministers or representatives of the community that has provided the articles to be blessed bring these to the celebrant.

1350 In the following or similar words, the celebrant prepares those present for the blessing.

**Brothers and sisters, these articles that have been brought forward will receive a special blessing, in order to indicate that they are to be set aside exclusively for divine worship. Together, then, let us pray that God will also strengthen us by his blessing. Let us ask that he who alone is holy may make us holy and worthy, so that we may celebrate the liturgy with reverence and devotion.**

## PRAYER OF BLESSING

1351 The celebrant then says:

**Let us pray.**

All pray briefly in silence; then, with hands outstretched, the celebrant says the prayer of blessing.

**Blessed are you, O God,**
**who through your Son, the Mediator of the New Testament,**
**graciously accept our praise**
**and generously bestow your gifts on us.**

Grant that these articles,
set aside for the celebration of divine worship,
may be signs of our reverence for you
and helps to our faithful service.

We ask this through Christ our Lord.

R/. Amen.

1352　Or, for liturgical vestments:

Blessed are you, O God,
for making your own Son the eternal High Priest
   of the New Covenant
and for choosing our own brothers
to be the stewards of your mysteries.
May your ministers who use these vestments,
prepared for the celebration of the liturgy
and set apart by your blessing,
wear them with reverence
and honor them by the holiness of their lives.

We ask this through Christ our Lord.

R/. Amen.

1353　For hymnals or service books                       USA

Lord God of glory,
your Church on earth joins with the choirs of heaven
in giving you thanks and praise.

As we gather to worship you in wonder and awe
may the songs on our lips
echo the music that swells in our hearts.

Bless us as we use these hymnals (service books)
and grant that we may glorify and praise you,
Father, Son, and Holy Spirit,
now and for ever.

R/. Amen.

# II. SHORTER RITE

1354 When the faithful have gathered, the celebrant begins in these words.

**Our help is in the name of the Lord.**

All reply:

**Who made heaven and earth.**

Or:

**The Lord be with you.**

All reply:

**And also with you.**

1355 As circumstances suggest, the celebrant may prepare those present for the blessing.

1356 One of those present or the celebrant reads a text of sacred Scripture, for example:

Romans 12:1

**I urge you therefore, brothers and sisters, by the mercies of God, to offer your bodies as a living sacrifice, holy and pleasing to God, your spiritual worship.**

Galatians 3:26-27

**For through faith you are all children of God in Christ Jesus. For all of you who were baptized into Christ have clothed yourselves with Christ.**

Acts 2:42

**They devoted themselves to the teaching of the apostles and to the communal life, to the breaking of the bread and to the prayers.**

John 4:23

**But the hour is coming, and is now here, when true worshipers will worship the Father in Spirit and truth; and indeed the Father seeks such people to worship him.**

**1357**  The celebrant then says:

**Let us pray.**

All pray briefly in silence; then, with hands outstretched, the celebrant says the prayer of blessing.

**Blessed are you, O God,**
**who through your Son, the Mediator of the New Testament,**
**graciously accept our praise**
**and generously bestow your gifts on us.**
**Grant that these articles,**
**set aside for the celebration of divine worship,**
**may be signs of our reverence for you**
**and helps to our faithful service.**

**We ask this through Christ our Lord.**

**R⁊. Amen.**


**1358**  Or, for liturgical vestments:

**Blessed are you, O God,**
**for making your own Son the eternal High Priest**
**  of the New Covenant**
**and for choosing our own brothers**
**to be the stewards of your mysteries.**
**May your ministers who use these vestments,**
**prepared for the celebration of the liturgy**
**and set apart by your blessing,**
**wear them with reverence**
**and honor them by the holiness of their lives.**

**We ask this through Christ our Lord.**

**R⊘. Amen.**


**1359**  Or, for hymnals or service books                    USA

**Lord God of glory,**
**your Church on earth joins with the choirs of heaven**
**in giving you thanks and praise.**

**As we gather to worship you in wonder and awe**
**may the songs on our lips**
**echo the music that swells in our hearts.**

Bless us as we use these hymnals (service books)
and grant that we may glorify and praise you,
Father, Son, and Holy Spirit,
now and for ever.

℞. Amen.

# CHAPTER 40

# ORDER FOR THE BLESSING OF A CHALICE AND PATEN[31]

USA

## INTRODUCTION

1360   The chalice and paten in which wine and bread are offered, consecrated, and received,[32] since they are intended solely and permanently for the celebration of the eucharist, become "sacred vessels."

1361   The intention, however, of devoting these vessels entirely to the celebration of the eucharist is made manifest before the community by a special blessing which is preferably imparted during Mass.

1362   Any bishop or priest may bless a chalice and paten, provided these have been made according to the norms laid down in the General Instruction of the Roman Missal, nos. 290–295.

1363   If it is a chalice or paten alone that is to be blessed, the text should be suitably adapted.

---

[31] This blessing is taken from The Roman Pontifical, *Dedication of a Church and an Altar,* ch. 7: Blessing of a Chalice and Paten.

[32] See The Roman Missal, General Instruction, no. 289.

# I. ORDER OF BLESSING WITHIN MASS

**1364** In the liturgy of the word, apart from the days listed on the Table of Liturgical Days, nos. 1-9, one or two readings may be taken from those given in no. 1365 below.

## LITURGY OF THE WORD

**1365** Readings:

1 Corinthians 10:14-22a—*Our blessing-cup is a communion with the blood of Christ.*

1 Corinthians 11:23-26—*This cup is the new covenant in my blood.*

Psalm 16:5, 8, 9-10, 11

℟. (v. 5) **The Lord is my inheritance and my cup.**

Psalm 23:1-3a, 3b-4, 5, 6

℟. (v. 5) **You prepare a banquet before me; my cup overflows.**

Matthew 20:20-28—*You shall indeed drink my cup.*

Mark 14:12-16, 22-26—*This is my body. This is my blood.*

## HOMILY

**1366** After the reading of the word of God the homily is given in which the celebrant explains the biblical readings and the meaning of the blessing of a chalice and paten that are used in the celebration of the Lord's Supper.

## GENERAL INTERCESSIONS

**1367** The general intercessions follow, either in the form usual at Mass or in the form provided here. The celebrant concludes the intercessions with the prayer of blessing. From the following intentions those best for the occasion may be used or adapted, or other intentions that apply to the particular circumstances may be composed.

The celebrant says:

Let us pray to the Lord Jesus who continuously offers himself for the Church as the bread of life and the cup of salvation. With confidence we make our prayer:

R⁊. **Lord, hear our prayer.**

Or:

R⁊. **Christ Jesus, bread of heaven, grant us eternal life.**

Assisting minister:

Savior of all, in obedience to the Father's will, you drank the cup of suffering; grant that we may share in the mystery of your death and thus win the promise of eternal life, and so we pray: R⁊.

Assisting minister:

Priest of the most high, hidden yet present in the sacrament of the altar, grant that we may discern by faith what is concealed from our eyes, and so we pray: R⁊.

Assisting minister:

Good Shepherd, you give yourself to your disciples as food and drink; grant that, fed by this mystery, we may be transformed into your likeness, and so we pray: R⁊.

Assisting minister:

Lamb of God, you commanded your Church to celebrate the paschal mystery under the signs of bread and wine; grant that this memorial may be the summit and source of holiness for all who believe, and so we pray: R⁊.

Assisting minister:

Son of God, you wondrously satisfy the hunger and thirst of all who eat and drink at your table; grant that through the mystery of the eucharist we may learn to live your command of love, and so we pray: R⁊.

The celebrant then says:

**Lord,
by the death and resurrection of your Son
you have brought redemption to the entire world.**

**Continue in us the work of your grace,
so that, ever recalling the mystery of Christ,
we may finally rejoice at your table in heaven.**

**Grant this through Christ our Lord.**

R̷. **Amen.**

## Presentation of the Chalice and Paten

1368　When the general intercessions are finished, ministers or representatives of the community that are presenting the chalice and paten place them on the altar. The celebrant then approaches the altar. Meanwhile the following antiphon is sung.

**I will take the cup of salvation and call on the name of the Lord.**

Another appropriate song may be sung.

## Prayer of Blessing

1369　When the singing is finished, the celebrant says:

**Let us pray.**

All pray in silence for a brief period. The celebrant then continues:

**Lord,
with joy we place on your altar
this cup and this paten,
vessels with which we will celebrate
the sacrifice of Christ's new covenant.**

**May they be sanctified,
for in them the body and blood of Christ
will be offered, consecrated, and received.**

**Lord,
when we celebrate Christ's faultless sacrifice on
　earth,**

may we be renewed in strength
and filled with your Spirit,
until we join with your saints
at your table in heaven.

Glory and honor be yours for ever and ever.

R̸. Blessed be God for ever.

## PREPARATION OF THE ALTAR AND GIFTS

1370 Afterward the ministers place a corporal on the altar. Some
of the congregation bring bread, wine, and water for the celebration of the Lord's sacrifice. The celebrant puts the gifts in the
newly blessed paten and chalice and offers them in the usual way.
Meanwhile the following antiphon may be sung with Psalm 116:
10-19.

**I will take the cup of salvation and offer a sacrifice of praise
(alleluia).**

Another appropriate song may be sung.

1371 When he has said the prayer "Lord God, we ask you to
receive us," the celebrant may incense the gifts and the altar.

1372 If the circumstances of the celebration permit, it is appropriate that the congregation should receive the blood of Christ from
the newly blessed chalice.

# II. ORDER OF BLESSING WITHIN A CELEBRATION OF THE WORD OF GOD

## INTRODUCTORY RITES

**1373** After the people have assembled, the priest, with alb or surplice and stole, goes to the chair. Meanwhile the following antiphon with Psalm 116:10-19 may be sung.

**I will take the cup of salvation and offer a sacrifice of praise (alleluia).**

Another appropriate song may be sung.

**1374** The priest greets the people saying:

**The grace of our Lord Jesus Christ,**
**who offered for us his body and blood,**
**the love of God,**
**and the fellowship of the Holy Spirit**
**be with you all.**

All reply:

**And also with you.**

Other suitable words taken preferably from sacred Scripture may be used.

## INTRODUCTION

**1375** Then the priest briefly addresses the people, preparing them to take part in the celebration and explaining to them the meaning of the rite. He may use these or similar words:

**The celebration of the mystery of the eucharist lies at the center of the Church's life. Christ nourishes and strengthens us with his living body and saving blood that we might be his witnesses in the world. The vessels which hold the bread and wine for the eucharist are treated with reverence and respect for they ultimately will contain the body and blood of the Lord. We ask for God's blessing on these vessels for the holy eucharist and upon us who will be fed from them.**

---

# Reading of the Word of God

1376  A reader, another person present, or the priest himself then reads a text of sacred Scripture.

**Brothers and sisters, listen to the words of the first letter of Paul to the Corinthians:**                                    10:14-21

*Our blessing-cup is a communion with the blood of Christ.*

**Therefore, my beloved, avoid idolatry. I am speaking as to sensible people; judge for yourselves what I am saying. The cup of blessing that we bless, is it not a participation in the blood of Christ? The bread that we break, is it not a participation in the body of Christ? Because the loaf of bread is one, we, though many, are one body, for we all partake of the one loaf.**

**Look at Israel according to the flesh; are not those who eat the sacrifices participants in the altar? So what am I saying? That meat sacrificed to idols is anything? Or that an idol is anything? No, I mean that what they sacrifice, they sacrifice to demons, not to God, and I do not want you to become participants with demons. You cannot drink the cup of the Lord and also the cup of demons. You cannot partake of the table of the Lord and of the table of demons.**

1377  Or:

1 Corinthians 11:23-26—*This cup is the new covenant in my blood.*

Matthew 20:20-28—*You shall indeed drink my cup.*

Mark 14:12-16, 22-26—*This is my body. This is my blood.*

1378  As circumstances suggest, one of the following responsorial psalms may be sung, or some other suitable song, or even a period of silence.

℟. **The Lord is my inheritance and my cup.**

Psalm 16

**O Lord, my allotted portion and my cup,
you it is who hold fast my lot.** ℟.

**I set the Lord ever before me;
with him at my right hand I shall not be disturbed.** ℟.

**Therefore my heart is glad and my soul rejoices,
my body, too, abides in confidence;**

Because you will not abandon my soul to the nether world,
nor will you suffer your faithful one to undergo corruption. ℟.

You will show me the path to life,
fullness of joys in your presence,
the delights at your right hand forever. ℟.

Psalm 23:1-3a, 3b-4, 5, 6

℟. (v. 5) **You prepare a banquet before me; my cup overflows.**

1379  After the reading of the word of God the homily is given,
in which the priest explains the biblical readings and the meaning of the blessing of a chalice and paten that are used in the
celebration of the Lord's Supper.

## PRESENTATION OF THE CHALICE AND PATEN

1380  After the homily the ministers or representatives of the
community that are presenting the chalice and paten place them
on the altar. The priest then approaches the altar. Meanwhile the
following antiphon may be sung.

**I will take the cup of salvation and call on the name of the Lord.**

Another appropriate song may be sung.

## PRAYER OF BLESSING

1381  The priest says:

**Let us pray.**

All pray in silence for a brief period. The priest continues:

**Father,
look kindly upon your children,
who have placed on your altar
this cup and this paten.**

**May these vessels be sanctified ✠ by your blessing,
for with them we will celebrate
the sacrifice of Christ's new covenant.**

And may we who celebrate these mysteries on earth
be renewed in strength
and filled with your Spirit
until we join with your saints
at your table in heaven.

Glory and honor be yours for ever and ever.

℟. Blessed be God for ever.


## INTERCESSIONS

1382 The intercessions are then said. The minister introduces
them and an assisting minister or one of those present announces
the intentions. From the following those best suited to the occasion may be used or adapted, or other intentions that apply to
the particular circumstances may be composed.

The minister says:

**Let us pray to the Lord Jesus who continuously offers himself
for the Church as the bread of life and the cup of salvation.
With confidence we make our prayer:**

℟. **Christ Jesus, bread of heaven, grant us eternal life.**

Assisting minister:

**Savior of all, in obedience to the Father's will, you drank the
cup of suffering; grant that we may share in the mystery of
your death and thus win the promise of eternal life, and so
we pray:** ℟.

Assisting minister:

**Priest of the most high, hidden yet present in the sacrament
of the altar, grant that we may discern by faith what is concealed from our eyes, and so we pray:** ℟.

Assisting minister:

**Good Shepherd, you give yourself to your disciples as food
and drink; grant that, fed by this mystery, we may be transformed into your likeness, and so we pray:** ℟.

Assisting minister:

**Lamb of God, you commanded your Church to celebrate the paschal mystery under the signs of bread and wine; grant that this memorial may be the summit and source of holiness for all who believe, and so we pray:** R⁊.

Assisting minister:

**Son of God, you wondrously satisfy the hunger and thirst of all who eat and drink at your table; grant that through the mystery of the eucharist we may learn to live your command of love, and so we pray:** R⁊.

1383 After the intercessions the priest, in the following or similar words, invites all present to sing or say the Lord's Prayer.

**Fastened to the cross, Christ was the way of salvation; in fulfilling the will of the Father he is acclaimed the master of prayer; let his prayer be the source of ours as we say:**

All:

**Our Father . . .**

## CONCLUDING PRAYER

1384 The priest then says:

**Lord,
by the death and resurrection of your Son
you have brought redemption to the entire world.**

**Continue in us the work of your grace,
so that, ever recalling the mystery of Christ,
we may finally rejoice at your table in heaven.**

**Grant this through Christ our Lord.**

R⁊. **Amen.**

## CONCLUDING RITE

1385 The priest concludes the rite by saying:

**May the Lord, who nourishes us with the body and blood
of his Son,**

**bless and keep you in his love,
now and for ever.**

℟. **Amen.**

Then he blesses all present.

**And may almighty God bless you all,
the Father, and the Son, + and the Holy Spirit.**

℟. **Amen.**

1386  Then he dismisses the people, saying:

**Go in peace.**

℟. **Thanks be to God.**

1387  It is preferable to end the celebration with a suitable song.

CHAPTER 41

# ORDER FOR THE BLESSING OF HOLY WATER OUTSIDE MASS

## INTRODUCTION

1388  On the basis of age-old custom, water is one of the signs that the Church often uses in blessing the faithful. Holy water reminds the faithful of Christ, who is given to us as the supreme divine blessing, who called himself the living water, and who in water established baptism for our sake as the sacramental sign of the blessing that brings salvation.

1389  The blessing and sprinkling of holy water usually take place on Sunday, in keeping with the rite given in the Roman Missal (Sacramentary).[33]

1390  But when the blessing of water takes place outside Mass, the rite given here may be used by a priest or deacon. While maintaining the structure and chief elements of the rite, the celebrant should adapt the celebration to the circumstances of the place and the people involved.

---

[33] See Roman Missal (Sacramentary), Appendix, "Rite of Blessing and Sprinkling Holy Water."

# ORDER OF BLESSING

## INTRODUCTORY RITES

1391   The celebrant begins with these words:

**In the name of the Father, and of the Son, and of the Holy Spirit.**

All make the sign of the cross and reply:

**Amen.**

1392   The celebrant greets those present in the following or other suitable words, taken mainly from sacred Scripture.

**May God, who through water and the Holy Spirit has given us a new birth in Christ, be with you all.**

All make the following or some other suitable reply.

**And also with you.**

1393   As circumstances suggest, the celebrant may prepare those present for the blessing in the following or similar words.

**The blessing of this water reminds us of Christ, the living water, and of the sacrament of baptism, in which we were born of water and the Holy Spirit. Whenever, therefore, we are sprinkled with this holy water or use it in blessing ourselves on entering the church or at home, we thank God for his priceless gift to us and we ask for his help to keep us faithful to the sacrament we have received in faith.**

## READING OF THE WORD OF GOD

1394   A reader, another person present, or the celebrant reads a short text of sacred Scripture.

**Brothers and sisters, listen to the words of the holy gospel according to John:**                                      7:37-39

*Let anyone who is thirsty come to me.*

**On the last and greatest day of the feast, Jesus stood up and exclaimed, ''Let anyone who thirsts come to me and drink. Whoever believes in me, as scripture says:**

**'Rivers of living water will flow from within him.'"**

**He said this in reference to the Spirit that those who came to believe in him were to receive. There was, of course, no Spirit yet, because Jesus had not yet been glorified.**

1395   Or:

Isaiah 12:1-6—*You will draw water joyfully from the springs of salvation.*

Isaiah 55:1-11—*Oh, come to the water, all you who are thirsty.*

Sirach 15:1-6—*She will give him the water of wisdom to drink.*

1 John 5:1-6—*Jesus Christ came by water and blood.*

Revelation 7:13-17—*The Lamb will lead them to the springs of living water.*

Revelation 22:1-5—*The river of life, rising from the throne of God and of the Lamb.*

John 13:3-15—*You too are clean.*

## Prayer of Blessing

1396   After the reading, the celebrant says:

**Let us pray.**

All pray briefly in silence; then, with hands outstretched, the celebrant says the prayer of blessing.

**Blessed are you, Lord, all-powerful God,**
**who in Christ, the living water of salvation,**
**blessed and transformed us.**
**Grant that, when we are sprinkled with this water**
**or make use of it,**
**we will be refreshed inwardly by the power of the**
**  Holy Spirit**
**and continue to walk in the new life we received**
**  at baptism.**

**We ask this though Christ our Lord.**

**R⁊. Amen.**

1397 Or:

**Lord, holy Father,**
**look with kindness on your children,**
**redeemed by your Son**
**and born to a new life by water and the Holy Spirit.**
**Grant that those who are sprinkled with this water**
**may be renewed in body and spirit**
**and may make a pure offering of their service to you.**

**We ask this through Christ our Lord.**

**R͡. Amen.**

1398 Or the celebrant says:

**O God, the Creator of all things,**
**by water and the Holy Spirit**
**you have given the universe its beauty**
**and fashioned us in your own image.**

**R͡. Bless and purify your Church.**

**O Christ the Lord, from your pierced side**
**you gave us your sacraments**
**as fountains of salvation.**

**R͡. Bless and purify your Church.**

**O Holy Spirit, giver of life,**
**from the baptismal font of the Church**
**you have formed us into a new creation**
**in the waters of rebirth.**

**R͡. Bless and purify your Church.**

1399 After the prayer of blessing, the celebrant sprinkles those present with holy water, as a suitable song is sung; as circumstances suggest, he may first say the following words.

**Let this water call to mind our baptism into Christ,**
**who has redeemed us by his death and resurrection.**

**R͡. Amen.**

# CHAPTER 42

# ORDER FOR THE BLESSING OF STATIONS OF THE CROSS

## INTRODUCTION

1400   When stations of the cross are erected in a church or oratory, it is preferable that the blessing and erection of the stations be carried out by means of the celebration provided for this, with the rector of the church as celebrant or a priest deputed by the rector. The people should take part and the celebration should immediately precede the devotion of the Way of the Cross. Stations of the cross that have been installed in a church that is to be dedicated or blessed do not require a distinct celebration of their erection.

1401   Whether the stations consist of images with crosses or simply of crosses, they should be set up in the church or in a place of their own, and in a manner convenient for the faithful.

1402   While maintaining the structure and chief elements of the rite, the celebrant should adapt the celebration to the circumstances of the place and the people involved.

# ORDER OF BLESSING

## Introductory Rites

1403   When the community has gathered, the hymn *Vexilla Regis* or some other suitable song may be sung.

1404   After the singing, the celebrant says:

**In the name of the Father, and of the Son, and of the Holy Spirit.**

All make the sign of the cross and reply:

**Amen.**

1405   The celebrant greets those present in the following or other suitable words, taken mainly from sacred Scripture.

**May the Lord Jesus, who suffered for us and by his paschal mystery redeemed us, be with you all.**

All make the following or some other suitable reply.

**And also with you.**

1406   In the following or similar words, the celebrant prepares those present for the blessing and for the devotion of the stations of the cross.

**The God of all mercy has saved us through the death and resurrection of his own Son. The Word became flesh and emptied himself, taking the form of a slave and obediently accepting even death, death on a cross.**

**As we remember the unmeasured outpouring of Christ's love, we are invited to follow the way of the cross with devout minds and hearts. Thankful to the Lord, who died for us on the cross, let us also die to sin and walk in newness of life.**

## Reading of the Word of God

1407   A reader, another person present, or the celebrant reads a text of sacred Scripture, taken preferably from the texts given in the Lectionary for Mass, Votive Masses, "Holy Cross,"[34] or from those given here.

---

[34] See Lectionary for Mass (2nd ed., 1981), nos. 969–975 (Votive Masses, "Holy Cross").

---

**Brothers and sisters, listen to the words of the first letter of the apostle Peter:**                    2:16-17, 19-25

*Christ suffered for you and left you an example.*

**Be free, yet without using freedom as a pretext for evil, but as slaves of God. Give honor to all, love the community, fear God, honor the king. For whenever anyone bears the pain of unjust suffering because of consciousness of God, that is a grace. But what credit is there if you are patient when beaten for doing wrong? But if you are patient when you suffer for doing what is good, this is a grace before God. For to this you have been called, because Christ also suffered for you, leaving you an example that you should follow in his footsteps.**

**"He committed no sin,
and no deceit was found in his mouth."**

**When he was insulted, he returned no insult; when he suffered, he did not threaten; instead, he handed himself over to the one who judges justly. He himself bore our sins in his body upon the cross, so that, free from sin, we might live for righteousness. By his wounds you have been healed. For you had gone astray like sheep, but you have now returned to the shepherd and guardian of your souls.**

1408   Or:

1 Peter 3:18—4:2—*Think of what Christ suffered in this life, and then arm yourselves with the same resolution that he had.*

Matthew 5:1-12a—*Blessed are those persecuted for holiness' sake.*

Luke 18:31-34—*All that was written by the prophets concerning the Son of Man will be accomplished.*

1409   As circumstances suggest, one of the following responsorial psalms may be sung or said, or some other suitable song.

℟. **My God, my God, why have you abandoned me?**

Psalm 22

**All who see me scoff at me;
they mock me with parted lips, they wag their heads:
He relied on the LORD; let him deliver him,
let him rescue him, if he loves him.** ℟.

Indeed, many dogs surround me,
a pack of evildoers closes in upon me;
They have pierced my hands and my feet;
I can count all my bones. R℣.

I will proclaim your name to my brethren;
in the midst of the assembly I will praise you:
''You who fear the Lord, praise him;
all you descendants of Jacob, give glory to him;
revere him, all you descendants of Israel!'' R℣.

Psalm 31:2 and 6, 12-13, 15-16

R℣. (Luke 23:46) **Father, I put my life in your hands.**

1410  As circumstances suggest, the celebrant may give those present a brief explanation of the biblical text, so that they may understand through faith the meaning of the celebration.

## INTERCESSIONS

1411  The intercessions are then said. The celebrant introduces them and an assisting minister or one of those present announces the intentions. From the following intentions those best suited to the occasion may be used or adapted, or other intentions that apply to the particular circumstances may be composed.

The celebrant says:

**Christ Jesus has loved us and redeemed us in his blood. With praise and thanksgiving to him who has died and risen for us, let us call upon him by saying:**

R℣. **O Lord, you have redeemed us in your blood.**

Or:

R℣. **Lord, hear our prayer.**

Assisting minister:

**You became a man and on the cross offered us the way of salvation; grant that, nailed to the cross with you, we may die with you and so rise with you. (For this we pray:)** R℣.

You said: "All who wish to come after me must take up their cross each day"; help us to follow you in your suffering, so that we may one day see you in your glory. (For this we pray:) ℟.

Assisting minister:

On the way to Calvary you did not refuse Simon's help to carry your cross; grant that we too may generously carry that cross for the good of the Church. (For this we pray:) ℟.

Assisting minister:

On your way to the cross you were comforted by the compassion of the women who wept for you; grant that in times of sorrow we may have the support and comfort of our brothers and sisters. (For this we pray:) ℟.

Assisting minister:

Through the blood of your cross you brought reconciliation to all things; unite all human beings to yourself, so that they may be free of all division and have you as their one shepherd in the one flock. (For this we pray:) ℟.

Assisting minister:

You promised that once you were lifted up from the earth you would draw all of us to yourself; turn all our hearts to love for you. (For this we pray:) ℟.

Assisting minister:

You willed to suffer on the cross, in order to bring help to all who are sorely tried; teach us the wisdom of the cross, so that as in grief we share in your suffering we may also rejoice exultantly in the vision of your glory. (For this we pray:) ℟.

Assisting minister:

On the cross you promised paradise to the good thief; stand by us in the sorrows of this life, so that we too may be glorified with you in heaven. (For this we pray:) ℟.

Assisting minister:

**As you hung on the cross, you gave us Mary, your Mother, through your disciple; grant that with her we may be at your side at the foot of the cross and in the glory of heaven. (For this we pray:) ℟.**

## PRAYER OF BLESSING

1412 With hands outstretched, the celebrant says the prayer of blessing:

**O God,**
**your Son was delivered up to death**
**and raised from the dead,**
**in order that we might die to sin and live lives**
**  of holiness.**
**By the favor of your blessing,**
**draw near with mercy to your faithful people,**
**who devoutly recall the mysteries of Christ's passion.**
**Grant that those who follow his footsteps**
**in bearing their cross patiently**
**may receive as their reward**
**the vision of Christ in his glory,**
**for he lives and reigns with you for ever and ever.**

**℟. Amen.**

1413 Or:

**Lord and Father all-holy,**
**you willed that your Son's cross**
**should become the source of all blessings,**
**the cause of all graces.**
**Grant that we who on earth hold fast to the mysteries**
**  of his sacred passion**
**may in heaven enter into the joys of his resurrection.**

**We ask this through Christ our Lord.**

**℟. Amen.**

1414 After the prayer of blessing, as circumstances suggest, the celebrant may place incense in the censer and incense the crosses or images of the stations; during this time the following antiphon or some other antiphon or song, for example, the *Stabat Mater*, is sung.

Ant. **We worship you, Lord, we venerate your cross, we praise your resurrection. Through the cross you brought joy to the world.**

1415   The devotion of the Way of the Cross then follows in the manner customary to the place.

## CONCLUDING RITE

1416   As a fitting conclusion there may be some reminder of the resurrection, for example, the singing of the hymn *Ad cenam Agni providi*. Then the celebrant blesses the people.

**Through the death and resurrection of his own Son,
the Father has given the human race
the great gift of redemption.
May he give you the grace
to meditate devoutly on Christ's passion
and to follow your crucified Lord,
so that you may come to the glory of his resurrection.**

R̸. **Amen.**

Then he blesses all present.

**And may almighty God bless you all,
the Father, and the Son, ✛ and the Holy Spirit.**

R̸. **Amen.**

1417   Or:

**May God,
who, through the cross and the blood of his Son,
has given us the gift of redemption and salvation,
send his blessing upon you.**

R̸. **Amen.**

**May God grant that with all his saints
you may grasp fully
the breadth, the length, the height, and the depth of the
cross of Christ.**

R̸. **Amen.**

**May God in his mercy look kindly upon you,
as you walk the way of the cross,
and listen compassionately to your prayers.**

R∕. **Amen.**

Then he blesses all present.

**And may almighty God bless you all,
the Father, and the Son, ✝ and the Holy Spirit.**

R∕. **Amen.**

# CHAPTER 43

# ORDER FOR THE BLESSING
# OF A CEMETERY

## INTRODUCTION

1418   The Church considers the cemetery to be a holy place and therefore wishes and urges that new cemeteries, established either by the Catholic community or by the civil authority in Catholic regions, be blessed and that a cross be erected as a sign to all of Christian hope in the resurrection.

"Neither place, language, nor their manner of civil life set the followers of Christ apart from other people,"[35] with whom they seek to live in harmony. Christians therefore offer prayers to the heavenly Father for all and when they pray to him they include all, both those "who have died in the peace of Christ and all the dead whose faith is known to God alone."[36]

In their cemeteries, therefore, Christians bury and show due honor to the bodies not only of their brothers and sisters in faith, but also of those to whom they are bound by the ties of a common humanity: in shedding his blood on the cross for all, Christ has redeemed us all.

1419   This rite should preferably be celebrated by the bishop of the diocese, but he may entrust the responsibility to a priest, particularly one who assists him in the pastoral care of the faithful who have established the cemetery.

When the bishop is the celebrant, everything is to be adapted accordingly.

1420   The blessing of a cemetery may be celebrated at any hour and on any day, except Ash Wednesday and the days of Holy Week. But the preferred day is one that permits a large attendance of the faithful, and especially a Sunday, since this weekly remembrance of Easter markedly expresses the paschal meaning that death has for a Christian.

1421   Sometimes either the civil government or a Christian community made up of both Catholics and other Christians separated from us may establish a cemetery specifically for the burial of the deceased members of the Christian communities. In such a case it is most desirable that the formal opening of the cemetery be marked by an ecumenical celebration, the parts of which are planned by all the parties involved. Everything in the celebration that relates to Catholics is regulated by the local Ordinary.

---

[35] *Epistula ad Diognetum*, 5: F. X. Funk, ed., *Didascalia et constitutiones apostolorum*, 2 vol. (1905), vol. 1, p. 397.

[36] Roman Missal, Eucharistic Prayer IV.

1422   If the Catholic community is invited to take part in the opening of a cemetery that belongs to a non-Christian religion or is purely secular, the Church does not refuse its presence or prayer for all the dead. The local Ordinary has responsibility for regulating the participation of Catholics.

When given the opportunity to do so, the Catholic priest and the faithful should choose scriptural readings, psalms, and prayers that plainly express the Church's teaching on death and the destiny of the human person, in whom there is a natural desire for the living and true God.

# ORDER OF BLESSING

## INTRODUCTORY RITES

1423   When feasible, a procession of the community from the church or other suitable place to the cemetery is preferable. When a procession is not feasible or not in keeping with circumstances, the faithful simply gather at the entrance of the cemetery.

When the people have gathered, before the procession or at the entrance of the cemetery, the celebrant greets them in the following or other suitable words.

**The grace of our Lord Jesus Christ, giver of life and conqueror of death, be with you all.**

All make the following or some other suitable reply.

**And also with you.**

1424   In the following or similar words, the celebrant prepares those present for the celebration.

**Brothers and sisters in Christ, a common Christian concern has brought us together to bless this cemetery, where our bodies and the bodies of others sealed with the name of Christ will lie at rest, awaiting the dawn of the Lord's coming in glory. After preparing this resting place for the dead, we should raise our hearts from earth to heaven and look to Christ, who suffered and rose again for our salvation. He has commanded that we keep watch for his coming and has promised to meet us when we rise again.**

1425   After his introductory remarks, the celebrant says:

**Let us pray.**

All pray briefly in silence; then, with hands outstretched, the celebrant continues:

**Lord,**
**you have made your people a pilgrim Church,**
**to be welcomed by you into its eternal home.**
**Bless us as we go in procession to this cemetery.**
**May this place, prepared in the sure hope of**
**the resurrection,**
**never cease to remind us**
**of the life that we are to share in Christ,**
**who will transform our earthly bodies**
**to be like his in glory,**
**for he is Lord for ever and ever.**

R̶/. **Amen.**

1426 After the prayer, the assisting deacon announces the procession.

**Let us proceed in peace.**

The procession to the cemetery is then formed; a crossbearer leads, walking between two servers carrying lighted candles; the clergy follow, then the celebrant with the assisting deacon and other ministers, then the faithful.

1427 During the procession one of the following antiphons with Psalm 118 or some other psalm, taken preferably from the *Order of Christian Funerals*,[37] or some other suitable song is sung.

Ant. **Lord, let my inheritance be in the land of the living.**

Or:

Ant. **Open for me the holy gates: I will enter and praise the Lord.**

Or:

Ant. **This is gate of the Lord; here the just shall enter.**

1428 When there is no procession, the celebrant with the ministers and the faithful enter the cemetery immediately after the opening prayer, as they sing the following antiphon with Psalm 134 or some other suitable song.

Ant. **I heard a voice from heaven saying to me: Blessed are those who have died in the Lord.**

---

[37] See Roman Ritual, *Order of Christian Funerals* (ICEL ed., 1985), Part III, 16.

# READING OF THE WORD OF GOD

**1429**  The procession moves to the place where the cemetery cross has been erected and there the reading of the word of God takes place; if this is not convenient the procession moves to the cemetery chapel or to another suitable place for the readings.

**1430**  One or more texts of Scripture are read, taken preferably from the readings given in the lectionary of the *Order of Christian Funerals*;[38] each reading is followed by a responsorial psalm, related to it, or an interval of silence. The gospel reading always holds the place of honor.

But when the celebration of the liturgy of the eucharist is to follow, then the readings include at least one other reading in addition to the gospel reading, both taken from those given in the Lectionary for Mass, Masses for the Dead,[39] and with a responsorial psalm between the readings and related to the reading that preceded it.

**1431**  After the readings, the celebrant in the homily explains both the biblical texts and the paschal meaning of death for the Christian.

**1432**  After the homily, the celebrant stands before the cross erected at the center of the cemetery and, with hands outstretched, blesses this cross as well as the cemetery grounds.

**God of all consolation,
by your just decree our bodies return to the dust
from which they were shaped,
yet in your way of mercy
you have turned this condition of darkness and death
into a proof of your loving care.
In your providence you assured Abraham, our father
   in faith,
of a burial place in the land of promise.
You extolled your servant Tobit
for his charity in burying the dead.
You willed that your own Son be laid to rest in
   a new tomb,
so that he might rise from it, the victor over death,
and offer us the pledge of our own resurrection.**

---

[38] See ibid., 13–15.

[39] See Lectionary for Mass (2nd ed., 1981), nos. 1011–1026 (Masses for the Dead).

Grant that this cemetery,
placed under the sign of the cross,
may, by the power of your blessing, ✢
be a place of rest and hope.
May the bodies buried here sleep in your peace,
to rise immortal at the coming of your Son.
May this place be a comfort to the living,
a sign of their hope for unending life.
May prayers be offered here continually
in supplication for those who sleep in Christ
and in constant praise of your mercy.

We ask this through Christ our Lord.

R̷. **Amen.**

1433   The celebrant places incense in the censer and incenses the
cross. He then sprinkles the cemetery and those present with holy
water. He may sprinkle the cemetery either as he stands at the
center or by walking around the grounds. In the second case the
following antiphon with Psalm 51 or some other suitable song
is sung.

Ant. **The bones that were broken shall leap for joy.**

# LITURGY OF THE EUCHARIST OR INTERCESSIONS

1434   After completion of the blessing, when the eucharistic sacrifice is to be offered for the dead, the celebrant, with the assisting ministers, makes the customary reverence to the altar, then
he kisses the altar. The ministers put the corporal, purificator,
chalice, and missal in place, then bring the bread and wine to
the celebrant, and Mass proceeds in the usual manner.

1435   When the altar of a cemetery chapel is to be dedicated or
blessed, everything is done, with the necessary adaptations, as
indicated in The Roman Pontifical.[40]

---

[40] See The Roman Pontifical, *Dedication of a Church and an Altar*, chs. 4 and 6.

**1436** If the eucharist is not to be celebrated, after the sprinkling of the cemetery with holy water the rite is concluded with intercessions. These may take the form usual at Mass or the form given here.

The celebrant says:

**Christ the Lord blotted out sin by dying on the cross and destroyed death by rising from the tomb. Let us therefore acclaim him in prayer and call upon him by saying:**

R⁄. **You are our life and resurrection.**

Or:

R⁄. **Lord, hear our prayer.**

Assisting minister:

**Christ, the Son of Man, dying on the cross, you made Mary the companion of your suffering and, rising, you filled her with gladness; lift up those who are distressed and strengthen them in hope. (For this we pray:)** R⁄.

Assisting minister:

**Christ, Son of the living God, you raised your friend Lazarus from the dead; raise up to life and glory the dead whom you have redeemed by your precious blood. (For this we pray:)** R⁄.

Assisting minister:

**Christ, consoler of those who mourn, you dried the tears of the widowed mother by raising her son to life; comfort those who mourn for their dead. (For this we pray:)** R⁄.

Assisting minister:

**Christ, Redeemer of those who have no hope because they do not know you, enlighten them with the gift of faith in the resurrection and in the life of the world to come. (For this we pray:)** R⁄.

Assisting minister:

**Christ, the light of the world, you revealed yourself to the blind man who begged that he might see; show your face to the dead who are still awaiting the light of your glory. (For this we pray:)** R⁄.

**1437**  The celebrant introduces the Lord's Prayer in the following or similar words.

**Let us now raise our thoughts to the Father in heaven, saying the Lord's Prayer to ask him for the coming of his kingdom and the forgiveness of our sins.**

All:

**Our Father . . .**

**1438**  Then he blesses the people.

**With a goodness beyond imagining God has created you**
**and in the resurrection of his Son**
**has filled you with the hope of rising again:**
**may the God of all consolation bless you,**
**now and for ever.**

℟. **Amen.**

**May he give us, the living, pardon for our sins,**
**and to our dead brothers and sisters**
**a resting place of light and peace,**
**now and for ever.**

℟. **Amen.**

**May we who believe in Christ's resurrection from the dead**
**live with him in glory for ever and ever.**

℟. **Amen.**

Then he blesses all present.

**And may almighty God bless you all,**
**the Father, and the Son, ✝ and the Holy Spirit.**

℟. **Amen.**

**1439**  The assisting deacon dismisses the people in the usual way.

# PART IV
# BLESSINGS OF ARTICLES MEANT TO FOSTER THE DEVOTION OF THE CHRISTIAN PEOPLE

PART IV

# BLESSINGS OF ARTICLES MEANT TO FOSTER THE DEVOTION OF THE CHRISTIAN PEOPLE

## INTRODUCTION

1440  In order to increase the piety of the Christian people, the Church has always favored devotional practices that are in accord with ecclesiastical laws and standards. Since certain articles are used in connection with liturgical prayer or popular devotions, for example, rosaries and the like, celebration of a blessing of such articles is a helpful means of recommending them to the faithful.

1441  Further, the faithful have developed the commendable practice of using religious articles as they pray, of having objects of piety on their person, of placing religious statues or pictures in their homes, or of keeping there certain other blessed objects, even food or drink.

In view of the existence of these forms of Christian piety, Part IV provides several models for the celebration of blessings in various circumstances.

# CHAPTER 44

# ORDER FOR THE BLESSING OF RELIGIOUS ARTICLES

## INTRODUCTION

1442   The present order is to be used to bless medals, small crucifixes, statues or pictures that will be displayed elsewhere than in a church or chapel, scapulars, rosaries, and other articles used for religious devotions.

1443   Particularly in shrines or places of pilgrimage where the faithful come together in large numbers, there should be a blessing of religious articles at certain times in a communal celebration. The blessing may be integrated in an appropriate manner into the celebrations held specially for pilgrims.

1444   The present order may be used by a priest or deacon. While maintaining the structure and chief elements of the rite, the celebrant should adapt the celebration to the circumstances of the place and the people involved.

1445   When a single religious article is to be blessed, the minister may use the shorter rite provided at the end of this chapter, nos. 1458–1461, or in special circumstances, the short formulary given in no. 1462.

# I. ORDER OF BLESSING

## INTRODUCTORY RITES

**1446** When the community has gathered, the celebrant says:

**In the name of the Father, and of the Son, and of the Holy Spirit.**

All make the sign of the cross and reply:

**Amen.**

**1447** The celebrant greets those present in the following or other suitable words, taken mainly from sacred Scripture.

**The grace, the mercy, and the peace of God, the Father, the Son, and the Holy Spirit, be with you all.**

All make the following or some other suitable reply.

**And also with you.**

**1448** In the following or similar words, the celebrant briefly addresses the faithful, in order to prepare them for the celebration and to explain the meaning of the rite.

**The symbols of religious devotion that you have brought to be blessed express your faith in various ways: they serve to bring to mind our Lord's great love for us or to increase our confidence in the power of Mary and the saints to help us.**

**When, therefore, we call down God's blessing on these religious articles, our foremost concern must be that our Christian lives bear out the kind of witness we give by using them.**

## READING OF THE WORD OF GOD

**1449** A reader, another person present, or the celebrant reads a text of sacred Scripture, taken preferably from those given here; but other texts relevant to the rite may also be chosen.

**Brothers and sisters, listen to the words of the second letter of Paul to the Corinthians:** 3:17b—4:2

*All of us, gazing on the Lord's glory, are being transformed into the very image of the Lord.*

**Where the Spirit of the Lord is, there is freedom. All of us, gazing with unveiled face on the glory of the Lord, are being transformed into the same image from glory to glory, as from the Lord who is the Spirit.**

**Therefore, since we have this ministry through the mercy shown us, we are not discouraged. Rather, we have renounced shameful, hidden things; not acting deceitfully or falsifying the word of God, but by the open declaration of the truth we commend ourselves to everyone's conscience in the sight of God.**

1450  Or:

Romans 8:26-31—*We do not know how to pray as we ought; but the Spirit makes intercession for us.*

1 Corinthians 13:8-13—*Now we see indistinctly in a mirror; then we shall see face to face.*

1 Corinthians 15:45-50—*Just as we resemble the first man from earth, so shall we bear the likeness of the man from heaven.*

2 Corinthians 4:1-7—*Christ is the image of God.*

Galatians 1:1, 3-5—2:19b-20—*I have been crucified with Christ.*

Ephesians 3:14-21—*God's power now at work in us can do immeasurably more than we ask or imagine.*

Colossians 3:14-17—*Whatever you do, do in the name of the Lord, giving thanks through him.*

Luke 11:5-13—*Ask and you shall receive. Seek and you shall find.*

Luke 18:1-8—*Pray always and do not lose heart.*

1451  As circumstances suggest, one of the following responsorial psalms may be sung or said, or some other suitable song.

℞. **Everlasting is God's love.**

Psalm 100

**Sing joyfully to the LORD, all you lands;**
**serve the LORD with gladness;**
**come before him with joyful song.** ℞.

**Know that the LORD is God;**
**he made us, his we are;**
**his people, the flock he tends.** ℞.

Enter his gates with thanksgiving,
his courts with praise;
Give thanks to him; bless his name. R℣.

For he is good:
the LORD whose kindness endures forever,
and his faithfulness, to all generations. R℣.

Psalm 123:1, 2, 3-4

R℣. (v. 1) I lift my eyes to you who dwell in the heavens.

Psalm 139:1-2, 3-4, 5-6, 7-8, 9-10

R℣. (v. 4b) O Lord, you know all things, through and through.

Psalm 150:1-2, 3-4, 5

R℣. (v. 2a) Praise the Lord for his abundant greatness.

1452 As circumstances suggest, the celebrant may give a homily in which he explains both the biblical text and the meaning of the rite.

## INTERCESSIONS

1453 As circumstances suggest, the prayer of blessing may be preceded by the intercessions. The celebrant introduces them and an assisting minister or one of those present announces the intentions. From the following intentions those best suited to the occasion may be used or adapted, or other intentions that apply to the particular circumstances may be composed. The intentions are followed immediately by the prayer of blessing, no. 1455.

The celebrant says:

Not making a pretense of religion, but in commitment to its true power, let us call on the name of the Lord, saying:

R℣. Give us , O Lord, the spirit of true piety.

Or:

R℣. Lord, hear our prayer.

Assisting minister:

Most merciful God, it is your wish that we be always mindful of your marvelous works; grant that the things we behold with our eyes may move our minds to dwell on the signs of your mercy. (For this we pray:) R℣.

Assisting minister:

**You seek worshipers who will worship in spirit and in truth; grant that with the aid of these articles and symbols we may follow the way of devotion and faith. (For this we pray:) ℟.**

Assisting minister:

**Through your Son you have commanded us to pray without ceasing; grant that steadfast prayer may help us to live pure and devout lives. (For this we pray:) ℟.**

Assisting minister:

**In your Church you generously provide us with every means of holiness and salvation; grant that whatever we receive through the ministry of the Church we may use for its upbuilding. (For this we pray:) ℟.**

1454 When there are no intercessions, the celebrant, before the prayer of blessing, says:

**Let us pray.**

As circumstances suggest, all may then pray for a moment in silence before the prayer of blessing.

## Prayer of Blessing

1455 With hands outstretched, the celebrant says the prayer of blessing.

**Blessed be your name, O Lord,**
**you are the fount and source of every blessing,**
**and you look with delight**
**upon the devout practices of the faithful.**
**Draw near, we pray, to these your servants**
**and, as they use this symbol of their faith and devotion,**
**grant that they may also strive to be transformed**
**into the likeness of Christ, your Son,**
**who lives and reigns with you for ever and ever.**

**℟. Amen.**

1456 The celebrant concludes the rite by saying:

**May God, who has revealed his glory to us in Christ,**
**bring your lives into conformity with the image**
  **of his Son,**
**so that you may reach the vision of his glory.**

R7. **Amen.**

Then he blesses all present.

**And may almighty God bless you all,**
**the Father, and the Son, + and the Holy Spirit.**

R7. **Amen.**

1457 It is preferable to end the celebration with a suitable song.

# II. SHORTER RITE

1458 To begin, the celebrant says:

**Lord, show us your mercy and love.**

All reply:

**And grant us your salvation.**

1459 As circumstances suggest, the celebrant may prepare those present for the blessing.

1460 One of those present or the celebrant reads a text of sacred Scripture, for example:

Romans 8:26b, 27

**For we do not know how to pray as we ought, but the Spirit itself intercedes with inexpressible groanings. And the one who searches hearts knows what is the intention of the Spirit, because it intercedes for the holy ones according to God's will.**

Colossians 3:17

**And whatever you do, in word or in deed, do everything in the name of the Lord Jesus, giving thanks to God the Father through him.**

Luke 11:9-10

**"And I tell you, ask and you will receive; seek and you will find; knock and the door will be opened to you. For everyone who asks, receives; and the one who seeks, finds; and to the one who knocks, the door will be opened."**

1461  With hands outstretched, the celebrant says:

**May the merciful Lord
enliven and strengthen by his blessing ✠
the spirit of devotion and filial love in your hearts,
so that you may walk blamelessly through this life
and happily reach life everlasting.**

R̶⁷. **Amen.**

## SHORT FORMULARY

1462  In special circumstances, a priest or deacon may use the following short blessing formulary.

**May this** (name of article) **and the one who uses it
be blessed,
in the name of the Father, and of the Son, ✠ and of
the Holy Spirit.**

R̶⁷. **Amen.**

# CHAPTER 45

# ORDER FOR THE BLESSING OF ROSARIES

## INTRODUCTION

1463  The blessing of a large number of rosaries is preferably carried out in a celebration that precedes the recitation of the rosary in which the people take part.

1464  The order for a communal celebration of this blessing may also be properly used on feasts or memorials of Mary or on the occasion of a pilgrimage. Rosaries may be blessed along with other religious articles by using the order provided in this chapter.

1465  The present order may be used by a priest or deacon. While maintaining the structure and chief elements of the rite, the celebrant should adapt the celebration to the circumstances of the place and the people involved.

1466  If a single rosary is to be blessed or just a few, the minister may use the shorter rite given at the end of this chapter, nos. 1482–1486; or in special circumstances the minister may use only the short formulary given in no. 1487.

# I. ORDER OF BLESSING

1467    When the community has gathered, the celebrant enters during the singing of a suitable hymn or song.[1]

1468    After the singing, the celebrant says:

**In the name of the Father, and of the Son, and of the Holy Spirit.**

All make the sign of the cross and reply:

**Amen.**

1469    The celebrant greets those present in the following or other suitable words, taken mainly from sacred Scripture.

**Through the Son, born of Mary, every blessing comes to us from God our Father. May his grace and peace be with you all.**

All make the following or some other suitable reply.

**And also with you.**

1470    In the following or similar words, the celebrant prepares those present for the blessing.

**Brothers and sisters, the blessed Virgin was chosen to be the Mother of God as part of the eternal plan for the incarnation of the Word of God. On this earth she was the cherished Mother of the Redeemer and in a unique way the companion of his saving work. The form of prayer that we call the rosary is a way of contemplating and extolling the plan of divine providence. This is the reason why the pastors of the Church have always praised the rosary and urged its use. The Church bestows a special blessing on rosaries and on those who, as they recite this prayer, reflect on the mysteries of our redemption. By this blessing the Church intends that with Mary and through Mary God's praises will be sung.**

---

[1] For example, *Te gestientem gaudiis* from the *Liturgia Horarum,* 7 October, memorial of Our Lady of the Rosary, morning prayer.

1471  A reader, another person present, or the celebrant reads a text of sacred Scripture, taken preferably from those given in the Lectionary for Mass in the Common of the Blessed Virgin Mary[2] or from those given here.

## Brothers and sisters, listen to the words of the holy gospel according to Luke: 2:46-52

*His mother meanwhile kept all these things in memory.*

After three days they found Jesus in the temple, sitting in the midst of the teachers, listening to them and asking them questions, and all who heard him were astounded at his understanding and his answers. When his parents saw him, they were astonished, and his mother said to him, "Son, why have you done this to us? Your father and I have been looking for you with great anxiety." And he said to them, "Why were you looking for me? Did you not know that I must be in my Father's house?" But they did not understand what he said to them. He went down with them and came to Nazareth, and was obedient to them; and his mother kept all these things in her heart. And Jesus advanced in wisdom and age and favor before God and man.

1472  Or:

## Brothers and sisters, listen to the words of the Acts of the Apostles: 1:12-14

*Together they devoted themselves to prayer with Mary, the Mother of Jesus.*

Then they returned to Jerusalem from the mount called Olivet, which is near Jerusalem, a sabbath day's journey away. When they entered the city they went to the upper room where they were staying, Peter and John and James and Andrew, Philip and Thomas, Bartholomew and Matthew, James son of Alphaeus, Simon the Zealot, and Judas son of James. All these devoted themselves with one accord to prayer, together with some women, and Mary the mother of Jesus, and his brothers.

---

[2] See Lectionary for Mass (2nd ed., 1981), nos. 707–712 (Commons, Common of the Blessed Virgin Mary).

1473 As circumstances suggest, one of the following responsorial psalms may be sung or said, or some other suitable song.

℟. **Blessed be the name of the Lord for ever.**

Psalm 113

**Praise, you servants of the LORD,**
**praise the name of the LORD.**
**Blessed be the name of the LORD**
**both now and forever.** ℟.

**From the rising to the setting of the sun**
**is the name of the LORD to be praised.**
**High above all nations is the LORD,**
**above the heavens is his glory.** ℟.

**Who is like the LORD, our God, who is enthroned on high**
**and looks upon the heavens and the earth below?** ℟.

**He raises up the lowly from the dust;**
**from the dunghill he lifts up the poor**
**To seat them with princes,**
**with the princes of his own people.** ℟.

Luke 1:46-47, 48-49, 50-51, 52-53, 54-55

℟. **(v. 49) The Almighty has done great things for me, and holy is his Name.**

1474 As circumstances suggest, the celebrant may give those present a brief explanation of the biblical text, so that they may understand through faith the meaning of the celebration and learn to pray more devoutly and intently through the use of the rosary.

## INTERCESSIONS

1475 As circumstances suggest, the prayer of blessing may be preceded by the intercessions. The celebrant introduces them and an assisting minister or one of those present announces the intentions. From the following intentions those best suited to the occasion may be used or adapted, or other intentions that apply to the particular circumstances may be composed. The intentions are followed immediately by the prayer of blessing, nos. 1477–1479.

The celebrant says:

**Because the rosary is rightly considered to be a preeminent sign of devotion to Mary, let us call upon the name of the Lord through the intercession of the one in whose honor we bless these rosaries.**

℟. **Through Mary, O Lord, join us more closely to Christ.**

Or:

℟. **Lord, hear our prayer.**

Assisting minister:

**Most compassionate Father, when Mary consented to your word you chose her as the companion of the Redeemer; grant that through her intercession your Church may abound in the fruits of Christ's redemption. (For this we pray:)** ℟.

Assisting minister:

**You joined the Virgin Mary to your Son in a close and unbreakable bond and showered her with the fullness of your grace; grant that we may always find her to be our advocate, pleading for the graces we need. (For this we pray:)** ℟.

Assisting minister:

**In Mary you have provided us with the perfect example of following Christ; help us to strive to reflect in our lives the mysteries that we devoutly recall in the rosary. (For this we pray:)** ℟.

Assisting minister:

**You taught Mary to keep all your words in memory; grant that, following her example, we may hold fast to the words of your Son in faith and carry them out in our lives. (For this we pray:)** ℟.

Assisting minister:

**You gave the Holy Spirit to your apostles as they were at prayer with Mary the Mother of Jesus; grant that, persevering in prayer, we may walk in the Spirit even as we live in the Spirit. (For this we pray:)** ℟.

**1476** When there are no intercessions, the celebrant, before the prayer of blessing, says:

**Let us pray.**

As circumstances suggest, all may then pray for a moment in silence before the prayer of blessing.

## PRAYER OF BLESSING

**1477** With hands outstretched, the celebrant says the prayer of blessing.

**Blessed be our God and Father,**
**who has given us the mysteries of his Son**
**to be pondered with devotion and celebrated with faith.**
**May he grant us, his faithful people,**
**that by praying the rosary**
**we may, with Mary the Mother of Jesus,**
**seek to keep his joys, sorrows, and glories**
**in our minds and hearts.**

**We ask this through Christ our Lord.**

**R⁊. Amen.**

**1478** Or:

**Grant, O Lord, we pray**
**that, in reciting the rosary,**
**your faithful may confidently seek the help of Mary.**
**As they meditate on the mysteries of Christ Jesus,**
**help them to affirm by their actions**
**the truths they treasure in their prayer.**

**We ask this through Christ our Lord.**

**R⁊. Amen.**

**1479** Or:

**Almighty and merciful God,**
**out of the immense love with which you have loved us**
**you willed that by the power of the Holy Spirit**
**your Son should be born of the Virgin Mary,**
**that he should suffer death through the cross,**
**and rise again from the dead.**

**Lord,
send your blessing
upon all who use these rosaries
to pray with lips and hearts
in honor of the Mother of your Son.
Grant that they may be filled with an enduring devotion
and at the end of their days
be led into your presence
by the Blessed Virgin Mary.**

**We ask this through Christ our Lord.**

**R̸. Amen.**

> 1480 The recitation of the rosary follows, in the manner customary in the place.

## CONCLUDING RITE

> 1481 After the recitation of the rosary, an antiphon, for example, *Salve Regina,* or some other suitable song may be sung. The celebrant then concludes the rite by saying:

**May God who has given joy to the world through
  the blessed Virgin Mary
shower you with his gracious kindness.**

**R̸. Amen.**

> Then he blesses all present.

**And may almighty God bless you all,
the Father, and the Son, ✚ and the Holy Spirit.**

**R̸. Amen.**

# II. SHORTER RITE

**1482** To begin, the celebrant says:

**Lord, show us your mercy and love.**

All reply:

**And grant us your salvation.**

**1483** As circumstances suggest, the celebrant may prepare those present for the blessing.

**1484** One of those present or the celebrant reads a text of sacred Scripture, for example:

Luke 2:51b-52

**Mary, his mother, kept all these things in her heart. And Jesus advanced in wisdom and age and favor before God and man.**

Acts 1:14

**All these devoted themselves with one accord to prayer, together with some women, and Mary the mother of Jesus, and his brothers.**

**1485** With hands outstretched, the celebrant says the prayer of blessing.

**Blessed be our God and Father,**
**who has given us the mysteries of his Son**
**to be pondered with devotion and celebrated with faith.**
**May he grant us, his faithful people,**
**that by praying the rosary**
**we may, with Mary the Mother of Jesus,**
**seek to keep his joys, sorrows, and glories**
**in our minds and hearts.**

**We ask this through Christ our Lord.**

**R̘. Amen.**

**1486** Or:

**In memory of the mysteries**
**of the life, death, and resurrection of our Lord**
**and in honor of the Virgin Mary,**
**Mother of Christ and Mother of the Church,**

may those who devoutly use this rosary to pray be blessed,
in the name of the Father, and of the Son, ✛ and of
  the Holy Spirit.

℟. Amen.

## Short Formulary

1487 In special circumstances, a priest or deacon may use the
following short blessing formulary.

**May this rosary and the one who uses it be blessed,
in the name of the Father, and of the Son, ✛ and of the Holy
Spirit.**

℟. Amen.

# CHAPTER 46

# ORDER FOR THE BLESSING AND CONFERRAL OF A SCAPULAR

## INTRODUCTION

1488   The blessing and conferral of a scapular should, if at all possible, be carried out in a communal celebration. Whenever the conferral is a way of receiving members of the faithful into a confraternity of a religious order or institute, this reception must be carried out by a member of that institute or else by a minister deputed by the competent authority of the institute.

1489   On the occasion of the blessing and conferral, the scapular itself, of prescribed design and material, must be used; afterwards a blessed medal may replace the scapular.

1490   Whenever a person joins a confraternity in order to share spiritually in the life of a religious institute, the particular norms established by each institute must be respected and followed exactly.

# ORDER OF BLESSING

## INTRODUCTORY RITES

1491   When the people or simply the members of the confraternity have gathered, the celebrant enters during the singing of a hymn suited to the particular celebration. After the singing, the celebrant says:

**In the name of the Father, and of the Son, and of the Holy Spirit.**

All make the sign of the cross and reply:

**Amen.**

1492   The celebrant greets those present in the following or other suitable words, taken mainly from sacred Scripture.

**Through the Son, born of Mary, every blessing comes to us from God our Father. May his grace and peace be with you all.**

All make the following or some other suitable reply.

**And also with you.**

1493   In the following or similar words, the celebrant prepares those present for the blessing.

**God uses ordinary things as signs to express his extraordinary mercy toward us. Through simple things as well we express our gratitude, declare our willingness to serve God, and profess the resolve to live up to our baptismal consecration.**

**(This scapular is a sign of entrance into the confraternity of N., approved by the Church. The scapular thus expresses our intention of sharing in the spirit of that Order. That intention renews our baptismal resolve to put on Christ with the help of Mary, whose own greatest desire is that we become more like Christ in praise of the Trinity, until, dressed for the wedding feast, we reach our home in heaven.)**

## READING OF THE WORD OF GOD

1494   A reader, one of those present, or the celebrant reads a text of sacred Scripture, taken preferably from the readings in the Lec-

1495  Or:

## Brothers and sisters, listen to the words of the second letter of Paul to the Corinthians:
4:13—5:10

*We do not wish to be stripped naked but rather to have the heavenly dwelling place envelop us.*

Since, then, we have the same spirit of faith, according to what is written, "I believed, therefore I spoke," we too believe and therefore speak, knowing that the one who raised the Lord Jesus will raise us also with Jesus and place us with you in his presence. Everything indeed is for you, so that the grace bestowed in abundance on more and more people may cause the thanksgiving to overflow for the glory of God.

Therefore, we are not discouraged; rather, although our outer self is wasting away, our inner self is being renewed day by day. For this momentary light affliction is producing for us an eternal weight of glory beyond all comparison, as we look not to what is seen but to what is unseen; for what is seen is transitory, but what is unseen is eternal.

For we know that if our earthly dwelling, a tent, should be destroyed, we have a building from God, a dwelling not made with hands, eternal in heaven. For in this tent we groan, longing to be further clothed with our heavenly habitation if indeed, when we have taken it off, we shall not be found naked. For while we are in this tent we groan and are weighed down, because we do not wish to be unclothed but to be further clothed, so that what is mortal may be swallowed up by life. Now the one who has prepared us for this very thing is God, who has given us the Spirit as a first installment.

So we are always courageous, although we know that while we are at home in the body we are away from the Lord, for we walk by faith, not by sight. Yet we are courageous, and we would rather leave the body and go home to the Lord. Therefore, we aspire to please him, whether we are at home or away. For we must all appear before the judgment seat of Christ, so that each one may receive recompense, according to what he did in the body, whether good or evil.

**1496** After the reading, the celebrant gives the homily in which he explains to those present the meaning of the celebration.

## INTERCESSIONS

**1497** The intercessions are then said. The celebrant introduces them and an assisting minister or one of those present announces the intentions. From the following intentions those best suited to the occasion may be used or adapted, or other intentions that apply to the particular circumstances may be composed.

The celebrant says:

**Relying on the intercession of Mary, who by the power of the Holy Spirit gave the Word our flesh, so that we might share in the grace of our firstborn brother and live for the glory of God, let us pray to the Father, saying:**

℟. **God, grant that we may put on Christ.**

Or:

℟. **Lord, hear our prayer.**

Assisting minister:

**Father, you willed to have your beloved Son take on our humanity, so that in him we might share in your own life; grant that we may be called and truly be your children. (For this we pray:)** ℟.

Assisting minister:

**You wished Christ to be in every respect like us, but without sin, so that in following him we might share in his filial image; grant that we may follow Christ so as to please you in all things. (For this we pray:)** ℟.

Assisting minister:

**You call those who are clothed in the wedding garment of the kingdom to the feast of your grace, where you reveal yourself to them; teach us to serve you loyally. (For this we pray:)** ℟.

---

Assisting minister:

**Through Saint Paul you urge us to be the sweet fragrance of Christ's goodness in the world; let us become the sign of Christ's presence for our brothers and sisters. (For this we pray:)** R⁊.

Assisting minister:

**You clothe us with the robe of righteousness and holiness, so that through the Holy Spirit we may live for you and show forth the holiness of your Church; through Christ make us grow in holiness, so that we may work together generously for the salvation of others. (For this we pray:)** R⁊.

Assisting minister:

**You continually bestow on us in Christ every spiritual blessing, until, clothed in the wedding garment, we go out to meet Christ at his coming; grant that through the prayers of Mary we may pass from death to life. (For this we pray:)** R⁊.

## PRAYER OF BLESSING

1498   With hands outstretched, the celebrant continues:

**O God,**
**the author and perfecter of all holiness,**
**you call all who are reborn of water and the Holy Spirit**
**to the fullness of the Christian life and**
  **the perfection of charity.**
**Look with kindness on those who devoutly receive**
  **this scapular**
**(in praise of the holy Trinity**
  *or* **in honor of Christ's passion**
  *or* **in honor of the blessed Virgin Mary).**
**As long as they live,**
**let them become sharers in the image of Christ your Son**
**and, after they have fulfilled their mission on earth**
**with the help of Mary, the Virgin Mother,**
**receive them into the joy of your heavenly home.**

**We ask this through Christ our Lord.**

R⁊. **Amen.**

# CONFERRAL OF THE SCAPULAR

**1499**  The celebrant puts the scapular on each of the candidates, saying either the words given here or similar words from the proper ritual of the religious family.

A    Scapular in honor of the Trinity or the mysteries of Christ

**Receive this scapular (*or* habit)
as the sign of your acceptance into the confraternity
of the religious family of N.,
which is dedicated to the blessed Trinity
(*or, for example,* to the passion of Jesus Christ).
Live in such a way that,
with the help of the Mother of God,
you may more and more put on Christ,
who redeemed us by his blood,
for the glory of the Trinity
and for the service of the Church and of your neighbor.**

**R̖. Amen.**

B    Scapular in honor of Mary

**Receive this scapular (*or* habit)
as the sign of your acceptance into the confraternity
of the religious family of N.,
which is dedicated to the blessed Virgin Mary.
Live in such a way that,
with the help of the Mother of God,
you may more and more put on Christ,
who redeemed us by his blood,
for the glory of the Trinity
and for the service of the Church and of your neighbor.**

**R̖. Amen.**

**1500**  As circumstances suggest, the celebrant may, in a clear voice, pronounce the formulary of conferral once for all the recipients. They all join in replying "Amen," then go one by one to receive the scapular from the celebrant.

**1501** After the conferral, the celebrant, facing the new confraternity members, says:

**By being clothed with this scapular (*or* habit)**
**you have been accepted into the religious family of N.**
**in order that you may more fully serve Christ and**
**  his Church**
**in the spirit of that community.**
**So that you may more completely achieve that goal,**
**I admit you, in virtue of the power entrusted to me,**
**into a participation in all the spiritual favors**
**belonging to this religious family.**

**1502** After stating the duties and obligations proper to the confraternity, the celebrant, in silence, sprinkles all present with holy water.

## CONCLUDING RITE

**1503** The celebrant concludes the rite either with the following words or with another blessing formulary related to the title of the scapular that has been received.

**May almighty God bless you with his gentle kindness**
**and give you the vision of his saving wisdom.**

**R̥. Amen.**

**May he continue to nourish you with the teaching of faith**
**and enable you to remain steadfast in doing what is right.**

**R̥. Amen.**

**May he turn your steps always toward him**
**and lead you along the pathway of peace and charity.**

**R̥. Amen.**

Then he blesses all present.

**And may almighty God bless you all,**
**the Father, and the Son, + and the Holy Spirit.**

**R̥. Amen.**

**1504** It is preferable to end the celebration with a suitable song.

# PART V
# BLESSINGS RELATED TO FEASTS AND SEASONS

# PART V

# BLESSINGS RELATED TO FEASTS AND SEASONS

## INTRODUCTION

1505   "The Church is conscious that it must celebrate the saving work of the divine Bridegroom by devoutly recalling it on certain days throughout the course of the year. Every week, on the day which the Church has called the Lord's Day, it keeps the memory of the Lord's resurrection, which it also celebrates once in the year, together with his blessed passion, in the most solemn festival of Easter

"Within the cycle of a year, moreover, the Church unfolds the whole mystery of Christ, from his incarnation and birth until his ascension, the day of Pentecost, and the expectation of blessed hope and of the Lord's return.

"Recalling thus the mysteries of redemption, the Church opens to the faithful the riches of the Lord's powers and merits, so that these are in some way made present in every age in order that the faithful may lay hold on them and be filled with saving grace."[1]

1506   The Church honors with special love Mary, the Mother of God and has also included in the annual cycle days devoted to the memory of the martyrs and other saints. By celebrating their passage from earth to heaven the Church proclaims the paschal mystery achieved in the saints, who have suffered and been glorified with Christ; it proposes them to the faithful as examples drawing all to the Father through Christ and pleads through their merits for God's favors.[2]

1507   In the various seasons of the year and according to its traditional discipline, the Church completes the formation of the faithful by means of devout practices for soul and body, by instruction, prayer, and works of penance and of mercy.[3]

1508   Accordingly, Part V contains blessings which are centered on the various feasts of the liturgical year. Some of these blessings serve to emphasize the great mysteries of our redemption in Christ, while others take their inspiration from the lives of the saints.

---

[1] SC, art. 102.

[2] See SC, art. 103 and 104.

[3] See SC, art. 105.

# CHAPTER 47

# ORDER FOR THE BLESSING OF
# AN ADVENT WREATH
## First Sunday of Advent

## INTRODUCTION

1509   The use of the Advent Wreath is a traditional practice which has found its place in the Church as well as in the home. The blessing of an Advent Wreath takes place on the First Sunday of Advent or on the evening before the First Sunday of Advent. The blessing may be celebrated during Mass, a celebration of the word of God, or Evening Prayer.

1510   Customarily the Advent Wreath is constructed of a circle of evergreen branches into which are inserted four candles. According to tradition, three of the candles are violet and the fourth is rose. However, four violet or white candles may also be used.

1511   The candles represent the four weeks of Advent and the number of candles lighted each week corresponds to the number of the current week of Advent. The rose candle is lighted on the Third Sunday of Advent, also known as Gaudete Sunday.

1512   If the Advent Wreath is to be used in church, it should be of sufficient size to be visible to the congregation. It may be suspended from the ceiling or placed on a stand. If it is placed in the presbyterium, it should not interfere with the celebration of the liturgy, nor should it obscure the altar, lectern, or chair.

1513   When the Advent Wreath is used in church, on the Second and succeeding Sundays of Advent the candles are lighted either before Mass begins or immediately before the opening prayer; no additional rites or prayers are used.

1514   When the blessing of the Advent Wreath is celebrated in the home, it is appropriate that it be blessed by a parent or another member of the family; the shorter rite may appropriately be used for this purpose.

1515   When the Advent Wreath is used in the home, the opening prayer of the Sunday Mass is recited when the candles are lighted. The lighting of the candles may be preceded or followed by an Advent hymn and a Scripture reading. The lighting of the Advent Wreath may fittingly be included as a part of the evening meal.

1516   The Advent Wreath may be blessed by a priest, deacon, or a lay minister.

# I. ORDER OF BLESSING WITHIN MASS

**1517** After the gospel reading, the celebrant in the homily, based on the sacred text and pertinent to the particular place and the people involved, explains the meaning of the celebration.

## GENERAL INTERCESSIONS

**1518** The general intercessions follow, either in the form usual at Mass or in the form provided here. The celebrant concludes the intercessions with the prayer of blessing. From the following intentions those best for the occasion may be used or adapted, or other intentions that apply to the particular circumstances may be composed.

The celebrant says:

**Christ came to bring us salvation and has promised to come again. Let us pray that we may be always ready to welcome him.**

R℣. **Lord, hear our prayer.**

Or:

R℣. **Come, Lord Jesus.**

Assisting minister:

**That the keeping of Advent may open our hearts to God's love, we pray to the Lord.** R℣.

Assisting minister:

**That the light of Christ may penetrate the darkness of sin, we pray to the Lord.** R℣.

Assisting minister:

**That this wreath may constantly remind us to prepare for the coming of Christ, we pray to the Lord.** R℣.

Assisting minister:

**That the Christmas season may fill us with peace and joy as we strive to follow the example of Jesus, we pray to the Lord.** R℣.

# PRAYER OF BLESSING

1519   With hands outstretched, the celebrant says the prayer of blessing:

**Lord God,
your Church joyfully awaits the coming of its Savior,
who enlightens our hearts
and dispels the darkness of ignorance and sin.**

**Pour forth your blessings upon us
as we light the candles of this wreath;
may their light reflect the splendor of Christ,
who is Lord, for ever and ever.**

R̶7. **Amen.**

1520   Or:

**Lord our God,
we praise you for your Son, Jesus Christ:
he is Emmanuel, the hope of the peoples,
he is the wisdom that teaches and guides us,
he is the Savior of every nation.**

**Lord God,
let your blessing come upon us
as we light the candles of this wreath.
May the wreath and its light
be a sign of Christ's promise to bring us salvation.
May he come quickly and not delay.**

**We ask this through Christ our Lord.**

R̶7. **Amen.**

The first candle is then lighted.

# II. ORDER OF BLESSING WITHIN A CELEBRATION OF THE WORD OF GOD

**1521** The present order may be used by a priest or a deacon, and also by a layperson, who follows the rites and prayers designated for a lay minister.

## INTRODUCTORY RITES

**1522** When the community has gathered, the minister says:

**In the name of the Father, and of the Son, and of the Holy Spirit.**

All make the sign of the cross and reply:

**Amen.**

**1523** A minister who is a priest or deacon greets those present in the following or other suitable words, taken mainly from sacred Scripture.

**May God, who enlightens every heart, be with you.**

And all reply:

**And also with you.**

---

**1524** A lay minister greets those present in the following words:

**Let us praise God, who enlightens every heart, now and for ever.**

**R̝. Amen.**

---

**1525** In the following or similar words, the minister prepares those present for the blessing.

**My brothers and sisters, today we begin the season of Advent. We open our hearts to God's love as we prepare to welcome Christ into our lives and homes. The candles of this wreath remind us that Jesus Christ came to conquer the darkness of sin and to lead us into the light of his glorious kingdom.**

---

# Reading of the Word of God

1526 A reader, another person present, or the minister reads a text of sacred Scripture.

**Brothers and sisters, listen to the words of the prophet Isaiah:**

9:1-2, 5-6

*The people who walked in darkness have seen a great light.*

**The people who walked in darkness
have seen a great light;
Upon those who dwelt in the land of gloom
a light has shone.
You have brought them abundant joy
and great rejoicing,
As they rejoice before you as at the harvest,
as men make merry when dividing spoils.
For a child is born to us, a son is given us;
upon his shoulder dominion rests.
They name him Wonder-Counselor, God-Hero,
Father-Forever, Prince of Peace.
His dominion is vast
and forever peaceful,
From David's throne, and over his kingdom,
which he confirms and sustains
By judgment and justice,
both now and forever.**

1527 Or:

Isaiah 63:16-17, 19; 64:2-7—*You, Lord, are our redeemer.*

Jeremiah 33:14-16—*I will cause a good seed to spring forth from David.*

1 John 1:5-7—*God is light; walk in the light.*

Matthew 1:18-25—*The birth of Jesus.*

1528 As circumstances suggest, one of the following responsorial psalms may be sung, or some other suitable song.

R̸. **Lord, make us turn to you, and we shall be saved.**

Psalm 80

**O shepherd of Israel, hearken,
O guide of the flock of Joseph!
From your throne upon the cherubim, shine forth
before Ephraim, Benjamin and Manasseh.** R̸.

---

Once again, O LORD of hosts,
look down from heaven, and see;
Take care of this vine,
and protect what your right hand has planted,
the son of man whom you yourself made strong. R⁷.

May your help be with the man of your right hand,
with the son of man whom you yourself made strong.
Then we will no more withdraw from you;
give us new life, and we will call upon your name. R⁷.

Psalm 8:2, 3, 4, 5, 6, 7, 8-9

R⁷. (v. 2) O Lord, our Lord, how great is your name over all the earth.

1529   As circumstances suggest, the minister may give those present a brief explanation of the biblical text, so that they may understand through faith the meaning of the celebration.

## INTERCESSIONS

1530   The intercessions are then said. The minister introduces them and an assisting minister or one of those present announces the intentions. From the following those best suited to the occasion may be used or adapted, or other intentions that apply to the particular circumstances may be composed.

The minister says:

Christ came to bring us salvation and has promised to come again. Let us pray that we may be always ready to welcome him.

R⁷. Come, Lord Jesus.

Assisting minister:

That the keeping of Advent may open our hearts to God's love, we pray to the Lord. R⁷.

Assisting minister:

That the light of Christ may penetrate the darkness of sin, we pray to the Lord. R⁷.

Assisting minister:

**That this wreath may constantly remind us to prepare for the coming of Christ, we pray to the Lord.** ℞.

Assisting minister:

**That the Christmas season may fill us with peace and joy as we strive to follow the example of Jesus, we pray to the Lord.** ℞.

1531 After the intercessions the minister, in the following or similar words, invites all present to sing or say the Lord's Prayer.

**With longing for the coming of God's kingdom, let us offer our prayer to the Father:**

All:

**Our Father . . .**

## Prayer of Blessing

1532 A minister who is a priest or deacon says the prayer of blessing with hands outstretched; a lay minister says the prayer with hands joined.

**Lord God,**
**your Church joyfully awaits the coming of its Savior,**
**who enlightens our hearts**
**and dispels the darkness of ignorance and sin.**

**Pour forth your blessings upon us**
**as we light the candles of this wreath;**
**may their light reflect the splendor of Christ,**
**who is Lord, for ever and ever.**

℞. **Amen.**

1533 Or:

**Lord our God,**
**we praise you for your Son, Jesus Christ:**
**he is Emmanuel, the hope of the peoples,**
**he is the wisdom that teaches and guides us,**
**he is the Savior of every nation.**

**Lord God,**
**let your blessing come upon us**
**as we light the candles of this wreath.**
**May the wreath and its light**
**be a sign of Christ's promise to bring us salvation.**
**May he come quickly and not delay.**

**We ask this through Christ our Lord.**

**R̶7. Amen.**

> The first candle is lighted.

## CONCLUDING RITE

1534 A minister who is a priest or deacon concludes the rite by saying:

**May the light of Christ lead you to the joy of his kingdom,**
**now and for ever.**

**R̶7. Amen.**

> Then he blesses all present.

**And may almighty God bless you all,**
**the Father, and the Son, ✝ and the Holy Spirit.**

**R̶7. Amen.**

---

1535 A lay minister concludes the rite by signing himself or herself with the sign of the cross and saying:

**May the light of Christ lead us to the joy of his kingdom, now and for ever.**

**R̶7. Amen.**

---

1536 It is preferable to end the celebration with a suitable song.

# III. SHORTER RITE

1537 All make the sign of cross as the minister says:

**Our help is in the name of the Lord.**

All reply:

**Who made heaven and earth.**

1538 One of those present or the minister reads a text of sacred Scripture, for example:

**Brothers and sisters, listen to the words of the prophet Isaiah:**
9:1-2, 5-6

*The people who walked in darkness have seen a great light.*

**The people who walked in darkness
have seen a great light;
Upon those who dwelt in the land of gloom
a light has shone.
You have brought them abundant joy
and great rejoicing,
As they rejoice before you as at the harvest,
as men make merry when dividing spoils.
For a child is born to us, a son is given us;
upon his shoulder dominion rests.
They name him Wonder-Counselor, God-Hero,
Father-Forever, Prince of Peace.
His dominion is vast
and forever peaceful,
From David's throne, and over his kingdom,
which he confirms and sustains
By judgment and justice,
both now and forever.**

1539 A minister who is a priest or deacon says the prayer of blessing with hands outstretched; a lay minister says the prayer with hands joined.

**Lord God,
your Church joyfully awaits the coming of its Savior,
who enlightens our hearts
and dispels the darkness of ignorance and sin.**

Pour forth your blessings upon us
as we light the candles of this wreath;
may their light reflect the splendor of Christ,
who is Lord, for ever and ever.

R⁄. **Amen.**

1540   Or:

Lord our God,
we praise you for your Son, Jesus Christ:
he is Emmanuel, the hope of the peoples,
he is the wisdom that teaches and guides us,
he is the Savior of every nation.

Lord God,
let your blessing come upon us
as we light the candles of this wreath.
May the wreath and its light
be a sign of Christ's promise to bring us salvation.
May he come quickly and not delay.

We ask this through Christ our Lord.

R⁄. **Amen.**

CHAPTER 48

# ORDER FOR THE BLESSING OF A CHRISTMAS MANGER OR NATIVITY SCENE

USA

## INTRODUCTION

1541  In its present form the custom of displaying figures depicting the birth of Jesus Christ owes its origin to Saint Francis of Assisi who made the Christmas crèche or manger for Christmas eve of 1223. However, as early as the fourth century representations of the nativity of the Lord were painted as wall decorations depicting not only the infancy narrative accounts of Christ's birth, but also the words of the prophets Isaiah and Habakkuk taken to mean that the Messiah would be born in the midst of animals in a manger.

1542  The blessing of the Christmas manger or nativity scene, according to pastoral circumstances, may take place on the Vigil of Christmas or at another more suitable time.

1543  The blessing may be given during a celebration of the word of God, during Mass, or even during another service, e.g., a carol service.

1544  If the manger is set up in the church, it must not be placed in the presbyterium. A place should be chosen that is suitable for prayer and devotion and is easily accessible by the faithful.

1545  When the manger is set up in the home, it is appropriate that it be blessed by a parent or another family member; the shorter rite may be used for this purpose.

A form of this rite is also found in *Catholic Household Blessings and Prayers*.

1546  The blessing may be given by a priest, deacon, or a lay minister.

# I. ORDER OF BLESSING WITHIN A CELEBRATION OF THE WORD OF GOD

1547 The present order may be used by a priest or a deacon, and also by a layperson, who follows the rites and prayers designated for a lay minister.

## INTRODUCTORY RITES

1548 When the community has gathered, a suitable song may be sung. After the singing, the minister says:

**In the name of the Father, and of the Son, and of the Holy Spirit.**

All make the sign of the cross and reply:

**Amen.**

1549 A minister who is a priest or deacon greets those present in the following or other suitable words, taken mainly from sacred Scripture.

**May the peace of our Lord Jesus Christ, who was born of the Virgin Mary, be with you all.**

And all reply:

**And also with you.**

---

1550 A lay minister greets those present in the following words:

**Praised be Jesus Christ, who dwells among us, now and for ever.**

℟. **Amen.**

---

1551 In the following or similar words, the minister prepares those present for the blessing.

**As we prepare to celebrate the birth of Christ, we pause to bless this Christmas manger scene. The practice of erecting such mangers was begun by Saint Francis of Assisi as a means to set forth the message of Christmas.**

---

When we look upon these figures, the Christmas gospel comes
alive and we are moved to rejoice in the mystery of the incarnation of the Son of God.

## READING OF THE WORD OF GOD

1552 A reader, another person present, or the minister reads a
text of sacred Scripture.

Brothers and sisters, listen to the words of the holy gospel
according to Luke:                                                   2:1-8

*The birth of Jesus.*

In those days a decree went out from Caesar Augustus that the
whole world should be enrolled. This was the first enrollment,
when Quirinius was governor of Syria. So all went to be enrolled, each to his own town. And Joseph too went up from
Galilee from the town of Nazareth to Judea, to the city of David
that is called Bethlehem, because he was of the house and family of David, to be enrolled with Mary, his betrothed, who was
with child. While they were there, the time came for her to
have her child, and she gave birth to her firstborn son. She
wrapped him in swaddling clothes and laid him in a manger,
because there was no room for them in the inn.

Now there were shepherds in that region living in the fields
and keeping the night watch over their flock.

1553 Or:

Isaiah 7:10-15—*Birth of Emmanuel.*

1554 As circumstances suggest, the following responsorial psalm
may be sung, or some other suitable song.

R⁊. **For ever I will sing the goodness of the Lord.**

Psalm 89

"I have made a covenant with my chosen one,
I have sworn to David my servant:
Forever will I confirm your posterity
and establish your throne for all generations." R⁊.

Happy the people who know the joyful shout;
in the light of your countenance, O LORD, they walk.
At your name they rejoice all the day,
and through your justice they are exalted. R⁊.

"He shall say of me, 'You are my father,
my God, the Rock, my savior.' R⁊.

"Forever I will maintain my kindness toward him,
and my covenant with him stands firm." R⁊.

> 1555 As circumstances suggest, the minister may give those
> present a brief explanation of the biblical text, so that they may
> understand through faith the meaning of the celebration.

## INTERCESSIONS

> 1556 The intercessions are then said. The minister introduces
> them and an assisting minister or one of those present announces
> the intentions. From the following those best suited to the occa-
> sion may be used or adapted, or other intentions that apply to
> the particular circumstances may be composed.

The minister says:

Let us ask for God's blessing on this Christmas manger and
upon ourselves, that we who reflect on the birth of Jesus may
share in the salvation he accomplished.

R⁊. Come, Lord, dwell with us.

Assisting minister:

For the Church of God, as we recall the circumstances surrounding the birth of Christ, that we may always proclaim his
gift of new life for all people, we pray to the Lord. R⁊.

Assisting minister:

For the world in which we live, that it may come to recognize
Christ who was greeted by the angels and shepherds, we pray
to the Lord. R⁊.

Assisting minister:

For our families and our homes, that Christ who was laid in
the manger may dwell with us always, we pray to the Lord. R⁊.

Assisting minister:

For parents, that their love for their children may be modeled
on that of the Virgin Mary and Saint Joseph, we pray to the
Lord. R⁊.

**1557** After the intercessions the minister, in the following or similar words, invites all present to sing or say the Lord's Prayer.

**Let us pray as our Lord Jesus Christ taught us:**

All:

**Our Father . . .**

## PRAYER OF BLESSING

**1558** A minister who is a priest or deacon says the prayer of blessing with hands outstretched; a lay minister says the prayer with hands joined.

**God of every nation and people,**
**from the very beginning of creation**
**you have made manifest your love:**
**when our need for a Savior was great**
**you sent your Son to be born of the Virgin Mary.**
**To our lives he brings joy and peace,**
**justice, mercy, and love.**

**Lord,**
**bless all who look upon this manger;**
**may it remind us of the humble birth of Jesus,**
**and raise up our thoughts to him,**
**who is God-with-us and Savior of all,**
**and who lives and reigns for ever and ever.**

**R⁊. Amen.**

## CONCLUDING RITE

**1559** A minister who is a priest or deacon concludes the rite by saying:

**May Christ our God enlighten your hearts and minds, now and for ever.**

**R⁊. Amen.**

Then he blesses all present.

**And may almighty God bless you all,**
**the Father, and the Son, ✛ and the Holy Spirit.**

**R⁊. Amen.**

---

1560    A lay minister concludes the rite by signing himself or herself with the sign of the cross and saying:

**May Christ our God enlighten our hearts and minds, now and for ever.**

℟. **Amen.**

1561    It is preferable to end the celebration with a suitable song.

# II. ORDER OF BLESSING WITHIN MASS

1562 After the gospel reading, the celebrant in the homily, based on the sacred text and pertinent to the particular place and the people involved, explains the meaning of the celebration.

## GENERAL INTERCESSIONS

1563 The general intercessions follow, either in the form usual at Mass or in the form provided here. The celebrant concludes the intercessions with the prayer of blessing. From the following intentions those best for the occasion may be used or adapted, or other intentions that apply to the particular circumstances may be composed.

The celebrant may introduce the intercessions with these or similar words:

**Let us ask for God's blessing on this Christmas manger and upon ourselves, that we who reflect on the birth of Jesus may share in the salvation he accomplished.**

R̸. **Lord, hear our prayer.**

Or:

R̸. **Come, Lord, dwell with us.**

Assisting minister:

**For the Church of God, as we recall the circumstances surrounding the birth of Christ, that we may always proclaim with joy his gift of new life for all people, we pray to the Lord.** R̸.

Assisting minister:

**For the world in which we live, that it may come to recognize Christ who was greeted by the angels and shepherds, we pray to the Lord.** R̸.

Assisting minister:

**For our families and our homes, that Christ who was laid in the manger may dwell with us always, we pray to the Lord.** R̸.

Assisting minister:

**For parents, that their love for their children may be modeled on that of the Virgin Mary and Saint Joseph, we pray to the Lord.** R̸.

1564 With hands outstretched, the celebrant says the prayer of blessing:

**God of every nation and people,**
**from the very beginning of creation**
**you have made manifest your love:**
**when our need for a Savior was great**
**you sent your Son to be born of the Virgin Mary.**
**To our lives he brings joy and peace,**
**justice, mercy, and love.**

**Lord,**
**bless all who look upon this manger;**
**may it remind us of the humble birth of Jesus,**
**and raise up our thoughts to him,**
**who is God-with-us and Savior of all,**
**and who lives and reigns for ever and ever.**

R̶⁊. **Amen.**

# III. SHORTER RITE

1565 This rite is especially appropriate for use when the blessing takes place in the home and is given by a family member.

1566 All make the sign of the cross as the minister says:

**Our help is in the name of the Lord.**

All reply:

**Who made heaven and earth.**

1567 One of those present or the minister reads a text of sacred Scripture, for example:

**Brothers and sisters, listen to the words of the holy gospel according to Luke:**                               2:1-8

*The birth of Jesus.*

**In those days a decree went out from Caesar Augustus that the whole world should be enrolled. This was the first enrollment, when Quirinius was governor of Syria. So all went to be enrolled, each to his own town. And Joseph too went up from**

Galilee from the town of Nazareth to Judea, to the city of David that is called Bethlehem, because he was of the house and family of David, to be enrolled with Mary, his betrothed, who was with child. While they were there, the time came for her to have her child, and she gave birth to her firstborn son. She wrapped him in swaddling clothes and laid him in a manger, because there was no room for them in the inn.

Now there were shepherds in that region living in the fields and keeping the night watch over their flock.

1568 Or:

Isaiah 7:10-15—*The birth of Emmanuel.*

1569 A minister who is a priest or deacon says the prayer of blessing with hands outstretched; a lay minister says the prayer with hands joined.

God of every nation and people,
from the very beginning of creation
you have made manifest your love:
when our need for a Savior was great
you sent your Son to be born of the Virgin Mary.
To our lives he brings joy and peace,
justice, mercy, and love.

Lord,
bless all who look upon this manger;
may it remind us of the humble birth of Jesus,
and raise up our thoughts to him,
who is God-with-us and Savior of all,
and who lives and reigns for ever and ever.

R̸. Amen.

# CHAPTER 49

# ORDER FOR THE BLESSING OF A CHRISTMAS TREE

USA

## INTRODUCTION

1570 The use of the Christmas tree is relatively modern. Its origins are found in the medieval mystery plays which depicted the tree of paradise and the Christmas light or candle which symbolized Christ, the Light of the world.

1571 According to custom, the Christmas tree is set up just before Christmas and may remain in place until the solemnity of Epiphany. Although the primary place for the Christmas tree is the home, at times one or more may also be placed in the church. In such a case, the decoration of the trees should be appropriate to their use in the church, and care should be taken that they do not interfere with the requirements of the liturgical space.

1572 The Christmas tree may be blessed on or before Christmas during a celebration of the word of God, or during Morning or Evening Prayer.

    If the blessing is celebrated during Morning or Evening Prayer, it takes place after the gospel canticle. The intercessions, Lord's Prayer, and prayer of blessing replace the intercessions and concluding prayer of Morning or Evening Prayer.

1573 The lights of the tree are illuminated after the prayer of blessing.

1574 In the home the Christmas tree may be blessed by a parent or another family member, in connection with the evening meal on the Vigil of Christmas or at another suitable time on Christmas Day; the shorter rite may be used for this purpose.

1575 These orders may be used by a priest or a deacon, and also by a layperson, who follows the rites and prayers designated for a lay minister.

# I. ORDER OF BLESSING

## INTRODUCTORY RITES

1576 When the community has gathered, a suitable song may be sung. After the singing, the minister says:

**In the name of the Father, and of the Son, and of the Holy Spirit.**

All make the sign of the cross and reply:

**Amen.**

1577 A minister who is a priest or deacon greets those present in the following or other suitable words, taken mainly from sacred Scripture.

**May the light of Christ, who is our peace and salvation, be always with you.**

And all reply:

**And also with you.**

---

1578 A lay minister greets those present in the following words:

**Let us glorify Christ our light, who brings salvation and peace into our midst, now and for ever.**

**R̂. Amen.**

---

1579 In the following or similar words, the minister prepares those present for the blessing.

**My brothers and sisters, amidst signs and wonders Christ Jesus was born in Bethlehem of Judea: his birth brings joy to our hearts and enlightenment to our minds. With this tree, decorated and adorned, may we welcome Christ among us; may its lights guide us to the perfect light.**

# Reading of the Word of God

**1580**  A reader, another person present, or the minister reads a text of sacred Scripture.

**Brothers and sisters, listen to the words of the apostle Paul to Titus:**  3:4-7

*His own compassion saved us.*

**But when the kindness and generous love
of God our savior appeared,
not because of any righteous deeds we had done
but because of his mercy,
he saved us through the bath of rebirth
and renewal by the holy Spirit,
whom he richly poured out on us
through Jesus Christ our savior,
so that we might be justified by his grace
and become heirs in hope of eternal life.**

**1581**  Or:

Genesis 2:4-9—*The tree of life in the center of the garden.*

Isaiah 9:1-6—*A son is given to us.*

Ezekiel 17:22-24—*I will plant a tender shoot on the mountain heights of Israel.*

**1582**  As circumstances suggest, the following responsorial psalm may be sung, or some other suitable song.

R℟. **Christ comes to enlighten us.**

Psalm 96

**Sing to the LORD a new song;
sing to the LORD, all you lands.
Sing to the LORD, bless his name;
announce his salvation, day after day.** R℟.

**Tell his glory among the nations;
among all peoples, his wondrous deeds.
For great is the LORD and highly to be praised;
awesome is he, beyond all gods.** R℟.

**For all the gods of the nations are things of nought,
but the LORD made the heavens.
Splendor and majesty go before him;
praise and grandeur are in his sanctuary.** R℟.

Give to the LORD, you families of nations,
give to the LORD glory and praise;
give to the LORD the glory due his name!
Bring gifts, and enter his courts;
worship the LORD in holy attire. R℣.

Tremble before him, all the earth;
say among the nations: The LORD is king.
He has made the world firm, not to be moved;
he governs the peoples with equity. R℣.

Let the heavens be glad and the earth rejoice;
let the sea and what fills it resound;
let the plains be joyful and all that is in them!
Then shall all the trees of the forest exult
before the LORD, for he comes;
for he comes to rule the earth. R℣.

He shall rule the world with justice
and the peoples with his constancy. R℣.

1583 As circumstances suggest, the minister may give those present a brief explanation of the biblical text, so that they may understand through faith the meaning of the celebration.

## INTERCESSIONS

1584 The intercessions are then said. The minister introduces them and an assisting minister or one of those present announces the intentions. From the following those best suited to the occasion may be used or adapted, or other intentions that apply to the particular circumstances may be composed.

The minister says:

**Let us ask God to send his blessing upon us and upon this sign of our faith in the Lord.**

**R℣. Lord, give light to our hearts.**

Assisting minister:

**That the Church may always reflect the joy of Jesus Christ who enlightens our hearts, let us pray to the Lord. R℣.**

Assisting minister:

**That this tree of lights may remind us of the tree of glory on which Christ accomplished our salvation, let us pray to the Lord. ℟.**

Assisting minister:

**That the joy of Christmas may always be in our homes, let us pray to the Lord. ℟.**

Assisting minister:

**That the peace of Christ may dwell in our hearts and in the world, let us pray to the Lord. ℟.**

1585 After the intercessions the minister, in the following or similar words, invites all present to sing or say the Lord's Prayer.

**With confident faith let us pray as Christ taught us:**

All:

**Our Father . . .**


## Prayer of Blessing

1586 A minister who is a priest or deacon says the prayer of blessing with hands outstretched; a lay minister says the prayer with hands joined.

**Lord our God,**
**we praise you for the light of creation:**
**the sun, the moon, and the stars of the night.**
**We praise you for the light of Israel:**
**the Law, the prophets, and the wisdom**
   **of the Scriptures.**
**We praise you for Jesus Christ, your Son:**
**he is Emmanuel, God-with-us, the Prince of Peace,**
**who fills us with the wonder of your love.**

**Lord God,**
**let your blessing come upon us**
**as we illumine this tree.**
**May the light and cheer it gives**
**be a sign of the joy that fills our hearts.**

May all who delight in this tree
come to the knowledge and joy of salvation.

We ask this through Christ our Lord.

℞. Amen.

1587 Or:

Holy Lord,
we come with joy to celebrate the birth of your Son,
who rescued us from the darkness of sin
by making the cross a tree of life and light.

May this tree, arrayed in splendor,
remind us of the life-giving cross of Christ,
that we may always rejoice
in the new life that shines in our hearts.

We ask this through Christ our Lord.

℞. Amen.

The candles or lights of the tree are then illuminated.

1588 During the illumination of the tree, the cantor or another minister leads the congregation in singing the following acclamations to Christ, or some other suitable hymn, such as "O Come, O Come, Emmanuel."

Lord Jesus, Son of God and Son of Mary.

℞. We welcome you, O Lord.

Lord Jesus, hope of the shepherds and the poor.

℞. We welcome you, O Lord.

Lord Jesus, glory of the angels.

℞. We welcome you, O Lord.

## CONCLUDING RITE

1589 A minister who is a priest or deacon concludes the rite by saying:

May the God of glory fill your hearts with peace and joy, now and for ever.

℞. Amen.

Then he blesses all present.

**And may almighty God bless you all,
the Father, and the Son, ✛ and the Holy Spirit.**

℟. **Amen.**

---

1590   A lay minister concludes the rite by signing himself or herself with the sign of the cross and saying:

**May the God of glory fill our hearts with peace and joy, now and for ever.**

℟. **Amen.**

---

1591   It is preferable to end the celebration with a suitable song.


# II. SHORTER RITE

1592   All make the sign of the cross as the minister says:

**Blessed be the name of the Lord.**

All reply:

**Now and for ever.**

1593   One of those present or the minister reads a text of sacred Scripture, for example:

**Brothers and sisters, listen to the words of the apostle Paul to Titus:**
3:4-7

*His own compassion saved us.*

**But when the kindness and generous love
of God our savior appeared,
not because of any righteous deeds we had done
but because of his mercy,
he saved us through the bath of rebirth
and renewal by the holy Spirit,
whom he richly poured out on us
through Jesus Christ our savior,
so that we might be justified by his grace
and become heirs in hope of eternal life.**

1594 Or:

Genesis 2:4-9—*The tree of life in the center of the garden.*

Isaiah 9:1-6—*A son is given to us.*

1595 A minister who is a priest or deacon says the prayer of blessing with hands outstretched; a lay minister says the prayer with hands joined.

Lord our God,
we praise you for the light of creation:
the sun, the moon, and the stars of the night.
We praise you for the light of Israel:
the Law, the prophets, and the wisdom
   of the Scriptures.
We praise you for Jesus Christ, your Son:
he is Emmanuel, God-with-us, the Prince of Peace,
who fills us with the wonder of your love.

Lord God,
let your blessing come upon us
as we illumine this tree.
May the light and cheer it gives
be a sign of the joy that fills our hearts.
May all who delight in this tree
come to the knowledge and joy of salvation.

We ask this through Christ our Lord.

R̸. Amen.

1596 Or:

Holy Lord,
we come with joy to celebrate the birth of your Son,
who rescued us from the darkness of sin
by making the cross a tree of life and light.

May this tree, arrayed in splendor,
remind us of the life-giving cross of Christ,
that we may always rejoice
in the new life that shines in our hearts.

We ask this through Christ our Lord.

R̸. Amen.

# CHAPTER 50

# ORDER FOR THE BLESSING OF HOMES DURING THE CHRISTMAS AND EASTER SEASONS

USA

## INTRODUCTION

1597   When the faithful wish to have their homes blessed, the priest or deacon should gladly assist them. The Christmas season, especially the feast of the Epiphany, and the Easter season are traditional times when homes may be blessed.

1598   The structure of the rite and its chief elements are always to be maintained, but the individual parts of the rite can be selected in such a way that the celebration is better adapted to the season and the other circumstances.

1599   A home should not be blessed unless those who live in it are present.

1600   These orders may be used by a priest or a deacon, and also by a layperson, who follows the rites and prayers designated for a lay minister.

# I. ORDER OF BLESSING

## INTRODUCTORY RITES

1601  When the community has gathered, a suitable song may
be sung. After the singing, the minister says:

**In the name of the Father, and of the Son, and of the Holy
Spirit.**

All make the sign of the cross and reply:

**Amen.**

1602  A minister who is a priest or deacon greets those present
in the following or other suitable words, taken mainly from sacred
Scripture.

**Peace be with this house and with all who live here.**

And all reply:

**And also with you.**

---

1603  A lay minister greets those present in the following words:

**Let us praise God, who fills our hearts and homes with peace.
Blessed be God for ever.**

℟. **Blessed be God for ever.**

---

1604  In the following or similar words, the minister prepares
those present for the blessing.

**The Word became flesh and made his dwelling place among
us. It is Christ who enlightens our hearts and homes with his
love. It is Christ, risen from the dead, who is our source of
hope, joy, and comfort. May all who enter this home find
Christ's light and love.**

---

# Reading of the Word of God

1605 A reader, another person present, or the minister reads a text of sacred Scripture.

(For Epiphany)

**Brothers and sisters, listen to the words of the holy gospel according to Luke:** 19:1-9

*Today salvation has come to this house.*

**Jesus came to Jericho and intended to pass through the town. Now a man there named Zacchaeus, who was a chief tax collector and also a wealthy man, was seeking to see who Jesus was; but he could not see him because of the crowd, for he was short in stature. So he ran ahead and climbed a sycamore tree in order to see Jesus, who was about to pass that way. When he reached the place, Jesus looked up and said to him, "Zacchaeus, come down quickly, for today I must stay at your house." And he came down quickly and received him with joy. When they all saw this, they began to grumble, saying, "He has gone to stay at the house of a sinner." But Zacchaeus stood there and said to the Lord, "Behold, half of my possessions, Lord, I shall give to the poor, and if I have extorted anything from anyone I shall repay it four times over." And Jesus said to him, "Today salvation has come to this house because this man too is a descendant of Abraham."**

1606 Or: (For Easter)

**Brothers and sisters, listen to the words of the holy gospel according to Luke:** 24:28-32

*Stay with us, Lord.*

**As the disciples approached the village to which they were going, Jesus gave the impression that he was going on farther. But they urged him, "Stay with us, for it is nearly evening and the day is almost over." So he went in to stay with them. And it happened that, while he was with them at table, he took bread, said the blessing, broke it, and gave it to them. With that their eyes were opened and they recognized him, but he vanished from their sight. Then they said to each other, "Were not our hearts burning within us while he spoke to us on the way and opened the scriptures to us?"**

1607 Or:

John 20:19-21—*Jesus came and said, "Peace be with you."*
(For Easter)

1608 As circumstances suggest, one of the following responsorial psalms may be sung, or some other suitable song.

R̸. **Happy are those who fear the Lord.**

Psalm 112

**Happy the man who fears the LORD,
who greatly delights in his commands.
His posterity shall be mighty upon the earth;
the upright generation shall be blessed.** R̸.

**Wealth and riches shall be in his house;
his generosity shall endure forever.
He dawns through the darkness, a light for
the upright!
he is gracious and merciful and just.** R̸.

**Well for the man who is gracious and lends,
who conducts his affairs with justice;
He shall never be moved;
the just man shall be in everlasting remembrance.** R̸.

**An evil report he shall not fear;
his heart is firm, trusting in the LORD.
His heart is steadfast; he shall not fear
till he looks down upon his foes.** R̸.

**Lavishly he gives to the poor;
his generosity shall endure forever;
his horn shall be exalted in glory.** R̸.

(For Epiphany)

R̸. **Lord, every nation on earth will adore you.**

Psalm 72

**O God, with your judgment endow the king,
and with your justice, the king's son;
He shall govern your people with justice
and your afflicted ones with judgment.** R̸.

Justice shall flower in his days,
and profound peace, till the moon be no more.
May he rule from sea to sea,
and from the River to the ends of the earth. R℣.

The kings of Tarshish and the Isles shall offer gifts;
the kings of Arabia and Seba shall bring tribute.
All kings shall pay him homage,
all nations shall serve him. R℣.

For he shall rescue the poor man when he cries out,
and the afflicted when he has no one to help him.
He shall have pity for the lowly and the poor;
the lives of the poor he shall save. R℣.

Psalm 127:1, 2, 3-4, 5

R℣. (see v. 1) May the Lord build us a home.

Psalm 128:1-2, 3, 4, 5-6

R℣. (v. 1) All those who fear the Lord will be blessed.

Psalm 118:2-4, 13-15, 22-24

R℣. (v. 1) Give thanks to the Lord, for he is good.

1609   As circumstances suggest, the minister may give those present a brief explanation of the biblical text, so that they may understand through faith the meaning of the celebration.

# INTERCESSIONS

1610   The intercessions are then said. The minister introduces them and an assisting minister or one of those present announces the intentions. From the following those best suited to the occasion may be used or adapted, or other intentions that apply to the particular circumstances may be composed.

The minister says:

**The Son of God made his home among us. With thanks and praise let us call upon him.**

**R℣. Stay with us, Lord.**

Assisting minister:

**Lord Jesus Christ, with Mary and Joseph you formed the Holy Family: remain in our home, that we may know you as our guest and honor you as our head. We pray: R℣.**

Assisting minister:

**Lord Jesus Christ, through you every dwelling is a temple of holiness: build those who live in this house into the dwelling place of God in the Holy Spirit. We pray: R℣.**

Assisting minister:

**Lord Jesus Christ, you taught your followers to build their houses upon solid rock: grant that the members of this family may live their lives in firm allegiance to your teachings. We pray: R℣.**

Assisting minister:

**Lord Jesus Christ, you had no place to lay your head, but in the spirit of poverty accepted the hospitality of your friends: grant that through our help the homeless may obtain proper housing. We pray: R℣.**

Assisting minister:

For Christmas

**Lord Jesus Christ, you became flesh of the Virgin Mary: grant that your presence may be known always in this home. We pray: R℣.**

Assisting minister:

For Epiphany

**Lord Jesus Christ, the three kings presented their gifts to you in praise and adoration: grant that those living in this house may use their talents and abilities to your greater glory. We pray: R℣.**

Assisting minister:

For Easter

**Lord Jesus Christ, the disciples recognized you in the breaking of the bread: grant that the members of this family may be open always to the presence of Christ in word and sacrament. We pray: R℣.**

Assisting minister:

For Easter

**Lord Jesus Christ, you appeared to the frightened apostles and said, ''Peace be with you'': grant that your abiding peace may remain with the members of this family. We pray: R℣.**

1611    After the intercessions the minister, in the following or similar words, invites all present to sing or say the Lord's Prayer.

**As children of God we confidently pray:**

All:

**Our Father . . .**

## Prayer of Blessing

1612    A minister who is a priest or deacon says the prayer of blessing with hands outstretched; a lay minister says the prayer with hands joined.

A        For the Christmas season

**Lord God of heaven and earth,**
**you revealed your only-begotten Son to every nation**
**by the guidance of a star.**

**Bless this house**
**and all who inhabit it.**
**Fill them with the light of Christ,**
**that their concern for others may reflect your love.**

**We ask this through Christ our Lord.**

**R̓. Amen.**

B        For the Easter season

**Lord,**
**we rejoice in the victory of your Son over death:**
**by rising from the tomb to new life**
**he gives us new hope and promise.**

**Bless all the members of this household**
**and surround them with your protection,**
**that they may find comfort and peace**
**in Jesus Christ, the paschal lamb,**
**who lives and reigns with you and the Holy Spirit,**
**one God, for ever and ever.**

**R̓. Amen.**

1613 As circumstances suggest, the minister in silence may sprinkle those present and the home with holy water. During the sprinkling the minister may say:

**Let this water call to mind our baptism in Christ, who by his death and resurrection has redeemed us.**

## CONCLUDING RITE

1614 A minister who is a priest or deacon concludes the rite by saying:

**May Christ Jesus dwell with you,**
**keep you from all harm,**
**and make you one in mind and heart,**
**now and for ever.**

**R̸. Amen.**

Then he blesses all present.

**And may almighty God bless you all,**
**the Father, and the Son, ✠ and the Holy Spirit.**

**R̸. Amen.**

1615 A lay minister concludes the rite by signing himself or herself with the sign of the cross and saying:

**May Christ Jesus dwell with us,**
**keep us from all harm,**
**and make us one in mind and heart,**
**now and for ever.**

**R̸. Amen.**

1616 It is preferable to end the celebration with a suitable song.

# II. SHORTER RITE

**1617**  All make the sign of the cross as the minister says:

**Blessed be the name of the Lord.**

All reply:

**Now and for ever.**

**1618**  One of those present or the minister reads a text of sacred Scripture, for example:

(For Epiphany)

**Brothers and sisters, listen to the words of the holy gospel according to Luke:** 19:1-9

*Today salvation has come to this house.*

**Jesus came to Jericho and intended to pass through the town. Now a man there named Zacchaeus, who was a chief tax collector and also a wealthy man, was seeking to see who Jesus was; but he could not see him because of the crowd, for he was short in stature. So he ran ahead and climbed a sycamore tree in order to see Jesus, who was about to pass that way. When he reached the place, Jesus looked up and said to him, "Zacchaeus, come down quickly, for today I must stay at your house." And he came down quickly and received him with joy. When they all saw this, they began to grumble, saying, "He has gone to stay at the house of a sinner." But Zacchaeus stood there and said to the Lord, "Behold, half of my possessions, Lord, I shall give to the poor, and if I have extorted anything from anyone I shall repay it four times over." And Jesus said to him, "Today salvation has come to this house because this man too is a descendant of Abraham."**

**1619**  Or: (For Easter)

**Brothers and sisters, listen to the words of the holy gospel according to Luke:** 24:28-32

*Stay with us, Lord.*

**As the disciples approached the village to which they were going, Jesus gave the impression that he was going on farther.**

But they urged him, "Stay with us, for it is nearly evening and the day is almost over." So he went in to stay with them. And it happened that, while he was with them at table, he took bread, said the blessing, broke it, and gave it to them. With that their eyes were opened and they recognized him, but he vanished from their sight. Then they said to each other, "Were not our hearts burning within us while he spoke to us on the way and opened the scriptures to us?"

**1620** Or:

John 20:19-21—*Jesus came and said, "Peace be with you."* (For Easter)

**1621** A minister who is a priest or deacon says the prayer of blessing with hands outstretched; a lay minister says the prayer with hands joined.

A        For the Christmas season

**Lord God of heaven and earth,
you revealed your only-begotten Son to every nation
by the guidance of a star.**

**Bless this house
and all who inhabit it.
Fill them with the light of Christ,
that their concern for others may reflect your love.**

**We ask this through Christ our Lord.**

**R̅. Amen.**

B        For the Easter season

**Lord,
we rejoice in the victory of your Son over death:
by rising from the tomb to new life
he gives us new hope and promise.**

**Bless all the members of this household
and surround them with your protection,
that they may find comfort and peace
in Jesus Christ, the paschal lamb,
who lives and reigns with you and the Holy Spirit,
one God, for ever and ever.**

**R̅. Amen.**

# CHAPTER 51

# ORDER FOR THE BLESSING OF THROATS ON THE FEAST OF SAINT BLASE
## February 3

## INTRODUCTION

1622   "Suffering and illness have always been among the greatest problems that trouble the human spirit. Christians feel and experience pain as do all other people; yet their faith helps them to grasp more deeply the mystery of suffering and to bear their pain with greater courage. . . . Part of the plan laid out by God's providence is that we should fight strenuously against all sickness and carefully seek the blessings of good health, so that we may fulfill our role in human society and in the Church."[4]

1623   "The blessing of the sick by ministers of the Church is a very ancient custom, rooted in imitation of Christ himself and his apostles."[5]

1624   In the United States the annual blessing of throats is a traditional sign of the struggle against illness in the life of the Christian. This blessing is ordinarily given during Mass or a celebration of the word of God on February 3, the memorial of Saint Blase.

1625   Saint Blase was the bishop of Sebaste in Armenia during the fourth century. Very little is known about his life. According to various accounts[6] he was a physician before becoming a bishop. His cult spread throughout the entire Church in the Middle Ages because he was reputed to have miraculously cured a little boy who nearly died because of a fishbone in his throat. From the eighth century he has been invoked on behalf of the sick, especially those afflicted with illnesses of the throat.

1626   The blessing of throats may be given by a priest, deacon, or a lay minister who follows the rites and prayers designated for a lay minister. If the blessing is conferred during Mass, the blessing follows the homily and general intercessions, or, for pastoral reasons, the prayer of blessing may take the place of the final blessing of the Mass. When the blessing is given outside Mass, it is preceded by a brief celebration of the word of God. If the blessing is to be celebrated at Morning Prayer or Evening Prayer, it is given after the reading and responsory (and homily) and before the gospel canticle.

---

[4] *Pastoral Care of the Sick: Rites of Anointing and Viaticum,* nos. 1, 3.

[5] *Rituale Romanum: De Benedictionibus,* Chapter 2: "Blessing of the Sick," no. 1.

[6] Metaphrastes, *Vita Sanctorum* in Migne, *Patrologia Graeca* 116:817. See also Roman Martyrology, February 3.

---

1627    The blessing may be given by touching the throat of each person with two candles blessed on the feast of the Presentation of the Lord (February 2) and which have been joined together in the form of a cross.

1628    If, for pastoral reasons, each individual cannot be blessed in the manner described in no. 1627, for example when great numbers are gathered for the blessing or when the memorial of Saint Blase occurs on a Sunday, a priest or deacon may give the blessing to all assembled by extending hands, without the crossed candles, over the people while saying the prayer of blessing. A lay minister says the prayer proper to lay ministers without making the sign of the cross.

1629    The blessing may also be given to the sick or the elderly in their homes when they cannot attend the parish celebration.

# I. ORDER OF BLESSING WITHIN MASS

## INTRODUCTORY RITES

1630    After the celebrant has greeted the people, he may introduce the celebration in these or similar words.

**Today we celebrate the feast of Saint Blase, who was bishop of Sebaste in Armenia in the fourth century. Before being martyred, he is said to have healed a boy who was choking. Since the eighth century, Saint Blase has been venerated as the patron of those who suffer from diseases of the throat. We pray in a special way today for protection from afflictions of the throat and from other illnesses. The blessing of Saint Blase is a sign of our faith in God's protection and love for us and for the sick.**

1631    After the gospel reading, the celebrant in the homily, based on the sacred text and pertinent to the particular place and the people involved, explains the meaning of the celebration.

# GENERAL INTERCESSIONS

**1632** The general intercessions follow, either in the form usual at Mass or in the form provided here. The celebrant concludes the intercessions with the prayer of blessing. From the following intentions those best for the occasion may be used or adapted, or other intentions that apply to the particular circumstances may be composed.

The celebrant says:

**Let us now pray for those who are sick and suffering, for those who care for the sick, and for all who seek the blessings of good health.**

℞. **Lord, hear our prayer.**

Or:

℞. **Lord, have mercy.**

Assisting minister:

**For those who suffer from sickness and disease, that they may receive healing, we pray to the Lord.** ℞.

Assisting minister:

**For the mentally ill and for their families, that they may receive comfort, we pray to the Lord.** ℞.

Assisting minister:

**For those with physical disabilities, that the strength of Christ may invigorate them, we pray to the Lord.** ℞.

Assisting minister:

**For doctors and nurses, and for all who care for the sick, we pray to the Lord.** ℞.

Assisting minister:

**For those who seek the prayers of Saint Blase today, that they may be protected from afflictions of the throat and other forms of illness, we pray to the Lord.** ℞.

## PRAYER OF BLESSING

**1633**  With the crossed candles touched to the throat of each person, the celebrant says immediately:

**Through the intercession of Saint Blase, bishop and martyr, may God deliver you from every disease of the throat and from every other illness:**

**In the name of the Father, and of the Son, ✛ and of the Holy Spirit.**

Each person responds:

**Amen.**

During the blessing suitable psalms or other suitable songs may be sung.

---

**1634**  A lay minister touches the throat of each person with the crossed candles and, without making the sign of the cross, says the prayer of blessing.

**Through the intercession of Saint Blase, bishop and martyr, may God deliver you from every disease of the throat and from every other illness:**

**In the name of the Father, and of the Son, and of the Holy Spirit.**

Each person responds:

**Amen.**

---

**1635**  If all cannot be blessed individually, the celebrant, without candles, extends his hands over the assembly and says the prayer of blessing.

# II. ORDER OF BLESSING WITHIN A CELEBRATION OF THE WORD OF GOD

1636 The present order may be used by a priest or a deacon, and also by a lay person, who follows the rites and prayers designated for a lay minister.

## INTRODUCTORY RITES

1637 When the community has gathered, a suitable song may be sung. After the singing, the minister says:

**In the name of the Father, and of the Son, and of the Holy Spirit.**

All make the sign of the cross and reply:

**Amen.**

1638 A minister who is a priest or deacon greets those present in the following or other suitable words, taken mainly from sacred Scripture.

**The grace and peace of God the Father and the Lord Jesus Christ be with you.**

And all reply:

**And also with you.**

---

1639 A lay minister greets those present in the following words:

**Let us praise the God and Father of our Lord Jesus Christ.**

**R̸. Blessed be God for ever.**

---

1640 In the following or similar words, the minister prepares those present for the blessing.

**Today we celebrate the feast of Saint Blase, who was bishop of Sebaste in Armenia in the fourth century. Before being martyred, he is said to have healed a boy who was choking. Since the eighth century, Saint Blase has been venerated as the patron of those who suffer from diseases of the throat. We pray in a special way today for protection from afflictions of the throat and from other illnesses. The blessing of Saint Blase is a sign of our faith in God's protection and love for us and for the sick.**

# Reading of the Word of God

1641  A reader, another person present, or the minister reads a text of sacred Scripture.

**Brothers and sisters, listen to the words of the holy gospel according to Mark:**  16:15-20

*They will place their hands on the sick and they will recover.*

**Jesus said to the eleven, "Go into the whole world and proclaim the gospel to every creature. Whoever believes and is baptized will be saved; whoever does not believe will be condemned. These signs will accompany those who believe: in my name they will drive out demons, they will speak new languages. They will pick up serpents with their hands, and if they drink any deadly thing, it will not harm them. They will lay hands on the sick, and they will recover."**

1642  Or:

Matthew 8:14-17—*Peter's mother-in-law is healed.*

1643  As circumstances suggest, one of the following responsorial psalms may be sung, or some other suitable song.

R̸. **Taste and see the goodness of the Lord.**

Psalm 34

**I will bless the LORD at all times;**
**his praise shall be ever in my mouth.**
**Let my soul glory in the LORD;**
**the lowly will hear me and be glad.** R̸.

**Glorify the LORD with me,**
**let us together extol his name.**
**I sought the LORD, and he answered me**
**and delivered me from all my fears.** R̸.

**Look to him that you may be radiant with joy,**
**and your faces may not blush with shame.**
**When the afflicted man called out, the LORD heard,**
**and from all his distress he saved him.** R̸.

**The angel of the LORD encamps**
**around those who fear him, and delivers them.**
**Taste and see how good the LORD is;**
**happy the man who takes refuge in him.** R̸.

Fear the LORD, you his holy ones,
for nought is lacking to those who fear him.
The great grow poor and hungry;
but those who seek the LORD want for no good thing. R℣.

Come, children, hear me;
I will teach you the fear of the LORD.
Which of you desires life,
and takes delight in prosperous days? R℣.

Keep your tongue from evil
and your lips from speaking guile;
Turn from evil and do good;
seek peace, and follow after it. R℣.

Psalm 27

R℣. (v. 14) **Put your hope in the Lord; take courage and be strong.**

1644   As circumstances suggest, the minister may give those present a brief explanation of the biblical text, so that they may understand through faith the meaning of the celebration.


# INTERCESSIONS

1645   The intercessions are then said. The minister introduces them and an assisting minister or one of those present announces the intentions. From the following those best suited to the occasion may be used or adapted, or other intentions that apply to the particular circumstances may be composed.

The minister says:

**Let us now pray for those who are sick and suffering, for those who care for the sick, and for all who seek the blessings of good health.**

R℣. **Lord, hear our prayer.**

Or:

R℣. **Lord, have mercy.**

Assisting minister:

**For those who suffer from sickness and disease, that they may receive healing, we pray to the Lord.** R℣.

Assisting minister:

**For the mentally ill and for their families, that they may receive comfort, we pray to the Lord. ℟.**

Assisting minister:

**For those with physical disabilities, that the strength of Christ may invigorate them, we pray to the Lord. ℟.**

Assisting minister:

**For doctors and nurses, and for all who care for the sick, we pray to the Lord. ℟.**

Assisting minister:

**For those who seek the prayers of Saint Blase today, that they may be protected from afflictions of the throat and other forms of illness, we pray to the Lord. ℟.**

1646 After the intercessions the minister, in the following or similar words, invites all present to sing or say the Lord's Prayer.

**With confidence we call upon the Lord, saying:**

All:

**Our Father . . .**


## PRAYER OF BLESSING

1647 A minister who is a priest or deacon touches the throat of each person with the crossed candles and says the prayer of blessing.

**Through the intercession of Saint Blase, bishop and martyr, may God deliver you from every disease of the throat and from every other illness:**

**In the name of the Father, and of the Son, ✝ and of the Holy Spirit.**

Each person responds:

**Amen.**

During the blessing suitable psalms or other suitable songs may be sung.

**1648** A lay minister touches the throat of each person with the crossed candles and, without making the sign of the cross, says the prayer of blessing.

**Through the intercession of Saint Blase, bishop and martyr, may God deliver you from every disease of the throat and from every other illness:**

**In the name of the Father, and of the Son, and of the Holy Spirit.**

Each person responds:

**Amen.**

**1649** After receiving the blessing each person may depart.

**1650** If all cannot be blessed individually, a minister who is a priest or deacon, without candles, may extend his hands over the assembly and say the prayer of blessing. A lay minister says the prayer proper to lay ministers without making the sign of the cross.

# III. SHORTER RITE

**1651** All make the sign of the cross as the minister says:

**Our help is in the name of the Lord.**

All reply:

**Who made heaven and earth.**

**1652** One of those present or the minister reads a text of sacred Scripture, for example:

**Brothers and sisters, listen to the words of the holy gospel according to Mark:** 16:15-20

*They will place their hands on the sick and they will recover.*

**Jesus said to the eleven, "Go into the whole world and proclaim the gospel to every creature. Whoever believes and is baptized will be saved; whoever does not believe will be condemned. These signs will accompany those who believe: in**

my name they will drive out demons, they will speak new languages. They will pick up serpents with their hands, and if they drink any deadly thing, it will not harm them. They will lay hands on the sick, and they will recover.''

1653  Or:

Matthew 8:14-17—*Peter's mother-in-law is healed.*

1654  A minister who is a priest or deacon touches the throat of each person with the crossed candles and says the prayer of blessing.

**Through the intercession of Saint Blase, bishop and martyr, may God deliver you from every disease of the throat and from every other illness:**

**In the name of the Father, and of the Son, ✠ and of the Holy Spirit.**

Each person responds:

**Amen.**

1655  A lay minister touches the throat of each person with the crossed candles and, without making the sign of the cross, says the prayer of blessing.

**Through the intercession of Saint Blase, bishop and martyr, may God deliver you from every disease of the throat and from every other illness:**

**In the name of the Father, and of the Son, and of the Holy Spirit.**

Each person responds:

**Amen.**

# CHAPTER 52

# ORDER FOR THE BLESSING AND DISTRIBUTION OF ASHES[7]
## Ash Wednesday

## INTRODUCTION

1656 The season of Lent begins with the ancient practice of marking the baptized with ashes as a public and communal sign of penance. The blessing and distribution of ashes on Ash Wednesday normally takes place during the celebration of Mass. However, when circumstances require, the blessing and distribution of ashes may take place apart from Mass, during a celebration of the word of God.

1657 This order may also be used when ashes are brought to the sick. According to circumstances, the rite may be abbreviated by the minister. Nevertheless, at least one Scripture reading should be included in the service.

1658 If already blessed ashes are brought to the sick, the blessing is omitted and the distribution takes place immediately after the homily. The homily should conclude by inviting the sick person to prepare himself or herself for the reception of the ashes.

1659 This rite may be celebrated by a priest or deacon who may be assisted by lay ministers in the distribution of the ashes. The blessing of the ashes, however, is reserved to a priest or deacon.

---

[7] This blessing is an adaptation of the rite for the blessing and distribution of ashes on Ash Wednesday in The Roman Missal.

# ORDER OF BLESSING

## INTRODUCTORY RITES

1660    When the community has gathered, a suitable song may be sung. After the singing, the minister says:

**In the name of the Father, and of the Son, and of the Holy Spirit.**

All make the sign of the cross and reply:

**Amen.**

1661    The minister greets those present in the following or other suitable words, taken mainly from sacred Scripture.

**The grace, the mercy, and the peace of God the Father and Christ Jesus our Savior be with you.**

And all reply:

**And also with you.**

---

1662    A lay minister greets those present in the following words:

**Praised be the God of grace, mercy, and peace. Blessed be God for ever.**

R̸. **Blessed be God for ever.**

---

1663    In the following words, the minister prepares those present for the blessing and distribution of the ashes.

**My brothers and sisters, the hour of God's favor draws near, the day of his mercy and of our salvation approaches, when death was destroyed and eternal life began. As we begin this season of Lent, we gather today to acknowledge that we are sinners. As we express our sorrow, may God be merciful to us and restore us to his friendship.**

## OPENING PRAYER

1664    The minister then says the opening prayer.

**Let us pray.**

After a brief period of silence, the minister continues:

Father in heaven,
the light of your truth bestows sight
to the darkness of sinful eyes.
May this season of repentance
bring us the blessing of your forgiveness
and the gift of your light.

Grant this through Christ our Lord.

R︦⁊. Amen.

## READING OF THE WORD OF GOD

1665  A reader, another person present, or the minister reads a
text of sacred Scripture.

**Brothers and sisters, listen to the words of the prophet Joel:**

2:12-18

*Let your hearts be broken, and not your garments torn.*

**Yet even now, says the LORD,
return to me with your whole heart,
with fasting, and weeping, and mourning;
Rend your hearts, not your garments,
and return to the LORD, your God.
For gracious and merciful is he,
slow to anger, rich in kindness,
and relenting in punishment.
Perhaps he will again relent
and leave behind him a blessing,
Offerings and libations
for the LORD, your God.**

**Blow the trumpet in Zion!
proclaim a fast,
call an assembly;
Gather the people,
notify the congregation;
Assemble the elders,
gather the children
and the infants at the breast;
Let the bridegroom quit his room,
and the bride her chamber.
Between the porch and the altar
let the priests, the ministers of the LORD, weep,**

And say, "Spare, O LORD, your people,
and make not your heritage a reproach,
with the nations ruling over them!
Why should they say among the peoples,
'Where is their God?'"

Then the LORD was stirred to concern for his land and took
pity on his people.

1666  Or:

2 Corinthians 5:20—6:2—*Be reconciled to God, now is the acceptable
time.*

Matthew 6:1-6, 16-18—*Your Father, who sees all that is done in se-
cret, will reward you.*

1667  As circumstances suggest, the following responsorial psalm
may be sung, or some other suitable song.

R⁊. Be merciful, O Lord, for we have sinned.

Psalm 51

Have mercy on me, O God, in your goodness;
in the greatness of your compassion wipe out my offense.
Thoroughly wash me from my guilt
and of my sin cleanse me. R⁊.

For I acknowledge my offense,
and my sin is before me always:
"Against you only have I sinned,
and done what is evil in your sight"—
That you may be justified in your sentence,
vindicated when you condemn. R⁊.

A clean heart create for me, O God,
and a steadfast spirit renew within me.
Cast me not out from your presence,
and your holy spirit take not from me. R⁊.

Give me back the joy of your salvation,
and a willing spirit sustain in me. R⁊.

O Lord, open my lips,
and my mouth shall proclaim your praise. R⁊.

1668  As circumstances suggest, the minister may give those
present a brief explanation of the biblical text, so that they may
understand through faith the meaning of the celebration.

## Prayer of Blessing

1669 After the homily the minister, if a priest or deacon, joins his hands and says:

**Dear friends in Christ, let us ask our Father to bless these ashes which we will use as the mark of our repentance.**

Pause for silent prayer.

**Lord,
bless the sinner who asks for your forgiveness
and bless ✝ all those who receive these ashes.
May they keep this lenten season
in preparation for the joy of Easter.**

**We ask this through Christ our Lord.**

℟. **Amen.**

1670 Or:

**Lord,
bless these ashes ✝
by which we show that we are dust.
Pardon our sins
and keep us faithful to the discipline of Lent,
for you do not want sinners to die
but to live with the risen Christ,
who reigns with you for ever and ever.**

℟. **Amen.**

He sprinkles the ashes with holy water in silence.

## Distribution of the Ashes

1671 The minister then places the ashes on those who come forward, saying to each:

**Turn away from sin and be faithful to the gospel.**

Or:

**Remember, you are dust
and to dust you will return.**

1672 Meanwhile some of the following antiphons or other appropriate songs are sung.

## Antiphon 1

**Come back to the Lord with all your heart;**
**leave the past in ashes,**
**and turn to God with tears and fasting,**
**for he is slow to anger and ready to forgive.**

## Antiphon 2

**Let the priests and ministers of the Lord**
**lament before his altar, and say:**
**Spare us, Lord; spare your people!**
**Do not let us die for we are crying out to you.**

## Antiphon 3

**Lord, take away our wickedness.**

These may be repeated after each verse of Psalm 51, "Have mercy on me, O God."

## Responsory

**Direct our hearts to better things, O Lord;**
**heal our sin and ignorance.**
**Lord, do not face us suddenly with death,**
**but give us time to repent.**

℟. **Turn to us with mercy, Lord: we have sinned against you.**

℣. **Help us, God our savior, rescue us for the honor of your name.**

℟. **Turn to us with mercy, Lord; we have sinned against you.**

1673 After the giving of ashes the minister's hands are washed; the rite concludes with the general intercessions and the final blessing.

## INTERCESSIONS

1674 The intercessions are then said. The minister introduces them and an assisting minister or one of those present announces the intentions. From the following those best suited to the occasion may be used or adapted, or other intentions that apply to the particular circumstances may be composed.

The minister says:

**Our merciful Father does not desire the death of sinners but rather that they should turn from their sins and have life. Let us pray that we who are sorry for our sins may fear no future evil and sin no more.**

℞. **Lord, hear our prayer.**

Assisting minister:

**By human weakness we have disfigured the holiness of the Church: pardon all our sins and restore us to full communion with our brothers and sisters. ℞.**

Assisting minister:

**Grant the forgiveness of sins and the gift of new life to those who will be baptized this Easter. ℞.**

Assisting minister:

**Your mercy is our hope: welcome us to the sacrament of reconciliation. ℞.**

Assisting minister:

**Give us the will to change our lives, and the lives of others, by charity, good example, and prayer. ℞.**

Assisting minister:

**Make us a living sign of your love for all to see: people reconciled with you and each other. ℞.**

1675 After the intercessions the minister, in the following or similar words, invites all present to sing or say the Lord's Prayer.

**Now, in obedience to Christ himself, let us join in prayer to the Father, asking him to forgive us as we forgive others.**

All:

**Our Father . . .**

The minister adds:

**Father, our source of life,**
**you know our weakness.**
**May we reach out with joy to grasp your hand**
**and to walk more readily in your ways.**

**We ask this through Christ our Lord.**

℟. **Amen.**

## Concluding Rite

1676 The minister concludes the rite by saying:

**May the Father bless us,**
**for he has adopted us as his children.**

℟. **Amen.**

**May the Son come to help us,**
**for he has received us as brothers and sisters.**

℟. **Amen.**

**May the Spirit be with us,**
**for he has made us his dwelling place.**

℟. **Amen.**

---

1677 A priest or deacon then blesses all present:

**And may almighty God bless you all,**
**the Father, and the Son, ✝ and the Holy Spirit.**

℟. **Amen.**

---

1678 It is preferable to end the celebration with a suitable song.

# CHAPTER 53

# ORDER FOR THE BLESSING OF SAINT JOSEPH'S TABLE
## March 19

## INTRODUCTION

1679   On the solemnity of Saint Joseph (March 19) it is the custom in some places to bless bread, pastries, and other food and give a large portion of it to the poor.

1680   The faithful should be encouraged to participate in the celebration of Mass on the solemnity of Saint Joseph.

1681   These orders may be used by a priest or a deacon, and also by a lay-person, who follows the rites and prayers designated for a lay minister.

# I. ORDER OF BLESSING

## INTRODUCTORY RITES

1682  When the community has gathered, a suitable song may be sung. After the singing, the minister says:

**In the name of the Father, and of the Son, and of the Holy Spirit.**

All make the sign of the cross and reply:

**Amen.**

1683  A minister who is a priest or deacon greets those present in the following or other suitable words, taken mainly from sacred Scripture.

**May God, who has called us to be saints, be with you all.**

And all reply:

**And also with you.**

---

1684  A lay minister greets those present in the following words:

**Praised be God, who gives us saints as models and examples. Blessed be God for ever.**

R̶̸. **Blessed be God for ever.**

---

1685  In the following or similar words, the minister prepares those present for the blessing.

**Today we honor the memory of Saint Joseph, husband of the Virgin Mary and patron of the universal Church. We rejoice at this table, which is a sign of God's generous blessings and of our call to serve the poor and hungry. We pray that through the intercession of Saint Joseph we too might join the saints at the banquet of the Lord in the heavenly kingdom.**

## READING OF THE WORD OF GOD

1686  A reader, another person present, or the minister reads a text of sacred Scripture.

**Brothers and sisters, listen to the words of the holy gospel according to Matthew:**                                    1:18-23

*Joseph did as the angel commanded him.*

**Now this is how the birth of Jesus Christ came about. When his mother Mary was betrothed to Joseph, but before they lived together, she was found with child through the holy Spirit. Joseph her husband, since he was a righteous man, yet unwilling to expose her to shame, decided to divorce her quietly. Such was his intention when, behold, the angel of the Lord appeared to him in a dream and said, "Joseph, son of David, do not be afraid to take Mary your wife into your home. For it is through the holy Spirit that this child has been conceived in her. She will bear a son and you are to name him Jesus, because he will save his people from their sins." All this took place to fulfill what the Lord had said through the prophet:**

**"Behold, the virgin shall be with child and bear a son, and they shall name him Emmanuel,"**

**which means "God is with us."**

1687  Or:

Matthew 13:54-58—*Is this not the carpenter's son?*

1688  As circumstances suggest, one of the following responsorial psalms may be sung, or some other suitable song.

**R̷. The Son of David will live for ever.**

Psalm 89

**The favors of the LORD I will sing forever;
through all generations my mouth shall proclaim
  your faithfulness. R̷.**

**For you have said, "My kindness is established forever";
in heaven you have confirmed your faithfulness:
"I have made a covenant with my chosen one.
I have sworn to David my servant: R̷.**

**"Forever will I confirm your posterity
and establish your throne for all generations." R̷.**

**The heavens proclaim your wonders, O LORD,
and your faithfulness, in the assembly of the holy ones.
For who in the skies can rank with the LORD?
Who is like the LORD among the sons of God? R̷.**

Psalm 112:1-2, 3-4, 5-7, 8-9

R︎. (v. 1) **Happy are they who fear the Lord.**

1689 As circumstances suggest, the minister may give those present a brief explanation of the biblical text, so that they may understand through faith the meaning of the celebration.

## INTERCESSIONS

1690 The intercessions are then said. The minister introduces them and an assisting minister or one of those present announces the intentions. From the following those best suited to the occasion may be used or adapted, or other intentions that apply to the particular circumstances may be composed.

The minister says:

**Let us call upon the name of the Lord through the intercession of Saint Joseph.**

R︎. **Lord, you are our hope and our strength.**

Assisting minister:

**That we who have listened to the word of God may do his will, let us pray to the Lord.** R︎.

Assisting minister:

**That we who have experienced doubt and fear may be helped in times of difficulty, let us pray to the Lord.** R︎.

Assisting minister:

**That we may hunger for justice and mercy, we pray to the Lord.** R︎.

Assisting minister:

**That we who seek God's way may complete our journey to God's kingdom, let us pray to the Lord.** R︎.

Assisting minister:

**That we who follow the example of Saint Joseph, patron of the universal Church, may strive always to build up the body of Christ, let us pray to the Lord.** R︎.

## LITANY OF SAINT JOSEPH

| | |
|---|---|
| Lord, have mercy | Lord, have mercy |
| Christ, have mercy | Christ, have mercy |
| Lord, have mercy | Lord, have mercy |
| God our Father in heaven | have mercy on us |
| God the Son, Redeemer of the world | have mercy on us |
| God the Holy Spirit | have mercy on us |
| Holy Trinity, one God | have mercy on us |
| Holy Mary | pray for us |
| Saint Joseph | pray for us |
| Noble son of the House of David | pray for us |
| Light of patriarchs | pray for us |
| Husband of the Mother of God | pray for us |
| Guardian of the Virgin | pray for us |
| Foster father of the Son of God | pray for us |
| Faithful guardian of Christ | pray for us |
| Head of the holy family | pray for us |
| Joseph, chaste and just | pray for us |
| Joseph, prudent and brave | pray for us |
| Joseph, obedient and loyal | pray for us |
| Pattern of patience | pray for us |
| Lover of poverty | pray for us |
| Model of workers | pray for us |
| Example to parents | pray for us |
| Guardian of virgins | pray for us |
| Pillar of family life | pray for us |
| Comfort of the troubled | pray for us |
| Hope of the sick | pray for us |
| Patron of the dying | pray for us |
| Terror of evil spirits | pray for us |
| Protector of the Church | pray for us |
| Lamb of God, you take away the sins of the world | have mercy on us |

**Lamb of God, you take away**
**the sins of the world**        **have mercy on us**
**Lamb of God, you take away**
**the sins of the world**        **have mercy on us**

1692   After the intercessions the minister, in the following or similar words, invites all present to sing or say the Lord's Prayer.

**Let us pray to the Father in the words our Savior gave us:**

All:

**Our Father . . .**

## PRAYER OF BLESSING

1693   A minister who is a priest or deacon says the prayer of blessing with hands outstretched; a lay minister says the prayer with hands joined.

**All-provident God,**
**the good things that grace this table**
**remind us of your many good gifts.**

**Bless this food,**
**and may the prayers of Saint Joseph,**
**who provided bread for your Son and food for the poor,**
**sustain us and all our brothers and sisters**
**on our journey towards your heavenly kingdom.**

**We ask this through Christ our Lord.**

**R̞. Amen.**

## CONCLUDING RITE

1694   A minister who is a priest or deacon concludes the rite by saying:

**Lord,**
**you have given us the saints as our intercessors in**
   **heaven.**
**May the prayers of Saint Joseph**
**always help us to do your will**
**and live in your love.**

**Grant this through Christ our Lord.**

**R̞. Amen.**

Then he blesses all present.

**And may almighty God bless you all,
the Father, and the Son, ✚ and the Holy Spirit.**

℟. **Amen.**

---

1695 A lay minister concludes the rite by signing himself or herself with the sign of the cross and saying:

**May almighty God, the Father, and the Son, and the Holy Spirit, bless and protect us.**

℟. **Amen.**

---

1696 It is preferable to end the celebration with a suitable song.

# II. SHORTER RITE

1697 All make the sign of the cross as the minister says:

**Our help is in the name of the Lord.**

All reply:

**Who made heaven and earth.**

1698 One of those present or the minister reads a text of sacred Scripture, for example:

**Brothers and sisters, listen to the words of the holy gospel according to Matthew:**                                    1:18-23

*Joseph did as the angel commanded him.*

**Now this is how the birth of Jesus Christ came about. When his mother Mary was betrothed to Joseph, but before they lived together, she was found with child through the holy Spirit. Joseph her husband, since he was a righteous man, yet unwilling to expose her to shame, decided to divorce her quietly. Such was his intention when, behold, the angel of the Lord appeared to him in a dream and said, ''Joseph, son of David, do not be afraid to take Mary your wife into your home. For it is through**

the holy Spirit that this child has been conceived in her. She will bear a son and you are to name him Jesus, because he will save his people from their sins." All this took place to fulfill what the Lord had said through the prophet:

"Behold, the virgin shall be with child and bear a son, and they shall name him Emmanuel,"

which means "God is with us."

1699  Or:

Matthew 13:54-58—*Is this not the carpenter's son?*

1700  A minister who is a priest or deacon says the prayer of blessing with hands outstretched; a lay minister says the prayer with hands joined.

All-provident God,
the good things that grace this table
remind us of your many good gifts.

Bless this food,
and may the prayers of Saint Joseph,
who provided bread for your Son and food for the poor,
sustain us and all our brothers and sisters
on our journey towards your heavenly kingdom.

We ask this through Christ our Lord.

R̸. Amen.

# CHAPTER 54

# ORDER FOR THE BLESSING OF FOOD
# FOR THE FIRST MEAL OF EASTER

USA

## INTRODUCTION

1701   The custom of blessing food for Easter arose from the discipline of fasting throughout Lent and the special Easter fast during the Easter Triduum. Easter was the first day when meat, eggs, and other foods could again be eaten. Although not of obligation, the special fast during the Triduum may still be observed as well as the tradition of blessing food for the first meal of Easter.

1702   According to custom, food may be blessed before or after the Easter Vigil on Holy Saturday[8] or on Easter morning for consumption at the first meal of Easter, when fasting is ended and the Church is filled with joy.

1703   The blessing may take place in the church or another suitable place.

1704   The food which is to be blessed may be placed on a table or held by those who bring it.

1705   The shorter rite may appropriately be used after the Easter Vigil.

1706   These orders may be used by a priest or a deacon, and also by a layperson, who follows the rites and prayers designated for a lay minister.

---

[8] Festive customs and traditions associated with this day on account of the former practice of anticipating the celebration of Easter on Holy Saturday should be reserved for Easter night and the day that follows (*Circular Letter Concerning the Preparation and Celebration of the Easter Feasts,* no. 76).

# I. ORDER OF BLESSING

## INTRODUCTORY RITES

1707 When the community has gathered, a suitable song may be sung.

The minister says:

**In the name of the Father, and of the Son, and of the Holy Spirit.**

All make the sign of the cross and reply:

**Amen.**

1708 The minister greets those present in the following or other suitable words, taken mainly from sacred Scripture.

A      Before the Easter Vigil

**For our sake Christ became obedient, accepting even death, death on a cross. Therefore God raised him on high and gave him the name above all other names. Blessed be God for ever.**

And all reply:

**Blessed be God for ever.**

B      After the Easter Vigil

**Christ is risen. Alleluia.**

And all reply:

**He is risen indeed. Alleluia.**

1709 In the following or similar words, the minister prepares those present for the blessing.

**Throughout Lent we have been preparing for the resurrection of the Lord by prayer, almsgiving, and fasting. Our lenten fasting is a reminder of our hunger and thirst for holiness which is satisfied only by Christ who feeds and nourishes us by his word and sacraments. When we gather at our first meal of Easter may this food be a sign for us of that heavenly banquet to which the Lord calls us.**

# READING OF THE WORD OF GOD

1710   One of those present, or the minister, then reads a text of
sacred Scripture.

**Brothers and sisters, listen to the words of the book of
Deuteronomy:**
16:1-8

*The passover of the Lord.*

**Observe the month of Abib by keeping the Passover of the
LORD, your God, since it was in the month of Abib that he
brought you by night out of Egypt. You shall offer the Passover sacrifice from your flock or your herd to the LORD, your
God, in the place which he chooses as the dwelling place of
his name. You shall not eat leavened bread with it. For seven
days you shall eat with it only unleavened bread, the bread
of affliction, that you may remember as long as you live the
day of your departure from the land of Egypt; for in frightened haste you left the land of Egypt. Nothing leavened may
be found in all your territory for seven days, and none of the
meat which you sacrificed on the evening of the first day shall
be kept overnight for the next day.**

**You may not sacrifice the Passover in any of the communities
which the LORD, your God, gives you; only at the place which
he chooses as the dwelling place of his name, and in the evening at sunset, on the anniversary of your departure from
Egypt, shall you sacrifice the Passover. You shall cook and eat
it at the place the LORD, your God, chooses; then in the morning you may return to your tents. For six days you shall eat
unleavened bread, and on the seventh there shall be a solemn
meeting in honor of the LORD, your God; on that day you shall
not do any sort of work.**

1711   Or:

Isaiah 55:1-11—*Come all you who are thirsty.*

Luke 24:13-35—*They knew Christ in the breaking of the bread.*

John 6:1-14—*Multiplication of the loaves.*

1712  As circumstances suggest, one of the following responsorial psalms may be sung, or some other suitable song.

R̰. **My soul is thirsting for God, the living God.**

Psalms 42 and 43

**Athirst is my soul for God, the living God.**
**When shall I go and behold the face of God?** R̰.

**Those times I recall,**
**now that I pour out my soul within me,**
**When I went with the throng**
**and led them in procession to the house of God,**
**Amid loud cries of joy and thanksgiving,**
**with the multitude keeping festival.** R̰.

**Send forth your light and your fidelity;**
**they shall lead me on**
**And bring me to your holy mountain,**
**to your dwelling-place.** R̰.

**Then will I go in to the altar of God,**
**the God of my gladness and joy;**
**Then will I give you thanks upon the harp,**
**O God, my God!** R̰.

Psalm 104:1-2, 5-6, 10, 12, 13-14, 24, 35

R̰. **(v. 1) Bless the Lord, O my soul.**

1713  As circumstances suggest, the minister may give those present a brief explanation of the biblical text, so that they may understand through faith the meaning of the celebration.

## INTERCESSIONS

1714  The intercessions are then said. The minister introduces them and an assisting minister or one of those present announces the intentions. From the following those best suited to the occasion may be used or adapted, or other intentions that apply to the particular circumstances may be composed.

The minister says:

**The Son of God who invites us to the Paschal feast stands ready**
**to help. Let us call upon him in our need.**

R̸. **Lord, prepare us for the feast of life.**

Assisting minister:

**That Easter may find us cleansed of sin and ready to live anew our Christian faith, we pray to the Lord.** R̸.

Assisting minister:

**That the bread we share may be a reminder of the bread of life we share in the eucharist, we pray to the Lord.** R̸.

Assisting minister:

**That we may be ready to give from our table to those who hunger and thirst, we pray to the Lord.** R̸.

Assisting minister:

**That we may one day enjoy the banquet of the Lord in the heavenly kingdom, we pray to the Lord.** R̸.

1715 After the intercessions the minister, in the following or similar words, invites all present to sing or say the Lord's Prayer.

**Christ taught us to pray for our daily bread and so we dare to say:**

All:

**Our Father . . .**

## PRAYER OF BLESSING

1716 A minister who is a priest or deacon says the prayer of blessing with hands outstretched; a lay minister says the prayer with hands joined.

**God of glory,**
**the eyes of all turn to you**
**as we celebrate Christ's victory over sin and death.**

**Bless us and this food of our first Easter meal.**
**May we who gather at the Lord's table**
**continue to celebrate the joy of his resurrection**
**and be admitted finally to his heavenly banquet.**

**Grant this through Christ our Lord.**

R̸. **Amen.**

## Concluding Rite

**1717**  A minister who is a priest or deacon concludes the rite by saying:

**May Christ always nourish you and strengthen you in faith and love,**
**now and for ever.**

℟. **Amen.**

Then he blesses all present.

**And may almighty God bless you all,**
**the Father, and the Son, ✝ and the Holy Spirit.**

℟. **Amen.**

---

**1718**  A lay minister concludes the rite by signing himself or herself with the sign of the cross and saying:

**May Christ nourish us and strengthen us in faith and love now and for ever.**

℟. **Amen.**

---

**1719**  It is preferable to end the celebration with a suitable song.

# II. SHORTER RITE

**1720**  The minister then greets those present in the following or other suitable words, taken mainly from sacred Scripture.

A          Before the Easter Vigil

**For our sake Christ became obedient, accepting even death, death on a cross. Therefore God raised him on high and gave him the name above all other names. Blessed be God for ever.**

And all reply:

**Blessed be God for ever.**

**Christ is risen. Alleluia.**

And all reply:

**He is risen indeed. Alleluia.**

1721    One of those present or the minister reads a text of sacred
Scripture, for example:

**Brothers and sisters, listen to the words of the book of
Deuteronomy:**                                    16:1-8

*The passover of the Lord.*

**Observe the month of Abib by keeping the Passover of the
LORD, your God, since it was in the month of Abib that he
brought you by night out of Egypt. You shall offer the Passover sacrifice from your flock or your herd to the LORD, your
God, in the place which he chooses as the dwelling place of
his name. You shall not eat leavened bread with it. For seven
days you shall eat with it only unleavened bread, the bread
of affliction, that you may remember as long as you live the
day of your departure from the land of Egypt; for in frightened haste you left the land of Egypt. Nothing leavened may
be found in all your territory for seven days, and none of the
meat which you sacrificed on the evening of the first day shall
be kept overnight for the next day.**

**You may not sacrifice the Passover in any of the communities
which the LORD, your God, gives you; only at the place which
he chooses as the dwelling place of his name, and in the evening at sunset, on the anniversary of your departure from
Egypt, shall you sacrifice the Passover. You shall cook and eat
it at the place the LORD, your God, chooses; then in the morning you may return to your tents. For six days you shall eat
unleavened bread, and on the seventh there shall be a solemn
meeting in honor of the LORD, your God; on that day you shall
not do any sort of work.**

1722    Or:

Isaiah 55:1-11—*Come all you who are thirsty.*

Luke 24:13-35—*They knew Christ in the breaking of the bread.*

**1723** A minister who is a priest or deacon says the prayer of blessing with hands outstretched; a lay minister says the prayer with hands joined.

**God of glory,**
**the eyes of all turn to you**
**as we celebrate Christ's victory over sin and death.**

**Bless us and this food of our first Easter meal.**
**May we who gather at the Lord's table**
**continue to celebrate the joy of his resurrection**
**and be admitted finally to his heavenly banquet.**

**Grant this through Christ our Lord.**

**R̹. Amen.**

# CHAPTER 55

# ORDER FOR THE BLESSING OF MOTHERS ON MOTHER'S DAY
## Second Sunday of May

USA

## INTRODUCTION

1724   The observance of Mother's Day has an important place in American life. Since it occurs on the second Sunday in May, during the Easter season, the Mass of the Sunday is always celebrated. However, in order to provide some recognition of this holiday, model intercessions and a prayer over the people are provided here.

1725   The intercessions are added to those of the day and may be adapted as necessary.

1726   The prayer over the people may replace the solemn blessing of the Easter season.

# ORDER OF BLESSING

## INTERCESSIONS

1727  The following intercessions may be added to those of the day.

**For our mothers, who have given us life and love, that we may show them reverence and love, we pray to the Lord.** ℟.

**For mothers who have lost a child through death, that their faith may give them hope, and their family and friends support and console them, we pray to the Lord.** ℟.

**For mothers who have died, that God may bring them into the joy of his kingdom, we pray to the Lord.** ℟.

## PRAYER OVER THE PEOPLE

1728  This prayer over the people may be used at the end of Mass or other liturgical services on Mother's Day.

**Loving God,
as a mother gives life and nourishment to her children,
so you watch over your Church.
Bless these women,
that they may be strengthened as Christian mothers.
Let the example of their faith and love shine forth.
Grant that we, their sons and daughters,
may honor them always
with a spirit of profound respect.**

**Grant this through Christ our Lord.**

℟. **Amen.**

Then he blesses all present.

**And may almighty God bless you all,
the Father, and the Son, ✝ and the Holy Spirit.**

℟. **Amen.**

# CHAPTER 56

# ORDER FOR THE BLESSING OF FATHERS ON FATHER'S DAY
## Third Sunday of June

## INTRODUCTION

1729   The observance of Father's Day has an important place in American life. Since it is celebrated on the third Sunday in June, the Mass of the Sunday is always celebrated. However, in order to provide some recognition of this holiday, model intercessions and a prayer over the people are provided here.

1730   The intercessions are added to those of the day and may be adapted as necessary.

1731   The prayer over the people may replace the solemn blessing of the Easter season.

# ORDER OF BLESSING

## INTERCESSIONS

**1732**  The following intercessions may be added to those of the day.

**For our fathers, who have given us life and love, that we may show them respect and love, we pray to the Lord.** ℞.

**For fathers who have lost a child through death, that their faith may give them hope, and their family and friends support and console them, we pray to the Lord.** ℞.

**For fathers who have died, that God may bring them into the joy of his kingdom, we pray to the Lord.** ℞.

## PRAYER OVER THE PEOPLE

**1733**  This prayer over the people may be used at the end of Mass or other liturgical services on Father's Day.

**God our Father,**
**in your wisdom and love you made all things.**
**Bless these men,**
**that they may be strengthened as Christian fathers.**
**Let the example of their faith and love shine forth.**
**Grant that we, their sons and daughters,**
**may honor them always**
**with a spirit of profound respect.**

**Grant this through Christ our Lord.**

℞. **Amen.**

Then he blesses all present.

**And may almighty God bless you all,**
**the Father, and the Son, + and the Holy Spirit.**

℞. **Amen.**

# ORDER FOR VISITING A CEMETERY ON ALL SOULS DAY (November 2), MEMORIAL DAY, OR ON THE ANNIVERSARY OF DEATH OR BURIAL USA

## Introduction

1734  This order is a solemn commemoration of the departed whose bodies lie in a cemetery. It may be used on All Souls Day, Memorial Day, on the anniversary of the death or burial of a particular deceased person, or when a gravestone or cemetery monument is erected. The service may also be adapted for use by individuals when they visit the grave of a relative or friend.

1735  The service may be used immediately following Mass or apart from Mass.

1736  If the service takes place immediately after Mass and there is to be a procession to the cemetery, the blessing and dismissal of the Mass are omitted. During the procession a psalm or other suitable song may be sung. The priest may wear the chasuble or a cope for the procession and for the service in the cemetery.

1737  This order may be used by a priest, deacon, or a lay minister.

1738  On those occasions when this service is used by a family, one of the family members takes the minister's parts.

# ORDER FOR VISITING A CEMETERY

## PROCESSION

1739  If the service is to take place immediately after Mass and the cemetery is close to the parish church, the blessing and dismissal of the Mass are omitted and the procession to the cemetery is formed. During the procession Psalm 25, Psalm 116, Psalm 118, or Psalm 42 may be sung. Other suitable songs may also be used. When all have reached the cemetery, the minister addresses the people, using the introduction in no. 1742, below.

If there is no procession, or the service takes place apart from Mass, a psalm or other suitable song may be sung after all have gathered at the cemetery.

## GREETING

1740  A minister who is a priest or deacon greets the people in the following or other words preferably taken from Scripture:

**The grace and peace of God our Father, who raised Jesus from the dead, be with you always.**

All reply:

**And also with you.**

---

1741  A lay minister greets those present in the following words:

**Praise be to God our Father, who raised Jesus Christ from the dead. Blessed be God for ever.**

**R℣. Blessed be God for ever.**

---

1742  The minister using these or similar words, says:

**My dear friends, we gather today to pray for our brothers and sisters whose bodies lie here in rest. They have passed from death to life in company with the Lord Jesus, who died and rose to new life, and are purified now of their faults. We pray that God may welcome them among all the saints of heaven.**

# READING OF THE WORD OF GOD

**1743** If Mass has not preceded, a reader, another person present, or the minister reads a text of sacred Scripture.

**Brothers and sisters, listen to the words of the first letter of Paul to the Thessalonians:** 4:13-18

*We shall stay with the Lord for ever.*

**We do not want you to be unaware, brothers and sisters, about those who have fallen asleep, so that you may not grieve like the rest, who have no hope. For if we believe that Jesus died and rose, so too will God, through Jesus, bring with him those who have fallen asleep. Indeed, we tell you this, on the word of the Lord, that we who are alive, who are left until the coming of the Lord, will surely not precede those who have fallen asleep. For the Lord himself, with a word of command, with the voice of an archangel and the trumpet of God, will come down from heaven, and the dead in Christ will rise first. Then we who are alive, who are left, will be caught up together with them in the clouds to meet the Lord in the air. Thus we shall always be with the Lord. Therefore, console one another with these words.**

**1744** Or one of the Scripture texts in Part III of the *Order of Christian Funerals* may be chosen.

**1745** As circumstances suggest, one of the following responsorial psalms may be sung, or some other suitable song.

℟. **To you, O Lord, I lift up my soul.**

Psalm 25

**In you I trust; let me not be put to shame,
let not my enemies exult over me.
No one who waits for you shall be put to shame;
those shall be put to shame who heedlessly break faith.** ℟.

**Your ways, O LORD, make known to me;
teach me your paths,
Guide me in your truth and teach me,
for you are God my savior,
and for you I wait all the day.** ℟.

Remember that your compassion, O LORD,
and your kindness are from of old.
The sins of my youth and my frailties remember not;
in your kindness remember me,
because of your goodness, O LORD. R̥.

Good and upright is the LORD;
thus he shows sinners the way.
He guides the humble to justice,
he teaches the humble his way. R̥.

All the paths of the LORD are kindness and constancy
toward those who keep his covenant and his decrees.
For your name's sake, O LORD,
you will pardon my guilt, great as it is. R̥.

Psalm 27:1, 2, 3, 4, 13

R̥. (v. 1) **The Lord is my light and my salvation.**

Psalm 130:1-2, 3-4, 5-6, 7-8

R̥. (v. 5) **My soul has hoped in the Lord.**

Psalm 143:1-2, 3-4, 5-6, 7, 9-10, 11-12

R̥. (v. 1) **O Lord, hear my prayer.**


## LITANY

**1746** While the following litany is sung or recited, the minister sprinkles the graves with holy water and, if desired, may also incense them.

| | |
|---|---|
| Lord, have mercy | Lord, have mercy |
| Christ, have mercy | Christ, have mercy |
| Lord, have mercy | Lord, have mercy |
| Holy Mary, Mother of God | pray for them |
| Saint Michael | pray for them |
| Saint John the Baptist | pray for them |
| Saint Joseph | pray for them |
| Saint Peter | pray for them |
| Saint Paul | pray for them |
| Saint Andrew | pray for them |
| Saint Stephen | pray for them |

| | |
|---|---|
| Saint Ann | pray for them |
| Saint Teresa | pray for them |
| Saint Catherine | pray for them |
| Saint Frances Cabrini | pray for them |
| Saint Elizabeth Seton | pray for them |

(The names of other saints may be added.)

| | |
|---|---|
| All holy men and women | pray for them |
| Christ, pardon all their faults | Lord, hear our prayer |
| Christ, remember the good they have done | Lord, hear our prayer |
| Christ, receive them into eternal life | Lord, hear our prayer |
| Christ, comfort all those who mourn | Lord, hear our prayer |
| Lord, have mercy | Lord, have mercy |
| Christ, have mercy | Christ, have mercy |
| Lord, have mercy | Lord, have mercy |

1747 The minister then invites those present to pray the Lord's Prayer, in these or similar words:

**With Christ there is mercy and fullness of redemption; let us pray as Jesus taught us:**

All:

**Our Father . . .**

## PRAYER

1748 The minister then says the following prayer or another taken from the *Order of Christian Funerals*, no. 398.

**All-powerful God,**
**whose mercy is never withheld**
**from those who call upon you in hope,**
**look kindly on your servants (N. and N.),**
**who departed this life confessing your name,**
**and number them among your saints for evermore.**

**We ask this through Christ our Lord.**

R⁷. **Amen.**

1749 Or:

**Almighty God and Father,**
**by the mystery of the cross, you have made us strong;**
**by the sacrament of the resurrection**
**you have sealed us as your own.**
**Look kindly upon your servants,**
**now freed from the bonds of mortality,**
**and count them among your saints in heaven.**

**We ask this through Christ our Lord.**

**R̷. Amen.**

1750    Or: For one person

**Almighty God and Father,**
**it is our certain faith**
**that your Son, who died on the cross, was raised from the**
   **dead,**
**the first fruits of all who have fallen asleep.**
**Grant that through this mystery**
**your servant N., who has gone to his/her rest in Christ,**
**may share in the joy of his resurrection.**

**We ask this through Christ our Lord.**

**R̷. Amen.**

1751    Or: For the blessing of a gravestone or monument

**O God,**
**by whose mercy the faithful departed find rest,**
**bless this gravestone**
**with which we mark the resting place of N.**
**May he/she have everlasting life**
**and rejoice in you with your saints for ever.**

**We ask this through Christ our Lord.**

**R̷. Amen.**


## CONCLUDING RITE

1752    The minister says:

**Eternal rest grant unto them, O Lord.**

**R̷. And let perpetual light shine upon them.**

**May they rest in peace.**

R⁊. **Amen.**

**May their souls and the souls of the faithful departed, through the mercy of God, rest in peace.**

R⁊. **Amen.**

---

1753  A priest or deacon adds:

**May the peace of God,**
**which is beyond all understanding,**
**keep your hearts and minds**
**in the knowledge and love of God**
**and of his Son, our Lord Jesus Christ.**

R⁊. **Amen.**

Then he blesses all present.

**And may almighty God bless you all,**
**the Father, and the Son, ✛ and the Holy Spirit.**

R⁊. **Amen.**

---

1754  The service may be concluded by a suitable psalm or other song.

# CHAPTER 58

# ORDER FOR THE BLESSING OF FOOD FOR THANKSGIVING DAY
## Fourth Thursday of November

## INTRODUCTION

1755   In the United States Thanksgiving Day is a holiday with special religious significance. Originally it was celebrated by the Pilgrims and the Native Americans to give thanks to God after the harvest of 1621. In 1863 President Abraham Lincoln declared the last Thursday of November should be a national day of thanksgiving.

1756   Individuals or families may bring food to be blessed for their Thanksgiving dinner. Food may also be blessed that will be distributed to the poor.

1757   This order may be celebrated in the church or some other suitable place. The blessing may take place during Mass or outside Mass.

1758   This blessing may be given by a priest, deacon, or a lay minister.

# I. ORDER OF BLESSING WITHIN MASS

1759 After the gospel reading, the celebrant in the homily, based on the sacred text and pertinent to the particular place and the people involved, explains the meaning of the celebration.

## GENERAL INTERCESSIONS

1760 The general intercessions follow, either in the form usual at Mass or in the form provided here. The celebrant concludes the intercessions with the prayer of blessing. From the following intentions those best for the occasion may be used or adapted, or other intentions that apply to the particular circumstances may be composed.

The celebrant says:

**The Son of God, who invites us to the Paschal feast, stands ready to help us. Let us call upon him in our need.**

R̝. **Lord, hear our prayer.**

Assisting minister:

**For the Church of God, that we may never cease to give thanks for all good gifts, we pray to the Lord.** R̝.

Assisting minister:

**For the poor of the world, that we may share with them our food and material goods, we pray to the Lord.** R̝.

Assisting minister:

**For farmers and all those who provide us with our food, that we may cherish their labor and love for the land, we pray to the Lord.** R̝.

Assisting minister:

**For the world and all it contains, that God may continue to bless creation and make all things fruitful, we pray to the Lord.** R̝.

## PRAYER OF BLESSING

**1761** With hands outstretched, the celebrant says the prayer of blessing:

**God most provident,**
**we join all creation**
**in raising to you a hymn of thanksgiving**
**through Jesus Christ, your Son.**

**For generation upon generation**
**peoples of this land have sung of your bounty;**
**we too offer you praise**
**for the rich harvest we have received at your hands.**

**Bless us and this food which we share with grateful hearts.**

**Continue to make our land fruitful**
**and let our love for you be seen**
**in our pursuit of peace and justice**
**and in our generous response to those in need.**

**Praise and glory to you, Lord God, now and for ever.**

R̸. **Amen.**

# II. ORDER OF BLESSING WITHIN A CELEBRATION OF THE WORD OF GOD

1762　The present order may be used by a priest or a deacon, and also by a lay person, who follows the rites and prayers designated for a lay minister.

## INTRODUCTORY RITES

1763　When the community has gathered, a suitable song may be sung. After the singing, the minister says:

**In the name of the Father, and of the Son, and of the Holy Spirit.**

All make the sign of the cross and reply:

**Amen.**

1764　A minister who is a priest or deacon greets those present in the following or other suitable words, taken mainly from sacred Scripture.

**May the Lord, who fills you with his bounty, be with you always.**

And all reply:

**And also with you.**

---

1765　A lay minister greets those present in the following words:

**Let us glorify the Lord who fills us with his bounty. Blessed be God for ever.**

℟. **Blessed be God for ever.**

---

1766　In the following or similar words, the minister prepares those present for the blessing.

**We gather today (this evening) to give thanks to God for his gifts to this land and its people, for God has been generous to us. As we ask God's blessing upon the food we will share with our families, may we be mindful of those in need.**

# READING OF THE WORD OF GOD

1767 A reader, another person present, or the minister reads a text of sacred Scripture.

**Brothers and sisters, listen to the words of the first letter of Paul to the Corinthians:** 1:3-9

*Thanks be to God who has bestowed on us every gift.*

**Grace to you and peace from God our Father and the Lord Jesus Christ.**

**I give thanks to my God always on your account for the grace of God bestowed on you in Christ Jesus, that in him you were enriched in every way, with all discourse and all knowledge, as the testimony to Christ was confirmed among you, so that you are not lacking in any spiritual gift as you wait for the revelation of our Lord Jesus Christ. He will keep you firm to the end, irreproachable on the day of our Lord Jesus Christ. God is faithful, and by him you were called to fellowship with his Son, Jesus Christ our Lord.**

1768 Or:

Sirach 50:22-24—*Let us bless the God of all.*

Deuteronomy 8:7-18—*Bless the Lord, your God, for the good country he has given you.*

Isaiah 63:7-9—*I will recall the favors of the Lord.*

Luke 17:11-19—*Has no one returned to give thanks?*

1769 As circumstances suggest, one of the following responsorial psalms may be sung, or some other suitable song.

℟. **I will give you thanks, O Lord, with all my heart.**

Psalm 138

**I will give thanks to you, O Lᴏʀᴅ, with all my heart,
for you have heard the words of my mouth;
in the presence of the angels I will sing your praise;
I will worship at your holy temple
and give thanks to your name, ℟.**

**Because of your kindness and your truth;
for you have made great above all things
your name and your promise.
When I called, you answered me;
you built up strength within me. ℟.**

---

All the kings of the earth shall give
thanks to you, O Lord,
when they hear the words of your mouth;
And they shall sing of the ways of the Lord:
"Great is the glory of the Lord." R̸.

Psalm 145:2-3, 4-5, 6-7, 8-9, 10-11

R̸. (v. 1) I will bless your name for ever and ever.

1770 As circumstances suggest, the minister may give those present a brief explanation of the biblical text, so that they may understand through faith the meaning of the celebration.

## INTERCESSIONS

1771 The intercessions are then said. The minister introduces them and an assisting minister or one of those present announces the intentions. From the following those best suited to the occasion may be used or adapted, or other intentions that apply to the particular circumstances may be composed.

The minister says:

The Son of God, who invites us to the Paschal feast, stands ready to help us. Let us call upon him in our need.

R̸. Lord, hear our prayer.

Assisting minister:

For the Church of God, that we may never cease to give thanks for all good gifts, we pray to the Lord. R̸.

Assisting minister:

For the poor of the world, that we may share with them our food and material goods, we pray to the Lord. R̸.

Assisting minister:

For farmers and all those who provide us with our food, that we may cherish their labor and love for the land, we pray to the Lord. R̸.

Assisting minister:

For the world and all it contains, that God may continue to bless creation and make all things fruitful, we pray to the Lord. R̸.

1772 After the intercessions the minister, in the following or similar words, invites all present to sing or say the Lord's Prayer.

**Let us pray to our loving Father as Jesus taught us:**

All:

**Our Father . . .**

## Prayer of Blessing

1773 A minister who is a priest or deacon says the prayer of blessing with hands outstretched; a lay minister says the prayer with hands joined.

**God most provident,
we join all creation
in raising to you a hymn of thanksgiving
through Jesus Christ, your Son.**

**For generation upon generation
peoples of this land have sung of your bounty;
we too offer you praise
for the rich harvest we have received at your hands.**

**Bless us and this food which we share with grateful hearts.**

**Continue to make our land fruitful
and let our love for you be seen
in our pursuit of peace and justice
and in our generous response to those in need.**

**Praise and glory to you, Lord God, now and for ever.**

**R̥. Amen.**

## Concluding Rite

1774 A minister who is a priest or deacon concludes the rite by saying:

**May Christ, the living bread, bring you to the banquet of eternal life.**

**R̥. Amen.**

Then he blesses all present.

**And may almighty God bless you all,
the Father, and the Son, ✝ and the Holy Spirit.**

℟. **Amen.**

---

1775   A lay minister concludes the rite by signing himself or herself with the sign of the cross and saying:

**May Christ, the living bread, bring us to the banquet of eternal life.**

℟. **Amen.**

---

1776   It is preferable to end the celebration with a suitable song.


# III. SHORTER RITE

1777   All make the sign of the cross as the minister says:

**Blessed be the name of the Lord.**

All reply:

**Now and for ever.**

1778   One of those present or the minister reads a text of sacred Scripture, for example:

**Brothers and sisters, listen to the words of the first letter of Paul to the Corinthians:**                                   1:3-9

*Thanks be to God who has bestowed on us every gift.*

**Grace to you and peace from God our Father and the Lord Jesus Christ.**

**I give thanks to my God always on your account for the grace of God bestowed on you in Christ Jesus, that in him you were enriched in every way, with all discourse and all knowledge, as the testimony to Christ was confirmed among you, so that**

you are not lacking in any spiritual gift as you wait for the revelation of our Lord Jesus Christ. He will keep you firm to the end, irreproachable on the day of our Lord Jesus Christ. God is faithful, and by him you were called to fellowship with his Son, Jesus Christ our Lord.

1779 Or:
Sirach 50:22-24—*Let us bless the God of all.*

Luke 17:11-19—*Has no one returned to give thanks?*

1780 A minister who is a priest or deacon says the prayer of blessing with hands outstretched; a lay minister says the prayer with hands joined and does not make the sign of the cross.

**God most provident,**
**we join all creation**
**in raising to you a hymn of thanksgiving**
**through Jesus Christ, your Son.**

**For generation upon generation**
**peoples of this land have sung of your bounty;**
**we too offer you praise**
**for the rich harvest we have received at your hands.**

**Bless us and this food which we share with grateful hearts.**

**Continue to make our land fruitful**
**and let our love for you be seen**
**in our pursuit of peace and justice**
**and in our generous response to those in need.**

**Praise and glory to you, Lord God, now and for ever.**

℟. **Amen.**

CHAPTER 59

# ORDER FOR THE BLESSING OF FOOD OR DRINK OR OTHER ELEMENTS CONNECTED WITH DEVOTION

## INTRODUCTION

1781   On the occasion of a feast or season of the liturgical year or in honor of Mary or other saints, it is customary in some places to celebrate a rite for the blessing of food or drink (for example, bread, water, wine, oil) or of other articles that the faithful devoutly present to be blessed. In such a celebration parish priests (pastors) are to ensure that the faithful have a correct understanding of the true meaning of the blessing. In his comments or homily the celebrant is as far as possible to take into account traditions and biographical information on the saints that may serve to clarify the origin and meaning of the special blessing celebrated in honor of a saint. There must always be respect for historical accuracy.

1782   Whenever a priest or a deacon carries out this kind of celebration in a church, a large attendance and the active participation of the faithful are desirable.

1783   When several kinds of food or drink or other articles are to be blessed, there is to be no duplication of rites, but everything is to be blessed in a single rite, in which the proper blessing formulary is used for each particular object.

1784   While maintaining the structure and chief elements of the rite, the celebrant should adapt the celebration to the circumstances of the place and the people involved.

1785   Celebration of these blessings within Mass, by use of the rite in nos. 1799–1804, is permitted only on feasts of Mary or the saints in places where there is a popular tradition for such a celebration and the faithful customarily attend Mass on these days. The blessing may be celebrated within Mass only once on any day.

# I. ORDER OF BLESSING OUTSIDE MASS

## INTRODUCTORY RITES

1786  When the community has gathered, a suitable song may
be sung. After the singing, the celebrant says:

**In the name of the Father, and of the Son, and of the Holy
Spirit.**

All make the sign of the cross and reply:

**Amen.**

1787  The celebrant greets those present in the following or other
suitable words, taken mainly from sacred Scripture.

**May God, who has chosen us to be saints, be with you all.**

All make the following or some other suitable reply.

**And also with you.**

1788  In the following or similar words, the celebrant prepares
those present for the blessing.

**God makes known his mighty power and his abounding good-
ness to all the ends of the earth; but he also directs his Church
to bless the simplest and most commonplace things. He does
so in order that all who devoutly make use of material things
(while invoking the name of Mary/of the saints) may be drawn
to the world that is not seen and may give glory to God, who
alone performs the wonders we call miracles, but who is wonderful also in his saints.**

## READING OF THE WORD OF GOD

1789  A reader, another person present, or the celebrant reads
a text of sacred Scripture, taken either from the Lectionary for
Mass or from those given here.

**Brothers and sisters, listen to the words of the holy gospel
according to Matthew:** 7:7-11

*Ask and you will receive.*

Jesus said to the crowds: "Ask and it will be given to you; seek and you will find; knock and the door will be opened to you. For everyone who asks, receives; and the one who seeks, finds; and to the one who knocks, the door will be opened. Which one of you would hand his son a stone when he asks for a loaf of bread, or a snake when he asks for a fish? If you then, who are wicked, know how to give good gifts to your children, how much more will your heavenly Father give good things to those who ask him."

1790   Or:

A   Blessing of water

Exodus 17:1-7—*Give us water to drink.*

2 Kings 2:19-22—*I have purified this water. Never again shall death or miscarriage spring from it.*

B   Blessing of bread

1 Kings 19:3b-8—*Strengthened by that food, he walked forty days and forty nights.*

Wisdom 16:20-21, 24-26—*That your children whom you loved might learn.*

John 6:27-35—*You should not be working for perishable food.*

C   Blessing of other foods

Genesis 1:27-31a—*He has given you all the trees with seed-bearing fruit; this shall be your food.*

Genesis 9:1-3—*Every living and crawling thing shall provide food for you.*

Exodus 12:1-4, 6-8, 11—*You shall eat the lamb like this: it is the Passover in honor of the Lord.*

Luke 11:9-13—*Ask and it will be given to you.*

D   Blessing of oil, wine, salt

Sirach 39:30-41 (Greek, 39:25-35)—*Chief of all the needs of human life.*

Matthew 5:13-16—*You are the salt of the earth.*

Mark 6:7-13—*They anointed the sick with oil and worked many cures.*

Luke 10:30-37—*He dressed his wounds, pouring in oil and wine.*

John 2:1-11—*You have kept the best wine till now.*

E       **Blessing of flowers (for example, roses, lilies)**

Sirach 24:1a, 17-31 (Greek, 24:1a, 13-22)—*Like a rosebush in Jericho.*

2 Corinthians 2:14-17—*We are an aroma of Christ for God's sake.*

Matthew 6:25-34—*Learn a lesson from the way the wild flowers grow.*

F       **Blessing of candles**

Matthew 4:13-17—*The people have seen a great light.*

Luke 2:27-33—*A revealing light to the Gentiles.*

John 1:6-10—*The real light which gives light to everyone.*

Ephesians 5:8-10—*Live as children of light.*

**1791**   As circumstances suggest, one of the following responsorial psalms may be sung or said, or some other suitable song.

℟. **O Lord, our God, how wonderful your name in all the earth!**

Psalm 8

**O LORD, our Lord,
how glorious is your name over all the earth!
You have exalted your majesty above the heavens.
Out of the mouths of babes and sucklings
you have fashioned praise because of your foes,
to silence the hostile and the vengeful.
When I behold your heavens, the work of your fingers,
the moon and the stars which you set in place—** ℟.

**What is man that you should be mindful of him,
or the son of man that you should care for him?
You have made him little less than the angels,
and crown him with glory and honor.
You have given him rule over the works of your hands,** ℟.

**Putting all things under his feet:
All sheep and oxen,
yes, and the beasts of the field,
The birds of the air, the fishes of the sea,
and whatever swims the paths of the seas.** ℟.

Psalm 23:1-3, 4, 5, 6

℟. **(v. 5) You spread a table before me, O Lord.**

Psalm 104:10-12, 13-15, 16-18, 19-21, 22-23

℟. **(v. 24) How many are your works, O Lord!**

Psalm 147:7-8, 9-11, 12-13, 14-16

℟. (v. 1) **O praise the Lord! How good to sing praise to our God.**

1792   In the homily the celebrant explains both the biblical text and the meaning of the rite.

## INTERCESSIONS

1793   As circumstances suggest, the prayer of blessing may be preceded by the intercessions. Intercessions that are best suited to the feast or liturgical season may be composed. The celebrant introduces them and an assisting minister or one of those present announces the intentions. The intentions are followed immediately by the prayer of blessing, no. 1795.

1794   When there are no intercessions, the celebrant, before the prayer of blessing, says:

**Let us pray.**

As circumstances suggest, all may then pray for a moment in silence before the prayer of blessing.

## PRAYER OF BLESSING

1795   With hands outstretched, the celebrant says the prayer of blessing.

A        Blessing of food                                                    USA

**Blessed are you, Lord God,**
**who have showered all creatures with your blessings.**
**Hear the prayers of these your servants:**
**that whenever they eat this food (bread)**
**(in honor of the blessed Virgin Mary *or* Saint N.)**
**(in the celebration of this festival)**
**they may be blessed with your heavenly blessing;**
**that striving always for what is holy,**
**they may continually grow in charity.**

**We ask this through Christ our Lord.**

℟. **Amen.**

B        Blessing of wine

**Blessed are you, Lord God,**
**who fill the hungry and satisfy the thirsty,**
**and give us wine to gladden our hearts.**
**Grant that all who drink this wine (in remembrance of**
**    the blessed Virgin Mary *or* Saint N.)**
**may rejoice in you**
**and be invited to sit at your heavenly banquet**
**for ever and ever.**

Ry. **Amen.**

C        Blessing of flowers

**Lord God,**
**creator of all that is beautiful,**
**the splendor of these flowers reflects your glory.**
**As we gather today (on this feast of _____ of Mary**
**    [*or* Saint N.]),**
**we ask you to bless ✛ these flowers,**
**so that the faithful who use them to adorn their homes**
**    (this church)**
**may praise you always for the beauty**
**with which you clothed your creation.**

**We ask this through Christ our Lord.**

Ry. **Amen.**

D        Blessing of candles

**God of power,**
**who enlightens the world**
**and dispels the darkness of ignorance and sin,**
**(as we remember the Virgin Mother of your Son [*or* Saint N.])**
**let the light of these candles**
**illumine our hearts and minds,**
**that they may reflect always the splendor of Christ,**
**who is Lord, for ever and ever.**

Ry. **Amen.**

E Blessing of oil USA

**God of compassion, mercy, and love,**
**in the midst of the pain and suffering of the world**
**your Son came among us**
**to heal our infirmities and soothe our wounds.**
**May all who use this oil (in honor of Saint** N.**)**
**be blessed with health of mind and body.**

**Grant this through Christ our Lord.**

℟. **Amen.**

F Blessing of other materials

**Lord God,**
**you beautify your Church**
**with the rich variety of the virtues of your saints.**
**Show your kindness to these your servants,**
**who with devotion wish to use this (these) sign (signs)**
**of your goodness**
**(in remembrance and in honor of the blessed Virgin Mary** *or*
**Saint** N.**).**
**Grant that they may be filled with the love**
**of your commandments**
**and that, sustained by the helps they need in the**
**present life,**
**they may progress toward the goal of life everlasting.**

**We ask this through Christ our Lord.**

℟. **Amen.**

G Blessing of several things at once

**God of power and goodness,**
**source of all grace and crown of all the saints,**
**through the intercession of Mary (***or* **Saint** N.**)**
**grant that as we use** *(the name of the things to be blessed)*
**brought here for your blessing,**
**we may be eager to imitate him/her**
**whose life we celebrate,**

and that our reward in heaven
may be the company of Mary (*or* **Saint N.**),
whose protection is our comfort on earth.

**We ask this through Christ our Lord.**

℟. **Amen.**

1796   If this is the local custom, the objects blessed may now be sprinkled with holy water.

## CONCLUDING RITE

1797   With hands outstretched over the faithful, the celebrant concludes the rite by saying:

**May God look with favor on your devotion**
**and in his goodness give you the help you need.**

℟. **Amen.**

**May he give you serenity in your life**
**and shower you with his blessings.**

℟. **Amen.**

**May he rule over you with his strength and tender care**
   **in this life,**
**so that he may raise you up to the reward of happiness**
   **in heaven.**

℟. **Amen.**

Then he blesses all present.

**And may almighty God bless you all,**
**the Father, and the Son, ✝ and the Holy Spirit.**

℟. **Amen.**

1798   It is preferable to end the celebration with a suitable song.

# II. ORDER OF BLESSING WITHIN MASS ON A FEAST DAY

**1799**  After the readings, the celebrant in the homily explains both the biblical texts and the meaning of celebrating a blessing in honor of Mary or of a saint.

**1800**  The general intercessions follow, either in the form usual at Mass or in the form given here. The celebrant concludes the general intercessions with the pertinent prayer of blessing, chosen from those indicated here and in no. 1795. The celebrant introduces the intercessions and an assisting minister or one of those present announces the intentions. From the following intentions those best suited to the occasion may be used or adapted, or other intentions that apply to the particular circumstances may be composed.

The celebrant says:

**Through the intercession of the blessed Virgin Mary (*or* Saint N.) let us praise God and call upon him by saying:**

℟. **Lord, you are glorious in your saints.**

Or:

℟. **Lord, hear our prayer.**

Assisting minister:

**Most merciful Father, you have marvelously made known your almighty power through the life of the blessed Virgin Mary (*or* Saint N.); grant that by the power of our baptismal grace we too may become more and more a new creation. (For this we pray:)** ℟.

Assisting minister:

**Through your holy servants you have given us a perception of your mercy; grant that the virtues we admire in them may become part of our own lives. (For this we pray:)** ℟.

Assisting minister:

**In your saints you give to all a living proof of the holiness of your Church; grant that we may always be intent on promoting your glory and assisting the salvation of our brothers and sisters. (For this we pray:)** ℟.

Assisting minister:

**You have made your saints our faithful intercessors; grant that, being delivered from present evils, we may come to share with them the inheritance of the life to come. (For this we pray:) R℣.**

The celebrant continues:

**God of power and goodness,**
**source of all grace and crown of all the saints,**
**through the intercession of Mary (*or* Saint N.)**
**grant that as we use (*the name of the things to be blessed*)**
**brought here for your blessing,**
**we may be eager to imitate him/her**
**whose life we celebrate,**
**and that our reward in heaven**
**may be the company of Mary (*or* Saint N.),**
**whose protection is our comfort on earth.**

**We ask this through Christ our Lord.**

**R℣. Amen.**

1801   Or one of the prayers of blessing provided in no. 1795 may also be used.

1802   At the end of Mass it is appropriate to use the solemn blessing provided in the Roman Missal for celebrations of the blessed Virgin Mary.

**Born of the blessed Virgin Mary,**
**the Son of God has redeemed all of us.**
**May he enrich you with his blessings.**

**R℣. Amen.**

**You received the author of life through Mary.**
**May you always rejoice in her loving care.**

**R℣. Amen.**

**You have come to rejoice at Mary's feast.**
**May you be filled with the joys of the Spirit**
**and the gifts of your eternal home.**

**R℣. Amen.**

Then he blesses all present.

**And may almighty God bless you all,
the Father, and the Son, ☩ and the Holy Spirit.**

℟. **Amen.**

1803   Or one of the prayers over the people for celebrations of the saints may be used.

**God our Father,
may all Christian people exult in your saints,
the glorious members of Christ, your Son.
Give us fellowship with them
and unending joy in your kingdom.**

**We ask this in the name of Jesus the Lord.**

℟. **Amen.**

Then he blesses all present.

**And may almighty God bless you all,
the Father, and the Son, ☩ and the Holy Spirit.**

℟. **Amen.**

1804   Or:

**Lord,
you have given us many friends in heaven.
Through their prayers we are confident
that you will watch over us always
and fill our hearts with your love.**

**Grant this through Christ our Lord.**

℟. **Amen.**

Then he blesses all present.

**And may almighty God bless you all,
the Father, and the Son, ☩ and the Holy Spirit.**

℟. **Amen.**

# PART VI
# BLESSINGS FOR VARIOUS
# NEEDS AND OCCASIONS

Part VI

# BLESSINGS FOR VARIOUS NEEDS
# AND OCCASIONS

## Introduction

USA

1805 Our life as the Christian faithful is enhanced when, in the Spirit of the Lord and in keeping with the divine commandments, we seek to extend whatever contributes to the harmony of human society and to make more available the products of nature and of human industry. The life of the faithful is also enhanced when we bless the Lord and are blessed by him.[1]

1806 In the life of a parish there are occasions when God's blessing is especially sought for those who are about to begin new roles of ministry and service within the parish.

1807 The plans given in Part VI also provide for various occasions of solemn prayer or thanksgiving and therefore should be adapted to meet particular circumstances.

---

[1] See Augustine, *Enarrat. in ps.* 66, 1: PL 36, 802; CCL 39, 856.

# CHAPTER 60

# ORDER FOR THE BLESSING OF THOSE WHO EXERCISE PASTORAL SERVICE

## INTRODUCTION

1808 In the life of a parish there is a diversity of services that are exercised by lay persons. It is fitting that as people publicly begin their service they receive the blessing of God who gives the gifts needed to carry out this work.

1809 This order may be celebrated during Mass or during a celebration of the word of God.

1810 This blessing may be given by a priest or a deacon.

# I. ORDER OF BLESSING WITHIN MASS

**1811**  After the gospel reading, the celebrant in the homily, based on the sacred text and pertinent to the particular place and the people involved, explains the meaning of the celebration.

## GENERAL INTERCESSIONS

**1812**  The general intercessions follow, either in the form usual at Mass or in the form provided here. The celebrant concludes the intercessions with the prayer of blessing. From the following intentions those best for the occasion may be used or adapted, or other intentions that apply to the particular circumstances may be composed.

The celebrant says:

**Let us now ask God to strengthen and bless our brothers and sisters as they begin their new pastoral service in this parish.**

℟. **Lord, hear our prayer.**

Or:

℟. **We beseech you, hear us.**

Assisting minister:

**That those who exercise a pastoral service may grow to a greater love of Christ, let us pray to the Lord.** ℟.

Assisting minister:

**That they may lighten the burdens of others and assist them in their struggles, let us pray to the Lord.** ℟.

Assisting minister:

**That the Holy Spirit may strengthen their hearts and enlighten their minds, let us pray to the Lord.** ℟.

Assisting minister:

**That through their endeavors this parish may grow in faith, hope, and love, let us pray to the Lord.** ℟.

## Prayer of Blessing

1813   With hands extended over the new ministers, the celebrant says immediately:

Lord God,
in your loving kindness
you sent your Son to be our shepherd and guide.
Continue to send workers into your vineyard
to sustain and direct your people.

Bless N.N. and N.N.
Let your Spirit uphold them always
as they take up their new responsibility
among the people of this parish.

We ask this through Christ our Lord.

R⁊. Amen.

# II. ORDER OF BLESSING WITHIN A CELEBRATION OF THE WORD OF GOD

1814  The present order may be used by a priest or a deacon.

## INTRODUCTORY RITES

1815  When the community has gathered, a suitable song may be sung. After the singing, the minister says:

**In the name of the Father, and of the Son, and of the Holy Spirit.**

All make the sign of the cross and reply:

**Amen.**

1816  The minister greets those present in the following or other suitable words, taken mainly from sacred Scripture.

**May the God of love and peace be with you all.**

And all reply:

**And also with you.**

1817  In the following or similar words, the minister prepares those present for the blessing.

**The needs of the Church are many and varied but God shows his goodness by sending pastoral workers to care for the Church. Today we ask God to bless our brothers and sisters who have declared their willingness to serve the Church.**

## READING OF THE WORD OF GOD

1818  A reader, another person present, or the minister reads a text of sacred Scripture.

**Brothers and sisters, listen to the words of the holy gospel according to Matthew:**                                      5:1-12

*Rejoice, for your reward in heaven is great.*

When Jesus saw the crowds, he went up the mountain, and after he had sat down, his disciples came to him. He began to teach them, saying:

"Blessed are the poor in spirit,
for theirs is the kingdom of heaven.
Blessed are they who mourn,
for they will be comforted.
Blessed are the meek,
for they will inherit the land.
Blessed are they who hunger and thirst for righteousness,
for they will be satisfied.
Blessed are the merciful,
for they will be shown mercy.
Blessed are the clean of heart,
for they will see God.
Blessed are the peacemakers,
for they will be called children of God.
Blessed are they who are persecuted for the sake of
    righteousness,
for theirs is the kingdom of heaven.

Blessed are you when they insult you and persecute you and utter every kind of evil against you falsely because of me. Rejoice and be glad, for your reward will be great in heaven. Thus they persecuted the prophets who were before you."

1819  Or:

Jeremiah 1:4-9—*To whomever I send you, you shall go.*

Romans 10:9-18—*How will they hear without someone preaching?*

Mark 16:15-20—*Go into the whole world and preach the gospel.*

1820  As circumstances suggest, one of the following responsorial psalms may be sung, or some other suitable song.

R̸. **Happy are those who trust in the Lord.**

Psalm 96

**Sing to the LORD a new song;**
**sing to the LORD, all you lands.**
**Sing to the LORD, bless his name.** R̸.

**Announce his salvation, day after day.**
**Tell his glory among the nations;**
**among all peoples, his wondrous deeds.** R̸.

**Give to the LORD, you families of nations,
give to the LORD glory and praise;
give to the LORD the glory due his name!** R̸.

Psalm 121:1-2, 3-4, 5-6, 7-8

R̸. (v. 2) **Our help is from the Lord, who made heaven and
earth.**

1821 As circumstances suggest, the minister may give those
present a brief explanation of the biblical text, so that they may
understand through faith the meaning of the celebration.

## INTERCESSIONS

1822 The intercessions are then said. The minister introduces
them and an assisting minister or one of those present announces
the intentions. From the following those best suited to the occasion may be used or adapted, or other intentions that apply to
the particular circumstances may be composed.

The minister says:

**Let us now ask God to strengthen and bless our brothers and
sisters as they begin their new pastoral service in this parish.**

R̸. **We beseech you, hear us.**

Assisting minister:

**That those who exercise a pastoral service may grow to a greater
love of Christ, let us pray to the Lord.** R̸.

Assisting minister:

**That they may lighten the burdens of others and assist them
in their struggles, let us pray to the Lord.** R̸.

Assisting minister:

**That the Holy Spirit may strengthen their hearts and enlighten
their minds, let us pray to the Lord.** R̸.

Assisting minister:

**That through their endeavors this parish may grow in faith,
hope, and love, let us pray to the Lord.** R̸.

1823  After the intercessions the minister, in the following or similar words, invites all present to sing or say the Lord's Prayer.

**Let us pray to the Father in the words Jesus gave us:**

All:

**Our Father . . .**


## Prayer of Blessing

1824  The minister says the prayer of blessing with hands outstretched over the new ministers.

**Lord God,
in your loving kindness
you sent your Son to be our shepherd and guide.
Continue to send workers into your vineyard
to sustain and direct your people.**

**Bless N.N. and N.N.
Let your Spirit uphold them always
as they take up their new responsibility
among the people of this parish.**

**We ask this through Christ our Lord.**

**R̴. Amen.**


## Concluding Rite

1825  The minister concludes the rite by saying:

**May almighty God bless you in his mercy,
and make you aware of his saving wisdom.**

**R̴. Amen.**

**May he strengthen your faith with proofs of his love,
so that you may persevere in good works.**

**R̴. Amen.**

**May he direct your steps to himself
and show you how to walk in charity and peace.**

**R̴. Amen.**

Then he blesses all present.

**And may almighty God bless you all,
the Father, and the Son, ✝ and the Holy Spirit.**

℟. **Amen.**

1826   It is preferable to end the celebration with a suitable song.

# CHAPTER 61

# ORDER FOR THE BLESSING OF READERS USA

## INTRODUCTION

1827  The word of God, as proclaimed in the sacred Scripture, lies at the heart of our Christian life and is integral to all our liturgical celebrations.

1828  This order is not intended for the institution of readers by the bishop, who uses the rite contained in the Roman Pontifical. Rather, this blessing is for parish readers who have the responsibility of proclaiming the Scriptures at Mass and other liturgical services. Care should be taken to see that readers are properly prepared for the exercise of their ministry before receiving this blessing. The functions of the reader are given in no. 66 of the General Instruction of the Roman Missal.

1829  If desired, each new reader may be presented with a lectionary or bible after the prayer of blessing.

1830  This blessing is given by the pastor, who may also delegate it to another priest or a deacon.

# I. ORDER OF BLESSING WITHIN MASS

**1831** After the gospel reading, the celebrant in the homily, based on the sacred text and pertinent to the particular place and the people involved, explains the meaning of the celebration.

## GENERAL INTERCESSIONS

**1832** The general intercessions follow, either in the form usual at Mass or in the form provided here. The celebrant concludes the intercessions with the prayer of blessing. From the following intentions those best for the occasion may be used or adapted, or other intentions that apply to the particular circumstances may be composed.

The celebrant says:

**The word of God calls us out of darkness into the light of faith. With the confidence of God's children let us ask the Lord to hear our prayers and to bless these readers:**

℟. **Lord, hear our prayer.**

Or:

℟. **Lord, graciously hear us.**

Assisting minister:

**For the Church, that we may continue to respond to the word of God which is proclaimed in our midst, we pray to the Lord. ℟.**

Assisting minister:

**For all who listen as the Scriptures are proclaimed, that God's word may find in them a fruitful field, we pray to the Lord. ℟.**

Assisting minister:

**For those who have not heard the message of Christ, that we may be willing to bring them the good news of salvation, we pray to the Lord. ℟.**

Assisting minister:

**For our readers, that with deep faith and confident voice they may announce God's saving word, we pray to the Lord. ℟.**

# PRAYER OF BLESSING

1833  With hands extended over the new readers the celebrant says immediately:

**Everlasting God,
when he read in the synagogue at Nazareth,
your Son proclaimed the good news of salvation
for which he would give up his life.**

**Bless these readers.
As they proclaim your words of life,
strengthen their faith
that they may read with conviction and boldness,
and put into practice what they read.**

**We ask this through Christ our Lord.**

**R̸. Amen.**

# II. ORDER OF BLESSING WITHIN A CELEBRATION OF THE WORD OF GOD

1834   The present order may be used by a priest or a deacon.

## INTRODUCTORY RITES

1835   When the community has gathered, a suitable song may be sung. After the singing, the minister says:

**In the name of the Father, and of the Son, and of the Holy Spirit.**

All make the sign of the cross and reply:

**Amen.**

1836   The minister greets those present in the following or other suitable words, taken mainly from sacred Scripture.

**May the Lord, whose word dwells in your hearts, be with you.**

And all reply:

**And also with you.**

1837   In the following or similar words, the minister prepares those present for the blessing.

**The word of God, proclaimed in the sacred Scripture, enlightens our minds and hearts. When the Scriptures are read in the liturgical assembly, God speaks to us and calls us to respond in faith and love. The ministry of the reader, then, is important to the life of the Church, for the reader proclaims God's living word. We ask God to bless these readers and all of us who now listen to the word of the Lord.**

## READING OF THE WORD OF GOD

1838   A reader proclaims a text of sacred Scripture.

**Brothers and sisters, listen to the words of the second letter of Paul to Timothy:**                                              3:14-17

*All Scripture is inspired by God and can be used for teaching.*

---

But you, remain faithful to what you have learned and believed, because you know from whom you learned it, and that from infancy you have known the sacred scriptures, which are capable of giving you wisdom for salvation through faith in Christ Jesus. All scripture is inspired by God and is useful for teaching, for refutation, for correction, and for training in righteousness, so that one who belongs to God may be competent, equipped for every good work.

1839  Or:

Isaiah 55:10-11—*The rain makes the earth fruitful.*

Nehemiah 8:1-4a, 5-6, 8-10—*They read from the book of the Law and understood what was read.*

2 Timothy 4:1-5—*Preach the Good News.*

1 John 1:1-4—*What we have seen and heard we are making known to you.*

Matthew 5:14-19—*You are the light of the world.*

John 7:14-18—*My teaching is not mine, but of him who sent me.*

1840  As circumstances suggest, one of the following responsorial psalms may be sung, or some other suitable song.

R̷. **Your words, Lord, are spirit and life.**

Psalm 19

**The law of the LORD is perfect,
refreshing the soul;
The decree of the LORD is trustworthy,
giving wisdom to the simple.** R̷.

**The precepts of the LORD are right,
rejoicing the heart;
The command of the LORD is clear,
enlightening the eye.** R̷.

**The fear of the LORD is pure,
enduring forever;
The ordinances of the LORD are true,
all of them just.** R̷.

**They are more precious than gold,
than a heap of purest gold;
Sweeter also than syrup
or honey from the comb.** R̷.

Psalm 119:9, 10, 11, 12

R℣. (v. 12b) **Lord, teach me your decrees.**

1841 As circumstances suggest, the minister may give those present a brief explanation of the biblical text, so that they may understand through faith the meaning of the celebration.

## INTERCESSIONS

1842 The intercessions are then said. The minister introduces them and an assisting minister or one of those present announces the intentions. From the following those best suited to the occasion may be used or adapted, or other intentions that apply to the particular circumstances may be composed.

The minister says:

**The word of God calls us out of darkness into the light of faith. With the confidence of God's children let us ask the Lord to hear our prayers and to bless these readers:**

R℣. **Lord, graciously hear us.**

Assisting minister:

**For the Church, that we may continue to respond to the word of God which is proclaimed in our midst, we pray to the Lord. R℣.**

Assisting minister:

**For all who listen as the Scriptures are proclaimed, that God's word may find in them a fruitful field, we pray to the Lord. R℣.**

Assisting minister:

**For those who have not heard the message of Christ, that we may be willing to bring them the good news of salvation, we pray to the Lord. R℣.**

Assisting minister:

**For our readers, that with deep faith and confident voice they may announce God's saving word, we pray to the Lord. R℣.**

1843 After the intercessions the minister, in the following or similar words, invites all present to sing or say the Lord's Prayer.

**With one voice we dare to say:**

All:

**Our Father . . .**

## PRAYER OF BLESSING

1844 The minister says the prayer of blessing with hands outstretched over the new readers:

**Everlasting God,
when he read in the synagogue at Nazareth,
your Son proclaimed the good news of salvation
for which he would give up his life.**

**Bless these readers.
As they proclaim your words of life,
strengthen their faith
that they may read with conviction and boldness
and put into practice what they read.**

**We ask this through Christ our Lord.**

℞. **Amen.**

## CONCLUDING RITE

1845 The minister concludes the rite by saying:

**May the word of God in all its richness
dwell in your hearts and minds,
now and for ever.**

℞. **Amen.**

Then he blesses all present.

**And may almighty God bless you all,
the Father, and the Son, ✝ and the Holy Spirit.**

℞. **Amen.**

1846 It is preferable to end the celebration with a suitable song.

CHAPTER 62

# ORDER FOR THE BLESSING OF ALTAR SERVERS, SACRISTANS, MUSICIANS, AND USHERS

USA

## INTRODUCTION

1847 The Church earnestly desires that all the faithful be led to that full, conscious, and active participation in liturgical celebrations called for by the very nature of the liturgy (Constitution on the Liturgy, art. 14). Within the community of the baptized, individual members are called to participate in the liturgy by undertaking liturgical roles.

1848 Among the liturgical ministries exercised by lay persons are those of altar server (acolyte), sacristan, musician, and usher (or minister of hospitality).

1849 Those who are to receive this blessing should be properly prepared for the exercise of their new ministry. The various functions of these liturgical ministers are described in nos. 63–73 of the General Instruction of the Roman Missal.

1850 This order may be used during Mass or in a celebration of the word of God.

1851 This blessing is normally given by the pastor. If necessary, he may delegate another priest or deacon to give the blessing.

# I. ORDER OF BLESSING WITHIN MASS

1852  After the gospel reading, the celebrant in the homily, based on the sacred text and pertinent to the particular place and the people involved, explains the meaning of the celebration.

## GENERAL INTERCESSIONS

1853  The general intercessions follow, either in the form usual at Mass or in the form provided here. The celebrant concludes the intercessions with the prayer of blessing. From the following intentions those best for the occasion may be used or adapted, or other intentions that apply to the particular circumstances may be composed.

The celebrant says:

**God provides the Church with suitable ministers to assist in divine worship. Let us pray for these new liturgical ministers, that God may bless them as they undertake their new roles of service to this parish.**

R℣. **Lord, hear our prayer.**

Or:

R℣. **Lord, graciously hear us.**

Assisting minister:

**For the Church of Christ and for this parish of N., that all Christians may offer themselves as living sacrifices, we pray to the Lord.** R℣.

Assisting minister:

**For all the liturgical ministers of our parish, that they may deepen their commitment to serve God and their neighbor, we pray to the Lord.** R℣.

Assisting minister:

For altar servers

**For these altar servers, that the light of Christ may shine in their hearts, we pray to the Lord.** R℣.

Assisting minister:

For sacristans

**For these sacristans, that the preparations they make for the celebration of the liturgy may remind us to prepare our hearts for worship, we pray to the Lord.** R̶⁊.

Assisting minister:

For musicians

**For these parish musicians, that the beauty which they create in song and praise may echo always in our hearts, we pray to the Lord.** R̶⁊.

Assisting minister:

For ushers

**For these ushers, that their presence may make all who enter this church always feel welcome in God's house, we pray to the Lord.** R̶⁊.

## Prayer of Blessing

1854 With hands extended over the new ministers the celebrant says immediately:

**God of glory,**
**your beloved Son has shown us**
**that true worship comes from humble and contrite hearts.**

**Bless our brothers and sisters,**
**who have responded to the needs of our parish**
**and wish to commit themselves to your service as**
    **(altar servers, sacristans, musicians, ushers).**
**Grant that their ministry may be fruitful**
**and our worship pleasing in your sight.**

**We ask this through Christ our Lord.**

R̶⁊. **Amen.**

# II. ORDER OF BLESSING WITHIN A CELEBRATION OF THE WORD OF GOD

**1855** The present order may be used by a priest or a deacon.

## INTRODUCTORY RITES

**1856** When the community has gathered, a suitable song may be sung. After the singing, the minister says:

**In the name of the Father, and of the Son, and of the Holy Spirit.**

All make the sign of the cross and reply:

**Amen.**

**1857** The minister greets those present in the following or other suitable words, taken mainly from sacred Scripture.

**The grace and favor of our Lord Jesus Christ be with you always.**

And all reply:

**And also with you.**

## INTRODUCTION

**1858** In the following or similar words, the minister prepares those present for the blessing.

**In the body of Christ there exists a wonderful variety of ministries, which are especially evident when we gather around the altar to worship God. By virtue of our baptism in Christ some of us are called to serve as ministers of the liturgical assembly: altar servers assist the priest and deacon, sacristans prepare and maintain that which is necessary for divine worship, musicians help to raise our spirits in joyful praise, and ushers provide welcome and dignified order to the celebration. Today we ask God to bless abundantly these new (altar servers, sacristans, musicians, ushers) as they begin their liturgical ministry in our parish.**

1859  A reader, another person present, or the minister reads a text of sacred Scripture.

For altar servers

**Brothers and sisters, listen to the words of the book of Numbers:**                                                     3:5-9

*The Levites carried out their duties.*

**Now the LORD said to Moses: "Summon the tribe of Levi and present them to Aaron the priest, as his assistants. They shall discharge his obligations and those of the whole community before the meeting tent by serving at the Dwelling. They shall have custody of all the furnishings of the meeting tent and discharge the duties of the Israelites in the service of the Dwelling. You shall give the Levites to Aaron and his sons; they have been set aside from among the Israelites as dedicated to me."**

1860  Or:

Acts 4:32-35—*The community of believers were of one heart and mind.*

1 Corinthians 12:1-31—*Set your hearts on the greater gifts.*

1 John 3:14-18—*Let us love in deed and in truth.*

Matthew 5:1-12—*The beatitudes.*

John 15:12-16—*The commandment of love.*

1861  For sacristans

**Brothers and sisters, listen to the words of the book of Numbers:**                                                     4:4-14

*Preparation of the meeting tent.*

**The LORD said to Moses and Aaron: "The service of the Kohathites in the meeting tent concerns the most sacred objects. In breaking camp, Aaron and his sons shall go in and take down the screening curtain and cover the ark of the commandments with it. Over these they shall put a cover of tahash skin, and on top of this spread an all-violet cloth. They shall then put the poles in place. On the table of the Presence they shall spread a violet cloth and put on it the plates and**

cups, as well as the bowls and pitchers for libations; the established bread offering shall remain on the table. Over these they shall spread a scarlet cloth and cover all this with tahash skin. They shall then put the poles in place. They shall use a violet cloth to cover the lampstand with its lamps, trimming shears, and trays, as well as the various containers of oil from which it is supplied. The lampstand with all its utensils they shall then enclose in a covering of tahash skin, and place on a litter. Over the golden altar they shall spread a violet cloth, and cover this also with a covering of tahash skin. They shall then put the poles in place. Taking the utensils of the sanctuary service, they shall wrap them all in violet cloth and cover them with tahash skin. They shall then place them on a litter. After cleansing the altar of its ashes, they shall spread a purple cloth over it. On this they shall put all the utensils with which it is served: the fire pans, forks, shovels, basins, and all the utensils of the altar. They shall then spread a covering of tahash skin over this, and put the poles in place.''

### 1862   For musicians

**Brothers and sisters, listen to the words of the apostle Paul to the Colossians:**                                            3:15-17

*Sing to God from your hearts.*

**And let the peace of Christ control your hearts, the peace into which you were also called in one body. And be thankful. Let the word of Christ dwell in you richly, as in all wisdom you teach and admonish one another, singing psalms, hymns, and spiritual songs with gratitude in your hearts to God. And whatever you do, in word or in deed, do everything in the name of the Lord Jesus, giving thanks to God the Father through him.**

### 1863   For ushers

**Brothers and sisters, listen to the words of the first letter of Paul to the Corinthians:**                                            13:1-13

*Hymn to love.*

**If I speak in human and angelic tongues, but do not have love, I am a resounding gong or a clashing cymbal. And if I have the gift of prophecy, and comprehend all mysteries and all knowledge; if I have all faith so as to move mountains, but do not have love, I am nothing. If I give away everything I**

own, and if I hand my body over so that I may boast but do not have love, I gain nothing.

Love is patient, love is kind. It is not jealous, love is not pompous, it is not inflated, it is not rude, it does not seek its own interests, it is not quick-tempered, it does not brood over injury, it does not rejoice over wrongdoing but rejoices with the truth. It bears all things, believes all things, hopes all things, endures all things.

Love never fails. If there are prophecies, they will be brought to nothing; if tongues, they will cease; if knowledge, it will be brought to nothing. For we know partially and we prophesy partially, but when the perfect comes, the partial will pass away. When I was a child, I used to talk as a child, think as a child, reason as a child; when I became a man, I put aside childish things. At present we see indistinctly, as in a mirror, but then face to face. At present I know partially; then I shall know fully as I am fully known. So faith, hope, love remain, these three; but the greatest of these is love.

1864 As circumstances suggest, one of the following responsorial psalms may be sung, or some other suitable song.

R̸. O Lord, my allotted portion and my cup,
    you it is who hold fast my lot.

Psalm 16

Keep me, O God, for in you I take refuge;
I say to the Lord, "My Lord are you.
Apart from you I have no good." R̸.

O Lord, my allotted portion and my cup,
you it is who hold fast my lot. R̸.

I bless the Lord who counsels me;
even in the night my heart exhorts me.
I set the Lord ever before me;
with him at my right hand I shall not be disturbed. R̸.

You will show me the path to life,
fullness of joys in your presence,
the delights at your right hand forever. R̸.

Psalm 19:8, 9, 10, 12

R̸. (see John 6:63b) Your words, O Lord, are spirit and life.

Psalm 34:2-3, 4-5, 6-7, 10-11, 12-13

R⁊. (v. 9) **Taste and see the goodness of the Lord.**

Psalm 112:1-2, 3-4, 5-7, 8-9

R⁊. (v. 1) **Happy those who fear the Lord,
who greatly delight in his commands.**

Psalm 147:1, 2, 3, 7, 12-13

R⁊. (v. 1) **Praise the Lord, for he is good.**

Psalm 149:1, 2, 3, 4, 5, 6

R⁊. (v. 1) **Sing to the Lord a new song.**

Psalm 150

R⁊. (v. 6) **Alleluia.** *Or:* **Let everything that has breath praise
the Lord.**

1865    As circumstances suggest, the minister may give those
present a brief explanation of the biblical text, so that they may
understand through faith the meaning of the celebration.


# INTERCESSIONS

1866    The intercessions are then said. The minister introduces
them and an assisting minister or one of those present announces
the intentions. From the following those best suited to the occasion may be used or adapted, or other intentions that apply to
the particular circumstances may be composed.

The minister says:

**God provides the Church with suitable ministers to assist in
divine worship. Let us pray for these new liturgical ministers,
that God may bless them as they undertake their new roles
of service to this parish.**

R⁊. **Lord, graciously hear us.**

Assisting minister:

**For the Church of Christ and for this parish of N., that all Chris-
tians may offer themselves as living sacrifices, we pray to the
Lord.** R⁊.

Assisting minister:

**For all the liturgical ministers of our parish, that they may deepen their commitment to serve God and their neighbor, we pray to the Lord. R℣.**

Assisting minister:

For altar servers

**For these altar servers, that the light of Christ may shine in their hearts, we pray to the Lord. R℣.**

Assisting minister:

For sacristans

**For these sacristans, that the preparations they make for the celebration of the liturgy may remind us to prepare our hearts for worship, we pray to the Lord. R℣.**

Assisting minister:

For musicians

**For these parish musicians, that the beauty which they create in song and praise may echo always in our hearts, we pray to the Lord. R℣.**

Assisting minister:

For ushers

**For these ushers, that their presence may make all who enter this church always feel welcome in God's house, we pray to the Lord. R℣.**

1867 After the intercessions the minister, in the following or similar words, invites all present to sing or say the Lord's Prayer.

**In the spirit of our common baptism, we cry out:**

All:

**Our Father . . .**

## Prayer of Blessing

1868 The minister says the prayer of blessing with hands outstretched over the new ministers.

**God of glory,**
**your beloved Son has shown us**
**that true worship comes from humble and contrite hearts.**

**Bless our brothers and sisters,**
**who have responded to the needs of our parish**
**and wish to commit themselves to your service as**
**(altar servers, sacristans, musicians, ushers).**
**Grant that their ministry may be fruitful**
**and our worship pleasing in your sight.**

**We ask this through Christ our Lord.**

℟. **Amen.**

## Concluding Rite

1869 The minister concludes the rite by saying:

**Lord God,**
**you give to each person**
**the gift of your Spirit for the building up of the Church.**
**Bless us and keep us all in your love.**

**We ask this through Christ our Lord.**

℟. **Amen.**

Then he blesses all present.

**And may almighty God bless you all,**
**the Father, and the Son, ✠ and the Holy Spirit.**

℟. **Amen.**

1870 It is preferable to end the celebration with a suitable song.

# CHAPTER 63

# ORDER FOR THE COMMISSIONING OF EXTRAORDINARY MINISTERS OF HOLY COMMUNION[2]

USA

## INTRODUCTION

1871 It is, first of all, the office of the priest and deacon to minister holy communion to the faithful who ask to receive it.[3] It is most fitting, therefore, that they give a suitable part of their time to this ministry of their order, depending on the needs of the faithful.[4]

It is the office of an acolyte who has been properly instituted to give communion as an extraordinary minister when the priest and deacon are absent or impeded by sickness, old age, or pastoral ministry or when the number of the faithful at the holy table is so great that the Mass or other service may be unreasonably protracted.[5]

The local Ordinary may give other extraordinary ministers the faculty to give communion whenever it seems necessary for the pastoral benefit of the faithful and a priest, deacon, or acolyte is not available.[6]

1872 Persons authorized to distribute holy communion in special circumstances should be commissioned by the local Ordinary or his delegate[7] according to the following rite. The rite should take place in the presence of the people during Mass or outside Mass.

1873 The pastor is the usual minister of this rite. However, he may delegate another priest to celebrate it, or a deacon when it is celebrated outside Mass.

---

[2] This order is taken from the *Rite of Commissioning Special Ministers of Holy Communion.*

[3] See Congregation of Rites, instruction *Eucharisticum mysterium,* no. 31: *AAS* 64 (1967).

[4] Roman Ritual, *Holy Communion and Worship of the Eucharist outside Mass,* no. 17.

[5] Roman Ritual, *Holy Communion and Worship of the Eucharist outside Mass,* no. 17; see Paul VI, apostolic letter *Ministeria quaedam,* August 15, 1972, no. VI: *AAS* 64 (1972) 532.

[6] Roman Ritual, *Holy Communion and Worship of the Eucharist outside Mass,* no. 17; see Congregation for the Discipline of the Sacraments, instruction *Immensae caritatis,* January 29, 1973, 1, I and II.

[7] See instruction *Immensae caritatis* I, nos. 1, 6.

# I. ORDER OF COMMISSIONING WITHIN MASS

**1874** After the gospel reading, the celebrant in the homily, based on the sacred text and pertinent to the particular place and the people involved, explains the meaning of the celebration.

## PRESENTATION OF THE CANDIDATES

**1875** Then he presents to the people those chosen to serve as special ministers, using these or similar words:

**Dear friends in Christ, our brothers and sisters N. and N. are to be entrusted with administering the eucharist, with taking communion to the sick, and with giving it as viaticum to the dying.**

The celebrant pauses, and then addresses the candidates:

**In this ministry, you must be examples of Christian living in faith and conduct; you must strive to grow in holiness through this sacrament of unity and love. Remember that, though many, we are one body because we share the one bread and one cup.**

**As ministers of holy communion be, therefore, especially observant of the Lord's command to love your neighbor. For when he gave his body as food to his disciples, he said to them: "This is my commandment, that you should love one another as I have loved you."**

## EXAMINATION

**1876** After the address the candidates stand before the celebrant, who asks them these questions:

**Are you resolved to undertake the office of giving the body and blood of the Lord to your brothers and sisters, and so serve to build up the Church?**

℟. **I am.**

---

Are you resolved to administer the holy eucharist with the utmost care and reverence?

R7. I am.


## Prayer of Blessing

1877  All stand. The candidates kneel and the celebrant invites the faithful to pray:

Dear friends in Christ, let us pray with confidence to the Father; let us ask him to bestow his blessings on our brothers and sisters, chosen to be ministers of the eucharist.


Pause for silent prayer. The celebrant then continues:

Merciful Father,
creator and guide of your family,
bless ✛ our brothers and sisters N. and N.

May they faithfully give the bread of life to your people.

Strengthened by this sacrament,
may they come at last to the banquet of heaven.

We ask this through Christ our Lord.

R7. Amen.


1878  Or:

Gracious Lord,
you nourish us with the body and blood
   of your Son,
that we might have eternal life.

Bless ✛ our brothers and sisters who have
   been chosen
to give the bread of heaven and the cup of salvation
to your faithful people.

May the saving mysteries they distribute
lead them to the joys of eternal life.

We ask this through Christ our Lord.

R7. Amen.

# General Intercessions

1879  The general intercessions follow, either in the form usual at Mass or in the form provided here. The celebrant concludes the intercessions with the prayer of blessing. From the following intentions those best for the occasion may be used or adapted, or other intentions that apply to the particular circumstances may be composed.

The celebrant says:

**The Lord feeds and nourishes us with his life-giving body and blood. Let us pray that these ministers of communion be ever faithful to their responsibility of distributing holy communion in our community.**

℞. **Lord, hear our prayer.**

Or:

℞. **Hear us, O Lord.**

Assisting minister:

**For our ministers of communion, that they witness by their deep faith in the eucharist to the saving mystery of Christ, let us pray to the Lord. ℞.**

Assisting minister:

**For the Church, that the eucharist we celebrate always be a bond of unity and a sacrament of love for all who partake, let us pray to the Lord. ℞.**

Assisting minister:

**For the sick who will receive holy communion from these ministers, that Christ heal and strengthen them, let us pray to the Lord. ℞.**

Assisting minister:

**For all who are present here, that the bread of life and cup of salvation we receive at the altar always be our nourishment, let us pray to the Lord. ℞.**

1880   The celebrant then says:

**Lord our God,**
**teach us to cherish in our hearts**
**the paschal mystery of your Son,**
**by which you redeemed the world.**

**Watch over the gifts of grace your love has given us**
**and bring them to fulfillment in the glory of heaven.**

**We ask this through Christ our Lord.**

R̷. **Amen.**


## LITURGY OF THE EUCHARIST

1881   In the procession at the presentation of gifts, the newly-commissioned ministers carry the vessels with the bread and wine, and at communion may receive the eucharist under both kinds.

# II. ORDER OF COMMISSIONING WITHIN A CELEBRATION OF THE WORD OF GOD

## INTRODUCTORY RITES

1882   When the community has gathered, a suitable song may be sung. After the singing, the minister says:

**In the name of the Father, and of the Son, and of the Holy Spirit.**

All make the sign of the cross and reply:

**Amen.**

1883   The minister greets those present in the following or other suitable words, taken mainly from sacred Scripture.

**May the Lord, who nourishes us with the bread of life, be with you.**

And all reply:

**And also with you.**

1884   In the following or similar words, the minister prepares those present for the blessing.

**Our brothers and sisters who have been chosen as extraordinary ministers of holy communion will be commissioned through our prayer and God's blessing. We pray that they may exercise this ministry with faith, devotion, and love.**

## READING OF THE WORD OF GOD

1885   A reader, another person present, or the minister reads a text of sacred Scripture.

**Brothers and sisters, listen to the words of the first letter of Paul to the Corinthians:**                                     10:16-17

*Though we are many, we form a single body because we share this one loaf.*

**The cup of blessing that we bless, is it not a participation in the blood of Christ? The bread that we break, is it not a participation in the body of Christ? Because the loaf of bread is one, we, though many, are one body, for we all partake of the one loaf.**

1886   Or:

Genesis 14:18-20—*Melchizedek brought bread and wine.*

Exodus 16:2-4, 12-15—*I will rain bread from heaven upon you.*

Exodus 24:3-8—*This is the blood of the covenant that the Lord has made with you.*

Deuteronomy 8:2-3, 14b-16a—*He gave you food which you and your fathers did not know.*

1 Kings 19:4-8—*Strengthened by the food, he walked to the mountain of the Lord.*

Proverbs 9:1-6—*Come and eat my bread, drink the wine I have prepared.*

Acts 2:42-47—*All who believed shared everything in common.*

Acts 10:34a, 37-43—*We have eaten and drunk with him after his resurrection from the dead.*

1 Corinthians 11:23-26—*Until the Lord comes, every time you eat this bread and drink this cup, you proclaim his death.*

Hebrews 9:11-15—*The blood of Christ will purify our inner selves.*

Mark 14:12-16, 22-26—*This is my body. This is my blood.*

Luke 9:11b-17—*They all ate and were filled.*

Luke 24:13-35—*They had recognized him in the breaking of the bread.*

John 6:1-15—*He distributed to those who were seated as much as they wanted.*

John 6:24-35—*Anyone who comes to me will never be hungry; anyone who believes in me will never thirst.*

John 6:41-52—*I am the living bread that came down from heaven.*

John 6:51-59—*My flesh is real food and my blood is real drink.*

John 21:1-14—*Jesus came and took the bread and gave it to them.*

1887   As circumstances suggest, one of the following responsorial psalms may be sung, or some other suitable song.

℟. **The Lord is my shepherd; there is nothing I shall want.**

Psalm 23

**The Lord is my shepherd; I shall not want.**
**In verdant pastures he gives me repose;**
**Beside restful waters he leads me;**
**he refreshes my soul. ℟.**

**He guides me in right paths**
**for his name's sake.**
**Even though I walk in the dark valley**
**I fear no evil; for you are at my side**
**With your rod and your staff**
**that give me courage. ℟.**

**You spread the table before me**
**in the sight of my foes;**
**You anoint my head with oil;**
**my cup overflows.**
**Only goodness and kindness follow me**
**all the days of my life;**
**And I shall dwell in the house of the Lord**
**for years to come. ℟.**

Psalm 34:2-3, 4-5, 6-7

℟. **(v. 9a) Taste and see the goodness of the Lord.**

Psalm 78:3, 4bc, 23-24, 25, 54

℟. **(v. 24) The Lord gave them bread from heaven.**

Psalm 145:10-11, 15-16, 17-18

℟. **(v. 16) The hand of the Lord feeds us; he answers all our needs.**

Psalm 147:12-13, 14-15, 19-20

℟. **(see John 6:58b) Whoever eats this bread will live for ever.**

**1888**  In the homily the minister first explains the reason for this ministry.

# PRESENTATION OF THE CANDIDATES

1889   Then he presents to the people those chosen to serve as extraordinary ministers, using these or similar words:

**Dear friends in Christ, our brothers and sisters N. and N. are to be entrusted with administering the eucharist, with taking communion to the sick, and with giving it as viaticum to the dying.**

The minister pauses, and addresses the candidates:

**In this ministry, you must be examples of Christian living in faith and conduct; you must strive to grow in holiness through this sacrament of unity and love. Remember that, though many, we are one body because we share the one bread and one cup.**

**As ministers of holy communion be, therefore, especially observant of the Lord's command to love your neighbor. For when he gave his body as food to his disciples, he said to them: "This is my commandment, that you should love one another as I have loved you."**

# EXAMINATION

1890   After the address the candidates stand before the minister, who asks them these questions:

**Are you resolved to undertake the office of giving the body and blood of the Lord to your brothers and sisters, and so serve to build up the Church?**

R̷. **I am.**

**Are you resolved to administer the holy eucharist with the utmost care and reverence?**

R̷. **I am.**

# PRAYER OF BLESSING

1891   All stand. The candidates kneel and the minister invites the faithful to pray:

**Dear friends in Christ, let us pray with confidence to the Father; let us ask him to bestow his blessings on our brothers and sisters, chosen to be ministers of the eucharist.**

Pause for silent prayer. The minister then continues:

**Merciful Father,**
**creator and guide of your family,**
**bless ✠ our brothers and sisters** N. **and** N.

**May they faithfully give the bread of life to your people.**

**Strengthened by this sacrament,**
**may they come at last to the banquet of heaven.**

**We ask this through Christ our Lord.**

℟. **Amen.**

1892 Or:

**Gracious Lord,**
**you nourish us with the body and blood**
**of your Son,**
**that we might have eternal life.**

**Bless ✠ our brothers and sisters who have**
**been chosen**
**to give the bread of heaven and the cup of salvation**
**to your faithful people.**

**May the saving mysteries they distribute**
**lead them to the joys of eternal life.**

**We ask this through Christ our Lord.**

℟. **Amen.**

## Intercessions

1893 The intercessions are then said. The minister introduces them and an assisting minister or one of those present announces the intentions. From the following those best suited to the occasion may be used or adapted, or other intentions that apply to the particular circumstances may be composed.

The minister says:

**The Lord feeds and nourishes us with his life-giving body and blood. Let us pray that these ministers of communion be ever faithful to their responsibility of distributing holy communion in our community.**

℟. **Hear us, O Lord.**

Assisting minister:

**For our ministers of communion, that they witness by their deep faith in the eucharist to the saving mystery of Christ, let us pray to the Lord.** ℟.

Assisting minister:

**For the Church, that the eucharist we celebrate always be a bond of unity and a sacrament of love for all who partake, let us pray to the Lord.** ℟.

Assisting minister:

**For the sick who will receive holy communion from these ministers, that Christ heal and strengthen them, let us pray to the Lord.** ℟.

Assisting minister:

**For all who are present here, that the bread of life and cup of salvation we receive at the altar always be our nourishment, let us pray to the Lord.** ℟.

1894  After the intercessions the minister, in the following or similar words, invites all present to sing or say the Lord's Prayer.

**Let us pray to the Father in the words our Savior gave us.**

All:

**Our Father . . .**

# Concluding Rite

1895 The minister concludes the rite by saying:

**Lord our God,
teach us to cherish in our hearts
the paschal mystery of your Son,
by which you redeemed the world.
Watch over the gifts of grace your love has given us
and bring them to fulfillment in the glory of heaven.**

**We ask this through Christ our Lord.**

**R⁷. Amen.**

Then he blesses all present.

**And may almighty God bless you all,
the Father, and the Son, ✝ and the Holy Spirit.**

**R⁷. Amen.**

1896 It is preferable to end the celebration with a suitable song.

CHAPTER 64

# ORDER FOR THE BLESSING OF
# A PARISH COUNCIL

USA

## INTRODUCTION

1897   The pastoral council of a parish provides valuable assistance and support to the pastor. Through the parish council the Christian faithful, along with those who share in the pastoral care of the parish in virtue of their office, give their help in fostering pastoral activity (*C.I.C.*, c. 536,1). Because of the importance of their role it is appropriate that the members of the council receive God's blessing as they begin their term of office.

1898   This order may be used during Mass or in a celebration of the word of God.

1899   This order is used by the pastor of the parish or by another priest who has been delegated by him.

# I. ORDER OF BLESSING WITHIN MASS

1900    After the gospel reading, the celebrant in the homily, based on the sacred text and pertinent to the particular place and the people involved, explains the meaning of the celebration.

## GENERAL INTERCESSIONS

1901    The general intercessions follow, either in the form usual at Mass or in the form provided here. The celebrant concludes the intercessions with the prayer of blessing. From the following intentions those best for the occasion may be used or adapted, or other intentions that apply to the particular circumstances may be composed.

The celebrant says:

**My dear friends, let us pray to God our Father who binds us together in the Holy Spirit.**

R̶⁊. **Lord, hear our prayer.**

Or:

R̶⁊. **Graciously hear us, O Lord.**

Assisting minister:

**For the holy Church of God, that we may grow in Christ and in the bond of common fellowship, we pray to the Lord.** R̶⁊.

Assisting minister:

**For the members of our parish council, that they may give witness to the presence of Christ by lives manifesting faith, hope, and love, we pray to the Lord.** R̶⁊.

Assisting minister:

**For all concerned with the welfare of this parish, that they may be open to the movement of the Holy Spirit and be always ready to carry out God's will, we pray to the Lord.** R̶⁊.

Assisting minister:

**For all gathered here, that we may reach out with compassion and care to those in need, we pray to the Lord.** R̶⁊.

# PRAYER OF BLESSING

1902 With hands extended over the council members, the celebrant says immediately:

**Ever-living God,
you gather us together
as the parish of** N.
**to carry the Gospel of Christ to all people.**

**Bless the members of this parish council.
Let your Spirit enlighten their minds
and guide all their actions
that they may be renewed in faith,
united in love,
and bring to fulfillment the work of your Church
to your greater honor and glory.**

**We ask this through Christ our Lord.**

R̸. **Amen.**

# II. ORDER OF BLESSING WITHIN A CELEBRATION OF THE WORD OF GOD

## INTRODUCTORY RITES

1903   When the community has gathered, a suitable song may be sung.

The priest then says:

**In the name of the Father, and of the Son, and of the Holy Spirit.**

All make the sign of the cross and reply:

**Amen.**

1904   The priest greets those present in the following or other suitable words, taken mainly from sacred Scripture.

**The grace of our Lord Jesus Christ, the love of God, and the fellowship of the Holy Spirit be with you.**

And all reply:

**And also with you.**

1905   In the following or similar words, the priest next prepares those present to receive the blessing.

**The parish council provides the pastor with the wisdom of the laity for the good of the parish. Because of their knowledge and competence the members of the council are called to share with one another and with the pastor their insights honestly, with courage and prudence. And so, the parish is strengthened by the unity of effort achieved in reverence and charity.**

## READING OF THE WORD OF GOD

1906   One of those present, or the priest himself, then reads a text of sacred Scripture.

**Brothers and sisters, listen to the words of the apostle Paul to the Philippians:**                                    2:1-4

*Have the same convictions, the same love, the concern for unity.*

---

If there is any encouragement in Christ, any solace in love, any participation in the Spirit, any compassion and mercy, complete my joy by being of the same mind, with the same love, united in heart, thinking one thing. Do nothing out of selfishness or out of vainglory; rather, humbly regard others as more important than yourselves, each looking out not for his own interests, but also everyone for those of others.

1907 Or:

Ephesians 4:1-6—*Do all you can to preserve the unity of the Spirit in the bond of peace.*

Matthew 18:15-20—*Where two or three meet in my name, I shall be there with them.*

John 14:23-29—*The Spirit of truth will teach you everything.*

1908 As circumstances suggest, one of the following responsorial psalms may be sung, or some other suitable song.

℟. **Lord, guard your people like a shepherd guarding his flock.**

Jeremiah 31

**Hear the word of the LORD, O nations,**
**proclaim it on distant coasts, and say:**
**He who scattered Israel, now gathers them together,**
**he guards them as a shepherd his flock.** ℟.

**The LORD shall ransom Jacob,**
**he shall redeem him from the hand of his conqueror.**
**Shouting, they shall mount the heights of Zion,**
**they shall come streaming to the LORD's blessings:**
**The grain, the wine, and the oil,**
**the sheep and the oxen;**
**They themselves shall be like watered gardens,**
**never again shall they languish.** ℟.

**Then the virgins shall make merry and dance,**
**and young men and old as well.**
**I will turn their mourning into joy,**
**I will console and gladden them after their sorrows.**
**I will lavish choice portions upon the priests,**
**and my people shall be filled with my blessings,**
**says the LORD.** ℟.

Psalm 100:2, 3, 4, 5

R̸. (v. 3) **We are his people: the sheep of his flock.**

1909   As circumstances suggest, after the reading the priest may give those present a brief explanation of the biblical text, so that they may understand through faith the meaning of the celebration.


## INTERCESSIONS

1910   The intercessions are then said. The priest introduces them and an assisting minister or one of those present announces the intentions. From the following those best suited to the occasion may be used or adapted, or other intentions that apply to the particular circumstances may be composed.


The priest says:

**My dear friends, let us pray to God our Father who binds us together in the Holy Spirit.**

R̸. **Graciously hear us, O Lord.**

Assisting minister:

**For the holy Church of God, that we may grow in Christ and in the bond of common fellowship, we pray to the Lord.** R̸.

Assisting minister:

**For the members of our parish council, that they may give witness to the presence of Christ by lives manifesting faith, hope, and love, we pray to the Lord.** R̸.

Assisting minister:

**For all concerned with the welfare of this parish, that they may be open to the movement of the Holy Spirit and be always ready to carry out God's will, we pray to the Lord.** R̸.

Assisting minister:

**For all gathered here, that we may reach out with compassion and care to those in need, we pray to the Lord.** R̸.

1911 After the intercessions the priest, in the following or similar words, invites all present to sing or say the Lord's Prayer.

**Let us pray to the Father in the words Jesus taught us:**

All:

**Our Father . . .**

## PRAYER OF BLESSING

1912 The priest says the prayer of blessing with hands outstretched over the parish council.

**Ever-living God,**
**you gather us together**
**as the parish of N.**
**to carry the Gospel of Christ to all people.**

**Bless the members of this parish council.**
**Let your Spirit enlighten their minds**
**and guide all their actions**
**that they may be renewed in faith,**
**united in love,**
**and bring to fulfillment the work of your Church**
**to your greater honor and glory.**

**We ask this through Christ our Lord.**

**R̃. Amen.**

## CONCLUDING RITE

1913 The priest concludes the rite by saying:

**Lord, bless us with your heavenly gifts**
**and in your mercy make us ready to do your will.**

**We ask this through Christ our Lord.**

**R̃. Amen.**

Then he blesses all present.

**And may almighty God bless you all,**
**the Father, and the Son, ✝ and the Holy Spirit.**

**R̃. Amen.**

1914 It is preferable to end the celebration with a suitable song.

# CHAPTER 65

# ORDER FOR THE BLESSING OF OFFICERS OF PARISH SOCIETIES

USA

## INTRODUCTION

1915   Part of the life of every parish is reflected in the work carried out by its various societies of the faithful. The officers of these societies may be blessed at the time of their installation.

1916   This blessing is celebrated during a meeting of the society in the context of a celebration of the word of God.

1917   The pastor is the usual minister of this blessing. However, he may delegate another priest or deacon to act in his behalf.

---

# ORDER OF BLESSING

## INTRODUCTORY RITES

1918   When the community has gathered, a suitable song may be sung. After the singing, the minister says:

**In the name of the Father, and of the Son, and of the Holy Spirit.**

All make the sign of the cross and reply:

**Amen.**

1919   The minister greets those present in the following or other suitable words, taken mainly from sacred Scripture.

**May the Lord, who confirms us in holiness, be with you.**

And all reply:

**And also with you.**

1920   In the following or similar words, the minister prepares those present for the blessing.

**Parish societies serve the parish community in various ways. The life and vitality of these societies depends on leaders who are willing to give their time and talent. We pray today for the new officers of the N. society of N. parish.**

## READING OF THE WORD OF GOD

1921   A reader, another person present, or the minister reads a text of sacred Scripture.

**Brothers and sisters, listen to the words of the holy gospel according to Luke:**           22:24-30

*Who is the greatest in the kingdom of God?*

**Then an argument broke out among the disciples about which of them should be regarded as the greatest. Jesus said to them, "The kings of the Gentiles lord it over them and those in authority over them are addressed as 'Benefactors'; but among you it shall not be so. Rather, let the greatest among you be as the youngest, and the leader as the servant. For who is**

greater: the one seated at table or the one who serves? Is it not the one seated at table? I am among you as the one who serves. It is you who have stood by me in my trials; and I confer a kingdom on you, just as my Father has conferred one on me, that you may eat and drink at my table in my kingdom; and you will sit on thrones judging the twelve tribes of Israel.''

1922 Or:

Hebrews 12:1-4—*Let us bear patiently the struggle placed upon us.*

Philippians 2:1-4—*Make my joy complete by your unanimity.*

Philippians 4:6-9—*The God of peace be with you.*

John 15:9-17—*I shall not call you servants anymore; I call you friends.*

1923 As circumstances suggest, one of the following responsorial psalms may be sung, or some other suitable song.

R℟. **Blessed be the name of the Lord for ever.**

Psalm 113

**Praise, you servants of the LORD,**
**praise the name of the LORD.**
**Blessed be the name of the LORD**
**both now and forever.** R℟.

**From the rising to the setting of the sun**
**is the name of the LORD to be praised.**
**High above all nations is the LORD,**
**above the heavens is his glory.** R℟.

**Who is like the LORD, our God, who is enthroned on high**
**and looks upon the heavens and the earth below?** R℟.

**He raises up the lowly from the dust;**
**from the dunghill he lifts up the poor**
**To seat them with princes,**
**with the princes of his own people.** R℟.

Psalm 31:3-4, 6, 7, 8, 17, 21

R℟. **(Ps. 34:5) The Lord has set me free from all my fears.**

1924 As circumstances suggest, the minister may give those present a brief explanation of the biblical text, so that they may understand through faith the meaning of the celebration.

# INTERCESSIONS

1925   The intercessions are then said. The minister introduces them and an assisting minister or one of those present announces the intentions. From the following those best suited to the occasion may be used or adapted, or other intentions that apply to the particular circumstances may be composed.

The minister says:

**God guides and protects his people in mercy and love. We pray with faith and trust for the N. society and its new officers.**

**R̷. Lord, hear our prayer.**

Assisting minister:

**God has shaped and formed us into his people; grant, Lord, that we may do your will in all things and so remain close to you. With faith we pray: R̷.**

Assisting minister:

**God's presence is found where unity and love prevail; grant, Lord, that we may strive to work together in harmony and peace. With faith we pray: R̷.**

Assisting minister:

**God is the strength and protector of his people; grant, Lord, to the officers of the N. society the strength and courage they need to serve our parish. With faith we pray: R̷.**

Assisting minister:

**God enriches the Church through its members; grant, Lord, that this parish benefit from the work done by the N. society. With faith we pray: R̷.**

1926   After the intercessions the minister, in the following or similar words, invites all present to sing or say the Lord's Prayer.

**We pray to the one Father who hears all our prayers, saying:**

All:

**Our Father . . .**

## PRAYER OF BLESSING

1927 The minister says the prayer of blessing with hands outstretched over the new officers.

**Almighty God,**
**we give you thanks**
**for the many and varied ways you build up your Church.**

**Bless these officers of the N. society.**
**Grant that through their vision and direction**
**they may be of service to this parish**
**and bring honor and glory to your name.**
**Grant this through Christ our Lord.**

℞. **Amen.**

## CONCLUDING RITE

1928 The minister concludes the rite by saying:

**Lord,**
**bless your people and fill them with zeal.**
**Strengthen them by your love to do your will.**

**We ask this through Christ our Lord.**

℞. **Amen.**

Then he blesses all present.

**And may almighty God bless you all,**
**the Father, and the Son, ✝ and the Holy Spirit.**

℞. **Amen.**

1929 It is preferable to end the celebration with a suitable song.

# CHAPTER 66

# ORDER FOR THE WELCOMING OF NEW PARISHIONERS

## INTRODUCTION

1930   When an individual or a family moves into a parish, it is appropriate that a formal welcome be extended by the parish community.

1931   The welcome of new parishioners, according to the circumstances, may take place occasionally at the Sunday Mass, or at another public celebration.

## ORDER FOR THE WELCOMING OF NEW PARISHIONERS

1932   When the welcome takes place at Mass, the pastor presents the new parishioners to the people after the greeting. If desired, the priest may invite the persons to stand at their places or come before the congregation. After the new parishioners have been presented the people may express their welcome by applause or in some other suitable way.

## INTERCESSIONS

1933   A petition for the new parishioners should be included in the general intercessions. The following petition may be used:

**For N.N. and N.N., that they may always be welcome in our parish family, we pray to the Lord.**

CHAPTER 67

# ORDER FOR THE BLESSING
# OF A DEPARTING PARISHIONER

## INTRODUCTION

1934  When an individual or a family leaves a parish to take up residence in another place, it is fitting that the parish express its farewell and pray for God's blessing upon the person or family.

1935  A petition for the departing parishioner should be included in the general intercessions.

1936  The blessing may take place at the end of Mass as a part of the final blessing.

## ORDER OF BLESSING

### INTERCESSIONS

1937  The following or a similar petition may be included in the general intercessions:

**For N.N., that as he/she leaves our community God's loving kindness may ever go with him/her, we pray to the Lord.**

1938  At the conclusion of the prayer after communion the priest invites the person who is leaving the parish to come before the people and, in his own words, he expresses the parish's farewell.

1939  He then greets the people in the usual manner and extends his hands over the departing parishioner and says:

**May almighty God keep you from all harm
and bless you with every good gift.**

R̷. **Amen.**

**May he set his word in your heart
and fill you with lasting joy.**

R̷. **Amen.**

May you walk in his ways,
always knowing what is right and good,
until you enter your heavenly inheritance.

R⁷. **Amen.**

Then he blesses all present, saying:

**And may almighty God bless you all,
the Father, and the Son,** ✠ **and the Holy Spirit.**

R⁷. **Amen.**

# CHAPTER 68

# ORDER FOR THE BLESSING OF THOSE RECEIVING ECCLESIASTICAL HONORS

## INTRODUCTION

1940   There are different gifts but the same Spirit; there are different ministries but the same Lord; there are different works but the same God who accomplishes all of them in everyone (1 Cor. 12:4-6). When we recognize the gifts and talents of another person we are, in fact, acknowledging God—the author and giver of all gifts.

1941   This order is intended for use on occasions when ecclesiastical honors are conferred. It is appropriate for use by a bishop when priests have been named as members of the papal household (protonotaries apostolic, honorary prelates, and honorary chaplains), and when laity have been granted papal honors.

 The blessing may also be used for the conferral of diocesan or parish honors.

1942   When priests are to receive ecclesiastical honors, they vest in choir cassock, sash, and surplice before the service begins. The rescript from the Apostolic See is presented at the conferral of the honor (no. 1955).

 When laity receive ecclesiastical honors they are presented with the rescript and the medal at the conferral of the honor (no. 1955).

1943   The blessing may be given outside Mass during a celebration of the word, during Mass, or during Morning or Evening Prayer.

1944   If the blessing is conferred during Mass, the Mass of the day is celebrated. The blessing is given following the homily, as indicated below, nos. 1954–1956, and 1958; the Lord's Prayer, no. 1957, is omitted. Priests who are to receive ecclesiastical honors are vested as concelebrants throughout the Mass.

1945   If the blessing is to be celebrated at Morning or Evening Prayer, the presentation (no. 1954) and conferral of the honor (no. 1955) takes place after the reading, responsory, and homily. The general intercessions of this rite (no. 1956) replace those of the office and the prayer of blessing (no. 1958) follows the Lord's Prayer (no. 1957); the concluding prayer of the office is omitted. The rite concludes with the blessing in no. 1959.

1946   This order may be used by a bishop or a priest delegated by him.

# ORDER OF BLESSING

## INTRODUCTORY RITES

1947  When the community has gathered, a suitable song may be sung. After the singing, the minister says:

**In the name of the Father, and of the Son, and of the Holy Spirit.**

All make the sign of the cross and reply:

**Amen.**

1948  The minister greets those present in the following or other suitable words, taken mainly from sacred Scripture.

**The grace of our Lord Jesus Christ, the love of God, and the fellowship of the Holy Spirit be with you all.**

And all reply:

**And also with you.**

1949  In the following or similar words, the minister prepares those present for the blessing.

**Brothers and sisters, we gather here today to acknowledge and honor our brothers and sisters for** *(reason for the conferral of the honor)*. **The Scriptures remind us that all good gifts come from God, who distributes them as he wills to build up the body of Christ. Let us listen now to the word of God.**

## READING OF THE WORD OF GOD

1950  A reader, another person present, or the presiding minister reads a text of sacred Scripture.

**Brothers and sisters, listen to the words of the apostle Paul to the Romans:**                                                              12:3-8

*Many members in one body.*

**For by the grace given to me I tell everyone among you not to think of himself more highly than one ought to think, but to think soberly, each according to the measure of faith that God has apportioned. For as in one body we have many parts,**

and all the parts do not have the same function, so we, though many, are one body in Christ and individually parts of one another. Since we have gifts that differ according to the grace given to us, let us exercise them: if prophecy, in proportion to the faith; if ministry, in ministering; if one is a teacher, in teaching; if one exhorts, in exhortation; if one contributes, in generosity; if one is over others, with diligence; if one does acts of mercy, with cheerfulness.

1951   Or:

1 Corinthians 1:4-9—*I thank God for the favor he has bestowed on you in Christ.*

1 Corinthians 9:24-25—*Run so as to win.*

1 Corinthians 12:1-11—*Variety and unity in the Church.*

1 Corinthians 12:27-31—*We are one body in Christ.*

1 Corinthians 12:31—13:13—*Excellence of the gift of love.*

Ephesians 1:3-10—*The Father's plan of salvation is fulfilled in Christ.*

1952   As circumstances suggest, one of the following responsorial psalms may be sung, or some other suitable song.

℟. **O Lord, our God, how wonderful your name in all the earth!**

Psalm 8

**You have exalted your majesty above the heavens.**
**Out of the mouths of babes and sucklings**
**you have fashioned praise because of your foes,**
**to silence the hostile and the vengeful.** ℟.

**When I behold your heavens, the work of your fingers,**
**the moon and the stars which you set in place—**
**What is man that you should be mindful of him,**
**or the son of man that you should care for him?** ℟.

**You have made him little less than the angels,**
**and crowned him with glory and honor.**
**You have given him rule over the works of your hands,**
**putting all things under his feet:** ℟.

**All sheep and oxen,**
**yes, and the beasts of the field,**
**The birds of the air, the fishes of the sea,**
**and whatever swims the paths of the seas.** ℟.

Psalm 65:2b-3, 5, 6, 7, 8, 9

℟. (v. 2) **To you we owe our hymn of praise, O God in Zion.**

Psalm 96:1-2, 3, 7-8a, 8b-9, 10

℟. (v. 8) **Give to the Lord the glory due his name.**

**1953** As circumstances suggest, the minister may give those present a brief explanation of the biblical text, so that they may understand through faith the meaning of the celebration.

## PRESENTATION OF THE CANDIDATES

**1954** After the homily those to be honored are presented to the presiding minister. Either the presiding minister or another minister may briefly explain the honor or award to be conferred and the reasons for its conferral.

## CONFERRAL OF THE HONOR

**1955** The minister then presents the honor (rescript, medal, etc.) to the recipient.

## INTERCESSIONS

**1956** The intercessions are then said. The minister introduces them and an assisting minister or one of those present announces the intentions. From the following those best suited to the occasion may be used or adapted, or other intentions that apply to the particular circumstances may be composed.

The minister says:

**Brothers and sisters, God is the giver of all good gifts; let us call upon him with faith and thanksgiving.**

℟. **Hear us, O Lord.**

Assisting minister:

**For our brothers and sisters whom we honor today, that their true reward may be in the kingdom of God, we pray to the Lord.** ℟.

Assisting minister:

**For those who use their talents and gifts for the good of others, that they may acknowledge God as their source, we pray to the Lord. ℟.**

Assisting minister:

**For all of us, that God may stir up in us the spirit of gratitude and thankfulness, we pray to the Lord. ℟.**

Assisting minister:

**For those in distress, that we respond to their need by sharing what God has given us, we pray to the Lord. ℟.**

1957 After the intercessions the minister, in the following or similar words, invites all present to sing or say the Lord's Prayer.

**God has shown us his love; with praise and thanks we pray:**

All:

**Our Father . . .**


## PRAYER OF BLESSING

1958 The minister says the prayer of blessing with hands outstretched over those who have been honored:

**Eternal God,**
**source of every gift and talent,**
**through your Son, Jesus Christ, you grant us your**
   **blessings**
**that the Church might be nourished and strengthened.**

**Bless N. and N. today,**
**and confer upon them the gifts of your Spirit**
**that they may remain humble in heart**
**as they serve your household the Church.**

**Bring us all into the peace of your kingdom,**
**where all honor and glory are yours, Lord our God,**
**for ever and ever.**

**℟. Amen.**

# CONCLUDING RITE

1959  The minister concludes the rite by saying:

**Lord, bless us with your heavenly gifts,
and grant us the grace to do your will.**

**We ask this through Christ our Lord.**

**R℣. Amen.**

Then he blesses all present.

**And may almighty God bless you all,
the Father, and the Son, ✝ and the Holy Spirit.**

**R℣. Amen.**

1960  It is preferable to end the celebration with a suitable song.

# CHAPTER 69

# PRAYER ON THE OCCASION OF THE INAUGURATION OF A PUBLIC OFFICIAL <small>USA</small>

## INTRODUCTION

1961   The inauguration of a public official is normally a civic function at which representatives of various religious traditions may be invited to offer public prayers.

1962   The usual pattern for such celebrations calls for an invocation prayer at the beginning and a benediction at the end. The prayer which follows may be used for either purpose.

1963   This prayer is an adaptation of the prayer for the Church and for civil authorities which was composed by Archbishop John Carroll for use on the occasion of the inauguration of George Washington in 1789.

1964   The whole prayer may be used or, in addition to the first and last paragraph, one or more of the three central paragraphs may be selected. Paragraph B is for the president, Paragraph C is for the members of Congress, and Paragraph D is for state governors, legislators, judges, and other civic officials.

# PRAYER FOR AN INAUGURATION

1965   The following prayer may be used at the inauguration of
a public official for either the invocation or the benediction.

Paragraphs B, C, or D may be used or omitted according to the
circumstances; paragraphs A and E are always used.

A     **Almighty and eternal God,**
      **you have revealed your glory to all nations.**
      **God of power and might, wisdom and justice,**
      **through you authority is rightly administered,**
      **laws are enacted, and judgment is decreed.**

B     **Assist with your spirit of counsel and fortitude**
      **the President of these United States,**
      **that his/her administration may be conducted in**
          **righteousness,**
      **and be eminently useful to your people over whom**
          **he/she presides.**
      **May he/she encourage due respect for virtue and**
          **religion.**
      **May he/she execute the laws with justice and mercy.**
      **May he/she seek to restrain crime, vice, and**
          **immorality.**

C     **Let the light of your divine wisdom**
      **direct the deliberations of Congress, (and**
          **especially of N.,)**
      **and shine forth in all the proceedings**
      **and laws framed for our rule and government.**
      **May they seek to preserve peace, promote national**
          **happiness,**
      **and continue to bring us the blessings of liberty**
          **and equality.**

D      We pray for N., the governor of this state
           (commonwealth, dominion),
      for the members of the legislature, (especially, N.,)
      for judges, elected civil officials, (especially, N.,)
        and all others
      who are entrusted to guard our political welfare.
      May they be enabled by your powerful protection
      to discharge their duties with honesty and ability.

E      We likewise commend to your unbounded mercy
      all citizens of the United States,
      that we may be blessed in the knowledge and sanctified in
        the observance of your holy law.
      May we be preserved in union and that peace which the
        world cannot give;
      and, after enjoying the blessings of this life,
      be admitted to those which are eternal.

      We pray to you, who are Lord and God,
      for ever and ever.

      R℣. Amen.

# Chapter 70

# ORDER FOR A BLESSING IN THANKSGIVING

## Introduction

1966 In the desire that the grace of the eucharistic celebration should reach deeply into their daily lives, Christians strive to remain in an attitude of thanksgiving. The gifts of God are a constant reminder to thank him at all times in return, and especially when he has granted some special favor to his faithful. On such occasions they should gather to praise him together and to bless him.

1967 The present order may be used by a priest or deacon. It may also be used by a layperson, who follows the rites and prayers designated for a lay minister. While maintaining the structure and chief elements of the rite, the minister should adapt the celebration to the circumstances of the place and the people involved.

1968 The present order is also useful in places where it is customary to celebrate a thanksgiving service at the end of each year, but where no priest is available.

# ORDER OF BLESSING

## Introductory Rites

1969 When the community has gathered, the minister says:

**In the name of the Father, and of the Son, and of the Holy Spirit.**

All make the sign of the cross and reply:

**Amen.**

1970 A minister who is a priest or deacon greets those present in the following or other suitable words, taken mainly from sacred Scripture.

**May God, who is rich in mercy and who has favored us in wonderful ways, be with you all.**

All make the following or some other suitable reply.

**And also with you.**

---

1971 A lay minister greets those present in the following words.

**Brothers and sisters, give praise to God, who is rich in mercy and who has favored us in wonderful ways. Blessed be God now and for ever.**

All reply:

**Amen**

---

1972 In the following or similar words, the minister prepares those present for the blessing.

**Let us open our hearts in thanks to God for the favors showered upon us. Saint Paul teaches us to give thanks to God the Father always through Christ, in whom he has given us everything. For when we became God's children in Christ, God gave us the riches of his grace, rescuing us from the powers of darkness and bringing us into the kingdom of his beloved Son. Whenever we acknowledge God's gifts, we prepare ourselves to take part more fully in the eucharist, which is the sum of all blessings and the crown and source of all thanksgiving.**

# Reading of the Word of God

1973  A reader, another person present, or the minister reads a text of sacred Scripture.

**Brothers and sisters, listen to the words of the apostle Paul to the Philippians:**  4:4-7

*Present your needs to God in every form of prayer and in petitions full of gratitude.*

**Rejoice in the Lord always. I shall say it again: rejoice! Your kindness should be known to all. The Lord is near. Have no anxiety at all, but in everything, by prayer and petition, with thanksgiving, make your requests known to God. Then the peace of God that surpasses all understanding will guard your hearts and minds in Christ Jesus.**

1974  Or:

1 Corinthians 1:4-9—*In Christ Jesus you have been richly endowed with every gift.*

Colossians 3:15-17—*Give thanks to God the Father through him.*

1 Thessalonians 5:12-24—*Render constant thanks; such is God's will for you.*

1 Timothy 2:1-10—*First of all I urge that thanksgiving be offered for all people.*

Luke 17:11-19—*They praised God with a loud voice.*

1975  As circumstances suggest, one of the following responsorial psalms may be sung or said, or some other suitable song.

℟. **All peoples, shout with joy to God.**

Psalm 47

**All you peoples, clap your hands,
shout to God with cries of gladness,
For the LORD, the Most High, the awesome,
is the great king over all the earth.** ℟.

**He chooses for us our inheritance,
the glory of Jacob, whom he loves.
God mounts his throne amid shouts of joy;
the Lord, amid trumpet blasts.** ℟.

Sing praise to God, sing praise;
sing praise to our king, sing praise.
For king of all the earth is God;
sing hymns of praise. ℟.

God reigns over the nations,
God sits upon his holy throne.
The princes of the peoples are gathered together
with the people of the God of Abraham.
For God's are the guardians of the earth;
he is supreme. ℟.

Psalm 66:1b-2, 8-9, 10-11, 13-14, 16-17, 19-20

℟. (see v. 16) **Come, listen as I tell you what God did for me.**

Psalm 118:1-2, 5-6, 8-9, 17-19, 26-27, 28-29

℟. (v. 1) **Give thanks to the Lord for he is good, his love is everlasting.**

1976 As circumstances suggest, the minister may give those present a brief explanation of the biblical text, so that they may understand through faith the meaning of the celebration.

## INTERCESSIONS

1977 As circumstances suggest, the intercessions may follow. The minister introduces them and an assisting minister or one of those present announces the intentions. From the following intentions those best suited to the occasion may be used or adapted, or other intentions that apply to the particular circumstances may be composed.

The minister says:

**The heavens declare the glory of God, our almighty Father, and every creature he has made extols his goodness. Mindful of our indebtedness, let us together with praise and thanksgiving call upon him by saying:**

℟. **Glory to you, O Lord, for all your gifts to us.**

Or:

℟. **Lord, hear our prayer.**

Assisting minister:

**Father most generous, in Christ Jesus, your Son, you have given us all things; grant that we may never fail to sing your praises. (For this we pray:) R℣.**

Assisting minister:

**Your loving response far exceeds the merits and expectations of those who pray to you; grant that with our lips and our hearts we may sing the wonders of your works. (For this we pray:) R℣.**

Assisting minister:

**You prepare and bestow upon us all countless signs of your love; grant that, as we receive your gifts, we may always see you as their giver. (For this we pray:) R℣.**

Assisting minister:

**You have told your disciples to share what they have with others; grant that our neighbors may share in your gifts to us, so that they may also share in our joy. (For this we pray:) R℣.**

1978    Instead of the intercessions, the hymn *Te Deum,* or the canticle *Bless the Lord, all you works of the Lord,* or the Canticle of Mary, or a suitable psalm may be sung.

## PRAYER OF BLESSING

1979    A minister who is a priest or deacon says the prayer of blessing with hands outstretched; a lay minister says the prayer with hands joined.

**Almighty Father,**
**you are lavish in bestowing all your gifts,**
**and we give you thanks for the favors you have given**
    **to us.**
**In your goodness you have favored us**
**and kept us safe in the past.**
**We ask that you continue to protect us**
**and to shelter us in the shadow of your wings.**

**We ask this through Christ our Lord.**

**R℣. Amen.**

1980  Or:

**O God,**
**your mercy is without measure,**
**the treasures of your goodness without limit.**
**We thank your gentle majesty**
**for the favors you have bestowed on us.**
**As we do so, we appeal to your compassion:**
**stay close to those whose petitions you have granted**
**and prepare them for the rewards of the life to come.**

**We ask this through Christ our Lord.**

Rʒ. **Amen.**

## CONCLUDING RITE

1981  A minister who is a priest or deacon concludes the rite by saying:

**May God the Father, with the Son and the Holy Spirit,**
**who has shown you such great mercy,**
**bless you with an everlasting blessing.**

Rʒ. **Amen.**

Then he blesses all present.

**And may almighty God bless you all,**
**the Father, and the Son, ✝ and the Holy Spirit.**

Rʒ. **Amen.**

1982  A lay minister concludes the rite by signing himself or herself with the sign of the cross and saying:

**May God the Father, with the Son and the Holy Spirit,**
**who has shown us such great mercy,**
**be praised and blessed for ever and ever.**

Rʒ. **Amen.**

1983  It is preferable to end the celebration with a suitable song.

CHAPTER 71

# ORDER FOR A BLESSING TO BE USED IN VARIOUS CIRCUMSTANCES

## INTRODUCTION

1984    Since the present rite provides a wide choice of texts, it can be readily adapted for use in various circumstances. The purpose of the rite is to sanctify through the celebration of a blessing those situations in life not explicitly indicated in the rites already given (for example, a gathering of family members or of a group for some special occasion; a collection of contributions for the poor, etc.).

1985    The present order is in no sense meant to violate principles concerning blessings; it is not fitting to turn every object or situation into an occasion for celebrating a blessing (for example, every monument erected no matter what its theme, the installation of military weapons, frivolous events). Rather every celebration must be considered with balanced pastoral judgment, particularly when there is any foreseeable danger of shocking the faithful or other people.

1986    The present order may be used by a priest or deacon. It may also be used by a layperson, who follows the rites and prayers designated for a lay minister. While maintaining the structure and chief elements of the rite, the minister should adapt the celebration to the circumstances of the place and the people involved.

# ORDER OF BLESSING

## Introductory Rites

1987    When the community has gathered, the minister says:

**In the name of the Father, and of the Son, and of the Holy Spirit.**

All make the sign of the cross and reply:

**Amen.**

1988    A minister who is a priest or deacon greets those present in the following or other suitable words, taken mainly from sacred Scripture.

**May God, who is the fountain of all goodness, be with you all.**

All make the following or some other suitable reply.

**And also with you.**

---

1989    A lay minister greets those present in the following words.

**Brothers and sisters, let us bless and praise the Lord, the fountain of all goodness. Blessed be God now and for ever.**

All reply:

**Amen.**

---

1990    In the following or similar words, the minister prepares those present for the blessing.

**All that God has created and sustains, all the events he guides, and all human works that are good and have a good purpose, prompt those who believe to praise and bless the Lord with hearts and voices. He is the source and origin of every blessing. By this celebration we proclaim our belief that all things work together for the good of those who fear and love God. We are sure that in all things we must seek the help of God, so that in complete reliance on his will we may in Christ do everything for his glory.**

# READING OF THE WORD OF GOD

1991 A reader, another person present, or the minister reads a text of sacred Scripture.

**Brothers and sisters, listen to the words of the apostle Paul to the Colossians:** 1:9b-14

*Multiplying good works of every sort.*

**We do not cease praying for you and asking that you may be filled with the knowledge of his will through all spiritual wisdom and understanding to live in a manner worthy of the Lord, so as to be fully pleasing, in every good work bearing fruit and growing in the knowledge of God, strengthened with every power, in accord with his glorious might, for all endurance and patience, with joy giving thanks to the Father, who has made you fit to share in the inheritance of the holy ones in light. He delivered us from the power of darkness and transferred us to the kingdom of his beloved Son, in whom we have redemption, the forgiveness of sins.**

1992 Or:

**Brothers and sisters, listen to the words of the apostle Paul to the Romans:** 8:24-28

*The Spirit too helps us in our weakness.*

**For in hope we were saved. Now hope that sees for itself is not hope. For who hopes for what one sees? But if we hope for what we do not see, we wait with endurance.**

**In the same way, the Spirit too comes to the aid of our weakness; for we do not know how to pray as we ought, but the Spirit itself intercedes with inexpressible groanings. And the one who searches hearts knows what is the intention of the Spirit, because it intercedes for the holy ones according to God's will.**

**We know that all things work for good for those who love God, who are called according to his purpose.**

1993 Or:

**Brothers and sisters, listen to the words of the first letter of Paul to Timothy:**                                                        4:4-5

*Everything God created is good.*

**For everything created by God is good, and nothing is to be rejected when received with thanksgiving, for it is made holy by the invocation of God in prayer.**

1994 Or:

Numbers 6:22-27—*So shall they invoke my name upon the Israelites and I will bless them.*

Deuteronomy 33:1, 13b-16a—*This is the blessing of Moses.*

Wisdom 13:1-7—*For from the greatness and beauty of created things, their original author, by analogy, is seen.*

Sirach 18:1-9—*Who can measure God's mighty deeds?*

1995 As circumstances suggest, one of the following responsorial psalms may be sung or said, or some other suitable song.

R℣. **The Lord led his people out with rejoicing.**

Psalm 105

**Give thanks to the LORD, invoke his name;
make known among the nations his deeds.
Sing to him, sing his praise,
proclaim all his wondrous deeds.** R℣.

**Glory in his holy name;
rejoice, O hearts that seek the LORD!
Look to the LORD in his strength;
seek to serve him constantly.** R℣.

**Recall the wondrous deeds that he has wrought,
his portents, and the judgments he has uttered.
He, the LORD, is our God;
throughout the earth his judgments prevail.** R℣.

**He remembers forever his covenant
which he made binding for a thousand generations—
Which he entered into with Abraham
and by his oath to Isaac.** R℣.

Psalm 106:2-3, 4-5, 45-46, 47, 48

R̘. (v. 1) **Give thanks to the Lord for he is good, his love is everlasting.**

Psalm 107:2-3, 8-9, 31-32, 42-43

R̘. (v. 6) **They cried to the Lord in their troubles and he delivered them from their anguish.**

**1996** As circumstances suggest, the minister may give those present a brief explanation of the biblical text, so that they may understand through faith the meaning of the celebration.

# INTERCESSIONS

**1997** As circumstances suggest, the prayer of blessing may be preceded by the intercessions. The minister introduces them and an assisting minister or one of those present announces the intentions. From the following intentions those best suited to the occasion may be used or adapted, or other intentions that apply to the particular circumstances may be composed. The intentions are followed immediately by the prayer of blessing, nos. 1999–2008.

The minister says:

**God loves his creation and his goodness sustains the universe. Let us pray now that he will bestow his blessing upon us and that he will renew and support us with his strength.**

R̘. **Lord, send us your blessing.**

Or:

R̘. **Lord, hear our prayer.**

Assisting minister:

**Everlasting God, you give life a nobler meaning when we try wholeheartedly to do your will; fill us with the spirit of your own holiness. (For this we pray:)** R̘.

Assisting minister:

**You want us to increase your gifts and to return them to you and to our neighbor; accept the offering of our loving service. (For this we pray:)** R̘.

*Assisting minister:*

**You watch over us with fatherly care; hear the cries of those who trust in you. (For this we pray:)** ℟.

*Assisting minister:*

**You sent your Son into the world to remove the curse of sin and replace it with your blessing; in Christ fill us with every heavenly blessing. (For this we pray:)** ℟.

*Assisting minister:*

**You have poured forth into our hearts your Son's Spirit, in whom we cry out, Abba, Father; hear your children as they acclaim and praise your goodness. (For this we pray:)** ℟.

*Assisting minister:*

**Through your Son's death and resurrection you have chosen us to be your people and your inheritance; remember us in our needs and bless your inheritance. (For this we pray:)** ℟.

1998   When there are no intercessions, the minister, before the prayer of blessing, says:

**Let us pray.**

As circumstances suggest, all may then pray for a moment in silence before the prayer of blessing.

## PRAYER OF BLESSING

1999   A minister who is a priest or deacon says the prayer of blessing with hands outstretched; a lay minister says the prayer with hands joined.

A         2000   Blessing of natural products

**Blessed are you, O God,**
**Creator of the universe,**
**who have made all things good**
**and given the earth for us to cultivate.**
**Grant that we may always use created things gratefully**
**and share your gifts with those in need,**
**out of love for Christ our Lord,**
**who lives and reigns with you for ever and ever.**

**℟. Amen.**

B      2001   Blessing of natural products

**Lord and Father all-holy,**
**we bless you,**
**for your word and power have made all things**
**and your gift has given us**
**what we need to live.**
**Grant that, in obedience to your law and will,**
**your faithful may always use created things**
**in a spirit of gratitude.**

**We ask this through Christ our Lord.**

**R⁊. Amen.**

C      2002   Blessing of natural products

**Almighty and everlasting God,**
**by your design for us**
**you have given us the temporal blessings we need,**
**in order to bring us to the blessings of eternity.**
**Grant us the goods of this world**
**sufficient to meet our needs**
**and lead us to the heavenly inheritance you have promised.**

**We ask this through Christ our Lord.**

**R⁊. Amen.**

D      2003   Blessing of manufactured things

**Almighty and ever-living God,**
**you made us stewards over the created world,**
**so that in all things we might honor the demands**
**   of charity.**
**Graciously hear our prayers,**
**that your blessing may come upon all those**
**who use these objects for their needs.**
**Let them always see you as the good surpassing every good**
**and love their neighbor with upright hearts.**

**We ask this through Christ our Lord.**

**R⁊. Amen.**

E        2004   Blessing for the special occasions of life

**Lord God,**
**from the abundance of your mercy**
**enrich your servants and safeguard them.**
**Strengthened by your blessing,**
**may they always be thankful to you**
**and bless you with unending joy.**

**We ask this through Christ our Lord.**

**R̢. Amen.**

F        2005   Blessing for the special occasions of life

**Lord,**
**let the effect of your blessing**
**remain with your faithful people**
**to give them new life and strength of spirit,**
**so that the power of your love**
**will enable them to accomplish what is right and good.**

**We ask this through Christ our Lord.**

**R̢. Amen.**

G        2006   Blessing for the special occasions of life

**Lord,**
**may the blessing they long for**
**be the strength of your faithful people,**
**so that they will never be in conflict with your will.**
**May your blessing always prompt them**
**to give thanks for your favors.**

**We ask this through Christ our Lord.**

**R̢. Amen.**

H        2007   Blessing for the special occasions of life

**Bless your people, Lord,**
**who wait for the gift of your compassion.**
**Grant that what they desire by your inspiration**
**they may receive through your goodness.**

**We ask this through Christ our Lord.**

**R̢. Amen.**

I      2008   Blessing for the special occasions of life

**Lord,
we, your people, pray for the gift of your holy blessing
to ward off every harm
and to bring to fulfillment every right desire.**

**We ask this through Christ our Lord.**

℟. **Amen.**


## CONCLUDING RITE

2009   A minister who is a priest or deacon concludes the rite by saying:

**May God, who is blessed above all,
bless you in all things through Christ,
so that whatever happens in your lives
will work together for your good.**

℟. **Amen.**

Then he blesses all present.

**And may almighty God bless you,
the Father, and the Son, ✝ and the Holy Spirit.**

℟. **Amen.**


2010   A lay minister concludes the rite by signing himself or herself with the sign of the cross and saying:

**May God, who is blessed above all,
bless us in all things through Christ,
so that whatever happens in our lives
will work together for our good.**

℟. **Amen.**


2011   It is preferable to end the celebration with a suitable song.

# APPENDICES

# APPENDIX I
# ORDER FOR THE
# INSTALLATION OF A PASTOR

# ORDER FOR THE INSTALLATION OF A PASTOR

## INTRODUCTION

2012   When a new pastor is appointed for a parish it is appropriate that he be publicly installed by a liturgical rite. The installation should, if possible, take place at one of the Masses on the first Sunday that his appointment is effective. The installation may also take place during a celebration of the word of God, or during Morning or Evening Prayer.

2013   The bishop is the usual celebrant of this rite. However, he may delegate a priest to preside in his place, e.g., a vicar or a dean. In this case, the *Order of Installation within Mass When a Priest Presides* is used.

2014   When the diocesan bishop is present, he is the celebrant of the eucharist and the new pastor concelebrates with him.

   If the bishop is not present, the priest who represents the bishop greets the people and presides over the rite of installation. The new pastor is the celebrant of the remainder of the liturgy, beginning with the opening prayer.

2015   The pastor-elect is presented to the bishop's delegate by a priest or deacon.

2016   The members of the parish council (and the parish trustees) should be seated in the front of the church and, if desired, they may take part in the entrance procession.

2017   The Mass of the day is celebrated.

2018   The required oaths are signed after Mass.

2019   The new pastor may briefly address the people immediately after the prayer after communion.

2020   If the rite of installation is celebrated outside Mass, a liturgy of the word is celebrated. The rite of installation follows the gospel (nos. 2022–2030). The installation rite concludes with a hymn, the general intercessions (no. 2031), the Lord's Prayer, and a blessing. The new pastor may briefly address the people before the general intercessions.

2021   According to pastoral circumstances, e.g., in smaller parishes, the diocesan bishop may adapt or omit particular elements of this rite.

# I. ORDER OF INSTALLATION WITHIN MASS WHEN THE BISHOP PRESIDES

## PRESENTATION OF THE PASTOR-ELECT

2022   After the gospel, the pastor-elect stands before the bishop, who addresses the people in these or similar words:

**My dear friends, because I am aware of your pastoral needs and am confident of Father N.'s qualifications for the office of pastor, I now commend Father N. to you as your new pastor.**

## WELCOME BY THE PEOPLE

2023   The bishop may then invite the people to express their approval and support of their new pastor.

## HOMILY

2024   The bishop in the homily, based on the sacred text and pertinent to the particular place and the people involved, explains the meaning of the celebration.

## PRESENTATIONS

2025   The pastor stands before the bishop who introduces him to various groups of the parish.

## PRESENTATION OF THE PARISH CLERGY AND STAFF

2026   The priests, deacons, and other members of the parish staff are presented to the new pastor by the bishop:

**N., my brother, Father N. N., Deacon N. N., and N. N. will assist you in the pastoral care of the people of this parish. Share this ministry in a spirit of mutual trust, common prayer, and genuine concern.**

The new pastor is greeted by his associates in the parish ministry.

## PRESENTATION OF THE PARISH COUNCIL

2027   The parish council stands and is presented to the pastor
by the bishop:

**Father N., this is the pastoral council of N. parish. It is the
voice of your people and will assist and counsel you as you
minister to this parish. Always be attentive to the needs they
express.**

Then the pastor faces the parish council and says:

**My friends, I pledge to seek your counsel, guidance, and ad-
vice in the spiritual and temporal care of my pastorate.**

The members of the parish council immediately come forward
and greet the new pastor.

### [PRESENTATION OF THE PARISH TRUSTEES]

2028   If there are parish trustees, they come forward and the
bishop presents them to the new pastor:

**Father N., N.N. and N.N. are the civil trustees of this parish.
As the lay officers of the parish corporation they will share
with you the responsibility for the parish's corporate and legal affairs.**

## PROFESSION OF FAITH AND OATH

2029   Next the bishop addresses the new pastor, who stands facing him:

**Remember, my brother N., always be a loving father, a gentle
shepherd, and a wise teacher of your people, so that you may
lead them to Christ who will strengthen all that you do.**

**As a teacher of that faith, I ask you now to lead your people
in the profession of their faith.**

2030 The pastor then faces the people and leads them in the profession of faith (Nicene Creed). At the conclusion of the profession of faith, the pastor faces the bishop and recites the following oath:

**With firm faith I also believe everything contained in God's Word,**
**written or handed down in tradition**
**and proposed by the Church,**
**whether in solemn judgment or in ordinary and universal magisterium,**
**as divinely revealed and calling for faith.**

**I also firmly accept and hold each and every thing**
**that is proposed by the Church definitively**
**regarding teaching on faith and morals.**

**Moreover, I adhere with religious submission of will and intellect**
**to the teachings which either the Roman Pontiff**
**or the college of bishops enunciate**
**when they exercise the authentic magisterium**
**even if they proclaim those teachings in an act**
**that is not definitive.**

## GENERAL INTERCESSIONS

2031 The bishop introduces the general intercessions using these or similar words. Additional intentions may be added, if desired.

**Let us now pray for the Church and its leaders, especially the new pastor of this parish, and for the needs of all people.**

**R̷. Lord, hear our prayer.**

Assisting minister:

**For N., our pope, for N., our bishop, and all the bishops of the Church, that they may lead us to a more faithful living of the gospel, we pray to the Lord. R̷.**

Assisting minister:

**For N., our new pastor, that he may always show us love and compassion, we pray to the Lord. R̷.**

Assisting minister:

**For all who contribute their time and talent to this parish, that their service to the Church may help us to know the message of Christ, we pray to the Lord.** ℟.

Assisting minister:

**For peace and justice in the world and for the conversion of those who have hardened their hearts to the needs of their brothers and sisters, we pray to the Lord.** ℟.

Assisting minister:

**For the poor of our community and throughout the world, that we may be responsive to their needs and share with them from our bounty, we pray to the Lord.** ℟.

Assisting minister:

**For ourselves, that we who form the parish of N. may work together to proclaim the good news of Christ's love, we pray to the Lord.** ℟.

2032　The bishop then says the concluding prayer:

**Gracious God,**
**you have nourished and protected your Church**
**by providing it with pastors**
**who are stewards of your word and sacraments.**
**Strengthen our brother N.**
**as he begins a new ministry among us,**
**and help us all to follow your Son, Jesus Christ,**
**who is Lord, for ever and ever.**

℟. **Amen.**

2033　The Mass continues with the preparation of the altar and the gifts.

# II. ORDER OF INSTALLATION WITHIN MASS WHEN A PRIEST PRESIDES

## PRESENTATION OF THE PASTOR-ELECT

2034    After the greeting, the pastor-elect stands before the priest who has been appointed by the bishop to preside at the installation and is presented to him by another priest or deacon who uses these or other appropriate words:

**Father N., after consulting with the clergy and laity of the diocese, Bishop N. has chosen the Reverend N. N. as the new pastor of this parish. I now have the pleasure of presenting him to you and to the people of this parish.**

## PROCLAMATION OF THE APPOINTMENT

2035    The presiding priest responds:

**My dear friends, because Bishop N. is aware of your pastoral needs and is confident of Father N.'s qualifications for the office of pastor, he has asked me to express, in his name, his pastoral concern for the people of this parish, and he commends Father N. to you as your new pastor.**

## WELCOME BY THE PEOPLE

2036    The presiding priest may then invite the people to express their approval and support of their new pastor.

## PRESENTATIONS

2037    The presiding priest introduces the new pastor to various groups of the parish.

## Presentation of the Parish Clergy and Staff

2038   The priests, deacons, and other members of the parish staff
are presented to the new pastor by the presiding priest:

**N., my brother, Father N. N., Deacon N. N., and N. N. will
assist you in the pastoral care of the people of this parish. Share
this ministry in a spirit of mutual trust, common prayer, and
genuine concern.**

The new pastor is greeted by his associates in the parish ministry.

## Presentation of the Parish Council

2039   The parish council stands and is presented to the pastor
by the presiding priest:

**Father N., this is the pastoral council of N. parish. It is the
voice of your people and will assist and counsel you as you
minister to this parish. Always be attentive to the needs they
express.**

Then the pastor faces the parish council and says:

**My friends, I pledge to seek your counsel, guidance, and advice in the spiritual and temporal care of my pastorate.**

The members of the parish council immediately come forward
and greet the new pastor.

## [Presentation of the Parish Trustees]

2040   If there are parish trustees, they come forward and the
presiding priest presents them to the new pastor:

**Father N., N.N. and N.N. are the civil trustees of this parish.
As the lay officers of the parish corporation they will share
with you the responsibility for the parish's corporate and legal affairs.**

# Conclusion of the Rite of Installation

**2041**  Next the presiding priest addresses the new pastor, who stands facing him:

**Remember, my brother N., always be a loving father, a gentle shepherd, and a wise teacher of your people, so that you may lead them to Christ who will strengthen all that you do.**

**2042**  The new pastor then takes his place at the celebrant's chair and, after inviting the people to pray, says the opening prayer of the Mass. The Mass continues as usual and the new pastor presides over the remainder of the celebration.


# Profession of Faith and Oath

**2043**  At the conclusion of the profession of faith (Nicene Creed), the pastor recites the following oath:

**With firm faith I also believe everything contained in God's Word,**
**written or handed down in tradition**
**and proposed by the Church,**
**whether in solemn judgment or in ordinary and universal magisterium,**
**as divinely revealed and calling for faith.**

**I also firmly accept and hold each and every thing**
**that is proposed by the Church definitively**
**regarding teaching on faith and morals.**

**Moreover, I adhere with religious submission of will and intellect**
**to the teachings which either the Roman Pontiff**
**or the college of bishops enunciate**
**when they exercise the authentic magisterium**
**even if they proclaim those teachings in an act**
**that is not definitive.**


# General Intercessions

**2044**  The following general intercessions may be used. Additional intentions may be added, if desired.

The celebrant says:

**Let us now pray for the Church and its leaders, for this parish, and for the needs of all people.**

**℟. Lord, hear our prayer.**

Assisting minister:

**For N., our pope, N., our bishop, and all the bishops of the Church, that they may lead us to a more faithful living of the gospel, we pray to the Lord. ℟.**

Assisting minister:

**For N., our new pastor, that he may always show us love and compassion, we pray to the Lord. ℟.**

Assisting minister:

**For all who contribute their time and talent to this parish, that their service to the Church may help us to know the message of Christ, we pray to the Lord. ℟.**

Assisting minister:

**For peace and justice in the world and for the conversion of those who have hardened their hearts to the needs of their brothers and sisters, we pray to the Lord. ℟.**

Assisting minister:

**For the poor of our community and throughout the world, that we may be responsive to their needs and share with them from our bounty, we pray to the Lord. ℟.**

Assisting minister:

**For ourselves, that we who form the parish of N. may work together to proclaim the good news of Christ's love, we pray to the Lord. ℟.**

2045  The celebrant then says the concluding prayer:

**Almighty and eternal God,
in Christ your Son
you have shown your glory to the world.**

Guide the work of your Church:
help it to proclaim your name,
to persevere in faith
and to bring your salvation to people everywhere.

We ask this through Christ our Lord.

℟. Amen.

# APPENDIX II
# SOLEMN BLESSINGS AND PRAYERS OVER THE PEOPLE

# SOLEMN BLESSINGS AND PRAYERS OVER THE PEOPLE[1]

## INTRODUCTION

2046   The following solemn blessings and prayers over the people may be used to conclude any of the blessings contained in this book. They may also be used for the blessing at the end of Morning or Evening Prayer of the *Liturgy of the Hours* or on any occasion when a priest or deacon is asked to give a blessing.

## SOLEMN BLESSINGS

2047   **I. Celebrations During the Proper of Seasons**

1      **ADVENT**

**You believe that the Son of God once came to us;
you look for him to come again.
May his coming bring you the light of his holiness
and free you with his blessing.**

R℣. **Amen.**

**May God make you steadfast in faith,
joyful in hope, and untiring in love
all the days of your life.**

R℣. **Amen.**

**You rejoice that our Redeemer came to live with us as
    man.
When he comes again in glory,
may he reward you with endless life.**

R℣. **Amen.**

---

[1] These solemn blessings and prayers over the people are taken from The Roman Missal.

May almighty God bless you,
the Father, and the Son, ✝ and the Holy Spirit.

R/. Amen.


2      CHRISTMAS

When he came to us as man,
the Son of God scattered the darkness of this world,
and filled this holy night (day) with his glory.
May the God of infinite goodness
scatter the darkness of sin
and brighten your hearts with holiness.

R/. Amen.

God sent his angels to shepherds
to herald the great joy of our Savior's birth.
May he fill you with joy
and make you heralds of his gospel.

R/. Amen.

When the Word became man,
earth was joined to heaven.
May he give you his peace and good will,
and fellowship with all the heavenly host.

R/. Amen.

May almighty God bless you,
the Father, and the Son, ✝ and the Holy Spirit.

R/. Amen.


3      BEGINNING OF THE NEW YEAR

Every good gift comes from the Father of light.
May he grant you his grace and every blessing,
and keep you safe throughout the coming year.

R/. Amen.

May he grant you unwavering faith,
constant hope, and love that endures to the end.

R/. Amen.

May he order your days and work in his peace,
hear your every prayer,
and lead you to everlasting life and joy.

R℣. Amen.

May almighty God bless you,
the Father, and the Son, ✠ and the Holy Spirit.

R℣. Amen.

4    EPIPHANY

God has called you out of darkness
into his wonderful light.
May you experience his kindness and blessings,
and be strong in faith, in hope, and in love.

R℣. Amen.

Because you are followers of Christ,
who appeared on this day as a light shining in
    darkness,
may he make you a light to all your sisters and
    brothers.

R℣. Amen.

The wise men followed the star,
and found Christ who is light from light.
May you too find the Lord
when your pilgrimage is ended.

R℣. Amen.

May almighty God bless you,
the Father, and the Son, ✠ and the Holy Spirit.

R℣. Amen.

5    LENT

May God, our merciful Father,
grant you all the joy of returning, like the
    prodigal son,
to the happiness of his house.

R℣. Amen.

May Christ, our model of prayer and of living,
guide you through the journey of Lent
to an authentic conversion of heart.

℟. Amen.

May the Spirit of wisdom and courage
sustain you in your struggle against the Evil One,
so that you may be able to celebrate with Christ the
    paschal victory.

℟. Amen.

May almighty God bless you,
the Father, and the Son, ✛ and the Holy Spirit.

℟. Amen.


6    PASSION OF THE LORD

The Father of mercies has given us an example of
    unselfish love
in the sufferings of his only Son.
Through your service of God and neighbor
may you receive his countless blessings.

℟. Amen.

You believe that by his dying
Christ destroyed death for ever.
May he give you everlasting life.

℟. Amen.

He humbled himself for our sakes.
May you follow his example
and share in his resurrection.

℟. Amen.

May almighty God bless you,
the Father, and the Son, ✛ and the Holy Spirit.

℟. Amen.

7    EASTER VIGIL AND EASTER SUNDAY

May almighty God bless you on this solemn feast of
   Easter,
and may he protect you against all sin.

R℣. Amen.

Through the resurrection of his Son
God has granted us healing.
May he fulfill his promises,
and bless you with eternal life.

R℣. Amen.

You have mourned for Christ's sufferings;
now you celebrate the joy of his resurrection.
May you come with joy to the feast which lasts for
   ever.

R℣. Amen.

May almighty God bless you,
the Father, and the Son, ✝ and the Holy Spirit.

R℣. Amen.


8    EASTER SEASON

Through the resurrection of his Son
God has redeemed you and made you his children.
May he bless you with joy.

R℣. Amen.

The Redeemer has given you lasting freedom.
May you inherit his everlasting life.

R℣. Amen.

By faith you rose with him in baptism.
May your lives be holy,
so that you will be united with him for ever.

R℣. Amen.

May almighty God bless you,
the Father, and the Son, + and the Holy Spirit.

R̴. **Amen.**

9    ASCENSION

May almighty God bless you on this day
when his only Son ascended into heaven
to prepare a place for you.

R̴. **Amen.**

After his resurrection, Christ was seen by his disciples.
When he appears as judge
may you be pleasing for ever in his sight.

R̴. **Amen.**

You believe that Jesus has taken his seat in majesty
at the right hand of the Father.
May you have the joy of experiencing
that he is also with you to the end of time,
according to his promise.

R̴. **Amen.**

May almighty God bless you,
the Father, and the Son, + and the Holy Spirit.

R̴. **Amen.**

10    HOLY SPIRIT

(This day) the Father of light
has enlightened the minds of the disciples
by the outpouring of the Holy Spirit.
May he bless you
and give you the gifts of the Spirit for ever.

R̴. **Amen.**

May that fire which hovered over the disciples
as tongues of flame
burn out all evil from your hearts
and make them glow with pure light.

R̴. **Amen.**

God inspired speech in different tongues
to proclaim one faith.
May he strengthen your faith
and fulfill your hope of seeing him face to face.

℞. Amen.

May almighty God bless you,
the Father, and the Son, ✠ and the Holy Spirit.

℞. Amen.

11  ORDINARY TIME I

May the Lord bless you and keep you.

℞. Amen.

May his face shine upon you,
and be gracious to you.

℞. Amen.

May he look upon you with kindness,
and give you his peace.

℞. Amen.

May almighty God bless you,
the Father, and the Son, ✠ and the Holy Spirit.

℞. Amen.

12  ORDINARY TIME II

May the peace of God
which is beyond all understanding
keep your hearts and minds
in the knowledge and love of God
and of his Son, our Lord Jesus Christ.

℞. Amen.

May almighty God bless you,
the Father, and the Son, ✠ and the Holy Spirit.

℞. Amen.

13    **ORDINARY TIME III**

May almighty God bless you in his mercy,
and make you always aware of his saving wisdom.

R⁷. Amen.

May he strengthen your faith with proofs of his love,
so that you will persevere in good works.

R⁷. Amen.

May he direct your steps to himself,
and show you how to walk in charity and peace.

R⁷. Amen.

May almighty God bless you,
the Father, and the Son, ✝ and the Holy Spirit.

R⁷. Amen.


14    **ORDINARY TIME IV**

May the God of all consolation
bless you in every way
and grant you peace all the days of your life.

R⁷. Amen.

May he free you from all anxiety
and strengthen your hearts in his love.

R⁷. Amen.

May he enrich you with his gifts of faith, hope, and
  love,
so that what you do in this life
will bring you to the happiness of everlasting life.

R⁷. Amen.

May almighty God bless you,
the Father, and the Son, ✝ and the Holy Spirit.

R⁷. Amen.

15    ORDINARY TIME V

May almighty God keep you from all harm
and bless you with every good gift.

R̶⁊. Amen.

May he set his Word in your heart
and fill you with lasting joy.

R̶⁊. Amen.

May you walk in his ways,
always knowing what is right and good,
until you enter your heavenly inheritance.

R̶⁊. Amen.

May almighty God bless you,
the Father, and the Son, ✝ and the Holy Spirit.

R̶⁊. Amen.


16    ORDINARY TIME VI

May our Lord Jesus Christ himself and God our Father,
who has loved us and has given us everlasting
    encouragement
and good hope through his grace,
comfort your hearts and make them strong
for every good deed and word.

R̶⁊. Amen.

May almighty God bless you,
the Father, and the Son, ✝ and the Holy Spirit.

R̶⁊. Amen.


17    ORDINARY TIME VII

The God of peace make you perfect in holiness,
keep you whole and entire, spirit, soul and body,
free from fault at the coming of Jesus Christ our Lord.

R̶⁊. Amen.

May almighty God bless you,
the Father, and the Son, ✝ and the Holy Spirit.

℟. Amen.

18 ORDINARY TIME VIII

May the God of peace,
who brought again from the dead our Lord Jesus Christ,
the great Shepherd of the sheep,
by the blood of the everlasting covenant,
make you perfect in every good work to do his will,
working in you that which is pleasing in his sight.

℟. Amen.

May almighty God bless you,
the Father, and the Son, ✝ and the Holy Spirit.

℟. Amen.

19 ORDINARY TIME IX

May the God of all grace,
who has called you to his eternal glory in Christ,
confirm you and make you strong and sure in your faith.

℟. Amen.

May almighty God bless you,
the Father, and the Son, ✝ and the Holy Spirit.

℟. Amen.

2048 II. CELEBRATIONS OF SAINTS

20 BLESSED VIRGIN MARY

Born of the blessed Virgin Mary,
the Son of God redeemed humankind.
May he enrich you with his blessings.

℟. Amen.

You received the author of life through Mary.
May you always rejoice in her loving care.

℟. Amen.

You have come to rejoice at Mary's feast.
May you be filled with the joys of the Spirit
and the gifts of your eternal home.

℟. Amen.

May almighty God bless you,
the Father, and the Son, ✝ and the Holy Spirit.

℟. Amen.

21    PETER AND PAUL

The Lord has set you firm within his Church,
which he built upon the rock of Peter's faith.
May he bless you with a faith that never falters.

℟. Amen.

The Lord has given you knowledge of the faith
through the labors and preaching of Saint Paul.
May his example inspire you to lead others to Christ
by the manner of your life.

℟. Amen.

May the keys of Peter, and the words of Paul,
their undying witness and their prayers,
lead you to the joy of that eternal home
which Peter gained by his cross, and Paul by the sword.

℟. Amen.

May almighty God bless you,
the Father, and the Son, ✝ and the Holy Spirit.

℟. Amen.

22    APOSTLES

May God who founded his Church upon the apostles
bless you through the prayers of Saint N. (and Saint N.)

℟. Amen.

May God inspire you to follow the example of the apostles,
and give witness to the truth before all people.

℟. Amen.

The teaching of the apostles has strengthened your
  faith.
May their prayers lead you
to your true and eternal home.

℟. Amen.

May almighty God bless you,
the Father, and the Son, ✝ and the Holy Spirit.

℟. Amen.

23  ALL SAINTS

God is the glory and joy of all his saints,
whose memory we celebrate today.
May his blessing be with you always.

℟. Amen.

May the prayers of the saints deliver you from present
  evil.
May their example of holy living
turn your thoughts to service of God and neighbor.

℟. Amen.

God's holy Church rejoices that her saints
have reached their heavenly goal,
and are in lasting peace.
May you come to share all the joys of our Father's
  house.

℟. Amen.

May almighty God bless you,
the Father, and the Son, ✝ and the Holy Spirit.

℟. Amen.

2049  III. OTHER BLESSINGS

24  DEDICATION OF A CHURCH

The Lord of earth and heaven
has assembled you before him this day

to dedicate this house of prayer
(to recall the dedication of this church).
May he fill you with the blessings of heaven.

℞. Amen.

God the Father wills that all his children
scattered throughout the world
become one family in his Son.
May he make you his temple,
the dwelling-place of his Holy Spirit.

℞. Amen.

May God free you from every bond of sin,
dwell within you and give you joy.
May you live with him for ever
in the company of all his saints.

℞. Amen.

May almighty God bless you,
the Father, and the Son, ✝ and the Holy Spirit.

℞. Amen.

25   THE DEAD

In his great love,
the God of all consolation gave us the gift of life.
May he bless you with faith
in the resurrection of his Son,
and with the hope of rising to new life.

℞. Amen.

To us who are alive
may he grant forgiveness,
and to all who have died
a place of light and peace.

℞. Amen.

As you believe that Jesus rose from the dead,
so may you live with him for ever in joy.

℞. Amen.

**May almighty God bless you,
the Father, and the Son, ✝ and the Holy Spirit.**

℟. **Amen.**


# PRAYERS OVER THE PEOPLE


**2050**  After the prayer over the people the priest or deacon always adds:

**May almighty God bless you,
the Father, and the Son, ✝ and the Holy Spirit.**

℟. **Amen.**


**2051**  PRAYERS FOR GENERAL USE

1  **Lord,
have mercy on your people.
Grant us in this life the good things
that lead to the everlasting life you prepare for us.**

**We ask this through Christ our Lord.**

℟. **Amen.**

2  **Lord,
grant your people your protection and grace.
Give them health of mind and body,
perfect love for one another,
and make them always faithful to you.**

**Grant this through Christ our Lord.**

℟. **Amen.**

3  **Lord,
may all Christian people both know and cherish
the heavenly gifts they have received.**

**We ask this in the name of Jesus the Lord.**

℟. **Amen.**

4      Lord,
       bless your people and make them holy
       so that, avoiding evil,
       they may find in you the fulfillment of their longing.

       We ask this through Christ our Lord.

       R℣. Amen.


5      Lord,
       bless and strengthen your people.
       May they remain faithful to you
       and always rejoice in your mercy.

       We ask this in the name of Jesus the Lord.

       R℣. Amen.


6      Lord,
       you care for your people even when they stray.
       Grant us a complete change of heart,
       so that we may follow you with greater fidelity.

       Grant this through Christ our Lord.

       R℣. Amen.


7      Lord,
       send your light upon your family.
       May they continue to enjoy your favor
       and devote themselves to doing good.

       We ask this through Christ our Lord.

       R℣. Amen.


8      Lord,
       we rejoice that you are our creator and ruler.
       As we call upon your generosity,
       renew and keep us in your love.

       Grant this through Christ our Lord.

       R℣. Amen.

9    **Lord,**
     **we pray for your people who believe in you.**
     **May they enjoy the gift of your love,**
     **share it with others,**
     **and spread it everywhere.**

     **We ask this in the name of Jesus the Lord.**

     R̼. **Amen.**


10   **Lord,**
     **bless your people who hope for your mercy.**
     **Grant that they may receive**
     **the things they ask for at your prompting.**

     **We ask this through Christ our Lord.**

     R̼. **Amen.**


11   **Lord,**
     **bless us with your heavenly gifts,**
     **and in your mercy make us ready to do your will.**

     **We ask this through Christ our Lord.**

     R̼. **Amen.**


12   **Lord,**
     **protect your people always,**
     **that they may be free from every evil**
     **and serve you with all their hearts.**

     **We ask this through Christ our Lord.**

     R̼. **Amen.**


13   **Lord,**
     **help your people to seek you with all their hearts**
     **and to deserve what you promise.**

     **Grant this through Christ our Lord.**

     R̼. **Amen.**

---

14 **Father,**
**help your people to rejoice in the mystery of**
**redemption**
**and to win its reward.**

**We ask this in the name of Jesus the Lord.**

℟. **Amen.**


15 **Lord,**
**have pity on your people;**
**help them each day to avoid what displeases you**
**and grant that they may serve you with joy.**

**We ask this through Christ our Lord.**

℟. **Amen.**


16 **Lord,**
**care for your people and purify them.**
**Console them in this life**
**and bring them to the life to come.**

**We ask this in the name of Jesus the Lord.**

℟. **Amen.**


17 **Father,**
**look with love upon your people,**
**the love which our Lord Jesus Christ showed us**
**when he delivered himself to evil men**
**and suffered the agony of the cross,**
**for he is Lord for ever.**

℟. **Amen.**


18 **Lord,**
**grant that your faithful people**
**may continually desire to relive the mystery of the**
**eucharist**
**and so be reborn to lead a new life.**

**We ask this through Christ our Lord.**

℟. **Amen.**

19    **Lord God,**
**in your great mercy,**
**enrich your people with your grace**
**and strengthen them by your blessing**
**so that they may praise you always.**

**Grant this through Christ our Lord.**

℟. **Amen.**

20    **May God bless you with every good gift from on high.**
**May he keep you pure and holy in his sight at all**
    **times.**
**May he bestow the riches of his grace upon you,**
**bring you the good news of salvation,**
**and always fill you with love for all people.**

**We ask this through Christ our Lord.**

℟. **Amen.**

21    **Lord,**
**make us pure in mind and body,**
**that we will avoid all evil pleasures**
**and always delight in you.**

**We ask this in the name of Jesus the Lord.**

℟. **Amen.**

22    **Lord,**
**bless your people and fill them with zeal.**
**Strengthen them by your love to do your will.**

**We ask this through Christ our Lord.**

℟. **Amen.**

23    **Lord,**
**come, live in your people**
**and strengthen them by your grace.**
**Help them to remain close to you in prayer**
**and give them a true love for one another.**

**Grant this through Christ our Lord.**

℟. **Amen.**

24 **Father,**
**look kindly on your children who put their trust in**
**you;**
**bless them and keep them from all harm,**
**strengthen them against the attacks of the devil.**
**May they never offend you**
**but seek to love you in all they do.**

**We ask this through Christ our Lord.**

℟. **Amen.**

2052 Prayers for Use on the Feasts of Saints

25 **God our Father,**
**may all Christian people rejoice in the glory of your**
**saints.**
**Give us fellowship with them**
**and unending joy in your kingdom.**

**We ask this in the name of Jesus the Lord.**

℟. **Amen.**

26 **Lord,**
**you have given us many friends in heaven.**
**Through their prayers we are confident**
**that you will watch over us always**
**and fill our hearts with your love.**

**Grant this through Christ our Lord.**

℟. **Amen.**